Practicing Strategy

SAGE was founded in 1965 by Sara Miller McCune to support the dissemination of usable knowledge by publishing innovative and high-quality research and teaching content. Today, we publish over 900 journals, including those of more than 400 learned societies, more than 800 new books per year, and a growing range of library products including archives, data, case studies, reports, and video. SAGE remains majority-owned by our founder, and after Sara's lifetime will become owned by a charitable trust that secures our continued independence.

Los Angeles | London | New Delhi | Singapore | Washington DC | Melbourne

SOTIRIOS PAROUTIS . LOIZOS HERACLEOUS . DUNCAN ANGWIN

Practicing Strategy
Text & Cases

2ND EDITION

Los Angeles | London | New Delhi
Singapore | Washington DC | Melbourne

Los Angeles | London | New Delhi
Singapore | Washington DC | Melbourne

SAGE Publications Ltd
1 Oliver's Yard
55 City Road
London EC1Y 1SP

SAGE Publications Inc.
2455 Teller Road
Thousand Oaks, California 91320

SAGE Publications India Pvt Ltd
B 1/I 1 Mohan Cooperative Industrial Area
Mathura Road
New Delhi 110 044

SAGE Publications Asia-Pacific Pte Ltd
3 Church Street
#10-04 Samsung Hub
Singapore 049483

Editor: Kirsty Smy
Editorial assistant: Molly Farrell
Production editor: Sarah Cooke
Copyeditor: Lynda Watson
Proofreader: Derek Markham
Indexer: Silvia Benvenuto
Marketing manager: Alison Borg
Cover design: Francis Kenney
Typeset by: C&M Digitals (P) Ltd, Chennai, India
Printed and bound by CPI Group (UK) Ltd,
Croydon, CR0 4YY

© Sotirios Paroutis, Loizos Heracleous and Duncan Angwin 2016

First published 2013
This second edition published 2016

Apart from any fair dealing for the purposes of research or private study, or criticism or review, as permitted under the Copyright, Designs and Patents Act, 1988, this publication may be reproduced, stored or transmitted in any form, or by any means, only with the prior permission in writing of the publishers, or in the case of reprographic reproduction, in accordance with the terms of licences issued by the Copyright Licensing Agency. Enquiries concerning reproduction outside those terms should be sent to the publishers.

All material on the accompanying website can be printed off and photocopied by the purchaser/user of the book. The web material itself may not be reproduced in its entirety for use by others without prior written permission from SAGE. The web material may not be distributed or sold separately from the book without the prior written permission of SAGE. Should anyone wish to use the materials from the website for conference purposes, they would require separate permission from us. All material is © Sotirios Paroutis, Duncan Angwin and Loizos Heracleous, 2016

Library of Congress Control Number: 2015950066

British Library Cataloguing in Publication data

A catalogue record for this book is available from the British Library

ISBN 978-1-4739-1285-4
ISBN 978-1-4739-1286-1 (pbk)

At SAGE we take sustainability seriously. Most of our products are printed in the UK using FSC papers and boards. When we print overseas we ensure sustainable papers are used as measured by the PREPS grading system. We undertake an annual audit to monitor our sustainability.

SUMMARY OF CONTENTS

1	Practicing Strategy: Foundations and Importance	1

Section A   PRACTITIONERS — 17

2	Chief Executive Officers	19
3	Chief Strategy Officers	30
4	Strategy Teams	44
5	Middle Managers	57
6	Strategy Consultants	68

Section B   PRACTICES — 81

7	Strategy Tools	83
8	Influencing Strategy through Discourse	93

Section C   PRAXIS — 107

9	Strategic Alignment: The ESCO Model	109
10	Practicing Strategy across Firms: Insights from M&As	127
11	Strategic Ambidexterity: Dealing with Tensions	145

Section D   Case Studies — 159

12	Teaching Strategy using the Strategy-as-Practice Approach	161
13	Strategic Leadership and Innovation at Apple Inc.	168
14	Centrica: Strategizing in a Multi-utility	191
15	Narayana Health: Bringing Quality Healthcare to the Masses	212
16	A "Reliable" Recovery? The Turnaround of the Reliant Group	235
17	Marconi: When Strategists Hit the Perfect Storm	245
18	Lafarge vs. Blue Circle: Practices in a Hostile Takeover	256
19	Room for Improvement? Relocating a Business School	262
20	Strategy-making 2.0: Strategy Development Process at the Wikimedia Foundation	279

Index   304

CONTENTS

List of Mini Case Studies — xii
Guided Tour of the Book — xiii
Companion Website — xv
About the Authors — xvi
Preface — xvii
Praise for the First Edition — xviii

1 Practicing Strategy: Foundations and Importance — 1

    Learning Objectives — 1
1.1 Overview — 1
1.2 Strategy-making Processes: The Search for Action — 2
1.3 From Strategy to Strategizing — 4
1.4 Finding Misalignments across Levels: The ESCO Framework — 6
1.5 The Strategy-as-Practice Perspective — 7
1.6 Practitioners, Practices, and Praxis: The 3P Framework — 9
1.7 Conclusion — 10
    Route-map to this textbook — 11
    Revision Activities — 12
    Guidelines for the Revision Activities — 12
    Further Readings — 13
    References — 13

Section A PRACTITIONERS — 17

2 Chief Executive Officers — 19

    Learning Objectives — 19
2.1 Leadership and Upper Echelons — 19
2.2 Leadership Discourse and Creating Myths — 22
    Revision Activities — 27
    Further Readings — 27
    References — 28

3 Chief Strategy Officers — 30

	Learning Objectives	30
3.1	Introduction	30
3.2	Role, Location, and Types	31
3.3	Activities, Capabilities, and Networks	34
3.4	Tools and Formal Outputs	38
3.5	Conclusion	40
	Revision Activities	42
	Further Readings	43
	References	43

4 Strategy Teams — 44

	Learning Objectives	44
4.1	Introduction	44
4.2	Composition	45
4.3	Activities	45
4.4	Level and Mode of Strategizing	49
4.5	Conclusion	55
	Revision Activities	55
	Further Readings	55
	References	56

5 Middle Managers — 57

	Learning Objectives	57
5.1	Central and Peripheral Practitioners	57
5.2	Middle-level Managers	59
5.3	Engaged Strategy Participation	61
5.4	Collaborating with Strategy Communities	63
5.5	Conclusion	65
	Revision Activities	65
	Further Readings	66
	References	66

6 Strategy Consultants — 68

	Learning Objectives	68
6.1	Introduction	68
6.2	Characteristics and Roles	69

6.3	Consulting Interventions	72
6.4	The Consulting Profession in Focus	76
6.5	Conclusion	78
	Revision Activities	78
	Further Readings	78
	References	78

Section B   PRACTICES   81

7   Strategy Tools   83

	Learning Objectives	83
7.1	Types of Strategy Tools	83
7.2	Using Strategy Tools	85
7.3	Strategy Tools as Cognitive Artifacts	88
7.4	Strategy Tools as Material Artifacts	89
7.5	Conclusion	90
	Revision Activities	90
	Further Readings	90
	References	91

8   Influencing Strategy through Discourse   93

	Learning Objectives	93
8.1	Introduction	93
8.2	Language and Meaning in Organizations	94
8.3	Corresponding Views of Strategy and Organizations	95
8.4	Applying Discursive Approaches to Strategy and Organization	97
8.5	Conclusion	102
	Revision Activities	102
	Further Readings	103
	References	103

Section C   PRAXIS   107

9   Strategic Alignment: The ESCO Model   109

	Learning Objectives	109
9.1	Introduction	109
9.2	Strategic Alignment and Performance	110
9.3	Strategic Misalignment and Failure	113
9.4	Understanding Corporate Failure	113
9.5	Cases in Point: Strategic Misalignments and Failure at Worldcom and Nortel Networks	116

	Revision Activities	122
	Further Readings	123
	References	123

10 Practicing Strategy across Firms: Insights from M&As — 127

	Learning Objectives	127
10.1	Introduction	127
10.2	A Strategy-as-Practice Approach to M&A	129
10.3	Mini Case	135
10.4	Conclusion	141
	Revision Activities	142
	Further Readings	142
	References	143

11 Strategic Ambidexterity: Dealing with Tensions — 145

	Learning Objectives	145
11.1	Organizational Ambidexterity	145
11.2	Individual-level Ambidexterity	147
11.3	A Paradox-based Approach	148
11.4	Strategic Ambidexterity: Managing Paradoxical Demands	150
11.5	Conclusion	154
	Revision Activities	154
	Further Readings	155
	References	155

Section D Case Studies — 159

12 Teaching Strategy using the Strategy-as-Practice Approach — 161

Toward a Practice-led Approach to Learning and Teaching	161
Analysis of Practice in Case Studies	165
References	166

13 Strategic Leadership and Innovation at Apple Inc. — 168

Jobs' Turnaround and Rebuilding an Innovative Organization	169
Redefining the PC Industry	171
Growing the Apple ecosystem: Breakthrough innovation in the consumer electronics and entertainment industries	172
The Competitive Landscape	174
Playing with Different Rules	176
Corporate Culture and Organization Design at Apple	179

	Steve Jobs' Leadership	182
	Entering a New Apple Era	185
	References	187
14	**Centrica: Strategizing in a Multi-utility**	**191**
	A Changing Industry	191
	Surviving the Early Years	193
	Developing and Expanding	197
	Case Study Questions	211
	References	211
15	**Narayana Health: Bringing Quality Healthcare to the Masses**	**212**
	Redefining the Healthcare Industry	212
	The Global and Indian Healthcare Industry	214
	Narayana Health's Vision and Organization	216
	Can the Low-cost, High-quality Business Model work outside India?	227
	Appendices	228
	References	231
16	**A "Reliable" Recovery? The Turnaround of the Reliant Group**	**235**
	Overview	235
	History	235
	Taking Charge	237
	Doing Things Differently	239
	Crisis	241
	Crisis Averted?	242
	The Future	243
	Questions	244
	Sources	244
17	**Marconi: When Strategists Hit the Perfect Storm**	**245**
	The Deep Historical Background: GEC plc	245
	The Strategic Re-positioning of GEC (1996–2001)	248
	The Telecommunications Boom and Bust	250
	Strategists Hitting the Storm	252

	The End Game	253
	Questions	254
	Sources	255
18	**Lafarge vs. Blue Circle: Practices in a Hostile Takeover**	**256**
	Introduction	256
	Backdrop	256
	Post Deal Analysis	260
	Questions	261
19	**Room for improvement? Relocating a Business School**	**262**
	Introduction	262
	Background	263
	Oxford Brookes University Business School (OBBS)	263
	City Campus	266
	Competing in Higher Education	268
	Future Location for OBBS	269
	A Question of Space?	271
	Room for Improvement?	272
	Questions	278
20	**Strategy-making 2.0: Strategy Development Process at the Wikimedia Foundation**	**279**
	Background – Launching Wikipedia	279
	The Wikimedia Foundation and Chapter Organizations	280
	The Wikimedia Community	281
	Communication and Coordination – The Wiki Model	282
	Policies and Guidelines	283
	Wikimedia's Strategic Planning Project	284
	Designing the Process: Openness and Flexibility vs. Centralization and Control	285
	Reflecting on the Conclusion of the Process	294
	Appendices	296
	References	300
Index		304

LIST OF MINI CASE STUDIES

ESOLAR – choosing a new CEO	20
Charismatic leadership: six lessons from the public speaking of Steve Jobs	23
New CEO position needed to tackle social and political issues	26
Tesco – the group finance and strategy director	41
The strategy team at CISCO	49
Hewlett-Packard – associate, corporate strategy	51
DELL – internal strategy consultant, corporate strategy	53
Beiersdorf UK – strategy in action in a global company	62
BT Group – a strategy community in action	64
Booz Allen Hamilton (BAH)	69
Bain & Company – what top management consulting is about	70
Bain & Company – strategy consulting expertise	73
How a label embodies layers of meaning that shape strategic decisions	99
German management accounting as a technology of power	101
Tools influencing text	133
Practitioners' "talk"	134
"Talk" interacts with "text"	135
Twitter – simplicity as a business model for users, and the market too	146
Nokia – the burning platform memo	149
Quantum strategy: what Apple and Singapore Airlines have in common	153

GUIDED TOUR OF THE BOOK

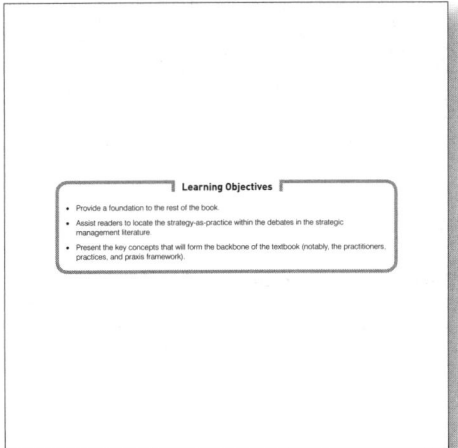

Learning Objectives
At the outset of each chapter is a useful list of the key aims and content covered to help you keep track of progress.

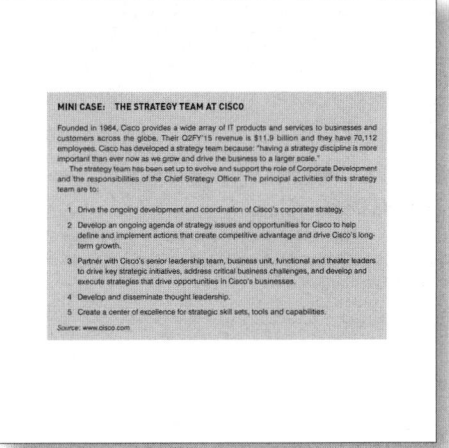

Mini Case Studies
Mini cases throughout the book highlight interesting real-life examples to help you link theory with practice.

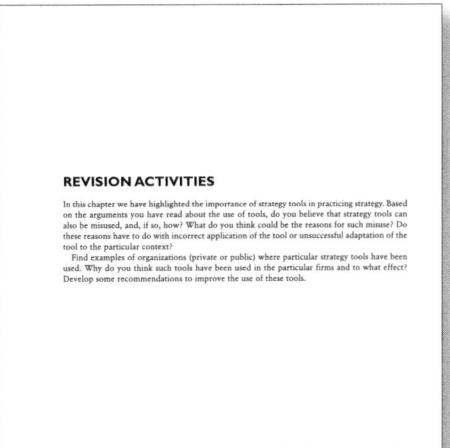

Revision Activities
Each chapter contains useful revision questions and guidelines to help you reflect on and check your understanding of what you have learned.

Additional Resources
At the end of each chapter you will find a suggested list of books, articles and websites so that you can explore key topics further.

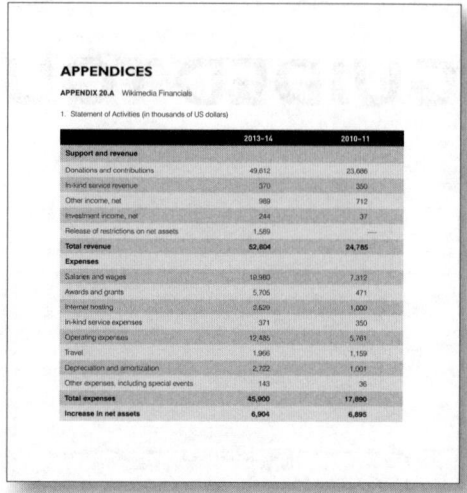

Extended Case Studies
Section D contains a series of in-depth case studies that cover a diverse range of organizations and contexts. The case studies are supported by useful appendices and exhibits.

COMPANION WEBSITE

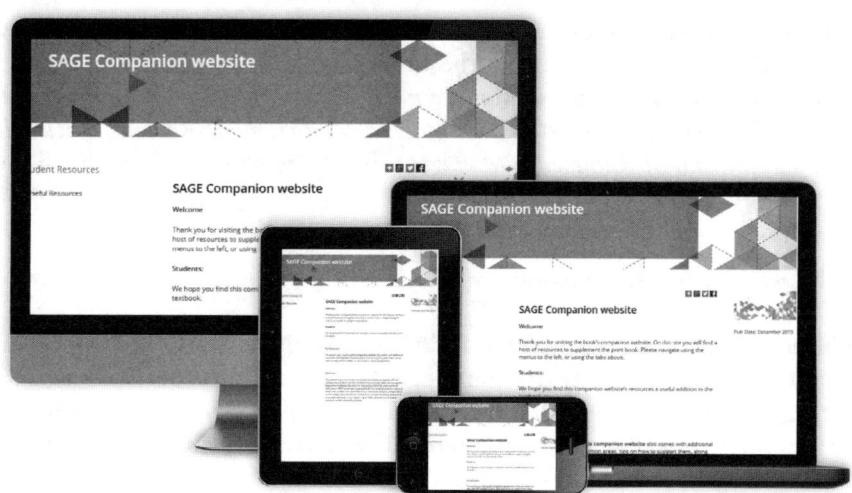

Practicing Strategy: Text and Cases is supported by a wealth of online resources for both students and lecturers to aid study and support teaching, which are available at https://study.sagepub.com/paroutispracticingstrategy2e

For Students

Author videos featuring discussions of key concepts offer insights into how the strategy-as-practice approach is applied to foster understanding and facilitate learning and bring theory to life.

Podcasts from the authors offer an alternative learning style to help you think more critically about the practicing strategy.

Additional online readings support the book, including free SAGE journal articles.

For Lecturers

Instructor's Manual provides you with suggested activities and examples to use in class or for assignments.

PowerPoint slides can be downloaded and customized for use in your own teaching.

ABOUT THE AUTHORS

Sotirios Paroutis is Associate Professor of Strategic Management and Assistant Dean at Warwick Business School. He earned his PhD from the University of Bath. His research has been published in journals such as the *Strategic Management Journal*, *Journal of Management Studies*, *Organization Studies*, *Human Relations*, *California Management Review*, *British Journal of Management*, and *Journal of Knowledge Management*. His research interests lie in the study of strategy practices and processes in challenging and complex organizational settings in the UK and globally. More information can be found at www.paroutis.org

Sotirios can be reached at sotirios.paroutis@wbs.ac.uk

Loizos Heracleous is Professor of Strategy and Organization at Warwick Business School. He earned his PhD from the University of Cambridge. His research has been published in leading journals such as the *Academy of Management Journal*, *Academy of Management Review*, *Strategic Management Journal*, *MIS Quarterly*, *Harvard Business Review*, and *MIT Sloan Management Review*. He researches strategic change processes, organization development, organizational discourse, corporate governance, and other related areas. More information can be found at www.heracleous.org

Loizos can be reached at loizos.heracleous@wbs.ac.uk

Duncan Angwin is the Sir Roland Smith Professor in Strategic Management at Lancaster University. He earned his PhD from the University of Warwick. He researches strategic practices in M&A and has recently completed a major EU-funded research project on European M&A. He holds a major research award at Said Business School, Oxford University, to study M&A communications practices. Duncan sits on the Advisory Boards of the M&A research centre, Cass Business School and a Grand Ecole business school, Paris and is senior judge for the Management Consulting Association. Duncan has published eight books and fifty journal articles on strategy and M&A. More information can be found at www.duncanangwin.com

Duncan can be reached at d.n.angwin@lancaster.ac.uk

PREFACE

Strategic management, as a discipline, has been undergoing exciting developments over the past few years. A number of theoretical, methodological, and empirical advancements have helped us gain new insights and renewed excitement about the way strategy is actually made and executed in organizations. One such stream of advancements has been made possible with the emergence of the "strategy-as-practice" perspective, which considers strategy not only as something an organization *has* but as something that its members *do*. As such, this perspective brings back to the surface of the debates in strategic management issues around agency, artifacts, processes and activities, among others.

The second edition of this textbook has been developed for those who want to gain insight into the strategy-as-practice perspective and its primary components: practitioners (the strategic actors), practices (their methods and tools), and praxis (their activities). In the chapters that follow we deal with a selective set of topics that have been nonetheless central in academic debates in the strategy-as-practice area and we have discovered them to be relevant to those studying practice-based issues in the business school classroom following our teaching experience. We approach each of these topics by using a mix of, mainly, academic studies and applied research aimed at practitioners. By doing so, we hope the reader will be inspired to seek out and investigate further practice issues and themes that are not included in this book. We also provide a set of case studies in the second part of this book that the reader can analyze to further appreciate how practice-related issues are applicable to real-life strategic situations. Compared to the first edition, this second edition is greatly enhanced and advanced on a number of areas. The structure of the textbook has been reshaped and better streamlined. We have made a number of enhancements and updates across the book and the case studies. There is also a lot of new content: we are now offering seven new chapters: in the first part of the book, chapters on: chief executive officers, middle level managers, strategic alignment, and strategic ambidexterity; and in the second part, new case studies about: the Narayana health, the turnaround of Reliant group and relocating a business school.

Our textbook is aimed at business school students, particularly at postgraduate level, as well as doctoral researchers and scholars of strategic management. It also serves as a reference point for advanced students and researchers of strategic management interested in studying and researching issues about the practicing of strategy. We hope that this second edition will receive the same exciting reception as our first edition.

A number of individuals have been supporting us during the process of developing this book. In particular, we would like to thank: Kirsty Smy, Molly Farrell, Lyndsay Aitken, Alison Borg, and Sarah Cooke for their publishing and marketing support. Also we would like to thank the community of strategy-as-practice scholars for their helpful comments, ideas, and insights on our first edition. Finally, we would like to thank our students – you are inspiring and stretching our thinking.

Sotirios, Loizos, and Duncan
July 2015

PRAISE FOR THE FIRST EDITION

'This book makes an important contribution by adopting a new stance of strategy as practice. It has a good mix of theory and practice and an excellent range of case studies.'
Professor Darren Calcher, CMI Management Book of the Year Category Judge

'A very interesting, absorbing and well-considered book that explores a subject often overlooked: that strategy must be executed and thus evolves in practice.'
Nigel Girling, CMI Management Book of the Year Category Judge

'This is a first: an academically rigorous textbook on the practicalities of strategizing. It will be a vital resource to all teachers and students interested in Strategy-as-Practice'
Richard Wittington, Professor of Strategy and Millmann Fellow, University of Oxford

'The book provides a step-by-step introduction to Strategy-as-Practice, a discussion of its main components and several exciting case studies. I am sure that both students and teachers will find the book of great value'
Professor David Seidl, Chair of Organization and Management, University of Zurich

'This is an outstanding strategy text that takes strategists and their work seriously. Students, practitioners and scholars who seek to understand the micro-levels of strategy including practitioners, practices and praxis will find this an invaluable reading'
Patrick Regnér, Professor of Strategic Management, Stockholm School of Economics

'This book is a welcome addition to the field of Strategic management. The case studies are original and really help to render the Strategy as Practice perspective accessible to practitioners and students alike'
Veronique Ambrosini, Professor of Management, Monash University, Australia

'The authors of this book have distilled the core messages of strategy-as-practice into a series of easy-to-read and easy-to-apply chapters. It has done well to retain sufficient sophistication for an academic audience, drawing on recent studies and explaining theoretical ideas, while also ensuring accessibility by presenting them in a format that is comprehensible for practitioners and students without prior knowledge in this area'
Jane Lê, University of Sydney Business School, University of Sydney

PRACTICING STRATEGY: FOUNDATIONS AND IMPORTANCE

Learning Objectives

- Provide a foundation to the rest of the book.
- Assist readers to locate the strategy-as-practice within the debates in the strategic management literature.
- Present the key concepts that will form the backbone of the textbook (notably, the practitioners, practices, and praxis framework).

OVERVIEW

1.1 The purpose of this chapter is to introduce the reader in the field of practice-based approaches to the study of strategy and organization, including its rationale and emergence. These will provide a basis for a clear identification of the key topics covered in the practice approach and a review of the main concepts involved in a key perspective to understand the practice of strategy: the strategy-as-practice perspective. By decoding the key concepts around the strategy-as-practice approach we encourage an appreciation of the micro-level aspects of strategy making and execution. Such micro-level aspects are not only of interest from a scholarly perspective, but also critical in any strategic review and can help practitioners develop a more nuanced understanding of the strengths and weaknesses of their strategy-making and execution processes. Overall, the key objective of this introductory chapter is to help the reader appreciate the micro-level foundations of strategy making and execution.

STRATEGY-MAKING PROCESSES: THE SEARCH FOR ACTION

1.2 The field of strategic management is often divided into different schools of thought. The planning and emergent schools are two fundamental schools that have shaped, and still influence, many debates in academia and practice. Based on the work of Chandler (1962), the planning (or rational) school considers strategy as the outcome of the sequential activities of strategic analysis, development, and implementation. The emergent school, on the other hand, led by Henry Mintzberg, considers strategy as not simply a plan but also a pattern that emerges over time based on experimentation and discussion (Mintzberg, 1973, 1978, 1987; Mintzberg and Waters, 1985). Mintzberg notes that "organizations develop plans for the future and they also evolve patterns out of their past" (1994: 24). Accordingly, strategy is perceived as more than just an intended outcome based on a top-down procedure and as a more complex, emergent, bottom-up process developed throughout the organization with the participation of multiple organizational members. Based on the foundations of these two schools, a number of frameworks have been developed concerned with the strategy-making processes that firms follow. Combining the learning around strategy-making processes, Hart (1992) developed an integrative framework consisting of five models (see Table 1.1). The main advantage of this model is that it integrates many of the insights from pre-existing strategy models by contrasting the roles of different management actors. In that way, strategy making is viewed as an organization-wide phenomenon.

Alongside Hart, the Bower–Burgelman (BB) process model of strategy making (Burgelman, 1983, 2002) has been a milestone in strategy process research. Bower (1970) developed a resource allocation process (RAP) model which was later modified and extended by Burgelman in the early 1980s using rich empirical insights. The result was the BB process model (Bower and Doz, 1979; Burgelman, 1983). The foundation of this process model was an evolutionary framework of the strategy-making process in established firms (see Figure 1.1). Burgelman's primary goal was to show the interactions between strategic behavior, corporate context, and the concept of corporate strategy. According to this model the strategy-making process is determined through strategic behavior that either is induced by top management or develops autonomously:

Autonomous strategic behavior introduces new categories for the definition of product or market opportunities. It develops from the bottom up within a company and covers project-championing efforts to mobilize corporate resources. Induced behavior on the other hand represents the guiding character of strategy. "The induced process concerns initiatives that are within the scope of the organization's current strategy and build on existing organizational learning" (Burgelman, 1991: 241).

Structural context determination means the top-down introduction of formal organizational structures (information, evaluation, reward systems, etc.) to shape the selection of strategic investments. Strategic context determination covers political activities of middle management that aim at combining autonomous strategic behavior on the product-market level with the current corporate strategy.

PRACTICING STRATEGY: FOUNDATIONS AND IMPORTANCE

TABLE 1.1 Hart's integrative framework

Contingency Factors	Command	Symbolic	Rational	Transactive	Generative
Environment	Simple; Low-level complexity	Dynamic; high velocity or radical change	Stable; Low degree of change	Complex; many stakeholders	Turbulent; Dynamic and complex
Firm Size	Small	Medium-Large	Medium-Large	Large	No relation
Stage of Firm Development	No relation	Rapid growth; reorientation	Steady growth	Mature	No relation
Strategic Orientation	No relation	Proactive change (Prospector / Analyzer)	Solidify position (Defender)	Continuous Improvement (Analyzer)	Innovation (Prospector)
Descriptors	**Command**	**Symbolic**	**Rational**	**Transactive**	**Generative**
Style	(Imperial) Strategy driven by leader or small top team	(Cultural) Strategy driven by mission and a vision of the future	(Analytical) strategy driven by formal structure and planning systems	(Procedural) strategy driven by internal process and mutual adjustment	(Organic) strategy driven by organizational actors' initiative
Role of Top Management	(Commander) Provide Direction	(Coach) Motivate and inspire	(Boss) Evaluate and control	(Facilitator) Empower and enable	(Sponsor) Endose and support
Role of Organizational Members	(Soldier) Obey orders	(Player) Respond to challenge	(Subordinate) Follow the system	(Participant) Learn and improve	(Entrepreneur) Experiment and take risks

Source: Hart (1992).

What is interesting about Burgelman's approach is that this autonomous process is perceived as an integral part of the strategy-making process:

> strategy making…involves keeping both processes (induced-autonomous) in play simultaneously at all times, even though one process or the other may be more prominent at different times in a company's evolution… A company rationally tolerates autonomous strategic initiatives because such initiatives explore and potentially extend the boundaries of the company's competencies and opportunities. (Burgelman, 2002: 14–15)

A deeper appreciation of the behavioral aspects shaping the strategy-making process comes from studies of managerial decision making. Miller and Friesen (1978) identified 11 strategy-making process dimensions including, for example, adaptiveness, analysis, expertise, integration, innovation, and risk taking. In his study, Fredrickson (1986) proposed dimensions such as proactiveness,

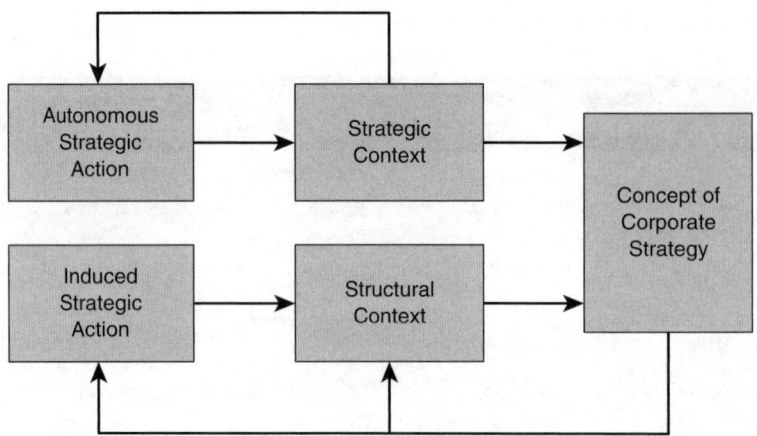

FIGURE 1.1 An evolutionary framework of the strategy-making process in established firms

Source: Adapted from Burgelman, 2002. Used with permission of Robert A. Burgelman.

rationality, comprehensiveness, risk taking, and assertiveness. Despite such developments most of our understanding of strategy making and execution has been mainly static, focusing on the macro, organizational level. As a result, a new approach, focusing on the micro-aspects of strategy or "strategizing," has emerged.

FROM STRATEGY TO STRATEGIZING

1.3 As indicated previously, in the present strategic management literature there is a limited analytical vocabulary to describe how managers practice strategy; as well as limited research attention to this topic as compared to the body of strategy scholarship, despite the emergence of the strategy-as-practice approach. Traditionally, conceptual and theoretical dichotomies within the strategy process area (think vs. act, content vs. process, micro vs. macro, rational process vs. political process) have bounded our understanding with respect to the day-to-day activities of strategy managers. Further, most process research has been fragmented, characterized by limited cumulative theory building and empirical testing (Rajagopalan et al., 1993).

Figure 1.2 summarizes the key areas in strategic content and process research presented across the macro and micro levels. Most research has been carried out at the macro-content level and to a lesser extent at the macro-process level. Accordingly, strategy academics realized that there was a need for an area of research that deals specifically with the actions and interactions of managers within and around the strategy process. The focus of such research is firmly at the "micro" level of Figure 1.2. This theoretical and empirical challenge has been pursued by researchers examining "strategizing" or "strategy-as-practice."

Strategizing refers to the strategy work (Vaara and Whittington, 2012) and encompasses all the continuous practices and processes through which strategy is conceived, maintained, renewed, and executed. An explicit and widely agreed definition of strategizing does not exist in the literature, however (the principal definitions are presented in Table 1.2). Strategizing focuses

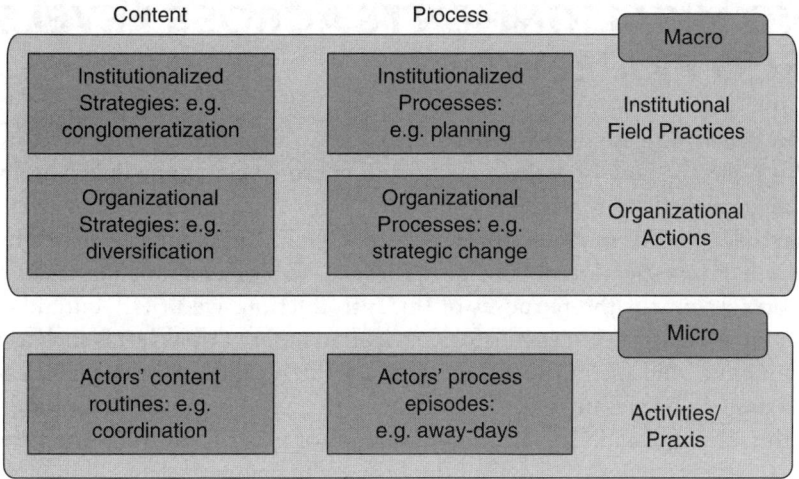

FIGURE 1.2 The micro and macro levels in strategic management research.

Adapted from: Whittington, Johnson and Melin (2004) Used with permission.

on the what, when, how, and why of making and executing strategy and demonstrates "the way strategies unfold over time, that is the way strategies are developed, realized, reproduced and transformed in an ongoing process" (Melin et al., 1999). Further, strategizing encapsulates the micro-level activities through which organizational members construct and enact strategies by utilizing both informal and formal means (Whittington, 1996). This approach also echoes the argument by Balogun et al. that "most strategy research has been about know what, whereas strategizing research looks for know how, know when and know where" (2003: 199).

TABLE 1.2 Definitions of the term strategizing

Definition	Source
"the detailed processes and practices which constitute the day-to-day activities of organizational life and which relate to strategic outcomes" (2003:3).	Johnson, Melin and Whittington (2003)
"the meeting, the talking, the form-filling and the number-crunching by which strategy actually gets formulated and implemented" (1996:732).	Whittington (1996)
"The concept of strategizing emphasizes the micro-level processes and practices involved as organizational members work to construct and enact organizational strategies, through both formal and informal means" (2003:111).	Maitlis and Lawrence (2003)
"an organizational learning process…new strategies evolve over time, not from discrete decisions but from indeterminate managerial behaviours embedded in a complex social setting" (2000:87).	Floyd and Wooldridge (2000)

Source: Paroutis (2006).

FINDING MISALIGNMENTS ACROSS LEVELS: THE ESCO FRAMEWORK

1.4 Before we investigate in more detail the strategy-as-practice perspective, it is important at this point to show how these macro and micro levels can be linked and what kind of insights can be generated for managers. There have been a number of frameworks that link the micro and macro levels. The model we present here is the ESCO model developed by Heracleous et al. (2009) in their investigation of Singapore Airlines. We will examine this framework in great detail in Chapter 9, but for the purposes of this introduction, we briefly outline the particular model. As shown in Figure 1.3, it stands for: Environment (at various levels such as the competitive, macroeconomic, and institutional), Strategy (at the business or corporate levels based on the kind of analysis to be conducted), Competencies (the core competencies of the organization that support the strategy), and Organization (the kinds of process, culture, structure, and people that operate in an integrated way to deliver the firm's core competencies). This model is scalable, and could be applied at the corporate, divisional, business, or functional levels as appropriate.

Heracleous and his colleagues note that: "Competencies must be aligned with the strategy and the organizational configuration must be aligned to deliver the desired competencies, all of this must support the strategy, which must be right for the competitive environment" (2009: 172).

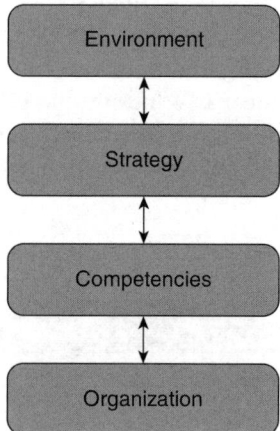

FIGURE 1.3 The ESCO model

Source: Heracleous, Wirtz, Pangarkar (2009).

Furthermore, according to Heracleous et al. (2009: 178–85) there can be a number of misalignments based on analysis through the ESCO model, namely:

Strategy is out of line with external competitive environment.

Organization and competencies fail to support strategy.

Incompatibilities and tensions exist within the organization level.

Reward misalignments, i.e., rewarding one thing but expecting another.

Failure to realign strategy and organization with environmental changes.

Misguided strategic actions leading to even greater misalignments.

The key message from this framework is that micro and macro levels are interrelated and managers need to be aware of these links. The classic problem of the separation between strategy formulation and strategy execution can be put in context when viewed from the perspective of the ESCO framework. The framework confirms that unless the strategy is translated into necessary competencies and appropriate organizational configuration, it will remain simply a plan. Secondly, a strategy plan is incomplete and most probably ineffectual unless it contains clear accountabilities and timeframes for the areas of competencies and organization. Finally, the framework suggests that identifying and dealing with misalignments represents a key task for the strategist.

THE STRATEGY-AS-PRACTICE PERSPECTIVE

1.5 **Strategy-as-practice** has been developed as an alternative perspective within the strategic management domain. Taking a leaf from a classic paper on the study of organizational culture (Smircich, 1983), this perspective recognizes that the traditional approach of the strategy discipline has been to treat strategy as a property of organizations – something an organization *has*. This has ignored that strategy is also something that executives *do* (Jarzabkowski, 2004). In this way, the type of research conducted in the "Mintzberg studies" on the nature of managerial work that we touched upon at the start of this chapter becomes once more the focus of the strategy field. According to strategy-as-practice scholars, there is a need to approach holistically "how managers and consultants act and interact in the whole strategy-making sequence" (Whittington, 1996: 732) and develop studies that focus more solidly on the practitioners of strategy (Angwin et al., 2009). As Johnson et al. stress: "In good part, the agenda for the micro-strategy and strategizing perspective is set by the limitations against which the process tradition has run" (2003: 13).

The strategy-as-practice perspective views strategizing "as a socially accomplished, situated activity arising from the actions and interactions of multiple level actors" (Jarzabkowski, 2005: 6). Practice researchers try to uncover the detailed actions and interactions that, taken together, over time constitute a strategy process (Paroutis and Pettigrew, 2007). Hence, the strategy-as-practice approach favors managerial agency, situated action, and both strategy stability and strategic change rather than focusing on a set of change events from a firm level of analysis, as most process studies tend to do. In addition to this anthropological orientation, where scholars are invited to delve deep into organizations to engage with executives' strategy activity in its intimate detail – sometimes described as "micro-strategy" (Johnson et al., 2003) – this perspective is also mindful of the aggregations of strategic activity into a bigger phenomenon.

Johnson et al. (2003) argued in favor of **activity theory** for studies investigating strategizing practice, but as yet empirical investigations utilizing activity theory have not been widespread.

According to activity theory, an organization can be regarded as an activity system comprising three main constituents: actors, collective social structures, and the practical activities in which they engage.

One of the first multi-level strategy-as-practice studies has been Jarzabkowski's research of three UK universities, which looked at the interaction between individual actions of top management team (TMT) actors and formal structures (Jarzabkowski, 2003; Jarzabkowski and Wilson, 2002). Regnér (2003) also investigated managers representing multiple levels across firms. His study of managerial actions at the center and the periphery of four multinational organizations suggests "a twofold character of strategy creation, including fundamentally different strategy activities in the periphery and centre, reflecting their diverse location and social embeddedness" (Regnér, 2003: 57). Further, Regnér's study focuses on the distinctiveness between central and peripheral managers and demonstrates "the great divide between periphery and centre" (2003: 77).

There have also been a number of other studies focusing on the micro-level aspects of strategizing. Oakes et al. (1998) studied the practices around a new business planning model in Canadian museums. Maitlis and Lawrence (2003) analyzed the failure of members of a UK symphony orchestra to construct an artistic strategy for their organization. These authors argue that failure in organizational strategizing can be understood as resulting from the interplay of certain elements of organizational discourse and specific kinds of political behavior. As indicated earlier, these empirical research efforts are attributed to the perceived failure of the traditional strategy process research to study the micro-level characteristics of how strategists actually think and act strategically in the whole strategy process of the firm. Alongside the growth in attention on this perspective, there have been calls for more critically oriented studies that focus on the fundamental issues of identity and power (Carter et al., 2008; Clegg, 2011). More recently, strategy-as-practice empirical studies have paid attention to topics such as: the role of discourse and rhetoric (Abdallah et al., 2011; Balogun et al., 2014; Bednarek et al., 2014; Dameron and Torset, 2014; Paroutis and Heracleous, 2013), and the role of materials, artefacts and tools (Dameron et al., 2015; Jarzabkowski et al., 2015a; Paroutis et al., 2015; Thomas and Ambrosini, 2015; Werle and Seidl, 2015; Wright et al., 2013).

Vaara and Whittington (2012) offer a comprehensive review of 57 strategy-as-practice empirical studies published since 2003 (24 studies relating to practices, 18 to praxis, and 15 to practitioners) and develop a set of five research directions for the strategy-as-practice perspective (placing agency in a web of practices, recognizing the macro-institutional nature of practices, focusing attention on emergence in strategy making, exploring how the material matters, and promoting critical analysis). Importantly, the authors note the distinctiveness of the "strategy-as-practice" label that:

> [it] carries with it a double meaning: "practice" signals both an attempt to be close to the world of practitioners and a commitment to sociological theories of practice ... its focus on the ways in which actors are enabled by organizational and wider social practices in their decisions and actions provides a distinctive contribution to research on strategic management. (2012: 2)

Overall, **strategy-as-practice scholars** examine the way in which actors interact with the social and physical features of context in the everyday activities that constitute practice. They investigate how managerial actors perform the work of strategy, both through their social interactions with other actors and through practices present within a context, as well as habits, tools, events, artifacts, and socially defined modes of acting through which the stream of strategic activity is constructed. Through their studies strategy-as-practice scholars aim to develop, "more precise and contextually sensitive theories about the enactment and impact of practices as well as about critical factors shaping differences in practice outcomes" (Jarzabkowski et al., 2015b).

PRACTITIONERS, PRACTICES, AND PRAXIS: THE 3P FRAMEWORK

1.6 Three key concepts have been used to encapsulate the strategy-as-practice approach: practitioners, practices, and praxis. This **3P framework** helps reveal the micro-level aspects of strategizing by focusing on the "who," "how," "where," and "when" of strategic actions (Figure 1.4).

Practitioners are the actors of strategizing, including managers, consultants, and specialized internal change agents. Overall, as Vaara and Whittington note:

> Practices refer to the various tools, norms, and procedures of strategy work, from analytical frameworks such as Porter's Five Forces to strategic planning routines such as strategy workshops. Praxis refers to the activity involved in strategy-making, for example, in strategic planning processes or meetings. Practitioners are all those involved in, or seeking to influence, strategy-making. (2012: 6)

FIGURE 1.4 The praxis, practitioners and practices framework

Adapted from Whittington, 2006. Used with permission.

The concept of **practices** refers to the various methods, tools, and techniques that practitioners utilize when they strategize. These methods, in many organizations over long periods of time, tend to become standardized and routinized ways of analyzing strategic issues. In other words, practices are "the shared routines of behaviour, including traditions, norms and procedures for thinking, acting and using 'things', this last in the broadest sense" (Whittington, 2006: 619).

Praxis refers to the activity comprising the work of strategizing. This work encompasses all the meeting, consulting, writing, presenting, communicating, and so on that are required in order to make and execute strategy. In other words, "all the various activities involved in the deliberate formulation and implementation of strategy" (Whittington, 2006: 619). Activities are defined as "the day to day stuff of management. It is what managers do and what they manage" (Johnson et al., 2003: 15).

Importantly, across these three concepts there are areas of overlap, as indicated in Figure 1.4. Each area of overlap raises a number of interesting questions about the conduct of strategy. For instance, in the area where the concepts of "Practices" and "Practitioners" meet we could raise a number of related questions, for instance "what kinds of methods do CEOs use to help them strategize?" or "how are particular planning techniques/tools/SWOT used in action by consultants?". Similarly, in the "Praxis" and "Practices" area of overlap we could raise questions such as "what kinds of actions do away-days encourage?" and "do particular strategy tools actually help us think in more innovative terms about our strategy?".

CONCLUSION

1.7 In this introductory chapter we have examined the move to study the micro levels of strategy paying particular attention to the strategy-as-practice perspective. We showed that this approach fundamentally moves away from modernist and positivist views of strategy that focus on the macro scale of organizational activity toward a more micro-level, humanistic, behavioral, interpretive approach to strategy making and execution. Integrating these insights with the ESCO model that we saw earlier, we arrive at the summary shown in Figure 1.5.

At the **macro level**, the more traditional approach to strategy, attention is on the environment and the key question is where to locate the organization among its competitors. At the level of the environment, the classic considerations of industrial organization (Porter, 1980, 1985) are relevant, but at the strategy level, the assumption is that managers and organizations have a choice on which environmental domains to compete in and how to position the organization (Child, 1972).

At the **micro level**, strategy is conceptualized as a *situated* and *socially constructed* activity involving multiple actors. The key question here is how to practice strategy and organize the culture, process, and structure in a way that supports the core competencies of the firm. At this level, considerations of the resource-based view (Barney, 1991) are relevant. The particular strategy actors, their tools, and their activities will be the focus of the following chapters.

PRACTICING STRATEGY: FOUNDATIONS AND IMPORTANCE

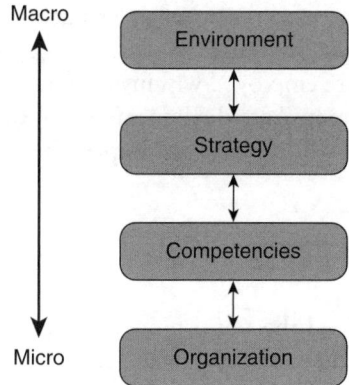

FIGURE 1.5 The ESCO model through the macro and micro lenses

ROUTE-MAP TO THIS TEXTBOOK

The purpose of this book is to deal with a number of topics that contribute to our understanding of strategy-as-practice. These topics are divided into two parts and four sections. The first part (sections A to C) aims to contribute to our understanding of the actors, methods and activities in and around the practice of strategy (Figure 1.6), and the second part (Section D) provides a number of case studies to illustrate the concepts presented in the first part. Section A deals with particular kinds of strategy practitioners, both internal and external to the organization (Chapters 2 to 6). The aim here is to highlight the importance of the individual strategists in making and

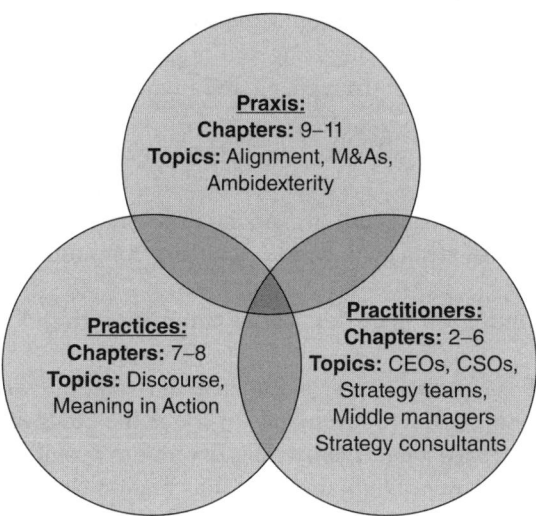

FIGURE 1.6 The chapters and key themes in the first part of the textbook

executing strategy. Section B focuses on the strategic artifacts and discursive practices employed by these practitioners to alter their organization's strategy (Chapters 7 and 8). Section C deals with the ways strategic activities are employed within and across organizations (Chapters 9 to 11). The objective of this part is to demonstrate the importance of the specific context within strategy that practitioners are called upon to formulate and implement.

REVISION ACTIVITIES

In this chapter we have highlighted the importance of micro-level aspects of strategy making and execution. Based on what you just read in the current chapter and your own experience, what kinds of questions would you be asking at the micro level as a student and researcher of strategy?

Select an organization that you are familiar with. Conduct an analysis of that organization's micro-level strategy using the ESCO and 3P models. What kinds of insights do you gain?

GUIDELINES FOR THE REVISION ACTIVITIES

Strategy at the micro level is a situated and socially constructed activity involving multiple actors. As such, the kinds of questions that we could raise relate to the kinds of actions, tools, and methods used to practice strategy and the ways to shape culture, processes, and structure to develop the core competencies of the firm.

Whittington (2003) provides the following questions related to the strategy-as-practice perspective at the micro level:

- How and where is strategizing and organizing work actually done?
- Who does the formal work of strategizing and organizing and how do they get to do it?
- What are the skills required for strategizing and organizing work and how are they acquired?
- What are the common tools and techniques of strategizing and organizing and how are these used in practice?
- How is the work of strategizing and organizing itself organized?
- How are the products of strategizing and organizing communicated and consumed?

Under each question Whittington provides a brief commentary (and references) that you can investigate further.

Using the ESCO and 3P frameworks you can gain at least two key types of insights: (a) about the way strategy is conducted at the micro level; and (b) about the kinds of potential misalignments that exist/have existed in the particular organization. In order to provide such analysis at the micro level you will appreciate that you need good-quality information from the particular organization (e.g., based on your own experience of that firm). Accordingly, micro-level analysis is demanding and should only be conducted if there is enough and good-quality information available.

FURTHER READINGS

- **Book**: Heracleous, L., Wirtz, J., and Pangarkar, N. (2009) *Flying High in a Competitive Industry*. Singapore: McGraw-Hill. An insightful investigation of one of the world's leading airlines, Singapore Airlines, and a number of strategy frameworks, including the ESCO model which we examined in Section 1.4.

- **Papers**: For four encompassing sets of theoretical and empirical papers on the strategy-as-practice perspective you can look at the following special issues: *Journal of Management Studies*, 40(1), 2003; *Human Relations*, 60(1), 2007; *Journal of Management Studies*, 51(2), 2014; and *British Journal of Management*, 26(S1), 2015.

- **Papers**: Jarzabkowski, P. and Spee, A. P. (2009) Strategy-as-practice: a review and future directions for the field. *International Journal of Management Reviews*, 11, 69–95; and Vaara, E. and Whittington, R. (2012) Strategy-as-practice: taking social practices seriously. *Academy of Management Annals*, 6(1), 285–336. Two comprehensive reviews of the strategy-as-practice area of research that provide classifications of papers employing the particular approach and avenues for future research.

- **Website**: For the latest announcements (for instance, for calls for special issues of journals, calls for conference papers, workshops and jobs advertisements), discussion forums, and journal publications about the strategy-as-practice area, you can register at the SAP-IN (Strategy as Practice International Network) at http://www.s-as-p.org

- **Website**: In order to find out more details about the aims, activities, and conferences offered by academic communities associated with the strategy-as-practice perspective you can visit: the Strategizing, Activities and Practices (SAP) interest group of the Academy of Management at http://sap.aomonline.org; the Strategy Practice interest group at the Strategic Management Society at http://practiceig.pbworks.com; and the Strategy-as-Practice special interest group at the British Academy of Management at http://www.bam.ac.uk/sigs-strategy-practice.

REFERENCES

Abdallah, C., Denis, J.-L., and Langley, A. (2011) Having your cake and eating it too: Discourses of transcendence and their role in organizational change dynamics. *Journal of Organizational Change Management*, 24(3): 333–48.

Angwin, D., Paroutis, S., and Mitson, S. (2009) Connecting up strategy: Are senior strategy directors (SSDs) a missing link? *California Management Review*, 51(3): 74–94.

Balogun, J., Huff, A. S., and Johnson, G. (2003) Three responses to the methodological challenges of studying strategizing. *Journal of Management Studies*, 40(1): 197–224.

Balogun, J., Jacobs, C., Jarzabkowski, P., Mantere, S., and Vaara, E. (2014) Placing strategy discourse in context: Sociomateriality, sensemaking, and power. *Journal of Management Studies*, 51(2): 175–201.

Barney, J. B. (1991) Firm resources and sustained competitive advantage. *Journal of Management*, 17: 99–120.

Bednarek, R., Paroutis, S., and Sillince, J. (2014) Practicing transcendence: Rhetorical strategies and constructing a response to paradox. *Academy of Management Best Paper Proceedings*. 2014 Strategizing, Activities and Practices (SAP) IG Best Paper Award.

Bower, J. L. (1970) *Managing the Resource Allocation Process: A Study of Corporate Planning and Investment*. Boston, MA: Harvard Business School Press.

Bower, J. L. and Doz, Y. (1979) Strategy formulation: A social and political process. In D. E. Schendel and C. W. Hofer (eds.), *Strategic Management*. Boston, MA: Little, Brown, 152–66.

Burgelman, R. A. (1983) A process model of internal corporate venturing in the diversified maker firm. *Administrative Science Quarterly*, 28(2): 223–44.

Burgelman, R. A. (1991) Intraorganizational ecology of strategy making and organizational adaption: Theory and field research. *Organization Science*, 2(3): 239–62.

Burgelman, R. A. (2002) *Strategy Is Destiny: How Strategy-Making Shapes a Company's Future*. New York: Free Press.

Carter, C. R., Clegg, S. R., and Kornberger, M. (2008) Strategy as practice? *Strategic Organization*, 6(1): 83–99.

Chandler, A. D. (1962) *Strategy and Structure: Chapters in the History of the American Industrial Enterprise*. Cambridge, MA: MIT Press.

Child, J. (1972) Organizational structure, environments and performance: The role of strategic choice. *Sociology*, 6: 1–22.

Clegg, S. R. (2011) Book Review: *Cambridge Handbook of Strategy as Practice*. *Organization Studies*, 32: 1587–9.

Dameron, S. and Torset, C. (2014) The discursive construction of strategists' subjectivities: Towards a paradox lens. *Journal of Management Studies*, 51(2): 291–319.

Dameron, S., Le, J., and LeBaron, C. (2015) Materializing strategy and strategizing material: Why matter matters. *British Journal of Management*, 26(S1): S1–S12.

Floyd, S. W. and Wooldridge, B. (2000) *Building Strategy from the Middle: Reconceptualizing Strategy Process*. Thousand Oaks, CA: Sage.

Fredrickson, J. W. (1986) The strategic decision process and organizational structure. *Academy of Management Review*, 11(2): 280–97.

Hart, S. L. (1992) An integrative framework for strategy-making processes. *Academy of Management Review*, 17(2): 327–51.

Heracleous, L., Wirtz, J., and Pangarkar, N. (2009) *Flying High in a Competitive Industry*. Singapore: McGraw-Hill.

Jarzabkowski, P. (2003) Strategic practices: An activity theory perspective on continuity and change. *Journal of Management Studies*, 40(1): 23–55.

Jarzabkowski, P. (2004) Strategy as practice: Recursiveness, adaptation and practices-in-use. *Organization Studies*, 25(4): 529–60.

Jarzabkowski, P. (2005) *Strategy as Practice: An Activity-Based View*. UK: Sage.

Jarzabkowski, P. and Spee, A. P. (2009) Strategy-as-practice: A review and future directions for the field. *International Journal of Management Reviews*, 11: 69–95.

Jarzabkowski, P. and Wilson, D. C. (2002) Top teams and strategy in a UK university. *Journal of Management Studies*, 39(3): 357–83.

Jarzabkowski, P., Burke, G., and Spee, P. (2015a) Constructing spaces for strategic work: A multimodal perspective. *British Journal of Management*, 26(S1): S26–S47.

Jarzabkowski, P., Kaplan, S., Seidl, D., and Whittington, R. (2015b) On the risk of studying practice in isolation: Linking what, who, and how in strategy research. *Strategic Organization*, published online before print August 27, 2015, doi: 10.1177/1476127015604125.

Johnson, G., Melin, L., and Whittington, R. (2003) Micro strategy and strategising: Towards an activity-based view. Guest Editors' Introduction. *Journal of Management Studies*, 40(1): 3–22.

Maitlis, S. and Lawrence, T. B. (2003) Orchestral manoeuvres in the dark: Understanding failure in organizational strategizing. *Journal of Management Studies*, 40(1): 109–39.

Melin, L., Ericson, T., and Müllern, T. (1999) Organizing in strategizing. Paper presented at the Nordfek Conference, Helsinki.

Miller, D. and Friesen, P. H. (1978) Archetypes of strategy formulation. *Management Science*, 24(9): 921–33.

Mintzberg, H. (1973) *The Nature of Managerial Work*. New York: Harper & Row.
Mintzberg, H. (1978) Patterns in strategy formation. *Management Science*, 24(9): 934–48.
Mintzberg, H. (1987) The strategy concept. 1: 5 Ps for strategy. *California Management Review*, 30(1): 11–24.
Mintzberg, H. (1994) *The Rise and Fall of Strategic Planning*. New York: Free Press.
Mintzberg, H. and Waters, J. A. (1985) Of strategies, deliberate and emergent. *Strategic Management Journal*, 6(3): 257–72.
Oakes, L. S., Townley, B., and Cooper, D. J. (1998) Business planning as pedagogy: Language and control in a changing institutional field. *Administrative Science Quarterly*, 43(2): 257–92.
Paroutis, S. (2006) Strategizing in the multi-business firm. Doctoral thesis, School of Management, University of Bath.
Paroutis, S. and Heracleous, L. (2013) Discourse revisited: Dimensions and employment of first-order strategy discourse during institutional adoption. *Strategic Management Journal*, 34(8): 935–56.
Paroutis, S. and Pettigrew, A. M. (2007) Strategizing in the multi-business firm: Strategy teams at multiple levels and over time. *Human Relations*, 60(1): 99–135.
Paroutis, S., Franco, A., and Papadopoulos, T. (2015) Visual interactions with strategy tools: Producing strategic knowledge in workshops. *British Journal of Management*, 26(S1): S48–S66.
Porter, M. E. (1980) *Competitive Strategy: Techniques for Analyzing Industries and Competitors*. New York: Free Press.
Porter, M. E. (1985) *Competitive Advantage: Creating and Sustaining Superior Performance*. New York: Free Press.
Rajagopalan, N., Rasheed, A. M. A., and Datta, D. K. (1993) Strategic decision processes: Critical review and future directions. *Journal of Management*, 19(2): 349–84.
Regnér, P. (2003) Strategy creation in the periphery: Inductive versus deductive strategy making. *Journal of Management Studies*, 40(1): 57–82.
Smircich, L. (1983) Concepts of culture and organizational analysis. *Administrative Science Quarterly*, 28: 339–58.
Thomas, L. and Ambrosini, V. (2015) Materializing strategy: The role of comprehensiveness and management controls in strategy formulation in volatile environments. *British Journal of Management*, 26 (S1): S105–S124.
Vaara, E. and Whittington, R. (2012) Strategy-as-practice: Taking social practices seriously. *Academy of Management Annals*, 6(1): 285–336.
Werle, F. and Seidl, D. (2015) The layered materiality of strategizing: Epistemic objects and the interplay between material artefacts in the exploration of strategic topics. *British Journal of Management*, 26 (S1): S67–S89.
Whittington, R. (1996) Strategy as practice. *Long Range Planning*, 29(5): 731–5.
Whittington, R. (2003) The work of strategizing and organizing: For a practice perspective. *Strategic Organization*, 1(1): 117–25.
Whittington, R. (2006) Completing the practice turn in strategy research. *Organization Studies*, 27(5): 613–34.
Whittington, R., Johnson, G., and Melin, L. (2004) The emerging field of strategy practice: Some links, a trap, a choice and a confusion. Paper presented at the European Group for Organization Studies Conference.
Wright, R., Paroutis, S., and Blettner, D. (2013) How useful are the strategic tools we teach in business schools? *Journal of Management Studies*, 50(1): 92–125.

PRACTITIONERS A

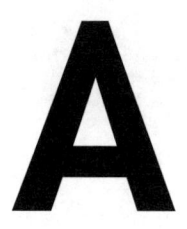

The purpose of Section A is to present the primary practitioners tasked to make and execute strategy. Our aim is not to provide an account of all available practitioners, but instead to focus on those who play key roles in the practicing of strategy. Based on our research and experience, we have decided to focus this part on five primary categories of actors: Chief Executive Officers (Chapter 2), Chief Strategy Officers (Chapter 3), strategy teams (Chapter 4), middle managers (Chapter 5), and strategy consultants (Chapter 6). These internal and external actors are often responsible for creating, communicating and executing strategic initiatives and oversee the strategy process in their organizations. Combined, these chapters showcase the multiple actors involved in the complex task that is the practice of strategy in the modern firm.

CHIEF EXECUTIVE OFFICERS

2

Learning Objectives

- Understand the characteristics of the chief executive officer role and its importance in modern firms.
- Appreciate the ways Chief Executive Officers (CEOs) influence the practice of strategy.
- Offer an additional lens to our understanding of CEOs, not only as decision makers, but as creators and communicators of strategy.

LEADERSHIP AND UPPER ECHELONS

2.1 Leadership has the potential to shape the ways organizations and their actors create and execute strategy, even in complex settings (Colville and Murphy, 2006; Jarzabkowski and Fenton, 2006). Within the leadership domain, the role and influence of Chief Executive Officers (CEOs) has been a central issue (Finkelstein and Hambrick, 1996; Hambrick and Mason, 1984; Pettigrew, 1992). The CEOs together with the top management team and other collective organizational actors and structures, have a decisive influence in building the history and culture of their firms (Weick and Roberts, 1993).

The work of Hambrick, Mason, and Finkelstein has pioneered the establishment of the *upper echelons* perspective. This perspective argues that the strategic choices and performance of an organization are directly related to the psychological (i.e., cognitive base and values) and observable (i.e., age, education, functional tracks) characteristics of its TMT (refer to Figure 2.1 below). Hambrick (2007) in an update to his seminal paper with Mason (Hambrick and Mason, 1984) notes that:

The central idea in our original paper, and the core of upper echelons theory, has two interconnected parts: (1) executives act on the basis of their personalized interpretations of the strategic situations they face, and (2) these personalized construals are a function of the executives' experiences, values, and personalities. As such, the theory is built on the premise of *bounded rationality* (Cyert and March, 1963) – the idea that informationally complex, uncertain situations are not objectively "knowable" but, rather, are merely interpretable (Mischel, 1977). If we want to understand why organizations do the things they do, or why they perform the way they do, we must consider the biases and dispositions of their most powerful actors – their top executives.

Research has also focused on the national differences of senior managers. For instance, a recent upper echelons study demonstrates that the effect of CEOs on firm performance is substantially greater in US firms than in German and Japanese firms (Crossland and Hambrick, 2007).

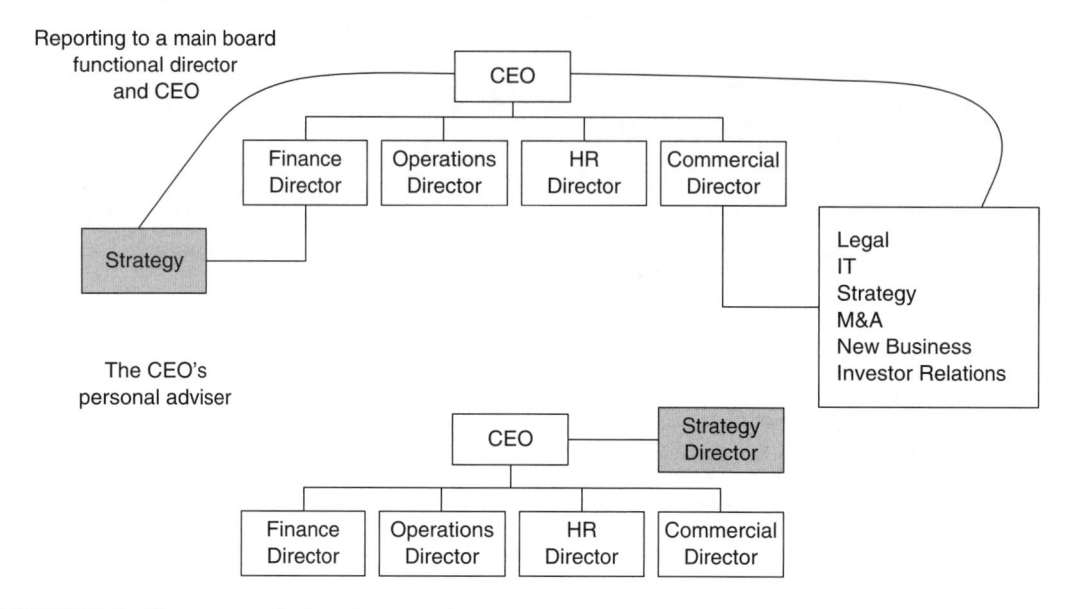

FIGURE 2.1 The upper echelons framework

Source: Hambrick and Mason, 1984.

MINI CASE: ESOLAR – CHOOSING A NEW CEO

eSolar is an Idealab company founded in 2007 and based in Pasadena, California. It develops, constructs, and deploys cost-effective, concentrating solar power (CSP) power plants. The approach the company follows marries a low-impact, prefabricated form factor with advanced optics and computer software engineering to meet the demands of utilities of any size for clean, renewable, and cost-competitive solar energy. By focusing on the key business obstacles that have characterized large solar installations – price, scalability, speed of deployment, and grid impact – eSolar has developed a proprietary solution to make a dramatic reduction in the cost of solar thermal technology.

CHIEF EXECUTIVE OFFICERS

The founder and first CEO of eSolar was Bill Gross. While still in college, he founded Solar Devices, a firm that sold plans and kits for solar energy products. He then acted as CEO of the technology incubator Idealab, which helped to found several successful companies, including Overture (acquired by Yahoo!), CarsDirect, and Picasa (acquired by Google). Idealab moved into the renewable energy market with Energy Innovations, a sister company to eSolar, that focuses on the retail rooftop solar market. Mr. Gross sits on the Board of Directors of the California Institute of Technology, where he obtained his BS in Mechanical Engineering.

In the period 2009–10, eSolar grew rapidly, gaining a global presence, especially in Asia. Its biggest licensing agreement was with Penglai Electric, a privately owned Chinese electrical power equipment manufacturer, to build solar thermal power plants of at least 2 gigawatt (GW) in China by 2021. The solar thermal power plants will be co-located with biomass electricity generation facilities. Penglai Electric will leverage local manufacturing to source some of the equipment. In total, the plants will eliminate 15 million tons of carbon dioxide emissions annually. "Using the power of the sun, eSolar's technology minimizes the environmental impact on manufacturing and deployment while maximizing land and cost efficiency," said Liu Guangyu, Chairman and CEO of Penglai Electric. "We are extremely grateful to the Chinese government for playing a major role in promoting zero-carbon renewable energy." "With Penglai as our partner and with the strong support of the Chinese government, eSolar is proud to be the first company to deliver the benefits of cost-effective solar thermal power to China," said Bill Gross.

With this growing momentum, eSolar transformed from a solutions-based, entrepreneurial firm to a global player in a highly competitive global power market. In order to deal with this change, the Board of the firm decided to appoint John Van Scoter as CEO. Mr. Van Scoter had 25 years of experience in the development and implementation of global market strategies for emerging technologies. He joined eSolar as the company matured from pioneering startup to global market leader. "John has a proven track record and invaluable expertise in bringing innovative technologies up through the business lifecycle," said Bill Gross:

> With our first plant online and key partnerships in place, eSolar is ready for its next phase of commercial growth and John is the best person to lead that effort. His previous work illustrates a successful formula that identifies winning technologies, develops them on a global scale, and cultivates close customer/partner relationships. John is a perfect match for eSolar as we transition to mainstream adoption.

Throughout his 25-year career at Texas Instruments, Mr. Van Scoter led several successful initiatives, most notably as Senior Vice President of the Digital Light Processing (DLP) product division, where he led product commercialization and the growth to profitability. Mr. Van Scoter developed Texas Instruments' alternative energy strategy, providing semiconductor solutions for smart grid/meter, solar, wind, and energy harvesting markets. He successfully transitioned new technologies through building new partner and customer relationships and executing large-scale global projects. "For two decades, I've helped promising new technologies thrive beyond the realm of R&D to make an impact on how the world operates," he said. "As we look for new and more efficient ways to meet growing energy needs, eSolar offers a cost-effective, highly reliable solution. I'm extremely excited to join eSolar and lead the next wave of hyper-growth." He holds a Bachelor's degree in Mechanical Engineering from the University of Vermont and has completed advanced courses at both Harvard University and the Wharton School of the University of Pennsylvania.

Source: www.esolar.com

As mentioned in Chapter 1, for the strategy-as-practice approach, strategy is conceptualized as a situated and socially constructed activity involving *multiple actors* who interact to accomplish the work of strategizing. Accordingly, there have been studies focusing on: top managers (Jarzabkowski, 2008), middle managers (Balogun, 2003; Mantere, 2008; Rouleau, 2005), strategy directors and their teams (Angwin et al., 2009; Paroutis and Heracleous, 2013; Paroutis and Pettigrew, 2007), strategy champions (Mantere, 2005), and expert personnel (Laine and Vaara, 2007).

LEADERSHIP DISCOURSE AND CREATING MYTHS

2.2 Studies have examined how managers utilize discourse to legitimize their position or encourage change (Hardy et al., 2000; Heracleous and Barrett, 2001; Suddaby and Greenwood, 2005). Johnson et al. (2008) propose that effective use of discourse can be a distinct advantage for an individual and note that it can help legitimize the CEO, as a credible strategist "making a difference" and dealing with the most important (i.e., strategic) areas of the business (2008: 43). Tsoukas (2005) argues that what is empirically interesting to explore is how the unit, between changes in language and changes in practices, works as well as through "what discursive strategies a new discourse is made to resonate with individuals?" (ibid., 2005: 99). A discursive approach makes this mediating role researchable in that the subjects, concepts, and objects of study are all accessible, or observable via words (Clegg et al., 2006; Fairclough, 1997; Heracleous, 2006). As such, a discursive approach to the study of particular strategists, such as the CEO or the chief strategy officer (Angwin et al., 2009), can help reveal how their performances relate to strategy and institutional phenomena (Brown et al., 2012; Paroutis and Heracleous, 2013).

In their critical reflection of strategy-as-practice Carter, Clegg and Kornberger (2008) argued that work in the strategy-as-practice perspective can help uncover the performative language games that are deployed in the creation of strategy. A deeper examination of these language games or the broader leadership discourse can help us reveal the mechanisms employed by key strategic actors, such as the CEOs, in making and executing strategy (Mckeown, 2010) and the resistance to these mechanisms (Vaara, 2010). While we examine in detail the ways discourse influences strategy in Chapter 8, below we consider more specifically the role of myths in practicing strategy.

Myths can be perceived as ideology in narrative form (Lincoln, 2006), in other words, as particular types of narratives or stories that have moral/ideological foundations, such as when particular actors from the past are perceived as heroes (for instance when an organizational myth is about the founders of the firm who are perceived as heroes because they used innovative methods, for their era, to grow the firm). Van Leeuwen (2008) distinguishes between moral tales in which actors are rewarded for doing what is considered good or for restoring order after facing difficulty and taking risks, with a happy ending for our heroes, whereas cautionary tales convey the negative consequences of being "bad," for failing to conform, or perform.

Paroutis et al. (2013) examined how successive CEOs in Hewlett-Packard used particular discursive mechanisms and myths over a 27-year period. They found that CEOs in HP committed to discourses of authorization, moral evaluation, rationalization and mythopoesis early in their tenure to shape the direction of their firm's strategic conversation. Such discourses tend to include at the clarification of the new strategy concepts adopted and a detailed explanation of the future strategy in relation to the predecessor CEO discourse. Overall, they found CEO discourse to be intertextually linked with external texts, in an effort to further strengthen the persuasive nature of internal texts. The authors also argue that the myths told by CEOs will be shaped by their identities (Boje, 2001; Brown, 2006) and their view of what needs to be said, done, and believed; but at the same time shape their own identities as strategists (Paroutis and Heracleous, 2013) who can have a legitimate and credible voice inside the firm.

Another study focusing on leadership discourse by Heracleous and Klaering (2014) entitled Charismatic Leadership and Rhetorical Competence: An Analysis of Steve Jobs' Rhetoric, published in *Group & Organization Management*, looked at how Jobs adapted his rhetoric for different situations. Using Aristotle's classic tools of persuasion – ethos, pathos, and logos – the study looked at how Jobs used each of them in different situations, from the courtroom, to a TV interview and a conference on digital technology. This study also informs our arguments for Chapter 8.

MINI CASE: CHARISMATIC LEADERSHIP: SIX LESSONS FROM THE PUBLIC SPEAKING OF STEVE JOBS

Steve Jobs provides business leaders with a perfect template of how to deliver expertly tailored rhetoric, according to Heracleous and Klaering (2014). The late Apple boss was a master of the art of effective and persuasive speaking, employing various strategies to adapt to differing scenarios and situations, while still delivering a constant message.

With his cool, calm exterior combined with a charismatic personality, Steve Jobs is often seen as the poster child for business leaders wanting to take center stage and win over audiences and customers with a compelling rhetoric. Jobs was instrumental in Apple becoming the world's most valuable publicly traded company within just over a decade after returning to the firm he co-founded. His "reality distortion field," in other words his ability to bring people round to his way of thinking, is well known and admired. Here, Loizos Heracleous, Professor of Strategy, reveals six lessons we can learn from Jobs' rhetorical style.

1. Know your audience

Jobs was brilliant at this and would adapt his style to suit his audience. Being able to gauge your audience is a vital skill for any business leader: a knack of knowing the language and rhetoric to use is an essential component of conveying leadership skills and getting the audience on your side. Of course, you only need to watch an Apple product launch presentation to see how Jobs played to a receptive audience, but in my research of Jobs I found he was also able to alter his rhetorical style, depending on the situation and audience in question, far beyond simply playing to the Apple fans. For example, when being interrogated by the US

(Continued)

(Continued)

Securities and Exchange Commission during a deposition – an audience which basically saw Jobs as a potential criminal and therefore paid little regard to his senior position at the firm – he used economical, descriptive, straightforward language, emphasizing emotional appeals (i.e., pathos). He mentioned that he was overworked, couldn't see his family and was eventually "fired." In other words he presented himself as just a human, as opposed to an all-powerful CEO of a huge tech company.

2. Practice, practice, practice

When looking at someone like Jobs, many people will inevitably ask "how can I develop rhetorical skills as a business leader like him?" I would suggest the answer is simple: effective language skills can be learned by watching great rhetoricians and learning from them. Of course that is easier said than done, but by taking the time to reflect on speeches that made an impact on you and trying to understand why this was the case, you'll really help yourself develop. Take this a step further and use any opportunities you can to practice public speaking. While my study focused on Jobs, who was unusual in his dedication and effectiveness of publicly presenting his company, you can focus on a leader who really inspires you. By doing this you can raise your self-awareness in order to use language more useful to the context of the situation at hand; while at the same time, consistently promoting themes that are instrumental to your company's future.

3. Choosing the right tool

Combined with knowing his audience, the late Apple boss was an excellent orator, utilizing Aristotle's classic tools of persuasion – ethos, pathos and logos to play to the differing audiences. This is a skill I found Jobs to be especially proficient at throughout my study. I found the driving factor in Jobs' rhetoric was his perceived ethos – his credibility in the situation – which significantly influenced how he used logos (logic) and pathos (emotion). For business leaders I would therefore suggest that it is wise to appreciate the situation and how the audience sees you, and customize your rhetoric to that situation. For example, in high-ethos situations use open, expansive and entertaining rhetoric. Jobs would certainly do this at product launches and at the *Wall Street Journal*'s D8: All Things Digital Conference where he was seen as a Silicon Valley icon, and therefore able to impart his knowledge with abandon.

At a low-ethos event like the SEC deposition that put Jobs under the microscope while Apple's alleged backdating of shares was investigated, the Apple guru adapted his style to use rhetoric that was descriptive, formal, and restricted to the facts. Using the right tool for the occasion, whether it is ethos, pathos or logos, and sometimes a combination of them, is another lesson business leaders can learn from Jobs. Business leaders should try to understand the level of their perceived ethos and how credible they are with that audience. They can then adapt as appropriate as Jobs did.

4. Re-purpose and reframe to remain in control

While researching Jobs' rhetoric I found the Apple icon was often able to re-direct a conversation if it seemed to be heading somewhere not in line with his objective or end goal. A CNBC TV interview featuring Jobs was a prime example of this. The interviewer took a hard line on Apple's shift from IBM to Intel as a supplier, but Jobs re-directed an aggressive line of questioning into his own way of seeing the situation. He was able to reframe the tone from the aggressive "business is war" line of the interviewer to more of a "business is a journey" theme, presenting the decision as one made in the normal course of business as the paths of Apple and IBM diverged, casting Apple in a more positive light and avoiding any inflammation of tensions with IBM. This ability to divert a potentially negative line of questioning and reframe situations can help you keep the audience on the message you aim to present.

5. A constant key message

Despite being able to customize his rhetorical style to different situations, Jobs was also able to present a set of constant messages or themes through all his public appearances, something I witnessed across a number of different scenarios involving the late Apple boss. Across a variety of situations Jobs often referred to his company as looking towards the future, being on a "journey," and he did this by using strategies such as reframing, using metaphors and evocative language. Similarly, Jobs often liked to refer to the people element of his firm, to highlight how important to Apple talent was, and Apple's commitment to getting the best people and keeping them happy. A third constant message was about Apple's pipeline of products, how Apple was focused on creating innovative products that the market loved, in order to create excitement and anticipation of what Apple would introduce next. It is important for you as a business leader to decide on the key messages that you want to share. These should ideally be consistent across situations and over time, no matter what the context.

6. Make strong use of metaphors, stories or imagery

A solid use of metaphors, stories, and more generally evocative language, especially in high-ethos situations, is another skill of the most charismatic leaders. Jobs often used the "business is a journey" metaphor, as well as the "circle of life" metaphor, that he used to structure his famous and influential Stanford commencement speech in 2005. Metaphors can help aid the understanding of even the most complex of topics and connect on an emotional level beyond typical conscious awareness. People will remember these long after they forget about numbers and statistics. The exception to this rule would be if you are speaking to a specialist audience that wants to hear numbers – in that case, use numbers as well as stories and metaphors. Even when using statistics, you are still selling a story, a vision of how things will be, and this is what brings the audience with you.

Source: www.wbs.ac.uk/news/steve-jobs-six-lessons-from-his-public-speaking/

Being part of the C-level suite, Chief Executive Officers also have a responsibility and get influenced by changes in the C-suite that is comprised around them, to support and oversee their work. In this textbook we will detail the emergence and role of one such group of C-level executives, the Chief Strategy Officers, in the chapter that follows. Before that, we will also examine the role of the Chief External Officers. Serious incidents such as the Deepwater Horizon oil spill and factory fires in India and Bangladesh highlight why some companies should create a new "Chief External Officer" role, according to the study by Doh et al. (2014). The new position in the C-suite would be part of an upgraded external affairs policy that can help align strategy and improve a firm's competitive advantage in a world that sees a greater need for nonmarket – social and political – strategies. More details about the Chief External Officers and their role are provided in the mini case below.

MINI CASE: NEW CEO POSITION NEEDED TO TACKLE SOCIAL AND POLITICAL ISSUES

Based on an analysis of case studies and interviews with executives at a wide range of companies, Doh et al. (2014) found that distributing the management of external affairs across several departments typically leads to disjointed, even contradictory corporate actions. On the other hand, developing deliberate, cohesive responses to outside pressures generally involves treating them like another important aspect of doing business, with a single office dedicated to aligning a firm's nonmarket strategies to its business interests.

For example, during the mid-1990s, airlines were faced with pressure from the newly formed European Union to boost their fuel efficiency, cut down on emissions, and commit to sustainability. In addition, the authority for overseeing European airspace slowly shifted from the capitals of countries to a centralized commission in Brussels. But one airline, in particular, had anticipated the changing winds.

Lufthansa had already established a nine-person "corporate embassy" to the E.U. – the first of its kind – to monitor and comply with policymaking. The office was headed by Thomas Kropp, effectively the company's chief external officer. Its contacts with legislators and governments gave the company an advantage over its competitors, and helped the airline develop a long-term, rather than reactionary, strategy for dealing with the E.U. The air carrier gained first-mover advantage by building a corporate strategy that closely aligned its business objectives and market positions with its political obligations and social responsibilities. In the process, Lufthansa established itself as the go-to industry representative for E.U. politicians and committees, and survived near failure in the early 1990s to become one of the most successful airlines in the world as the E.U. evolved.

Another case is Tata Consultancy Services, which is present in 85 countries and seven industries, as a multinational company that took advantage of its proactive stance. From 2001 to 2013, the late Malcolm Lane oversaw the Indian firm's office of European external affairs, pushing TCS's green agenda and creating valuable ties with governmental agencies. Lane's award-winning work on the firm's antipoverty programs also dovetailed with the establishment of an adult literacy program that tapped into the company's business objectives and helped create a healthier, better educated customer base.

Doh and his colleagues provide a four-stage plan for companies looking to implement this new structure. In the first initiation phase, the top management team should lay out the rationale and time frame for elevating and integrating the external affairs role. During the second phase, executives should identify the resources required, specify budgets, and define functions for the external affairs team. The new office should be established during the third phase, with its responsibilities and scope clearly spelled out. Finally, the external affairs team's strategy should be developed, its communication channels with other departments opened, and its purpose communicated to the rest of the company. Whether an enhanced external affairs office takes the shape of close partnerships with governments or informal collaborations with nonprofits or individual experts, companies should develop a conscious, well-integrated way to deal with nonbusiness issues.

Overall, a realistic stance for most companies is a balanced approach to corporate strategy, political activity, and social responsibility, which emphasizes alignment across these priorities and the functions that are responsible for them. By increasing the stature and influence of the external affairs function, firms can achieve more effective strategic actions and policies, ultimately serving to increase their competitive advantage.

Source: Doh et al. (2014) and Palmquist (2014).

REVISION ACTIVITIES

In this introduction we have highlighted the importance of having a wider set of actors involved in strategy making and execution. Find examples of organizations (private or public) where you believe there is increased participation in strategizing. What do you think are the benefits and drawbacks to that particular organization from such increased participation? Do you think this will lead to higher financial performance in the particular industry?

What would be the benefits and drawbacks from choosing an internal CEO at eSolar? What do you think would be some of the benefits from hiring an external CEO at eSolar?

FURTHER READINGS

- **Papers:** More details about the upper echelons perspective can be found in the following papers: Hambrick, D. C. and Mason, P. A. (1984) Upper echelons: the organization as a reflection of its top managers. *Academy of Management Review*, 9, 193–206; and Finkelstein, S. and Hambrick, D. C. (1990) Top management team tenure and organizational outcomes: the moderating role of managerial discretion. *Administrative Science Quarterly*, 35, 484–503.

REFERENCES

Angwin, D., Paroutis, S., and Mitson, S. (2009) Connecting up strategy: Are senior strategy directors (SSDs) a missing link? *California Management Review*, 51(3): 74–94.

Balogun, J. (2003) From blaming the middle to harnessing its potential: Creating change intermediaries. *British Journal of Management*, 14: 69–84.

Boje, D. (2001) *Narrative Methods for Organizational and Communication Research*. London: Sage.

Brown, A. D. (2006) A narrative approach to collective identities. *Journal of Management Studies*, 43(4): 731–53.

Brown, A. D., Ainsworth, S., and Grant, D. (2012) The rhetoric of institutional change. *Organization Studies*, 33(3): 297–321.

Carter, C., Clegg, S. R., and Kornberger, M. (2010) Re-framing strategy: Power, politics and accounting. *Accounting, Auditing & Accountability Journal*, 23: 573–94.

Clegg, S. R., Courpasson, D., and Phillips, N. (2006) *Power and Organizations*. London: Sage.

Colville, I. D. and Murphy, A. J. (2006) Leadership as the enabler of strategizing and organizing. *Long Range Planning*, 39(6): 663–77.

Crossland, C. and Hambrick, D. C. (2007) How national systems differ in their constraints on corporate executives: A study of CEO effects in three countries. *Strategic Management Journal*, 28: 767–89.

Cyert, R. M. and March, J. G. (1963) *A Behavioral Theory of the Firm*. Englewood Cliffs, NJ: Prentice Hall.

Doh, J., Lawton, T., Rajwani, T., and Paroutis, S. (2014) Why your company may need a chief external officer: Upgrading external affairs can help align strategy and improve competitive advantage. *Organizational Dynamics*, 43: 96–104.

Fairclough, N. (1997) Discourse across disciplines: Discourse analysis in researching social change. *AILA Review*, 12: 3–17.

Finkelstein, S. and Hambrick, D. C. (1996) *Strategic Leadership: Top Executives and Their Effects on Organizations*. Minneapolis, MN: West Publishing Co.

Hambrick, D. C. (2007) Upper echelons theory: An update. *Academy of Management Review*, 32(2): 334–43.

Hambrick, D. C. and Mason, P. A. (1984) Upper echelons: The organization as a reflection of its top managers. *Academy of Management Review*, 9: 193–206.

Hardy, C., Palmer, I., and Phillips, N. (2000) Discourse as a strategic resource. *Academy of Management Review*, 22: 1227–48.

Heracleous, L. (2006) *Discourse, Interpretation, Organization*. Cambridge: Cambridge University Press.

Heracleous, L. and Barrett, M. (2001) Organizational change as discourse: Communicative actions and deep structures in the context of IT implementation. *Academy of Management Journal*, 44: 755–78.

Heracleous, L. and Klaering, L. A. (2014) Charismatic leadership and rhetorical competence: An analysis of Steve Jobs' rhetoric. *Group and Organization Management*, 39: 131–61.

Jarzabkowski, P. (2008) Shaping strategy as a structuration process. *Academy of Management Journal*, 51(4): 621–50.

Jarzabkowski, P. and Fenton, E. (2006) Strategizing and organizing in pluralistic contexts. *Long Range Planning*, 39(6): 631–48.

Johnson, G., Scholes, K., and Whittington, R. (2008) *Exploring Corporate Strategy*. London: Prentice Hall.

Laine, P. M. and Vaara, E. (2007) Struggling over subjectivity: A discursive analysis of strategic development in an engineering group. *Human Relations*, 60(1): 29–58.

Lincoln, B. (2006) An early moment in the discourse of "terrorism": Reflections on a tale from Marco Polo. *Comparative Studies in Society and History*, 48(2): 242–59.

Mantere, S. (2005) Strategic practices as enablers and disablers of championing activity. *Strategic Organization*, 3(2): 157–84.

Mantere, S. (2008) Role expectations and middle manager strategic agency. *Journal of Management Studies*, 45(2): 294–316.

Mckeown, M. (2010) The constitution of strategic change by insider and outsider CEOs: Language games and discursive bets. Doctoral dissertation, University of Warwick.

Mischel, W. (1977) The interaction of person and situation. In D. Magnusson and N. S. Endler (eds.), *Personality at the Crossroads: Current Issues in Interactional Psychology*. Hillsdale, NJ: Lawrence Erlbaum, 217–47.

Palmquist, M. (2014) A different kind of C(E)O. Strategy+Business. December 11. Available at: www.strategy-business.com/blog/A-Different-Kind-of-CEO?gko=f4bea (date accessed: March, 2015).

Paroutis, S. and Heracleous, L. (2013) Discourse revisited: Dimensions and employment of first-order strategy discourse during institutional adoption. *Strategic Management Journal*, 34(8): 935–56.

Paroutis, S. and Pettigrew, A. M. (2007) Strategizing in the multibusiness firm: The role of strategy teams at multiple levels and over time. *Human Relations,* 60(1): 99–135.

Paroutis, S., Mckeown, M. and Collinson, S. (2013) Building Castles from Sand: Unlocking CEO Mythopoetical Behaviour in Hewlett Packard from 1978 to 2005. *Business History*, Special Issue 'The Age of Strategy: Strategy, Organizations and Society', 55(7): 1200–27.

Pettigrew, A. (1992) On studying managerial elites. *Strategic Management Journal*, 13(S2): 163–82.

Rouleau, L. (2005) Micro-practices of strategic sensemaking and sensegiving: How middle managers interpret and sell change every day. *Journal of Management Studies*, 42(7): 1413–41.

Suddaby, R. and Greenwood, R. (2005) Rhetorical strategies of legitimacy. *Administrative Science Quarterly*, 50: 35–67.

Tsoukas, H. (2005) Why language matters in the analysis of organizational change. *Journal of Organizational Change Management*, 18: 96–104.

Vaara, E. (2010) Taking the linguistic turn seriously: Strategy as a multifaceted and interdiscursive phenomenon. *Advances in Strategic Management*, 27: 29–50.

Van Leeuwen, T. (2008) *Discourse and Practice: New Tools for Critical Discourse Analysis*. Oxford: Oxford University Press.

Weick, K. and Roberts, K. (1993) Collective mind in organizations: Heedful interrelating on flight decks. *Administrative Science Quarterly*, 38: 357–81.

CHIEF STRATEGY OFFICERS

3

Learning Objectives

- Understand the location and roles of Chief Strategy Officers (CSO).
- Appreciate how these executives interact with other levels of management inside the firm and with stakeholders outside the firm.
- Become aware of the diversity of the CSO role.
- Demonstrate the insights that can be gained by using the 3P model (practitioners, praxis and practices) to analyze the role of particular strategic actors.

INTRODUCTION

3.1 Senior functional executives often have titles such as head of strategic marketing, director of strategic IT, global strategic operations director, head of global strategic HR and within functions and business units many executives now have strategy titles. With this proliferation of "strategists" it is timely to enquire about those senior executives specifically tasked with being "Chief Strategy Officers" (CSOs) or "Strategy Directors" (SDs) – defined as senior board level (non-CEO) executives whose very job is about the strategy of the firm. It seems we have little idea about their role and purpose – a particularly pertinent issue if everyone else is now a strategist. What distinctive role does the Strategy Director perform and what specific capabilities do they bring to the organization? With the spread of strategy to other functional areas, is there a need for Strategy Directors? Are they now obsolete or do they carry out a critical and largely unsung function? This chapter aims to provide answers for these questions and focuses upon the role of strategists in firms and how they are involved in the connectedness of strategy. The CSOs ought to be closely involved with the connectedness of strategy in all its aspects and yet we know very little about their role, activities and purpose. In what follows, we briefly review the limited empirical studies on Chief Strategy Officers, from the established strategic decision-making literature the CEO-Adviser model. We then present insights into the practices of Chief Strategy Officers using the 3P framework.

ROLE, LOCATION, AND TYPES

3.2 The large strategic planning departments of the 1980s have currently been replaced in most firms by flexible teams of strategists specifically tasked to make and execute strategy. These teams are led by senior executives, often named as "strategy officers or directors." However, there have been only limited studies on Strategy Directors. One of the early studies identifying the role and offering insights into their influence was presented in a Strategic Management Society (SMS) conference in the University of Connecticut in 2003 and later in a chapter in the SMS book series (Paroutis and Pettigrew, 2003, 2005).

For their *Harvard Business Review* article Breene et al. (2007) surveyed 200 senior managers in the USA who considered themselves as strategy officers. They collected media data on 100 of them and then carried out a series of interviews. These Chief Strategy Officers (CSOs) had a multiplicity of titles and diverse backgrounds but the authors observed that despite these differences there were common aspects to the role. CSOs are involved in strategy formulation, strategy refinement and its implementation. These insights were also confirmed by a study by BCG (Kachaner and Stewart, 2013) that found CSOs to have the least-defined role among the C-suite executives. The BCG team conducted a series of in-depth interviews with 48 CSOs in firms from around the world, representing a wide set of industries. BCG found that the CSOs responsibilities:

> fall into three categories – strategy development, resource allocation, and strategy execution – but activities within these three categories vary widely. Most CSOs are responsible for identification of growth opportunities (84 percent of the executives we interviewed), strategic planning (82 percent), and M&A and divestments (82 percent). Other common responsibilities include monitoring long-term trends and outlook, gathering competitive intelligence, driving cross-business-unit initiatives, and sustaining business model innovation. Far fewer CSOs are involved with identifying cost improvement opportunities and managing postmerger integration (23 and 20 percent, respectively). (Kachaner and Stewart, 2013)

In Mintzbergian terms, Strategy Directors straddle the classic divide in strategy, between formulation and implementation. This breadth of activity means CSOs need to be able to tackle a wide range of challenges such as consumer innovation, international expansion, mergers and acquisitions, communications, business process redesign – a range which most people in functional oriented careers have not experienced. They also need to be able to work with and influence a wide range of executives across the whole organization. This broad mix of skills and experience is rare and highly valued. Although CSOs are often involved in strategy formulation, their main efforts are directed at getting buy-in to the strategy, its refinement and implementation. As "no strategy can just be handed down to an organization" (Kirk Klasson, former vice president of strategy for Novell) CSOs must engender commitment by building a federation for change and getting shared alignment. In the words of Breene et al. (2007: 87) "fundamentally, these are people that wield the authority and have a complex range of skills to make strategy happen – they act as realisteurs." They are often given carte blanche to tackle company-wide challenges and seize new business opportunities (Breene at al., 2007: 86). A sizeable portion of respondents in Breene et al.'s survey said they used direct authority to achieve their aims and a few influenced others through reflected authority – the implicit or explicit support of the CEO, although the authors remark that this probably severely underestimates the true extent of this influencing mechanism. This portrayal of the CSO could be characterized as the Eminence Grise view – a powerful figure in its own right, acting behind the scenes to directly influence and organize managers in order to achieve strategic alignment. In this image, the CSO is a star player, with a strong track record of achievement and a CEO in-waiting.

Dye (2008) in *McKinsey Quarterly* reports findings from a round table of strategy officers. Variously titled senior vice presidents of strategy and investor relations; strategy and business development; strategy and execution, the round table identifies that these CSOs feel there are certain commonalities in the role:

- Firstly, they all comment upon the centrality and importance of the CEO as chief strategist and recognize the CSO's role is dependent upon the CEO for sign-off decisions. The critical role of the CEO means that the CSO needs to be able to complement their specific skills and tendencies and add value by being able to explore facts and alternatives around the various strategic choices which face them.
- Secondly, CSOs have one foot in the corporate suite and the other deep in business units. Although there were differences in emphasis, with some strategies more head-office driven and others where the strategy was driven by businesses, there was agreement that CSOs get feedback from businesses, overlay global trends and then prioritize opportunities.
- Thirdly, balancing short- and long-term goals was perceived as an important challenge and some felt it the most important one. This would vary from emphases on expansion to restructuring depending upon the state of the market. Despite these pressures CSOs had to always maintain some sort of balance and perspective between long- and short-term issues.

Angwin et al. (2009) in their *California Management Review* paper, reveal that CSOs need to have a Janus-like propensity – the ability to face in two directions simultaneously, balancing short and long term as well as balancing transmitting from the top of the organization with feeding back from business units and other embedded interests. From this analysis, a unique insight into what Strategy Directors regard as "strategy" and "strategic activity" has emerged together with rich data on their practices and routines. Their view of social forces acting upon the strategy process has also enabled a broader view of the role of CSOs than is current in the literature. As noted in the previous section and in order to interpret and organize our findings we utilize the practitioners/praxis/practices framework in what follows. They also used the 3P model to analyze the praxis, practices, and practitioners around the role of the strategy director. In what follows, and based on the findings of research by Angwin et al. (2009), we present more details about the role of Strategy Directors using the 3P model.

The focus of this chapter is strategists at senior managerial positions. There are a profusion of labels to describe them. For instance, in our research the following were often encountered: Global Strategy Director, Head of Strategy, Global Business Development Director, Strategy and M&A Director, Strategic Planning Director. In one large multinational there were 40 strategy titles alone. A US study estimated over 90 job descriptors for strategy officers (Breene et al., 2007). Despite this complexity of titles, UK Strategy Directors reported the actual labels as not very important and in practice the activities beneath the titles overlap very significantly. Indeed in discussing this point with CSOs and how their titles came about most commented on it being on a rather ad-hoc basis with little intention of deep resonance with the job. Another complexity was that CSOs are located at different places on organizational charts. The following (Figure 3.1) illustrates their main locations.

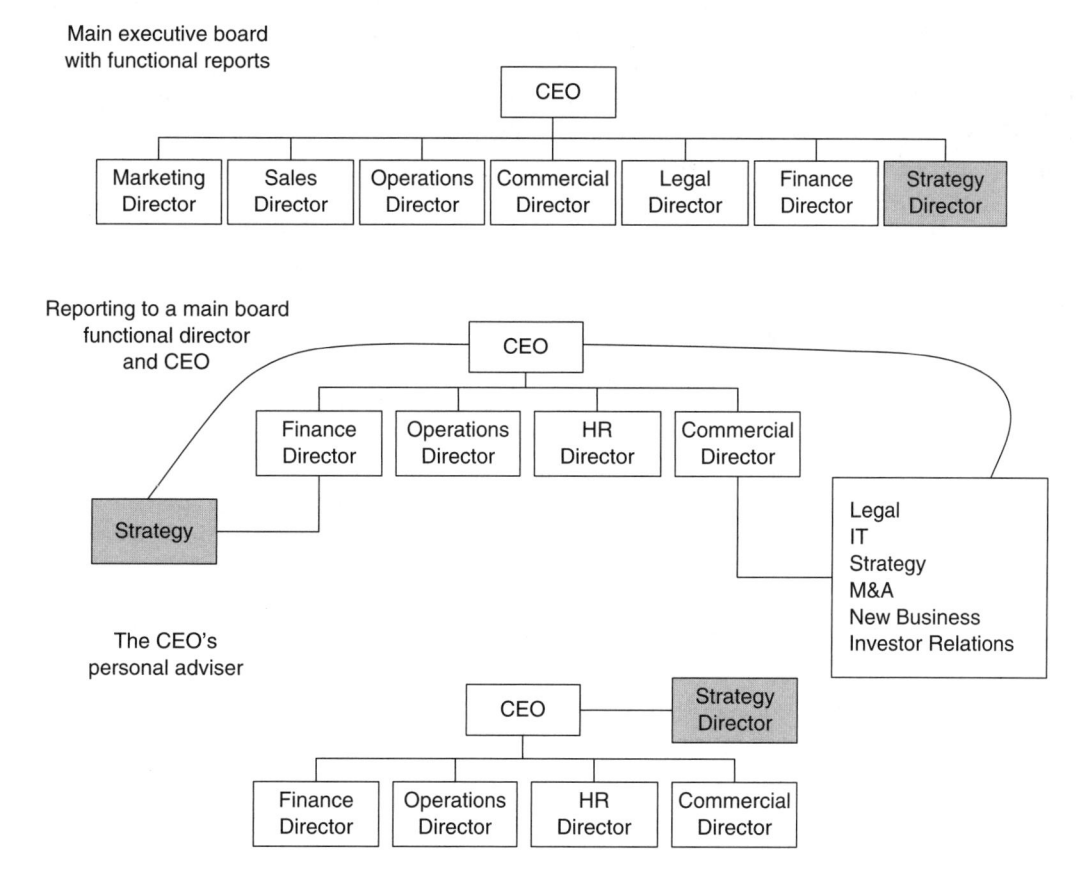

FIGURE 3.1 The location of CSOs in large firms

Source: Angwin, Paroutis, and Mitson, 2009.

These organizational charts show that a primary direct report is with the CEO – sometimes as the only report and sometimes with another report. We identified **three different types** of Strategy Director in terms of their position on organizational charts:

1. The CSO sitting on the main board in their own right is often a long-serving executive of the organization with substantial previous line experience;
2. The CSO reporting to a main Board Director and also working with the CEO is frequently a high-powered management consultant brought into the business for their industry knowledge and superior analytical skills. This outside person may have been brought in at a more junior level in the strategy group and been promoted to this position[1];
3. The CSO who is not on the main board but is the right-hand confidant of the CEO is frequently the ex-senior partner of a major consulting firm who brings a rich external perspective to the business, or a senior industry figure from outside the firm.

Despite our attempts to depict the CSO's position in large firms, the more important observation is that these sorts of organizational charts do not tell the whole story. Characteristic of CSOs is that they have more fluid positions than conventional schema can show. Whereas other divisional heads are atop of a vertical chain of command consisting of large numbers of direct reports, this is not the case with CSOs who generally have very few direct reports and yet have multiple links across multiple divisions and departments as well as vertically within them. This means CSOs are in many "locations." For instance they may well be nominally "above" line managers in organizational hierarchical terms, but it is absolutely clear that line managers are more powerful individuals in the firm and they do not report to CSOs. The location of CSO is therefore difficult to represent in classical organizational chart form.

The extensive social linkages between CSOs and all key executives in the firm are a distinguishing characteristic of these executives. They are embedded in very extensive social networks across multiple levels of the business as well as being in very close contact with the CEO. This high internal connectedness is critical for the CSO to be able to perform the role of engaging across the firm in all issues with strategic impact. Interestingly, although CSOs did interact with external experts such as lawyers, accountants, investment bankers for specific projects such as an acquisition, their social networks were heavily oriented towards internal connectedness.

ACTIVITIES, CAPABILITIES, AND NETWORKS

3.3 The role of CSOs is nuanced in terms of the complexities mentioned above, but the similarities between them are more striking than the differences. In all cases CSOs were engaged in a broad mix of strategy issues such as formulating strategies "de nuevo"; acting as a sounding board for strategies; translating strategies articulated by the CEO into practical implementable plans; communicating strategies to a broad range of stakeholders; aligning

---

[1] Often companies place their smartest young executives in a strategy function but they are then rotated out back into line positions. It is unusual for them to remain and rise to board level in this way.

internal stakeholders to strategies; acting as a strategy broker for in-company interest groups; guiding and managing the implementation of strategies.

Although CSOs sometimes came up with new strategies for the firm, it was more often the case that their primary role would be to work alongside the CEO in debating, refining, and articulating strategy. Their role was generally one of an objective sounding board – an "organizational conscience" that would remind top management of overall aims, objectives, and balance. In the words of one CSO, "I am the Jiminy Cricket[2] of the Organization. I am forever saying what about balance, what about the long term?"[3]

Otherwise CSOs would generate a more limited set of **strategic initiatives** within a broad direction set from above. These initiatives, however, could embrace a bewildering array of activities causing most CSOs to comment upon the huge span of the job. One described their work as "The Director of everything." It seems that they need to be able to engage with a very broad set of issues and many remarked that "The biggest challenge is breadth – a critical skill." Paradoxically maintaining the big picture, while also being able to bring about micro implementation, was also a major challenge. In the words of one CSO, "You need a helicopter perspective and mustn't get sucked into the day to day but the day of the egghead strategy director, removed from actual implementation, is long gone … The way in which a lot is achieved is not in a sort of ivory tower." Coping with these tensions of breadth and depth it is not surprising that the job comes with significant time pressure "Four hours' sleep in 72 hours! I can't even get to read the FT."

CSOs are embedded in **very extensive social networks** of strategy stakeholders. Internally these included primarily the CEO, divisional heads, functional heads, strategy teams at head office, within divisional and within business units as well as numerous other senior executives who became relevant depending upon the strategic episode. The CSOs primary role is to be i) close to the CEO, supporting their activities, **and** ii) to be highly embedded in the business across multiple levels. For i) the closeness to the CEO is well illustrated by comments such as "we are constantly popping in and out of each others offices." In several cases CSOs' offices were located next to the CEO's office and most of them met with the CEO almost every day. For ii) the importance of being highly embedded in the business is being aware of all strategy issues in the firm. This can only be achieved by being highly connected horizontally and vertically. In this way the CSO is distinctive in working across silos of interests and connecting multiple stakeholders in fluid ways.

Externally, CSOs did interact with experts such as lawyers, accountants, investment bankers, and consultants for specific projects such as an acquisition or a restructuring, but in all cases these links tended to be on a project-by-project basis. Although the CSO was fully informed of the progress on strategic projects, they were not always the ones working most closely with these advisers. Overall CSOs' social networks were heavily oriented towards internal strategy practitioners rather than external ones.

The **day-to-day job** is very varied with a mix of formal, informal, and opportunistic work. For instance there might be a formal process of identifying a market segment based upon rational

---

[2]Jiminy Cricket is a character in a Disney movie and depicts the conscience of the main character Pinocchio.

[3]All interviewee comments have been anonymized to protect their identities. Some are sourced by Angwin et al. (2009).

analysis, but then an opportunity might surface which achieves the original objectives better or provides better avenues for expansion: "We had selected one opportunity for acquisition based upon rational analysis but suddenly an opportunity arose which met the objectives more effectively and also added something."

No CSOs have a **typical day**. They each lived a very fragmented process consisting of many meetings, periods of time spent thinking, analyzing and getting information and time spent visiting parts of the business where they learn through listening and observing. "I spent most of my time in meetings because, frankly, that was the role." "If I was to estimate how much time I spent on different parts of the job it would be approximately 40% in meetings; 30% thinking, analyzing, getting information and 30% visiting parts of the business."

Being involved in many **workshops** is a characteristic of this fragmented job. These might be "intense, reflective workshops where we would encourage managers to think about the future" or workshops designed to interrogate initiatives. Another major aspect of the job was making presentations – "There is always one more presentation to make." Much of the work of CSOs was ad hoc activity in which a wide variety of tasks could be involved, such as making acquisitions, disposals, entering new markets, or marketing initiatives. In all cases the CSOs in this study had very few real resources with which to perform their jobs. Most had small teams of between two and five executives and no profit and loss (P&L) responsibility. As one put it, "I only have L responsibility." Next we turn our attention to the capabilities required for such a complicated role. CSOs also have to be sensitive to the **timing of initiatives**. There are times of the year when divisional heads are not receptive to new ideas. As one CSO put it "Timing is key – at this time of year they would sell their own grandmothers to hit targets as it directly affects their bonuses – so we don't communicate at the moment."

In all cases CSOs had **low positional power**. None of them believed they had the power to tell any divisional or line manager what to do and none of them tried based on their own authority: "I didn't have any positional power as it were over the divisional heads." Although all of them said that they could call upon support from the CEO on a particular issue and they also resorted to reflected power on rare occasions, they felt this undermined their own credibility. They also stressed they often resorted to raising "power barriers" between themselves and line managers and interfered with their ability to really be embedded in the business: "Although they never forgot I saw the CEO every day and that I worked with the board and the CEO, this could be a barrier if I was perceived as the CEO's henchman." Divisional heads valued the CSOs' access to the CEO and Board and often used them as sounding boards for their presentations and initiatives, but only if some sort of trust had been established. In many cases executives sought out the CSO as the right place to advise on new ideas and initiatives and how these might be presented to the board. In some instances CSOs would co-present these initiatives as they were able to communicate more effectively at this level than the originators of the ideas. This "incubator role" or "business angel" is a good example of a mechanism for connecting initiatives from the grass roots of the organization to the very top.

In order to carry out their hugely demanding and varied job with low actual power and few real resources, CSOs required high sociopolitical and technical skills. Being perceived as astute or wise, socially connected, technically smart, and contextually sensitive is critical for the credibility of a CSO. Interpersonal skills are vital and indeed were rated above analytical ones, which were seen as hygiene factors. "Those with very, very strong rational intellectual skills sometimes don't have the soft skills and contextual awareness that allows them to do the right things." "I went in thinking I would do that role well through my brilliant strategic ideas. I came out realising how important the inter-personal side was."

Communicating across multiple vertical, horizontal, and organizational levels with tact and diplomacy was viewed as a critical skill. In vertical terms this meant being able to work at big picture and pragmatic levels – "from 10,000 to 10 metres." Horizontally it meant being able to communicate effectively with different functional areas and for international operations, also to be sensitive to national cultural differences: "with Germans they will respond to a neat email but with Greeks you have to visit them." "Strategy Directors have to be good listeners, translators and influencers." They have to be able "to work every angle."

Central to the role of CSO is managing tensions across multiple levels. One that seemed most common was between head office and the rest of the company.

> One of my best achievements, and one of the things I'm proudest of was making the firm operate more smoothly than any other time in its history – there are generally not happy relationships between Head office and the company ... There's always disagreement um ... [Laughs] sorry if I haven't made that clear ... if I at any time suggested that this was a smooth process! These steering groups, you know, they were not sort of smooth meetings where some manager would present uh his five point plan and he'd get them ticked off, it was generally the CEO pulling his hair out – it was *always* a negotiation process.

In the words of another CSO: "I *am* the lubricant!"

Critical **capabilities** for CSOs were the ability to persuade, negotiate, influence, and collaborate. As one put it "You have to work through divisional heads." Persuasion had to be upward and downward as well as horizontally across the business: "There are lots and lots of meetings and informal communications." An example of upward management "to ease the decision making process for the CEO" is getting an approval related to an important marketing initiative. "I translated the Chinese name we would use on our boxes for the CEO as 'silk'. In Chinese it actually meant 'fresh jasmine' – he would have had a fit!" Explaining this action, the CSO said that "in the interests of moving forward, I didn't want the CEO getting hung up on a detail." Other CSOs have commented upon using their sifting and judgmental abilities to identify those things which are material and those which are not, so messages can be delivered with clarity. CSOs are continuously "interpreting" and "translating" strategic impulses in multiple directions.

Concluding, CSOs have to be adept at constructing and managing effective social networks of strategy practitioners. This means building multi-level alignment between different and often conflicting interest groups. One CSO characterized this as being like "the reins between husky dogs and sledge driver" where the top management team might be the sledge driver, the line managers the husky dogs, and the CSO working to transmit intentions and energy in several directions; absorbing and diffusing tensions while attempting to maintain directional coherence. More than the Janus paradox, where an executive is confronted with two opposing tensions, the CSO has a "Polycephalous problem" – of facing multiple tensions in space and time – where the biggest skill is to balance different temporal horizons and conflicting initiatives among a diverse set of strategic stakeholders.

TOOLS AND FORMAL OUTPUTS

3.4 Every CSO said that they either used **very basic models** such as SWOT or didn't really use models or frameworks at all even though many of them were experts in strategy models and techniques: "We don't really use models – even though I have written papers on the balanced score card. I hardly use this now – it tends to be the wise man approach to critiquing reports." "You'll be shocked to hear that in a company of this size and complexity, which ought to have the latest in techniques and tools for analysis, we generally rely on the good old SWOT." "I can't think of anything specific we might use." "We strip back to the basics" – unpick the general.

In terms of **formal output**, the CSOs did create substantial numbers of reports for the Board and CEO – often at short notice: "there is always another PowerPoint presentation to prepare." In most cases companies were very particular about formats and style. One company for instance insisted on a story book of PowerPoint slides with only one text caption per slide, so that someone could read through all the slides rapidly with the headers forming a story line.

In terms of shared routines, the **main routine** for some CSOs was the planning cycle, which ran on an annual basis. The beginning of the new planning cycle would be characterized by "intense, reflective workshops around various kind of key drivers and making sure people are thinking about the future. That's quite difficult to be frank because they've only just set budgets and targets." After around three months, "initiatives would be thrashed out" and approximately six months into the cycle these would be presented to the Board and CEO. Following the Board meeting "strategy is translated into budget and plan process and this then becomes more the world of financial guys." The cycle concludes with the meeting of targets and budgets. Interestingly a number of CSOs preferred to remove themselves from this process and just concentrate on strategic initiatives as and when they occurred, leaving the formal budgeting and assessment entirely to the finance function.

The general impression of practices for CSOs is a large number **of routine micro-processes** such as the format for working up an initiative, the approach to presenting materials to the Board and investors, and sitting on committees where there would be processes for decision making on investments. Overall, however, the day-to-day job is more remarkable for the lack of "routines" than their presence. A number of CSOs showed diaries where every day and every week was quite different. Strategic episodes could arise at any time in any area and require the application of substantially different skill sets. Committees on which CSOs sat were often ephemeral, such as an integration team that would slowly dissolve as the area being integrated became part of the normal business. Despite variety being the characteristic of these jobs there was a much broader rhythm in the general annual strategy planning cycle and on a two or three strategic horizon basis. Interestingly, not all CSOs were heavily involved in the strategy planning cycle, some even choosing to avoid its detail. For these reasons the role is characterized more by variety than sameness on a day-to-day or week-by-week basis.

Flexibility is also demanded in working closely with CEOs who are very varied in their personalities and demands. The CSO role is to cope with huge variety and scope and to recognize that CSOs are not concerned with the everyday normality of running a business but with change and difference, responding to and anticipating multiple internal and external pressures within and upon the firm. To embrace difference requires an openness and flexibility – to be able to think and act differently, rather than follow routines. Table 3.1 presents the main insights provided by our analysis of the praxis and practices of CSOs.

TABLE 3.1 The Role of the CSO through the 3P framework.

Dimensions	Description	Key Insights	Representative quotes
Practitioners	The CSOs	• They can have three distinctive organizational locations: a) functional, b) line, or c) adviser • They have various titles (group strategy director, chief strategy officer, director of strategic planning/development) • They have multiple career paths	• I didn't have any positional power as it were over the divisional heads • You have to work through divisional heads
Practices	The methods, routines, and tools adopted by the CSO to solve strategy issues	• Their formal output is in the form of reports to the top management team • They tend not to use complicated strategy tools • Their social networks are heavily oriented towards internal strategy practitioners	• There are lots and lots of meetings and informal communications • You'll be shocked to hear that in a company of this size and complexity, which ought to have the latest in techniques and tools for analysis, we generally rely on the good old SWOT • I can't think of anything specific [tool] we might use • Timing is key – at this time of year they would sell their own grandmothers to hit targets as it directly affects their bonuses – so we don't communicate at the moment
Praxis	The activities adopted by the CSO	• Their primary role is to be i) close to the CEO, supporting their activities, and ii) to be highly embedded in the business across multiple levels • Their role requires a polycephalous propensity: balancing short- and long-term goals as well as interacting with multiple strategy stakeholders	• Although they never forgot I saw the CEO every day and that I worked with the board and the CEO, this could be a barrier if I was perceived as the CEO's henchman • Those with very, very strong rational intellectual skills sometimes don't have the soft skills and contextual awareness that allows them to do the right things • I went in thinking I would do that role well through my brilliant strategic ideas. I came out realizing how important the inter-personal side was • [my role is being] the reins between husky dogs and sledge driver

Adapted by: Angwin, Paroutis, and Miston, 2009

CONCLUSION

3.5 This chapter has analyzed a specific category of "internal adviser", the CSO (Strategy Director). By providing empirical insights into the roles of the SDs we have unpacked the complexity of their role and begun to generate some tentative insights into the relationship between these kinds of internal advisers and the CEO. Our findings show that the CSO is not a homogeneous category even at senior director level. Numerous titles are used to describe these executives, differences are detected in their prior backgrounds and they appear to occupy different "locations" within the firm. However, through the use of multiple research methods, striking similarities in terms of their roles and capabilities were far more evident than differences. It is the identification of these capabilities and the nature of the CSO role that is distinctive in this study and to which we now turn.

In this chapter we have also addressed the questions: what is the role of the CSO; and what capabilities do they deploy. Rather provocatively we also enquire whether CSOs really perform a useful function in large organizations. Through the use of a novel multi-level research approach involving many interviews with Board-level CSOs in the UK over time, and with other strategy practitioners, we revealed a unique set of insights into the role and capabilities of CSOs. Key findings include the need for CSOs to build alignment horizontally and vertically across multiple levels in an organization – in other words, their role is to deal with many "polycephalous" problems. As mentioned, they are the reins connecting the driver of a sledge to the dog team – sensitively transmitting and responding to numerous strategic impulses in order for overall coherence in direction to be achieved. It is this role that the CSO performs which enables organizations to be flexible, responsive, and efficient. In order to perform this role, CSOs require critical capabilities such as influencing, negotiating, planning, and analytical skills. It is the skillful deployment of these capabilities which enables the CSO to mediate day-to-day strategizing practices in order to enable organizational change and continuity. In performing this role the CSO fulfills a vital and largely unsung task within large organizations. It is the CSO who resides among the most profound tensions within an organization, attempting to address multiple conflicting views and holding everything together as the organization flexes to accommodate internal and external pressures. In connecting strategy stakeholders over time the CSO is a micro-cosmos of complex strategizing within large firms. For researchers they may be proxies for understanding larger/macro-level ways of strategizing.

Prior research in the US on Chief Strategy Officers suggests that the CSO's considerable directive power is wielded to achieve strategic aims for the firm – a recursive actor working within, and reinforcing, structure. In this chapter we have also shown that UK CSOs generally have to rely on a considerable array of influencing skills (political, negotiating, technical) to achieve their ends. They have to win credibility as they generally lack positional power. The activities of UK CSOs are more exploratory, transformative, and creative. Here there is much less emphasis upon routine and structure and more upon initiating or managing change. The CSO's credibility is not achieved through position but rather through the demonstration of wisdom, connectedness, and the earning of credibility.

CSOs' praxis is characterized by: a) the close interactions and strong ties between the CEO and her/his advisers, and particularly the CSO, who act as a sounding board and provide support for the CEO; and b) the kind of interactions between the CEO and the SDs, that we found to be mainly informal and based on their interpersonal relationships instead of the more formal and prescribed interactions. In more detail:

a We found that the role of the SDs as internal advisers extends beyond the confines of the decision-making process, involving a lot of interactions with other advisers and managers across the firm once the decision has been taken in terms of communicating the message of strategy and, in effect, "connecting" strategy across organizational levels. In that way, SDs act as carriers and disseminators of the strategic discourse across the firm.

b We also found that SDs tend to have strategic skills that are complementary in nature to the skills of the CEO. This might be an avenue for further investigation and could potentially provide insights into the SD selection process and help us understand how some SDs become especially relied on by their CEOs.

c Our findings also highlight the importance of the SD's social network, beyond and alongside the CEO's social network. The SD's social ties were particularly important in terms of communicating the overall strategic discourse, especially after a key strategic decision. This brings to the forefront questions about the SD's adviser network in its own right, for example: what is its size; what is the intensity of ties across the network; how is it formed; and how does it grow? Investigating these strategists' intra- and inter-firm social networks has the potential to help us understand better how strategy tools, ideas, and discourses become institutionalized across firms and industries.

MINI CASE: TESCO – THE GROUP FINANCE AND STRATEGY DIRECTOR

Andrew Higginson joined Tesco in 1997 as Finance and Strategy Director and stayed in the role for 11 years. Following Tesco's purchase of RBS's 50% stake in Tesco Personal Finance for £950m in 2008, he moved to lead its retailing services division, which includes the Tesco Bank. Along with former boss Sir Terry Leahy, Higginson is one of the team of senior executives credited with masterminding the group's rise to the world's third-largest retailer with annual sales of £67.6bn.

Higginson is a graduate from Birmingham Poly and worked as Finance Director at Laura Ashley and Burton Group before joining the supermarket group. In an interview with *Accountancy Age* he said in 2008:

> My internal debate when I was offered the Tesco job was not "Do I want to be FD of Tesco, or do I want to be FD of Burton Group?" – that was obvious because Tesco is massive in comparison. But Terry persuaded me at the time that he could fulfil those aspirations at Tesco. I'm very glad he did because I've loved every minute of it.

He won the 2006 award for Outstanding Industry Contribution awarded by *Accountancy Age*. The award recognized that:

(Continued)

(Continued)

his strategic flair has been a huge influence on the decision-making of chief executive Sir Terry Leahy, and the two men are essentially treated as a pair in terms of the brains behind Tesco's incredible expansion, which includes successful moves into non-food, financial services and its international reach.

After Sir Terry Leahy's retirement in March 2011, concluding his 14-year period as CEO, Philip Clarke, the company's International Director, was announced as the incoming CEO. The supermarket's Chairman, David Reid, retired and was replaced by Sir Richard Broadbent, Barclays' deputy chairman, in November 2011. In the summer of 2011, Higginson also informed the company of his intention to retire from the board and executive committee on 1 September 2012.

Higginson commented about his departure:

> You get to a point when it is time to go and do something different. I have had a wonderful career with Tesco and am very proud of the part I have played in the company's success. Next year, I will be 55 and will have completed 15 years on the board ... We will have completed the creation of the bank as a standalone entity, and that seems an appropriate moment to hand over, and move on to the next phase of my career. I'd like to do a big CEO role if the right thing came up or even a chairmanship if there was a company that needed sorting out.

Shore Capital analyst Darren Shirley said Higginson's leaving was a "surprise" and a "loss" for the business: "He worked in a period under the leadership of chief executive Sir Terry Leahy that transformed the business from a domestic grocer into a truly multichannel and international business." Tesco had a large talent pool to draw from to replace him, added Shirley, but said: "Losing someone of Higginson's capability and experience can only be regarded as a loss to the business."

Source: Accountancy Age, guardian.co.uk

REVISION ACTIVITIES

In this chapter we have described the role and activities of CSOs in connecting strategy making and execution. Based on what you have just read in the current chapter, what do you think is the impact of these directors on large firms? Could such a role be applicable to organizations of smaller size (for instance, family businesses)?

Select an organization that you are familiar with. Do they have a CSO role? Is this role attached to an independent department or aligned with another department (for example, finance or marketing)? What is the career background of this CSO? Do you find any similarities with the Tesco mini case?

Note: This chapter is based on work originally presented in two conferences (Paroutis and Angwin, 2008; and Angwin and Paroutis, 2009) and published in Angwin et al. (2009).

FURTHER READINGS

- **Paper:** Angwin, D., Paroutis, S., and Mitson, S. (2009) Connecting up strategy: Are senior strategy directors (SSDs) a missing link? *California Management Review*, 51(3), Spring: 74–94. The authors provide a detailed explanation of the method employed to study Chief Strategy Officers that might be useful to researchers and students seeking to study further these actors.

- **Paper:** Brunsman, B., DeVore S., and Houston, A. (2011) The corporate strategy function: improving its value and effectiveness, *Journal of Business Strategy*, 32(5): 43–50. Offers a matrix that helps classify the contributions of the corporate strategy function and ways to increase the impact of the function (by changing the function's organization, processes and people competencies).

- **Paper:** Menz, M. (2012) Functional top management team members: A review, synthesis and research agenda, *Journal of Management*, January, 38(1): 45–80. A comprehensive review of the literature on functional top executives, with a number of options for future research in this area.

- **Paper:** Menz, M. and Scheef, C. (2014) Chief strategy officers: Contingency analysis of their presence in top management teams, *Strategic Management Journal*, 35(3): 461–71. Examined a sample of S&P 500 firms over a five-year period and found that diversification, acquisition activity, and TMT role interdependence are positively associated with CSO presence. However, they also find that the structural choice to have a CSO in the TMT does not significantly affect a firm's financial performance.

- **Website**: For a global community and think-tank for Chief Strategy Officers and senior-level strategic planners you can refer to the IEG. Strategy network at: http://strategy.theiegroup.com/about. They organize a number of industry-led summits involving CSOs and strategy officers from a variety of firms.

REFERENCES

Angwin, D. and Paroutis, S. (2009) Understanding the Role of Senior Strategy Directors: Connecting Strategy in Large Firms. Paper presented at the *25th EGOS Colloquium*, 2–4 July, Barcelona.

Angwin, D., Paroutis, S., and Mitson, S. (2009) Connecting up strategy: Are senior strategy directors (SSDs) a missing link? *California Management Review*, 51(3), Spring: 74–94.

Breene, T. R. S., Funes P. F., and Shill, W. E. (2007) The chief strategy officer. *Harvard Business Review*, 85(10): 84–93.

Burgoyne, J. (1989) *Management Development: Context and Strategies*. Aldershot: Gower.

Dye, R. (2008) How chief strategy officers think about their role. *The McKinsey Quarterly*, May: 1–8.

Kachaner, N. and Stewart, S. (2013) Understanding the role of the Chief Strategy Officer. December. BCG.Perspectives. Available at: www.bcgperspectives.com/content/articles/strategic_planning_business_unit_strategy_understanding_role_chief_strategy_officer/#chapter1.

Meldrum, M. and Atkinson, S. (1998) Meta-abilities and the implementation of strategy: Knowing what to do is simply not enough. *Journal of Management Development*, 17: 564–75.

Paroutis, S. and Angwin, D. (2008) The Roles of Strategy Directors and Strategy Teams in Large Firms. Paper presented at the *Strategic Management Society (SMS) 28th Annual International Conference*. Cologne, Germany. Winner of the SMS Best Conference Paper Prize for Practice Implications.

Paroutis, S. and Pettigrew, A. M. (2003) Making Strategy in the Multi-business Firm: Some Early Findings. Mini SMS conference, Connecticut, USA.

Paroutis, S. and Pettigrew, A. M. (2005) Making strategy in the multi-business firm. In S. W. Floyd, J. Roos, C. Jacobs, and F. W. Kellermanns (eds.), *Innovating Strategy Processes*. Oxford: Blackwell, pp. 97–110.

Winterton, J. and Winterton, R. (1999) *Developing Managerial Competence*. London: Routledge.

STRATEGY TEAMS

4

Learning Objectives

- Reveal the composition and activities of strategy teams.
- Understand how strategy teams interact with other parts of the business to make and execute strategy.
- Investigate the application of the 3P model (practitioners, praxis and practices) to analyze teams (instead of individuals).
- Appreciate how micro-level activities constitute an integral aspect of practicing strategy.

INTRODUCTION

4.1 The purpose of this chapter is to continue the investigation into the key strategic actors, their tools and capabilities involved in strategizing. Specifically we examine the composition of strategy teams and the ways they develop and deliver strategy. Within the strategy literature, recent studies have highlighted the importance of studying organizational structures and corporate strategies as continuous and intertwined processes of organizing and strategizing. It is claimed that in dealing with these dynamic processes the roles of those involved in strategy are also changing and so are their actions. Yet, our understanding about these activities remains scarce. Accordingly, the key question we address in this chapter is: what are the activities employed by strategy teams during their work?

COMPOSITION

4.2 The large strategic planning departments of the 1980s have currently been replaced in most firms by flexible teams of strategists specifically tasked to make and execute strategy. These teams are led by the **strategy directors** (Chief Strategy Officers) we saw in the previous chapter. Beyond the strategy director, strategy teams are often comprised of two other kinds of strategist: strategy analysts and strategy managers.

Strategy analysts have responsibility for preparing strategy-related reports and conduct strategic analysis using a variety of strategy tools. Their work is primarily desk-based and involves providing support for strategy managers through analysis of strategy-related data. They tend to have strong technical skills and quantitative-based educational backgrounds.

Strategy managers' principal role is to engage with various stakeholders within and outside the firm and oversee the formulation and implementation of strategy across the firm. The interactive nature of their work means that they spend a lot of time traveling while their diary commitments tend to be highly variable. They have strong interaction and social skills, and many of them have previously worked for a consultancy firm. In many firms they are perceived as internal consultants expected to provide high-level strategy support for senior and middle-level managers.

Overall, strategy teams are comprised of a strategy director and a group of strategy managers and analysts. In most firms strategy teams tend to be either small (not more than 10 members) or very large. The precise numbers of strategy analysts and managers depends on a number of factors: mainly, the internal and external conditions in the particular firm; plus the nature of the strategy planning process employed. It seems that a key determinant in terms of their size is whether the strategy team has to engage with regulators (which can lead to large teams). Accordingly, state sector and quasi-state-sector organizations can have very large teams, i.e., more than 50 members. Within the organizational chart, strategy teams tend to be considered as a supporting function or as direct reports to senior management. In large firms with multiple business units, strategy teams can be found not only at the corporate center but also within the business units. The study by BCG (Kachaner and Stewart, 2013) we saw in Chapter 3, confirms that the size of the central strategy team varies depending primarily on the size of the company itself, but this central team tends to be smaller than strategy teams in the business units. In most cases (68%) central strategy teams were found to consist of 10 or fewer members, with a median size of seven. The BCG study also found that teams who are accountable for mergers and acquisitions (M&A) or innovation tended to be larger compared to teams without those responsibilities.

ACTIVITIES

4.3 But what are the specific activities employed by strategy teams? Paroutis and Pettigrew (2007) developed an approach to study the praxis of strategy teams. Drawing upon an in-depth longitudinal case study of a FTSE-100 multi-business firm this study points to the importance of both actions and interactions of corporate center and business unit strategy teams during the strategy process. Their study reveals seven principal categories of activities employed by strategy teams (refer to Table 4.1 below).

The first three categories of *executing*, *reflecting*, and *initiating* refer to activities conducted within the setting of a single strategy team. Here, knowledge is generated among the inner members of the team and the interactions between them. Other strategy teams are not directly involved in these activities but, as the rest of the organizational members, can be influenced by them. Consequently, these three kinds of strategizing praxis correspond to activities that reflect the particular expertise, creativity, and capabilities of the strategy team members. The next three categories of *coordinating*, *supporting*, and *collaborating* refer to activities involving more than one strategy team. Accordingly, the settings of these types of praxis are mainly meetings,

TABLE 4.1 Activities employed by strategy teams

Practice	Definition	Activities comprising the practice
Executing	The strategy team undertakes day-to-day, routine activities	Developing new strategic ideas Starting new strategy initiatives/ projects
Reflecting	The strategy team reflects on and modifies past ways of conducting (or not conducting) strategy	Preparing strategy documents/ reports/ presentations Developing the strategy knowledge base
Initiating	The strategy team initiates or shapes new ideas about changes in the content and process of strategy	Investing in personal development Tweaking the strategy process and model
Coordinating	The strategy team leads and controls the activities of other teams or managers	Providing knowledge base and strategy toolkit support Conducting complex strategic analysis
Supporting	The strategy team provides strategy knowledge and resources to other managers or teams	Using common strategy model/ method/ framework Developing a common language around strategy
Collaborating	The strategy team jointly develops strategic reports and ideas across organizational levels	Sharing strategy related resources and information Working in cross-functional teams
Shaping context	The strategy team changes the contextual conditions within which other teams strategize	Deciding on the standards of strategy related output Building a network of relationships across the firm

Source: Paroutis and Pettigrew, 2007.

teleconferences, virtual teams, and away days. Here the emphasis is on the interactions between teams and the social construction of knowledge through exchange of information between team members. The final practice, *shaping context*, refers to activities undertaken by strategy teams that eventually change the structural and organizational context within which strategy is conducted. In what follows we examine in more detail these seven categories of practice using the insights by Paroutis and Pettigrew (2007).

Executing is conceptualized as the set of activities referring to instances when a strategy team undertakes day-to-day, routine activities. It includes activities such as: "preparing strategy documents/reports/presentations"; and "developing the strategy knowledge base." These activities are examples of what Whittington calls the "nitty-gritty, often tiresome and repetitive routines of strategy" (1996: 732). For strategy managers, such activities consume a large part of their day. The preparation of strategy documents and reports by strategy teams can also be directly linked with the use of appropriate strategy tools, frameworks, and models. We examine the use of strategy tools in more detail in section 4.4 below.

Reflecting refers to activities within the strategy team when members reconsider, learn from, and modify past ways of conducting (or not conducting) strategy. The two activities associated with reflecting were "investing in personal development" and "tweaking the strategy process and model." Over time, people improvise new activities as they invent, slip into, or learn new ways of interpreting and experiencing the world. Schön (1983) demonstrates that situated practice often involves reflection and experimentation. According to West (1996) team reflexivity is the extent to which team members collectively reflect upon the team's objectives, strategies, and processes as well as their wider objectives, and adapt them accordingly. High reflexivity exists when team planning is characterized by greater detail, inclusiveness of potential problems, hierarchical ordering of plans, and long- as well as short-range planning. In many firms, personal development programs are often used to establish the conditions for reflection within strategy teams. Another set of activities related to reflection by strategy teams refers to changes in the strategy process or model. Such changes are often the result of reflection by the strategy team director or the whole team during informal or formal meetings.

Initiating refers to activities by strategy teams that initiate or shape new ideas about changes in the established content and process of strategy. In this case, actions by strategy team members result in the adoption of new ways of strategizing either globally across the firm or in particular locations within the firm. The timing of these activities often occurs in the early stages of the development of new strategy initiatives, when the strategy team provides the necessary expertise and backing for new strategy ideas to emerge. As Porter (1991) stresses, strategic initiatives are new managerial actions that are specifically undertaken for the purpose of validating old or creating new strategies. Developing strategic initiatives can also be perceived as a systematic way for establishing and sustaining social relationships across managers from different business units of the firm.

Coordinating occurs when activities by one team directly influence the behaviors of another team or teams toward using a specific set of strategy tools or language. Hence, the specific coordinating activities identified during the interviews referred to "using common strategy model and method" and "developing a common language around strategy." From the viewpoint of the strategy team at the corporate center, the direction of these activities refers to interactions with the business unit strategy teams and central senior management teams. Another set of coordinating activities by the central strategy team refer to the firm's strategic model. In a similar fashion, peripheral strategy teams located in business units could also utilize coordinating activities during their interactions with local teams leading specific strategic initiatives or programs or the local top management team.

Supporting occurs when one strategy team provides strategy knowledge and resources to other managers or teams. More specifically, one team provides specific strategic information to other teams, assists them in utilizing the firm's strategy toolkit, or conducts strategic analysis that cannot be prepared by other teams. The ongoing practice of *supporting* allows central strategy teams to distribute strategic information, resources and models across business unit strategy teams. Often, central strategy teams are asked to provide expert support to peripheral strategy teams. The peripheral strategy teams also utilize similar activities to either support local teams working on business unit related programs or the local strategy team during their decision making process.

Collaborating concerns the development of strategic reports and ideas jointly with other teams across organizational levels. Two types of activities related to collaborating emerged from the data analysis: "actively sharing strategy related resources and information"; and "working in cross-functional teams." These activities allow strategy managers at the business-unit level to cooperate with their colleagues at the corporate center and exchange valuable information in preparing strategy related presentations and reports. Typically, such actions are associated with strategy events when the strategy team interacts with middle-level managers and teams, for example away-days or workshops. Strategy managers also often participate in cross-functional teams. Participating in these cross-functional teams allows strategy managers to engage with managers whose primary responsibility is not strategy and, hence, help them to understand the broad aspects of strategy and the specifics of how to utilize strategy frameworks and tools. In the mini case of Cisco below, the strategy team is expected to drive the ongoing development and coordination of Cisco's corporate strategy.

It is important to note that *supporting* is different from *collaborating* based on the level of interaction between strategy teams. Hence, supporting occurs when one team provides knowledge support to another team without being directly involved in debate (i.e., during joint meetings). This latter type of active (often face-to-face) interaction between teams corresponds to the collaborating practice. Overall, supporting refers to the simple exchange of strategic resources and information whereas collaborating involves active exchange of ideas and debate during face-to-face interaction.

Shaping context refers to activities taken by a strategy team aimed towards shaping the contextual conditions within which other teams are operating. The two activities related to this practice were "deciding on the standards of strategy related output" and "building a network of relationships across the firm." More specifically, the central strategy teams tend to be responsible for either creating or changing the majority of the standards related to the strategic output from peripheral strategy teams (i.e., length and type of reports, numerical outcomes, and presentations). Central strategy teams also actively create both formal and informal networks with peripheral strategy teams. These connections are then expected to facilitate the distribution of knowing both from the center to the periphery and across the peripheries of the firm.

Overall, strategy teams behave in a dynamic, collective, and distributed way using routine (recursive) and non-routine (adaptive) activities. For example, the Cisco strategy team (see mini case below) is responsible for coordinating Cisco's corporate strategy; developing the agenda of strategy issues (routine/recursive activities); and also interacting with leaders across the firm to develop initiatives that address emergent business challenges and opportunities; disseminating thought leadership; and creating a center of excellence (adaptive/non-routine activities). What also becomes clear is that an integral part of their daily practice involves using strategy tools (activity number 6 of the Cisco strategy team). We focus on this topic in Chapter 7.

MINI CASE: THE STRATEGY TEAM AT CISCO

Founded in 1984, Cisco provides a wide array of IT products and services to businesses and customers across the globe. Their Q2FY'15 revenue is $11.9 billion and they have 70,112 employees. Cisco has developed a strategy team because: "having a strategy discipline is more important than ever now as we grow and drive the business to a larger scale."

The strategy team has been set up to evolve and support the role of Corporate Development and the responsibilities of the Chief Strategy Officer. The principal activities of this strategy team are to:

1. Drive the ongoing development and coordination of Cisco's corporate strategy.
2. Develop an ongoing agenda of strategy issues and opportunities for Cisco to help define and implement actions that create competitive advantage and drive Cisco's long-term growth.
3. Partner with Cisco's senior leadership team, business unit, functional and theater leaders to drive key strategic initiatives, address critical business challenges, and develop and execute strategies that drive opportunities in Cisco's businesses.
4. Develop and disseminate thought leadership.
5. Create a center of excellence for strategic skill sets, tools and capabilities.

Source: www.cisco.com

LEVEL AND MODE OF STRATEGIZING

4.4 In order to examine in more detail the question about the actions employed by strategy teams, we developed the following matrix (Paroutis and Pettigrew, 2007). This matrix is informed by theories about groups of individuals from social psychology (McGrath, 1997; Moreland et al., 1994) and more specifically the work of McGrath, Arrow and Berdahl (2000). They describe three levels of dynamic causal interactions that continually shape a group of individuals: local dynamics, global dynamics and contextual dynamics. Local dynamics involve the activity of a group's constituent elements: members engaged in tasks using tools and resources. Global dynamics refer to the behavior of system-level variables (i.e., norms and status structures, group identity and group cohesiveness, and task performance effectiveness) that emerge from and subsequently shape and constrain local dynamics. Contextual dynamics are determined in part by the context in which the group is embedded and reflect the impact of system-level parameters on the overall trajectory of global group dynamics over time. These contextual dynamics (i.e., levels of organizational support, supply of potential members, demand for group outputs) continuously shape and constrain the local and global dynamics of a group. Hence, groups are regarded as open and complex systems that interact with the smaller systems (i.e., the members) embedded within them and the larger systems (e.g., organizations) within which they are embedded.

This understanding from social psychology theories can be applied to the work of strategy teams and helps us to develop two key dimensions: the level of strategizing; and the mode of strategizing. The **level of strategizing** concerns the location of the activity and whether it concerns one or multiple teams. The **mode of strategizing** is based on the extent of recursiveness or adaptation underpinning the daily activities of managers (Jarzabkowski, 2004). Recursiveness refers to recurrent, habitual, or routinized activities, while adaptation refers to exploratory, transformative, and creative activities that initiate or change the socially accomplished ways of acting (Paroutis and Pettigrew, 2007).

We combine these dimensions into the **2x2 matrix** below (Figure 4.1), which helps us map the sets of activities we presented earlier. Regarding the vertical axis and as described earlier, *executing*, *reflecting*, and *initiating* refer to activities conducted within the setting of a single strategy team, while *coordinating*, *supporting*, and *collaborating* refer to activities involving more than one strategy team. The practice *shaping context* is located in the middle of the diagram since it refers to activities that shape and constrain the context within which strategy teams operate. *Coordinating* and *executing* were found to refer to habitual activities aimed at maintaining the current way of acting and interacting around the strategy process. Hence, they are placed in the recursive section of the matrix. On the other hand, *collaborating* and *initiating* concern activities within or across strategy teams seeking to change the content and process of strategy. Finally, *supporting*, *reflecting*, and *shaping context* refer to activities that either sustain the present ways of conducting strategy or spark new ways of thinking and acting around strategy. Accordingly, they are located partially within the recursive and the adaptive section of the matrix. This matrix is helpful in furthering our understanding into the practice of strategy teams because it provides the basis for investigating the recursive or adaptive nature of their practice across different levels and over time.

In terms of the **capabilities** required by strategy teams, they include both technical and interaction skills (Paroutis and Pettigrew, 2005). *Technical* abilities refer to the knowledge and skills that enable strategy teams to deal with the day-to-day strategic activities, participate in the daily strategy discourse, and utilize strategy tools. *Interaction* abilities refer to the skills that allow them to communicate across the firm with other managers. As one member of a strategy team notes: "I will answer the skills question in two senses. One is the indoor technical skills that are required in the job, you know, in a factory that would be screwing knots and bolts together. The other kind of softer skills of teamwork, presentation etc" (Angwin et al., 2009). The job advertisements of firms aiming to recruit at the strategy team level also provide a lot of insights about these kinds of capabilities. In the first job posting below, Hewlett-Packard is seeking highly talented individuals to join their strategy team with strong technical (analyzing industry trends, testing hypotheses, conducting research) and interaction abilities (prepare communication

STRATEGY TEAMS

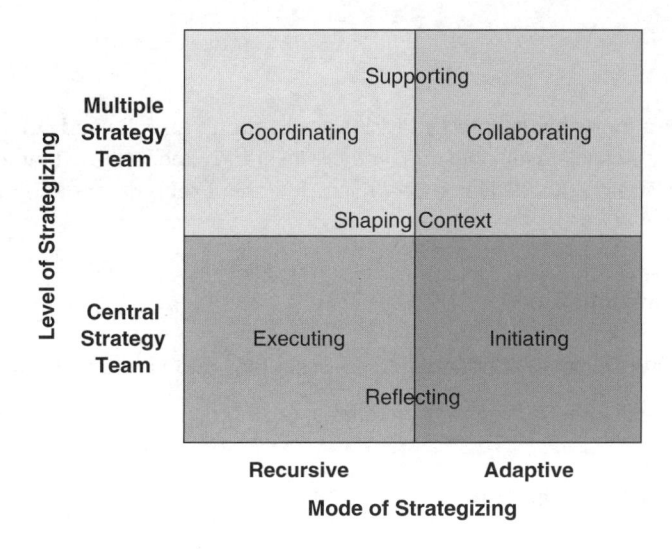

FIGURE 4.1 Levels and mode of strategizing activities matrix

Source: Paroutis and Pettigrew, 2007.

materials, strong communication skills). In the second job posting, Dell is seeking experienced managers for their small strategy team with strong technical (very strong understanding of business strategies and drivers, outstanding problem solving, and quantitative analytical skills) and interaction abilities (competent to effectively work at all levels of the organization, excellent written and verbal communication skills). Another notable aspect to these job advertisements is the need to be able to visually communicate using PowerPoint presentations (Kaplan, 2011).

MINI CASE: HEWLETT-PACKARD – ASSOCIATE, CORPORATE STRATEGY

Job Location: Palo Alto, CA

Come join Hewlett-Packard, the largest technology company in the world with a market-leading portfolio spanning personal computing, printing, software, services and IT infrastructure.

HP's Corporate Strategy team works directly with HP's executives to define, analyze, and shape HP's direction. We deliver analytically rigorous, pragmatic solutions to senior executives and work on high profile initiatives that help HP deliver game-changing results.

The Corporate Strategy team is widely respected across HP and regarded as a seeding ground for top talent. We work as a "meritocracy" that appeals to, and rewards, high achievers.

Your success paves the way for promotion inside Corporate Strategy or entry into one of HP's businesses, as your network of contacts become the "who's-who" across HP's executive ranks. Many of our alumni are now in key management positions across the company.

(Continued)

(Continued)

We are looking for highly talented individuals with strong analytic and communication skills to join our team as Associates. In this role, you will leverage experience in management consulting or business strategy to deliver data-driven, insightful recommendations to HP's senior management team.

Role and Responsibilities:

- Support pan-HP initiatives spanning growth strategy and operational excellence
- Analyze industry trends, competitive threats, growth opportunities and internal performance
- Test hypotheses through analytical rigor, data modeling, and collaboration with business unit stakeholders
- Conduct research and analysis to make recommendations that influence project outcomes
- Prepare communication materials (primarily PowerPoint presentations) used at the executive/Board level
- Actively participate in building team capability such as knowledge management and recruiting

Qualifications:

- 2–3 years in investment banking, management consulting, corporate strategy or business strategy preferred
- Demonstrable business acumen and maturity in discussing, solving and presenting complex business issues
- Strong communication skills in developing presentations through logical reasoning and structuring
- Ability to learn quickly and assimilate to new teams and projects
- Ability to work well under pressure in time-sensitive situations
- High level of attention to detail and professional rigor regarding work deliverables
- Comfortable in a high-demand work environment and responsive to rapid changes
- Organized, deliberate, and reliable in structuring work
- Highly proficient in data analysis using Excel, and visual communication using PowerPoint

Source: job posting from h30631.www3.hp.com

STRATEGY TEAMS

MINI CASE: DELL – INTERNAL STRATEGY CONSULTANT, CORPORATE STRATEGY

Location: Round Rock, TX

Dell's Corporate Strategy group is seeking exceptional leaders and forward-thinkers to help us drive the transformation of the company. We are a small team who works closely with the CEO's office and the Executive Leadership Team, and who collaborates across business segments to develop and implement solutions which deliver tangible results.

As a key member of the Corporate Strategy team, you will be:

- Consultant to internal clients
- Key part of a team leading projects to tackle issues and opportunities identified by the CEO's office and the Executive Leadership Team
- Expected to analyse, deliver insights, provide actionable/practical recommendations, and drive implementation to transform Dell

In the role, you will

- Work on highly complex problems
- Provide insight into the strategic issues which are forefront in the minds of the Executive Leadership Team
- Gain exposure to senior-level decision-making; and
- Establish relationships across all areas of the company

Job/Education Requirements:

- 10+ years of experience, including at least two years of strategy consulting experience at a top-tier management consulting firm OR 6+ years of experience at a large technology company in a strategy role
- Proficiency leading and managing smaller teams (1–2 person) teams
- Very strong understanding of business strategies and drivers
- Outstanding problem solving and quantitative analytical skills
- Ability to structure large, ambiguous business problems, and prioritize issues to address
- Excellent written and verbal communication skills
- Drive for results and ability to learn on the fly
- Self-direction and motivation, and ability to operate independently

(Continued)

(Continued)

- Ability to effectively work at all levels of the organization
- Flexibility to quickly adapt to new challenges
- Experience in enterprise hardware, services, and / or software
- Proficiency in using Microsoft tools – Powerpoint, Excel, Word, and Outlook
- MBA or equivalent work experience preferred.

Source: job posting from jobs.dell.com

Combining our insights about chief strategy officers in Chapter 3 and strategy teams in the current chapter, we can present an extended version of the 3P model that provides insights into the praxis, practices, and practitioners of internal strategy actors (see Figure 4.2).

Praxis:
Initiating, Executing, Reflecting, Coordinating, Supporting, Collaborating
-Building and managing social networks

Practices:
Strategy cycle(s)
Non-routine
-flexibility
-ad-hoc
-creativity

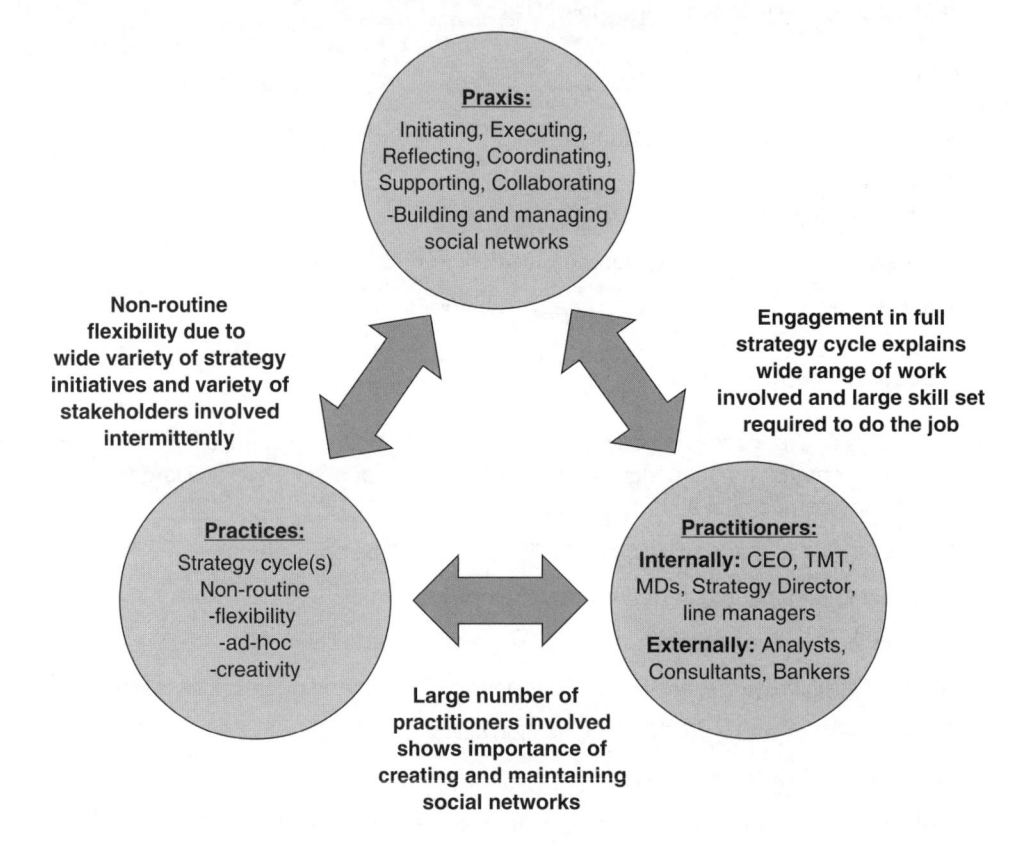

Practitioners:
Internally: CEO, TMT, MDs, Strategy Director, line managers
Externally: Analysts, Consultants, Bankers

Non-routine flexibility due to wide variety of strategy initiatives and variety of stakeholders involved intermittently

Engagement in full strategy cycle explains wide range of work involved and large skill set required to do the job

Large number of practitioners involved shows importance of creating and maintaining social networks

FIGURE 4.2 Applying the praxis, practitioners and practices framework for internal strategists

Source: Angwin, Paroutis and Mitson, 2009.

CONCLUSION

4.5 In this chapter we have explored the activities employed by strategy teams when they are practicing strategy. We show that these teams are involved in a **plethora of activities**. They are performing a complicated role across multiple levels. On one hand, they are *executing*, *reflecting*, and *initiating* strategy within the central strategy team they are directly supervising – here, knowledge is generated among the members of the team and the interactions between them. On the other hand, they are also *coordinating*, *supporting*, and *collaborating* with multiple strategy stakeholders – here, the emphasis is on interactions between strategists representing various organizational levels and the construction of knowledge during meetings, teleconferences, virtual teams, and away-days. The insights of this chapter complement the learning from the previous chapter and provide us with a more complete picture about the roles of internal strategy practitioners. In the next chapter we turn our attention on external strategists: the strategy consultants.

REVISION ACTIVITIES

In this chapter we discussed the role and activities of strategy teams. Based on what you just read in the current chapter and the previous chapter about chief strategy officers, what do you think are some of the challenges in the role of strategy teams? Could there be drawbacks in the use of strategy teams and why?

Find a job posting about a strategy-related position. How does this description compare with the cases of Hewlett-Packard and Dell in this chapter? Can you find differences in the description of these roles when you compare industries and sizes of firms?

FURTHER READINGS

- **Paper:** Evans, P. and Wolf, B. (2005) Collaboration rules. *Harvard Business Review*, 83(7): 96–104. Shows how an organizational environment designed to produce cheap, plentiful transactions unleashes collaborations (particularly around energized teams) that break conventional firm barriers.
- **Paper:** Senge, P. M., Lichtenstein, B. B., Kaeufer, K., Bradbury, H., and Carroll, J. S. (2007) Collaborating for systemic change. *Harvard Business Review*, 83(3): 70–9. Demonstrates that firms will increasingly require cross-sector collaboration across three realms: the conceptual, the relational, and the action-driven.
- **Paper:** Uzzi, B. and Dunlap, S. (2005) How to build your network. *Harvard Business Review*, 83(12): 53–60. Shows how managers can diagnose their personal network, create a more effective one, and then actively manage it. These insights are particularly relevant for managers in strategy teams.

REFERENCES

Angwin, D., Paroutis, S., and Mitson, S. (2009) Connecting up strategy: Are Senior Strategy Directors (SSDs) a missing link? *California Management Review*, 51(3): 74–94.

Jarzabkowski, P. (2004) Strategy as practice: Recursiveness, adaptation, and practices-in-use. *Organization Studies*, 25(4): 529–60.

Kachaner, N. and Stewart, S. (2013) Understanding the role of the Chief Strategy Officer. December. BCG.Perspectives. Available at: www.bcgperspectives.com/content/articles/strategic_planning_business_unit_strategy_understanding_role_chief_strategy_officer/#chapter1

Kaplan, S. (2011) Strategy and PowerPoint: An inquiry into the epistemic culture and machinery of strategy-making. *Organization Science*, 22(2): 320–46.

McGrath, J. E. (1997) Small group research, that once and future field: An interpretation of the past with an eye to the future. *Group Dynamics: Theory, Research, and Practice*, 1: 1–27.

McGrath, J. E., Arrow, H., and Berdahl, J. L. (2000) The study of groups: Past, present, and future. *Personality and Social Psychology Review*, 4(1): 95–105.

Moreland, R. L., Hogg, M. A., and Hains, S. C. (1994) Back to the future: Social psychological research on groups. *Journal of Experimental Social Psychology*, 30: 527–55.

Paroutis, S. and Pettigrew, A. M. (2005) Making strategy in the multi-business firm. In S. W. Floyd, J. Roos, C. Jacobs, and F. W. Kellermanns (eds.), *Innovating Strategy Processes*. Oxford: Blackwell, pp. 97–110.

Paroutis, S. and Pettigrew, A. M. (2007) Strategizing in the multibusiness firm: The role of strategy teams at multiple levels and over time. *Human Relations*, 60(1): 99–135.

Porter, M. E. (1991) Towards a dynamic theory of strategy. *Strategic Management Journal*, 12: 95–117.

Schön, D. A. (1983) *The Reflective Practitioner*. New York: Basic Books.

West, M. A. (1996) Reflexivity and work group effectiveness: A conceptual integration. In M. A. West (ed.), *Handbook of Work Group Psychology*. Chichester, UK: Wiley, 555–79.

Whittington, R. (1996) Strategy as practice. *Long Range Planning*, 29(5): 731–5.

MIDDLE MANAGERS

Learning Objectives

- Demonstrate the importance of central and peripheral practitioners for practicing strategy.
- Appreciate the role and importance of middle managers in the strategy process.
- Reveal the importance of engaged strategy participation and collaboration for practicing strategy.
- Showcase the growing importance of strategy communities.

CENTRAL AND PERIPHERAL PRACTITIONERS

5.1 As we explained in the introductory chapter, strategy-as-practice investigates how managerial actors perform the work of strategy, both through their social interactions with other actors and through practices present within a context (Hendry, 2000), as well as habits, tools, events, artifacts, and socially defined modes of acting through which the stream of strategic activity is constructed (Turner, 1994). One of the central arguments of the strategy-as-practice perspective is that strategy is not the analytical preserve of the CEO and the top team, or the visionary and charismatic domain of the entrepreneur. Instead of being solely a top-down process, strategizing is inherently more complex involving multiple tools and actors. This is particularly the case in large organizations which are characterized by an inner context (Pettigrew, 1987; Pettigrew and Whipp, 1991) of increased complexity compared to other organizations. In these firms the key question is: who is actually involved in practicing strategy?

TABLE 5.1 The role of central and peripheral strategists through the 3P framework

Dimensions	Description	Key insights
Practitioners	Central and peripheral strategists	• They have multiple career paths, some of them being former strategy consultants • They are organized in teams across the firm to allow better communication and efficient ways of working
Practices	Following a uniform template and set frameworks	• Their formal output is in the form of presentations and reports to the top and business unit management teams • Using a uniform template allows for a common language to develop between central and peripheral strategists
Praxis	Routine activities based on central framework but also customization to local requirements	• Their primary role is to: (a) provide technical and analytical support when new strategic issues emerge; and (b) help develop solutions for ongoing strategic issues • Their role requires high analytical skills but also the social skills to collaborate horizontally and vertically across the organization chart

In order to answer this question, empirical studies in the strategy-as-practice area are increasingly providing us with rich accounts of the ways managers act while formulating and implementing strategy. However, most of these studies focus on the activities of a single group of practitioners. Yet, in complex organizational settings, strategizing is constituted by the ongoing activities and interactions of diverse and distributed groups of individuals. Studying the practices of strategists in complex organizations also raises the issue of *distributed activity* (Orlikowski, 2002; Tsoukas, 1996). Here, the activities of distributed communities across multiple organizational levels are central in developing, maintaining, and renewing strategy. Using the practice approach, Regnér (2003) investigated managerial actions at the center and the periphery of multinational organizations. His findings suggest "a twofold character of strategy creation, including fundamental different strategy activities in the periphery and centre, reflecting their diverse location and social embeddedness" (2003: 57).

An example of an organization of increased complexity is the multi-business firm, which is characterized by the plethora of business units, organizational levels, and hence by a multitude of contextual pressures. In this setting, scholars have been primarily interested in the role of the corporate center (Goold et al., 1994). At the same time, within the multi-business firm business units may act as local political silos where teams of individuals and single individuals (like the business units' MDs, acting as "regional barons") try to maintain their local routines and practices when they are challenged by corporate center managers to follow group-wide standards. For example, when a new strategy process is introduced across a multi-business firm, a resistant context at the periphery may result in the local strategy team utilizing certain strategizing activities to alleviate this resistant behavior. Accordingly, the multi-business firm is an organizational setting in which the practice of strategy is an ongoing social process, involving processes of consent and resistance by central and peripheral strategists.

Overall, the key argument posed in this chapter is that in complex organizational settings strategy is practiced across a community of strategists. Using the 3P framework, we can see that peripheral and central strategy actors are involved (Regnér, 2003) in practicing strategy (see Table 5.1). By combining the insights of the current chapter with the learning we gained in Chapter 2 (CEOs), Chapter 3 (Chief Strategy Officers) and Chapter 4 (Strategy Teams), we can also gain an understanding about the activities of strategists at the periphery of organizations, particularly middle-level managers.

MIDDLE-LEVEL MANAGERS

5.2 Professor Steven Floyd and his colleagues have provided us with a number of insights and models about the strategic roles played by managers across different managerial levels (Floyd and Lane, 2000; Floyd and Wooldridge, 1992, 2000). This stream of work has provided a number of great insights, particularly into the activities of *middle-level managers* and the nature of their influence in the strategy-making process. For example, in their 1992 paper, Floyd and Wooldridge provide a model of middle managers' roles in the strategy process. They find four main roles: championing strategic alternatives; synthesizing information; facilitating adaptability; and implementing deliberate strategy (refer to Figure 5.1), across two dimensions: behavioral activity (upward and downward influence); and cognitive influence (integrative and divergent thinking). More recently, Floyd and Lane (2000) mapped previous studies into 10 managerial roles, each of them involving both processing of information and taking action. Regarding the three main managerial roles, they found that: (a) top management has decision-making roles of ratifying, directing, and recognizing; (b) middle managers' role is to communicate between the operating and top levels of management in the forms of championing, facilitating, synthesizing, and implementing; and (c) operating managers react to information by experimenting, conforming, or responding.

As mentioned in Chapter 1, for the strategy-as-practice approach, strategy is conceptualized as a situated and socially constructed activity involving *multiple actors* who interact to accomplish the work of strategizing. Accordingly, there have been studies focusing on: top managers (Jarzabkowski, 2008); middle managers (Balogun, 2003; Mantere, 2008; Rouleau, 2005); strategy directors and their teams (Angwin et al., 2009; Paroutis and Pettigrew, 2007); strategy champions (Mantere, 2005); and expert personnel (Laine and Vaara, 2007).

Key insights from these studies have been not only the focus on particular strategy practitioners, but also the realization of the multi-layered, contested nature of strategic cognition (Kaplan, 2008) and action that involves multiple practitioners and has particular *strategic outcomes*. For instance, practice studies have shown that activity and cognition differences between managers at the center and periphery in multinational companies have diverse capability creation

		Behavioral Activity	
		Upward Influence	**Downward Influence**
Cognitive influence	**Divergent**	Championing Strategic Alternatives	Facilitating Adaptability
	Integrative	Synthesizing Information	Implementing Deliberate Strategy

FIGURE 5.1 Typology of middle managers' roles in strategy

Source: Floyd and Wooldridge 1992. Used with permission of John Wiley and Sons.

effects (Regnér, 2003), that intertwined sense making and action have important consequences for strategy outcome (Balogun and Johnson, 2004), and that middle-level managers draw on tacit knowledge and discourse in everyday activities to understand and sell strategic change (Rouleau, 2005; Rouleau and Balogun, 2011). Further highlighting the importance of middle-level managers, Wooldridge et al. (2008) provide an informative review and future research agenda on what they term a middle-management perspective on strategy process. These studies showcase the theoretical and methodological advancements in our understanding of strategy process and practice. They also reflect the challenging and complex nature of the strategy task for many organizations.

THE END OF THE MIDDLE MANAGER (?)

Lynda Gratton, a Professor of Management Practice at London Business School, reflects in her *Harvard Business Review* article about the challenges new technologies pose for the role, and very survival, of the middle-level managers. She argues that the technological revolution has provided firms with the ability to utilize technological solutions to fulfill tasks that were traditionally held by middle-level managers, notably: monitoring performance; providing live feedback; and creating reports and presentations. Professor Gratton then notes that: "Technology itself has become the great general manager. It can monitor performance closely, provide instant feedback, even create reports." This new reality means that current middle-level managers need to consider developing their skill sets and develop new areas of proficiency.

Source: Gratton (2011).

ENGAGED STRATEGY PARTICIPATION

5.3 In the previous section we highlighted the importance of central and peripheral strategists; in this section we turn our attention to how exactly to engage these multiple actors in strategizing. In other words, the key question here is: how do we develop managers to engage really well in a shared strategy process? Nichols and Paroutis (2008) note that if an organization's strategy is merely a plan or a vision that people need to understand and buy into, then probably this firm is not being strategically engaged enough. They recommend three key actions to get active strategy participation, in other words to get employees to keep their eyes and ears open, constantly looking for new opportunities to improve the strategy and improve its effectiveness in action:

> Change the emphasis of your engagement process from "selling strategy" to teams toward **inviting involvement**. Top management must set the intent, but top management can never "own" the points of contact with the world where strategy is enacted. Everyone must be developed to be able to contribute well to strategy in action at the frontier of contact. The first act is to get this clear in your head and in the conversation within the most senior management groups.

> Invite **participation in strategy**. Management should not do this by e-mail or by engaging an internal communications team – though such teams will play a valuable role. Instead, all levels of management should treat their team members as people with valuable roles in making strategy real. They might also offer a series of events to share the strategic intent if it is unclear – and it is often less clear than you think to staff far from the boardroom. They should invite staff to join in a conversation about how "we all, together" purpose this intent well, and learn together from the process.

> Finally, management should invest in developing the **strategic capability** of people at all levels. This is not just about tools and analytical models – though this may be very important. It is also about the ability to listen and share – and about the development of a strategic mindset. And for the most senior managers it will be about the hard work of letting go of a heroic version of strategy in which they lead and others follow, and creating a more participatory and learning-based view of real strategy that reflects the fact that the people who know how the strategy is working in practice are rarely in the boardroom.

The third action point raises the question about the kinds of skills and capabilities required by strategists. Cunningham et al. (2007), through the use of focus groups in an Irish software company, identified four key skills for a strategist, namely: (1) a structured and analytical mind; (2) an entrepreneurial ability – to think outside the box; (3) the ability to network and communicate effectively; (4) leadership – to provide direction and take decisions.

Recent research on the knowledge and skills that enable managers to practice strategy (termed *strategizing capabilities*) supports the notion of the three-dimensional strategic manager (Paroutis, 2007; Paroutis and Palmer, 2007; Paroutis and Pettigrew, 2001, 2005):

Technical abilities refer to the knowledge and skills that enable managers to deal with day-to-day strategic activities, participate in the daily strategy discourse, and utilize strategy tools.

Interaction abilities allow strategists to interact with other managers and work in strategy teams. Furthermore, two sub-categories of interaction abilities were discovered: political and communication skills.

Meta-level abilities enable strategists to utilize their knowledge in novel ways and to provide critical insights during the strategy process. Within this broad category, two sub-categories of meta-level abilities were exposed: conceptual skills (the ability to translate figures and facts into strategic objectives and alternatives) and creativity (the ability to discover novel strategic solutions).

The importance of developing strategizing capabilities is illustrated through the following mini case of Beiersdorf UK. This case demonstrates one possible way to gain improved capability to engage teams in making strategy happen through a combination of development workshops and management support.

MINI CASE: BEIERSDORF UK – STRATEGY IN ACTION IN A GLOBAL COMPANY

"Beiersdorf UK" is the UK arm of a global skin care organization based in Hamburg, Germany. Corporate strategy clearly emanates from Hamburg, but the strategy is played out in different markets worldwide. So the actual strategy of the "Nivea for Men" brand in the UK is a combination of the stated intent of Hamburg and the local implementation strategy in the hands of Brand Manager Graham Taylor and UK Marketing Director Andrew Frost. "Every time we mount a marketing campaign, innovate with a key customer or consider a joint sales promotion," says Andrew Frost, "we are contributing to forming strategy in action."

This is why developing the team's ability to think strategically is so important. As Andrew Frost says:

> Everyone working on the brands, acting on consumer insights and negotiating with the major retailers – must be capable of seeing the strategic picture and be aware that their decisions shape an effective approach. Day to day decisions based on judgment and the refining of our stance is strategy – without it, strategic intent means little more than just words on paper.

Andrew Patterson is HR Director of Beiersdorf UK. He says, "We focus on developing the strategic thinking ability of our managers. Through our Step-Up Development program all managers have the opportunity to attend an elective on Strategic Thinking." This workshop covers the essential toolkit for awareness and analysis in competitive markets – context analysis, thinking about segmentation and sources of competitive advantage, and organizing for strategic effect. The workshop is practical: "Everything is focused on our business," says Andrew Patterson, "we make ourselves and our customers the case study."

Each Step-Up workshop is a two-day workshop with a single day follow-up six weeks later. In the intermodular period, participants carry out a live strategic project in their area of the business. Projects have considered new product evaluation and launch, supply chain and logistics strategy, and major customer relationship positioning – all aspects of strategy for the firm. Teams commonly discuss their ideas with the board or relevant members of senior management, who usually act as "sponsors" for the project work.

"The tools of the strategy workshop are only part of the learning," says Andrew Patterson:

> Participants are challenged, by the facilitators, by their colleagues and by sponsoring Directors, to think deeply and bring in alternative perspectives. We try hard to show that good participation in strategy is more than knowing the tools. Learning to challenge each other's mindsets, and learning to find and listen to different views, are both important parts of the strategic skill set. Our managers can also elect to take part in Step-Up workshops on Creativity and Innovation to help them broaden their field of vision where this would be helpful.

"What we have noticed above all," he says, "is that the inter-personal skills of our managers really matter. This is not the same as being polite or being 'fluffy', it is about having the ability to deal well with conflict, to give and receive feedback, to have difficult conversations about tough matters that make a difference in the business." Beiersdorf invests through its Step-Up program in coaching and feedback skills, the ability to deal with conflict, and assertiveness and personal impact skills:

> Everyone from our assistant brand managers to Board level has to be able to participate well in conversations about putting strategy into action. We find that many people have a reluctance to appreciate that everyone has power and that making conscious choices about the use of power is what makes for effective collaboration and effective teams. We want people, especially senior people, to be aware of their patterns of acting and ways of thinking so that we get more out of everyone in thinking together about our success. To help this everyone in the group has had 360-degree feedback and coaching sessions and some managers have also taken part in action learning sets, again to surface patterns and assumptions and increase self awareness.

What has been the result of all this investment in Step-Up? "We never imagined that sending people on workshops was a silver bullet," says Andrew Patterson, "but it does give a common grounding in tools and models and a shared vocabulary and expectations about how we interact. Every time I see someone coaching well in the business, when I see someone causing a colleague to re-examine their assumptions and examine a different angle, then I know we are making progress."

Source: Nichols and Paroutis (2008).

COLLABORATING WITH STRATEGY COMMUNITIES

5.4 A key implication from the previous two sections on the strategy practitioners involved in complex settings is about the nature of their interactions. In large firms, these interactions take the form of collaborations between central and peripheral teams (Paroutis and

Pettigrew, 2007), instead of coordinating activities from the corporate center. In these conditions strategy making and execution is an ongoing change process involving multiple actors. Middle-level managers play a key role in developing and disseminating the key messages of strategic change (Balogun and Johnson, 2004; Rouleau, 2005), while the close interaction between central and peripheral managers leads to the creation of strategic capabilities (Regnér, 2003). This multi-layered, interactive, and collaborative nature of the strategy task has led strategists to introduce a number of technologies in their practice (Orlikowski, 2000); for example, collaborative online communities or Web 2.0 (Paroutis and Al Saleh, 2009), together with more established methods of interaction, such as workshops (Hodgkinson et al., 2006; Johnson et al., 2010) and away-days. An illustration of this complexity, requiring a strategy community to be created, is the following mini case study on the BT Group.

MINI CASE: BT GROUP – A STRATEGY COMMUNITY IN ACTION

BT Group is one of the world's leading communications services companies, serving the needs of customers in the UK and in more than 170 countries worldwide. The firm's main activities are the provision of fixed-line services, broadband, mobile, and TV products and services, as well as networked IT services. In the UK, BT is a leading communications services provider, selling products and services to consumers, small and medium-sized enterprises (SMEs), and the public sector. It also sells wholesale products and services to communications providers in the UK and around the world. Globally, it supplies managed networked IT services to multinational corporations, domestic businesses, and national and local government organizations.

In the past few years there have been a number of structural and leadership changes to the group. The firm has been restructured along market lines, rather than the traditional product and technology lines. This market-facing structure has been important to help the firm be more responsive to the environment. An obvious example that underlines this change in organizational structure is the formation of a global services business division, which had previously been staffed by delivery-focused technology specialists. This division was restructured in 2005 in order to include client-facing business development managers and client managers and is organized along market lines and geographically in order to drive business overseas.

Ian Livingston (aged 46) was appointed Chief Executive of BT Group on June 1, 2008. Previously, he was Chief Executive of BT Retail, a position he held from February 2005. Prior to this, Ian was Group Finance Director for BT Group from April 2002. The Chairman of the Board is Michael Rake (aged 63) and he was appointed on September 26, 2007.

The process for strategy development in BT can be summarized as evolving. The current practice of strategy development has changed, supported by the new organizational structure. There is a headquarters' located strategy team consisting of approximately one dozen individuals. This corporate strategy team is typically working on projects that are brought to its attention by the market-facing units. Strategic options, especially those that might be considered disruptive or transformational, are largely driven by people who act in the capacity of strategy actors from within the market-facing units.

The corporate strategy team reacts to specific needs of the firm and the directions of the senior leadership team. If an opportunity that has been scoped out by market-facing units requires significant time commitment, often the corporate strategy team may invest one or two personnel to commit full time to the program of work, but the initial inspiration is not commonly theirs. A good example was the recommendation from the Retail Division that looks after SME and residential customers, to invest in the TV service market in order to support their competing with triple-play offerings in the telecommunications marketplace. TV is now one of the key strategic objectives for the firm driven by corporate strategy, but the innovation was developed elsewhere.

Under the guidance of the corporate strategy team, a strategy community has been established that helps unify and coordinate the work of the various strategy managers within all of the lines of business. This is designed to introduce information and ideas from bottom up, to balance the top-down direction and communication already in existence.

In addition, strategy away-days are facilitated for the company's Board twice annually. These sessions were good for review in the past, but now have become vehicles for strategic decision making in the newly evolving process. The strategy community is engaged in detailed preparatory work in readiness for these sessions, and options are presented to the Board as a whole for debate and decision. Various levels of management within the organization are consulted as part of this preparation.

Source: www.bt.com, primary research in BT.

CONCLUSION

5.5 The purpose of this chapter was to investigate the role and influence of strategic actors that tend to act 'in the middle' between the top and operational levels of organizations, often termed as middle-level managers. The key message is that strategy is not solely the exclusive domain of the CEO and the top management team. Instead, based on the strategy-as-practice perspective, multiple actors from various levels, at the center and the periphery, get involved in strategy making and execution. Further, in practice "strategy" is rarely implemented in the way the originator expects. The actual strategy pursued frequently ends up different from the plan. As such, strategists need to be aware of the kinds of tools and capabilities they require to improve the participation in strategy, to achieve engaged strategy participation. Overall, this chapter suggests that strategizing is an ongoing practice involving multiple actors, including middle-level managers, and that strategic capability needs to be developed to effectively execute the firm's strategic objectives.

REVISION ACTIVITIES

In this chapter we have highlighted the importance of central and peripheral actors in practicing strategy in complex organizational settings. Find examples of firms (private or public) where you expect middle-level managers to be playing a key role in strategy. Why do you think these firms rely on middle-level managers for their strategy making and execution? Provide recommendations to some of these firms on how they can improve their strategy practice.

What do you find interesting about the BT Group mini case? What do you think the firm achieves by having such a wide set of actors involved in the strategy process? What kind of resources are required to sustain such a process in the long run?

FURTHER READINGS

- **Book**: Floyd, S. W. and Wooldridge, B. (2000) *Building Strategy from the Middle: Reconceptualizing Strategy Process*. Thousand Oaks, CA: Sage. Develops an approach to the study of the role, influence, and impact of middle-level managers in the strategy process. A number of theoretical and methodological insights are provided for future studies of these managers, whose role is central in complex firms.

- **Paper**: Hope Hailey, V. and Balogun, J. (2002) Devising context sensitive approaches to change: the example of Glaxo Welcome. *Long Range Planning*, 35(2): 153–78. Provides a framework (change kaleidoscope) that can assist managers in developing context-sensitive implementation approaches.

- **Paper**: Laamanen, T. and Wallin, J. (2009) Cognitive dynamics of capability development paths. *Journal of Management Studies*, 46(6): 950–81. Offers a comprehensive study of three software firms, and shows that cognition–capability links can be detected at three levels of capability development: individual operational capabilities, capability portfolios, and capability constellations.

REFERENCES

Angwin, D., Paroutis, S., and Mitson, S. (2009) Connecting up strategy: Are senior strategy directors (SSDs) a missing link? *California Management Review*, 51(3): 74–94.

Balogun, J. (2003) From blaming the middle to harnessing its potential: Creating change intermediaries. *British Journal of Management*, 14: 69–84.

Balogun, J. and Johnson, G. (2004) Organizational restructuring and middle manager sensemaking. *Academy of Management Journal*, 47(5): 523–49.

Cunningham, J., Harney, B., and O'Dea, E. (2007) In search of the strategist. Paper presented at the Strategic Management Society Conference, San Diego, California, October.

Floyd, S. W. and Lane, P. J. (2000) Strategizing throughout the organization: Managing role conflict in strategic renewal. *Academy of Management Review*, 25(1): 154–77.

Floyd, S. W. and Wooldridge, B. (1992) Middle management involvement in strategy and its association with strategic type: A research note. *Strategic Management Journal*, 13: 153–67.

Floyd, S. W. and Wooldridge, B. (2000) *Building Strategy from the Middle: Reconceptualizing Strategy Process*. Thousand Oaks, CA: Sage.

Goold, M., Campbell, A., and Alexander, M. (1994) *Corporate-Level Strategy: Creating Value in the Multibusiness Company*. New York: Wiley.

Gratton, L. (2011) Column: The end of the middle manager. *Harvard Business Review*, January-February. Available at: http://hbr.org/2011/01/column-the-end-of-the-middle-manager/ar/1 (date accessed: March, 2015).

Hendry, J. (2000) Strategic decision making, discourse, and strategy as social practice. *Journal of Management Studies*, 37: 955–77.

Hodgkinson, G., Whittington, R., Johnson, G., and Schwarz, M. (2006) The role of strategy workshops in strategy development processes: Formality, communication, co-ordination and inclusion. *Long Range Planning*, 39(5): 479–96.

Jarzabkowski, P. (2008) Shaping strategy as a structuration process. *Academy of Management Journal*, 51(4): 621–50.

Johnson, G., Prashantham, S., Floyd, S. W., and Bourque, N. (2010) The ritualization of strategy workshops. *Organization Studies*, 31: 1589–618.

Kaplan, S. (2008) Framing contests: Strategy-making under uncertainty. *Organization Science*, 19(5): 729–52.

Laine, P. M. and Vaara, E. (2007) Struggling over subjectivity: A discursive analysis of strategic development in an engineering group. *Human Relations*, 60(1): 29–58.

Mantere, S. (2005) Strategic practices as enablers and disablers of championing activity. *Strategic Organization*, 3(2): 157–84.

Mantere, S. (2008) Role expectations and middle manager strategic agency. *Journal of Management Studies*, 45(2): 294–316.

Nichols, C. and Paroutis, S. (2008) Engaged strategy participation: Going beyond "buy-in". *Critical Eye Review*. Available at: http://criticaleye.net/insights-detail.cfm?id=1409 (date accessed: February, 2012).

Orlikowski, W. (2000) Using technology and constituting structure: A practice lens for studying technology in organizations. *Organization Science*, 12: 404–28.

Orlikowski, W. J. (2002) Knowing in practice: Enacting a collective capability in distributed organizing. *Organization Science*, 13(3): 249–73.

Paroutis, S. (2007) Strategizing capabilities: Conceptual and empirical insights from a multi-method study. Paper presented at the Strategic Management Society Conference, San Diego, California, October.

Paroutis, S. and Al Saleh, A. (2009) Determinants of knowledge sharing using Web 2.0 technologies. *Journal of Knowledge Management*, 13(4): 52–63.

Paroutis, S. and Palmer, G. (2007) Developing capabilities for practice: Do we really teach MBAs how to be effective strategists? Paper presented at the Third Organizational Studies Summer Workshop, Crete, Greece, June.

Paroutis, S. and Pettigrew, A. M. (2001) Practicing strategy and developing strategising capabilities: A research prospect. Paper presented at the 17th EGOS Colloquium, Lyons, France.

Paroutis, S. and Pettigrew, A. M. (2005) Studying strategizing and organizing within the multibusiness firm: Capabilities, evidence and learning. Paper presented at the First Organization Studies Summer Workshop, Santorini, Greece, June.

Paroutis, S. and Pettigrew, A. M. (2007) Strategizing in the multibusiness firm: The role of strategy teams at multiple levels and over time. *Human Relations*, 60(1): 99–135.

Pettigrew, A. M. (1987) Context and action in the transformation of the firm. *Journal of Management Studies*, 24(6): 649–70.

Pettigrew, A. M. and Whipp, R. (1991) *Managing Change for Competitive Success*. Oxford: Blackwell.

Regnér, P. (2003) Strategy creation in the periphery: Inductive versus deductive strategy making. *Journal of Management Studies*, 40(1): 57–82.

Rouleau, L. (2005) Micro-practices of strategic sensemaking and sensegiving: How middle managers interpret and sell change every day. *Journal of Management Studies*, 42(7): 1413–41.

Rouleau, L. and Balogun, J. (2011) Middle managers, strategic sensemaking, and discursive competence. *Journal of Management Studies*, 48(5): 953–83.

Tsoukas, H. (1996) The firm as a distributed knowledge system: A constructionist approach. *Strategic Management Journal*, 17: 11–25.

Turner, S. (1994) *The Social Theory of Practices: Tradition, Tacit Knowledge, and Presuppositions*. Chicago, IL: University of Chicago Press.

Wooldridge, B., Schmid, T., and Floyd, S. W. (2008) The middle management perspective on strategy process: Contributions, synthesis, and future research. *Journal of Management*, 34(6): 1190–221.

STRATEGY CONSULTANTS

6

> **Learning Objectives**
> - Provide insights into the characteristics and roles of strategy consultants.
> - Understand the role of strategy consultants as a strategy profession.
> - Appreciate the way consulting interventions are designed and executed.
> - Showcase how to analyze the work of strategy consultants through the 3P model.

INTRODUCTION

6.1 So far, we have focused our attention on the internal strategy actors (CEO, CSO, strategy teams and middle managers). In this chapter we turn our attention to external actors: the strategy consultants and their role in practicing strategy. While there are a number of studies concerning the consulting profession overall, the purpose of this chapter is to focus on the role of strategy consultants and reveal the ways they are involved in strategizing and with what effect. This chapter also allows the reader to start considering the complex relationships between internal and external strategists in their efforts to make and execute strategy. Our aim is to show how strategy consultants, as external strategic actors, become engaged in organizational activities and, ultimately how they influence the way strategy is practiced. We use the 3P framework to structure the present chapter. First we deal with the roles and characteristics of strategy consultants and the methods they employ (Practitioners and Practices) and finally we discuss their activities in the context of the consulting engagement (Praxis).

CHARACTERISTICS AND ROLES

6.2 Management consultants have grown to become an important external stakeholder in making and executing strategy for a large number of organizations, in various industries and on a global scale. This increasing use of consultants is evident in the market growth observed in this industry (Armbruester and Kipping, 2001). The global management & marketing consultancy market grew by 5.5% in 2010 to reach a value of $270 billion, while the compound annual growth rate of the market in the period 2006–10 was 2.7% (Datamonitor, 2011). Operations management is the largest segment of this market, accounting for 29.1% of the market's total value. The information technology segment accounts for a further 21.2% of the market, while corporate strategy comes third representing a 16.5% share (Datamonitor, 2011). This final segment is comprised of strategy consultancy firms, such as McKinsey, Boston Consulting Group, Bain, and Booz Allen Hamilton.

Strategy consultancies focus on assisting their clients to solve strategic problems. Boston Consulting Group provides the following questions as indicative of high-level, strategic questions within a complex business environment that strategy consultants are called upon to answer: Should an automotive manufacturer acquire its biggest competitor? How can a large pharmaceutical company achieve major cost savings in its global supply chain? What is the most effective way for a leading financial-services player to significantly expand its retail-banking business? Should a technology firm offshore some, most, or all of its R&D function? (BCG, 2012). They note that in dealing with these questions, clients expect "more than simply an accurate diagnosis of the problem: they want a practical, effective path to implement – one that can generate real bottom-line results and sustainable competitive advantage" (BCG, 2012). An insight into Booz Allen Hamilton (BAH) is provided in the box below where the CEO also provides an insight into the methods and technology employed by BAH consultants.

MINI CASE: BOOZ ALLEN HAMILTON (BAH)

Booz Allen Hamilton (BAH) is a strategy and technology consulting firm. The company offers a range of consulting services including organization and strategy, economic and business analysis, supply chain and logistics, intelligence and operations analysis, information technology, systems engineering and integration, assurance and resilience, and modeling and simulation. Its clients include government agencies, corporations, institutions, and infrastructure organizations. The company has 80 offices spanning North America, Europe, the Middle East and Asia Pacific. It is headquartered in McLean, Virginia and employs about 25,000 people.

The company recorded revenues of $5,591.3 million during the financial year ended March 2011 (FY2011), an increase of 9.1% over FY2010. The operating profit of the company was $128.1 million in FY2011, as compared to $48.9 million in FY2010. The net profit was $84.7 million ($84.7 million) in FY2011, as compared to $25.4 million in FY2010.

In the firm's 2011 annual report, Ralph W. Shrader, Chairman and Chief Executive Officer of Booz Allen Hamilton stated that:

(Continued)

(Continued)

Our important work springs from an entrepreneurial culture where ideas flourish – and where people grow and pursue their passions inside and outside of work … Today's professional services landscape is changing, and we must continue to evolve the way we work to create greater flexibility, more efficiency, and more personal and professional growth. Our "Way We Work" strategy combines face-to-face teaming, telework, remote delivery, and hoteling to foster greater work–life balance, reduced commuting times, and a smaller carbon footprint. Our people and our clients benefit from advanced computing centers, videoconferencing, and other technologies that support collaboration and improve product and service delivery.

Source: www.bah.com and 2011 Booz Allen Hamilton annual report.

After dealing with the broad role of consultants, we can now examine, more specifically, the career paths of the principal actors in strategy consultancies. Often consultants move into firms as strategy directors (into the role we saw in Chapter 3) and are valued for their methodologies, diagnostic skills and broader industry knowledge. Strategy consultancies are also known for their very substantial network of senior directors (often strategy directors) in large firms that they tap into as clients and which help them maintain close links between consulting and industry. For example, the McKinsey Alumni numbers nearly 24,000 members in 120 countries (McKinsey, 2011). For prospective strategy consultants, the profession provides the following positives: strong alumni networks; potential for fast and international careers; exposure to top management issues and generalist early career. On the negative side: there is the "up or out policy" (members either make progress within a specific period, often two years, or are asked to leave); high workload; and tendency to be a tough environment during economic downturns as client work tends to decrease then (Kitten, 2004). The box below outlines the details of the strategy consultant's role in Bain & Company and the skill set required for those wanting to join the profession.

MINI CASE: BAIN & COMPANY – WHAT TOP MANAGEMENT CONSULTING IS ABOUT

It seems that nowadays, everyone calls himself a consultant, from the wine specialist at your local supermarket to the football commentator on TV. Strategy consultants specialize in … strategy, business strategy to be more precise. Business strategy consulting is done at a very high level in the organization, typically the Board and the CEO. These are the ones making the choices. Below, the organization focuses on implementing the decisions (sometimes assisted by other consultants). Business strategy consulting is about facts and common sense much more than vision or dreams. Facts make decisions easier. Dreams without facts make them tougher. Business strategy consulting is tailor-made thinking. What works for one company will not necessarily work for the other, even in the same industry. Strategists use tools, but tools don't make the strategist. Only the quality of the people matters in this business.

> Having said that, what can you really expect from the job just after leaving university?
>
> Let's be honest, you will not immediately meet the CEO of your client, nor create multi-billion-dollar-recommendations on your own. First you will need to learn the job. Don't worry about formal training, as most firms have highly effective training programs in place. They could even finance your MBA. But it is the day-to-day, on-the-job coaching that will be most important in your development. So be very careful in selecting the right firm.
>
> Typically, a junior analyst will spend their day collecting facts on which to build solid recommendations. One day they will build a financial model. Then they will conduct literature searches on specialized databases to analyze industry trends. They might interview the client's staff members or customers. They might even conduct discussions with his client's competitors. The list is endless. As you develop your skills, your assignments will become more and more complex, but you will interact with more senior client representatives.
>
> Now, are you made for this job? First, one word of caution about lifestyle: strategy consultants are not die-hard workaholics, but it is not unusual for a consultant to work 55–60 hours a week, with highs and lows. Keep that in mind if your lifestyle requires a lot of personal time. The opportunities offered by strategy consulting firms are quite exceptional, but in return those firms only hire a few, exceptional people. The #1 requirement for the job is outstanding analytics. Some firms will only invite students with outstanding academic records. All will thoroughly test your analytical capabilities during real life "case interviews." Then, interpersonal skills are also very important, as the job involves a lot of teamwork and external contacts. In any case, make sure your CV contains the "signs of excellence" that might grant you a first round interview.
>
> Source: Thibaut and Faelli (2015).

After joining a strategy consultancy, there are a number of key stages in the career of a strategy consultant from the analyst to the partner level (see Table 6.1). Normally, analysts would have an undergraduate degree and would spend two to three years in the role before they can be considered for the consultant role. Consultants would be normally required to work two to four years in their role before moving to become engagement managers. Finally, engagement managers would spend three to five years delivering projects before being considered for the partner role (Kitten, 2004). In terms of the topics a strategy consultant tends to cover, these can range from corporate and business unit strategy to sustainability.

A number of studies are providing very useful insights about the challenging environment inside consultancy firms. Sturdy (2003) argues that in this "insecure business," defined by pressures from demanding clients and premature burn-out, consultants tend to share in the existential anxiety of the managerial task. Due to their location outside client organizations, consultants operate in the liminal spaces of project teams (Czarniawska and Mazza, 2003) and develop particular forms of language (Merilainen et al., 2004) to deal with the uncertainty about their position and identity. Consultants also often have to deal with forms of knowledge that is complex, esoteric and beset by uncertainties, making the effort to deliver diagnoses and solutions to clients' problems very challenging (Sturdy et al., 2009). Next we shed light into the nature and activities during consulting interventions.

TABLE 6.1 Principal roles in strategy consultancies.

Roles	Description of Roles
Partner	Acquires and manages senior client.
	Arranges contracts and bills.
	Supervises teams.
Engagement Manager	Leads project and delivery of solution.
	Liaises with partners and coaches team members.
	Often conducts presentation.
Consultant	Manages work streams and client team members.
	Coaches analysts.
	Liaises with information and industry specialists.
Analyst	Initial focus on interviewing and modelling.
	Takes part in problem solving.
	Often takes responsibility for logistics.

Adapted from: Kitten, 2004. Used with permission

CONSULTING INTERVENTIONS

6.3 In the previous section we examined the growth of the management consulting industry, the services provided by and the career roles in strategy consultancies. Despite these insights, there is no consensus in studies on consultancy about the best way of describing consulting interventions and, more particularly, the actions of strategy consultants. For client organizations, the intervention allows interaction with consultants who are widely perceived as importers of outside expertise (Sturdy et al., 2009) or as agents of change (Czarniawska and Joerges, 1996). Trigo et al. (2006) examine in more detail the consulting intervention and note that consultants influence top management teams in the process of making strategy and decision making (rather than taking the decisions themselves).

The consulting interventions are run by a client team consisting of a core group of consultants and members from the client side. As shown in Figure 6.1, the **strategy consulting team** is often comprised of a mix of the roles we presented in Table 6.1 (partners, engagement managers, consultants, and analysts) as well as internal knowledge experts who have experience of particular industries or operations. According to McKinsey (2012a), the team is responsible for planning and conducting the engagement, maintaining relationships with the client, participating in every phase of the engagement, and ensuring the ultimate quality of the work and the impact delivered to the client. The work in these teams involves the collection of data, exchange of ideas, analysis of data, and development of conclusion and recommendations aimed at dealing with the client issue. As we will see next, the structure and rules of operation of the client team are

STRATEGY CONSULTANTS

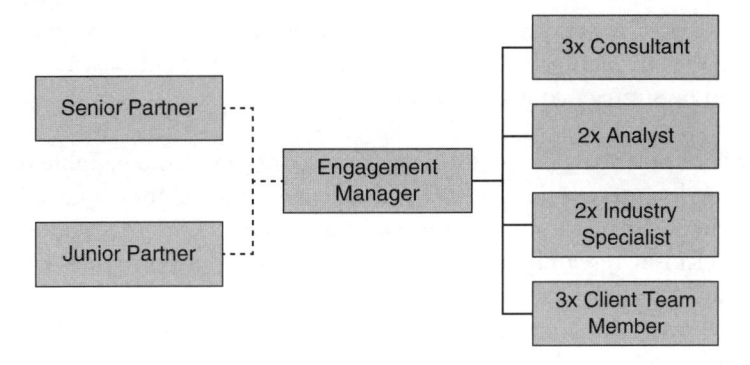

FIGURE 6.1 Composition of a strategy consulting team

Source: Adapted from Kitten, 2004. Used with permission.

decided at the start of the consulting project to ensure the client is clear of the consultants' role during the engagement. Strategy consultancies also tend to offer support across a number of strategic areas, from corporate strategy to mergers and acquisitions. The box below provides a detailed look at the topics the strategy arm of Bain and Company supports.

MINI CASE: BAIN & COMPANY – STRATEGY CONSULTING EXPERTISE

Fundamentals of growth: Only one in ten companies succeeds in achieving sustained growth. We help companies grow by defining and focusing on their core.

Business unit strategy: Effective strategy for business units requires making proprietary decisions about where to play and how to win. The goal is to enable a business to reach its full economic potential.

Corporate strategy: Corporate strategy involves a proprietary set of actions that enables a company to be worth more than just the sum of its parts. The most critical role of the center is to help business units achieve leadership positions.

Founder's Mentality: To win in the long term, most companies need the cost advantages and scale of global incumbents. Yet, in achieving that scale, companies often lose what we call the Founder's Mentality[SM] – the very core strengths and values that helped them succeed.

BothBrain Innovation: Bain works with clients to transform innovation for new product development and make big ideas actionable by combining creative strategy and analytic approaches.

Emerging markets: Home to most of the world's population and recording double-digit growth, emerging markets in Asia, Latin America, and Eastern Europe are must-win areas for multinational companies. Bain helps companies navigate this unfamiliar terrain and successfully compete against indigenous companies and other multinationals.

Sustainability: Bain helps companies develop renewable energy policies, realize the full potential of recycling processes and identify the impact of new trends and regulations, among other things.

Source: http://bain.com/consulting-services/strategy/index.aspx

An insight into the precise actions during a consulting intervention is provided by McKinsey (2012b). Despite the diversity of consulting projects and interventions, there are **five stages** normally followed by strategy consulting teams:

1. **Initiate**: where principals (the equivalent of the consultant role in Table 6.1), create new projects using long-term relationships with clients. There is often a negotiation process where the client issue and objectives are discussed, and a letter of proposal is provided by initial McKinsey research on the problem. This letter also provides details of the required team structure from McKinsey and the client.
2. **Start-up**: following the proposal, a team is created from McKinsey's diverse, global pool of staff. The team meets the client and prepares the project objectives. A project plan is developed and initial data is collected to assist the team in their analysis of the client problem and their position in the particular industry. This process is supported by internal industry specialists and internal practice research documentation.
3. **Develop a solution**: this is the most intense phase, requiring close collaboration and interaction with the client. Consultants collect more in-depth data through interviews and team meetings, and conduct extensive analysis of the data to develop a set of recommendations.
4. **Present recommendations**: the close collaboration of the McKinsey team with client executives occurs during the duration of the project. As a result, the client managers engage actively in the recommendations developed by the consulting team. Several formal interim progress reviews and a final presentation to the top management serve to communicate the recommendations developed.
5. **Launch change**: in this phase the recommendations of the team are implemented by the client. The team will often transform the recommendations into specific projects and offer an implementation and communication plan with clear steps to achieve the required change. Block (1981) also developed a five-stage model to describe consulting interventions (see Table 6.2 below).

TABLE 6.2 Stages in consulting interventions.

Consulting Stage	Indicative Consulting Practices
Entry and Contracting	Initial contact about the client issue. Exploring the problem, skills suitability, and client expectations.
Discovery and Dialogue	Consultants engage with the organization and begin to collect data to analyze the problem.
Feedback and Decision to Act	Reporting back of findings. Managing client expectations about the forthcoming recommendations.
Engagement and Implementation	Delivery of recommendations by the organization, with or without the consultants.
Extension, Recycle or Termination	Evaluation of delivery to assess whether to expand the program across wider organizational segments.

Adapted from: Block, 1981

STRATEGY CONSULTANTS

From the **client's perspective**, the consulting intervention provides the opportunity to acquire specific information needed to take strategic decisions. Clients often require accurate and up-to-date information, which they cannot access, or, having the possibility to access it, choose not to because they are unwilling to spare the necessary resources and time to obtain it (Turner, 1982). This information is relevant to clients to the extent that it reduces their anxiety and uncertainty concerning the strategic issue under analysis (Ford, 1985). Furusten (2009) also notes that management consultants help reduce clients' feelings of uncertainty and function rather as agents of stability rather than as agents of change. Fincham and Clark point out that:

> Uncertainty has long been seen as integral to management, which revolves around skills that are social and political in character. Correspondingly any agent who takes up these tasks inherits this uncertainty, adding to the quota of "agency problems". In this sense, the consultant role is seen as reproducing in heightened form the uncertainties of managerial work. (2002: 68)

Beyond reducing uncertainty, consulting interventions might also help: legitimize an already selected course of action in the client firm (Saxton, 1995); overcome resistance to change (Ginsberg and Abrahamson, 1991; Ginsberg, 1989); build consensus (Turner, 1982); and promote innovative perspectives (Appelbaum, 2004). Overall, taken together, the learning from the previous two sections allows us to apply the 3P framework. The result of this analysis is a deeper understanding of the strategy consultants and their teams as external agents who are involved in practicing strategy (refer to Table 6.3).

TABLE 6.3 Understanding strategy consultants through the 3P framework

Dimensions	Description	Key Insights
Practitioners	Strategy Consultants	• They have multiple career paths, and tend to have an MBA. • They are hired by clients to solve particular strategic issues. • They also tend to support non-profit organizations.
Practices	The methods, routines, and tools adopted by Strategy Consultants	• Their formal output is in the form of presentations and reports to their clients. They are often involved in implementing their recommendations. • They tend not to use customized strategic tools and adapt them to the particular issue facing their client. • Their social networks are heavily oriented across private and public organizations.
Praxis	The activities adopted by Strategy Consultants	• Their primary role is to: i) analyze the strategic issues they have been hired to tackle and provide concrete solutions; and ii) engage with the internal strategy actors who are related to this particular strategic issue. • Their role requires high analytical skills but also the ability to extract information and collaborate with multiple internal actors.

THE CONSULTING PROFESSION IN FOCUS

6.4 In order to appreciate the role of strategy consultants, we now turn our attention on two perspectives that have studied the impact of consultants on organizations: the dominant **organizational development** (OD) approach and the more recent **critical perspective** (Fincham and Clark, 2002). Within these perspectives, there are positive and negative views on consultants. In the positive view, consultants bring good problem solving and coaching skills along with a more unprejudiced view of the environment (Ginsberg and Abrahamson, 1991). Payne and Lumsden (1987) report CEOs to be predominantly satisfied with consultants' work and with interventions' outcomes. McLarty and Robinson (1998) also argue that hiring consultants on a temporary basis to deal with particular projects may be more cost effective than hiring high-calibre managers. In the negative view, consultants are even compared to "witch doctors" (Alvesson and Johansson, 2002). Overall, the more positive stream of literature is dominated by the traditional pro-consultancy texts, which tend to be written by consultants and that are strongly normative and self-promoting (Alvesson and Johansson, 2002). Contributions by academics assume a rather more unfavorable angle, occasionally being strongly negative towards consultants (refer to the box below). Overall, there are both negative and positive views about the role of consultants. Alvesson and Johansson also note on the issue:

> Interestingly, the general image of management consultants in contemporary society is, for different groups, provocative as well as appealing. Few occupations and activities trigger such strong reactions, both positive and negative. For many people consultancy signals interesting, significant, dynamic and prestigious work. [...] For others, however consultancy means the absence of deeper knowledge, shallowness partly associated with fashions and fads as well as overpayment and an almost immoral attitude. Some people even ascribe management consultants the blame for major corporate problems. (2002: 229)

CRITICAL VIEWS ON MANAGEMENT CONSULTING

There have been studies questioning the benefits of consultancy interventions (Appelbaum, 2004). Some go even further by describing business-people's perceptions on consultants as leading to heated discussions, where consultants are portrayed as "crooks," "incompetents," and "conmen" (Ford, 1985).

Often the reasons behind these negative assessments of consultants stems from clients' disappointment towards the outcomes or results that emerged from the consultancy intervention. This lack of satisfaction is connected, at a more immediate level, to consultants' inability to deliver what they had promised (Ford, 1985), as well as to implementation difficulties (Appelbaum, 2004). Frustrations also become visible at the level of interventions' consequences for the company as a whole. Researchers reported clients' dissatisfaction with consultants' failure to make the client company more competitive (Appelbaum, 2004), and their inability to lead to improved performance (Gibb, 1985).

Another set of reasons behind consultants' negative image is connected with clients' lack of confidence in their competence or expertise (Ford, 1985). Finally, the dissatisfaction was also

> linked to consultants' behaviors during the interventions. Aspects such as the following were put forward: lack of customization (Appelbaum, 2004); consultants' attitude of promising too much too soon; and their over-confidence concerning their ability to solve problems (Ford, 1985). A similar argument emerged from Karantinou and Hogg's (2001) study – these authors describe the pursuit of different or even conflicting agendas by clients and consultants as a relevant negative aspect of consultancy interventions.
>
> Saxton (1995) argues that consultants' benefits or disadvantages depend on the specific circumstances in which their engagement takes place. Werr and Linnarsson (2001) concluded that clients tended to have an ambiguous view of consultants, based on several tensions, such as clients valuing consultants' energy and initiative to force a high pace, on the one hand, and their need to control the process, on the other.
>
> Adapted from: Trigo et al. (2006).

Examining what led to the bankruptcy of Michael Porter's Monitor Group in November 2012, Denning (2012) writing in Forbes, notes that: "Ultimately what killed Monitor was the fact that its customers were no longer willing to buy what Monitor was selling. Monitor was crushed by the single dominant force in today's marketplace: the customer." Denning explains that, after the financial crisis of 2008, large firms have little interest in paying large fees to strategists to find sustainable competitive advantage from studying the structure of the industry or by analyzing the numbers. In this context, he argues that strategy consulting has a future, but this needs to evolve away from the view of strategy as defeating rivals by finding sustainable competitive:

> Consultancies that can guide large firms to move into the world of continuous innovation in the 21st Century have a bright future ... Managers and consultants are going to have to get their hands dirty understanding what happens on the front lines where work gets done and where customers experience the firm's products and services. To prosper, everyone has to become both more creative and more down-to-earth.

This view is also echoed by Clayton Christensen and colleagues in their *Harvard Business Review* article (Christensen et al., 2013), where they note that the consulting profession, more broadly, is facing a period of disruption for a number of reasons, for example the changing needs of their clients and the new services and technologies available to these firms. They go on to note that there are four implications from this disruption for the consulting profession and industry:

> 1. A consolidation – a thinning of the ranks – will occur in the top tiers of the industry over time, strengthening some firms while toppling others. 2. Industry leaders and observers will be tempted to track the battle for market share by watching the largest, most coveted clients, but the real story will begin with smaller clients – both those that are already served by existing consultancies and those that are new to the industry. 3. The traditional boundaries between professional services are blurring, and the new landscape will present novel opportunities. 4. The steady invasion of hard analytics and technology (big data) is a certainty in consulting, as it has been in so many other industries.

CONCLUSION

6.5 In this chapter we focused on one set of external strategy practitioners: the strategy consultants and investigated their role in the practice of strategy. By contrasting these insights with the learning we gained about internal strategy practitioners in Chapters 2 and 4, we motivate the reader to identify the differences in the role, methods, and activities adopted by external and internal strategy practitioners.

REVISION ACTIVITIES

In this chapter we have investigated the role and activities of strategy consultants in practicing strategy. Based on what you have just read in the current chapter, what do you think is the impact of these consultants in public and in not-for-profit organizations?

Select a consultancy firm that you are familiar with. Do they provide services related to strategic issues? What are the industries they support and do they have particular tools they are using in their practice? Do you think they are effective in having a distinctive identity compared to other consultancy firms, how do they achieve that?

FURTHER READINGS

- **Books**: Friga, P. N. (2008) *The McKinsey Engagement*. McGraw-Hill Professional. Rasiel, E. M. and Friga, P. N. (2001) *The McKinsey Mind* McGraw-Hill Professional. Provide insights into the realities of working for McKinsey and Company.

- **Website**: The Management Consultancies Association (MCA) is the representative body for management consultancy firms in the UK, it consists of 46 member companies (around 60% of the UK consulting industry, employing around 30,000 consultants): http://www.mca.org.uk. MCA publishes a series of reports. One of these reports demonstrates the value that consultants bring to their clients with example case studies from MCA member firms. The case studies were all taken from entries to the MCA Management Awards: http://www.mca.org.uk/sites/default/files/VoC in Practice FINAL.pdf

- **Websites**: One way to appreciate the requirements and nature of the consulting industry is to investigate the characteristics of recruiting in sites such as: www.top-consultant.com and http://www.consultancyrolefinder.com

REFERENCES

Alvesson, M. and Johansson, A. (2002) Professionalism and politics in management consultancy work. In T. Clark and R. Fincham (eds.), *Critical Consulting: New Perspectives on the Management Advice Industry*. Oxford: Blackwell Publishers, pp. 228–46.

Appelbaum, S. H. (2004) Critical success factors in the client-consultant relationship. *Journal of the American Academy of Business*, 4(1/2): 184–91.

Armbruester, T. and Kipping, M. (2001) Strategic change in top management consulting: Market evolution and current challenges in a knowledge-based perspective. *Academy of Management Proceedings*, August, A1–A6, doi: 10.5465/APBPP.2001.6133463.

BCG (2012) What is strategic consulting? Available at: www.bcg.com/careers/working_at_bcg/ strategy_consulting/default.aspx (date accessed: February 18, 2012).

Block, P. (1981) *Flawless Consulting: A Guide to Getting your Expertise Used*. Austin, TX: Learning Concepts.

Christensen, C. M., Wang, D., and van Bever, D. (2013) Consulting on the cusp of disruption. *Harvard Business Review*, October: 106–15.

Czarniawska, B. and Joerges, B. (1996) Travels of ideas. In B. Czarniawska and G. Sevón (eds) *Translating Organizational Change*. Berlin: de Gruyter, pp. 13–48.

Czarniawska, B. and Mazza, C. (2003) Consulting as a liminal space. *Human Relations*, 56(3): 267–90.

Datamonitor (2011) Global Management & Marketing Consultancy. Industry profile published in October. Reference Code: 0199-0424.

Denning, S. (2012) What killed Michael Porter's Monitor group? The one force that really matters. Forbes. Available at: http://www.forbes.com/sites/stevedenning/2012/11/20/what-killed-michael-porters-monitor-group-the-one-force-that-really-matters/ (date accessed: February 18, 2015).

Fincham, R. and Clark, T. (2002) Introduction: The emergence of critical perspectives on consulting. In T. Clark and R. Fincham (eds.), *Critical Consulting: New Perspectives on The Management Advice Industry*. Oxford: Blackwell Publishers, pp. 1–18.

Ford, C. H. (1985) Developing a successful client-consultant relationship. In C. R. Bell and L. Nadler (eds.), *Client and Consultants: Meeting and Exceeding Expectations* (2nd edn.). Houston: Gulf Publishing Company, pp. 8–21.

Furusten, S. (2009) Management consultants as improvising agents of stability, *Scandinavian Journal of Management*, 25(3): 264–74.

Gibb, J. R. (1985) Is help helpful? In C. R. Bell and L. Nadler (eds.), *Client and Consultants: Meeting and Exceeding Expectations* (2nd edn.). Houston: Gulf Publishing Company, pp. 140–5.

Ginsberg, A. (1989) Assessing the effectiveness of strategy consultants. *Group and Organization Studies*, 14(3): 281–98.

Ginsberg, A. and Abrahamson, E. (1991) Champions of change and strategic shifts: The role of internal and external change advocates. *Journal of Management Studies*, 28(2): 173–91.

Karantinou, K. M. and Hogg, M. K. (2001) Exploring relationship management in professional services: A study of management consultancy. *Journal of Marketing Management*, 17: 263–86.

Kitten, M. (2004) Introduction to Strategy Consulting (Candesic). Presentation to Chicago MBA, Barcelona, 20 October.

McKinsey (2011) Alumni. Available at: http://www.mckinsey.com/Alumni (date accessed: December 11, 2011).

McKinsey (2012a) Structure of the Team. Available at: http://www.mckinsey.com/locations/athens/ourwork/structureoftheteam/ (date accessed: February 18, 2012).

McKinsey (2012b) Project Phases. Available at: http://www.mckinsey.com/locations/ athens/ourwork/projectphases/ (date accessed: February 18, 2012).

McLarty, R. and Robinson, T. (1998) The practice of consultancy and a professional development strategy. *Leadership and Organization Development Journal*, 19(5): 256–63.

Merilainen, S., Tienari, J., Thomas, R. and Davies, A. (2004) Mangaement Consultant talk: A cross-cultural comparison of normalizing discourse and resistance. *Organization*, 11(4): 539–64.

Payne, A. and Lumsden, C. (1987) Strategy consulting – a shooting star? *Long Range Planning*, 20(3): 53–64.

Saxton, T. (1995) The impact of third parties on strategic decision making. *Journal of Organizational Change Management*, 8(3): 47–62.

Sturdy, A. (2003) The Consultancy Process – An Insecure Business? *Journal of Management Studies*, 34(3): 389–413.

Sturdy, A., Handley, K., Clark, T. and Fincham, R. (2009) *Management Consulting: Boundaries and Knowledge in Action*. Oxford: Oxford University Press.

Thibaut, P. and Faelli, F. (2015) What is top management consulting all about? Bain & Company. Available at: http://www.stopwondering.be/bainweb/localoffices/brussels/stopwondering/what_is_consulting.asp? (date accessed: February, 2015).

Trigo, S. P., Angwin D., and Wilson, D. (2006) Consultants as 'preying mantises'? Exploring consultants' contributions to strategizing practices. Paper presented at the EGOS conference, Bergen, Norway.

Turner, A. N. (1982) Consulting is more than giving advice. *Harvard Business Review*, Sept–Oct, 60(5): 120–9.

Werr, A. and Linnarsson, H. (2001) Management Consulting for Client Learning? Clients' Perceptions on Learning in Management Consulting. *Fenix: Working Papers*, WP 2001: 12 Version 2.

PRACTICES   B

The purpose of Section B is to present some of the practices (methods) strategy practitioners use to influence the way strategy is made and executed inside and across their firms. In Chapter 7 we focus on work about the use of strategy tools and how this can help us appreciate the multidimensional nature of the strategists' daily task. Our aim is not to provide an account of all available strategy tools, but instead motivate the reader to consider and then reflect on how tools are used (and sometimes misused) when practicing strategy. In Chapter 8 we further argue that language and discourse play a fundamental role in the way tools (and the broader "practices" of the 3P framework) are used. In Chapter 9 we focus our attention on the role of strategy workshops as arenas where important strategic work takes place. Combined, these chapters showcase the multi-dimensional nature of the methods practitioners can employ when practicing strategy.

STRATEGY TOOLS

7

Learning Objectives

- Consider the development and role of tools in practicing strategy
- Demonstrate that strategy tools play multiple roles in the way strategy is made and executed
- Understand the process through which strategy tools are created, developed and consumed within and across organizations
- Raise awareness of the material aspects of practicing strategy and their impact in the way actors develop strategy

TYPES OF STRATEGY TOOLS

7.1 Existing studies on strategy tools primarily focus on inventories of strategy and organizational tools and classifications of their popularity in different organizational settings (Clark, 1997; Gunn and Williams, 2007). The consultancy Bain and Company has been producing a survey since 1993 entitled "The Bain management tool survey," which studies the use of 25 tools by executives around the world and their performance (Rigby and Bilodeau, 2011). The tools included in this survey need to be relevant to senior management, topical, and measurable. Bain has built a large database of 11,163 responses (Rigby and Bilodeau, 2011) that allows for classification of the most popular tools according to various criteria (size of company, geographical location, industry, etc.). In their *Harvard Business Review* paper, Rigby and Bilodeau (2007) discuss some of the Bain survey results categorizing the tools into four sections: rudimentary tools, specialty tools, blunt instruments, and power tools:

- *Rudimentary* tools are usually new and underdeveloped, often surrounded by buzz but delivering little in overall satisfaction.
- *Specialty* tools and *blunt instruments* are on opposite sides of the coin. Specialty tools are highly effective when employed appropriately and blunt instruments seek to attack large problems in a cumbersome way (the example given is of knowledge management due to its historically poor implementation).
- *Power* tools are those with a proven track record of both use and satisfaction. The most pervasively used example of this is strategic planning, which has been consistently rated highly. The Bain study also demonstrates that the regional and national context is one of the central factors causing strategic tool usage variation in practice. For example, Asian firms were found to utilize fewer tools than the rest of the world. Similarly, other studies reveal the importance of various contextual factors influencing the use of strategy tools, such as the regional, macroeconomic, microeconomic and organizational contexts.

In the Bain survey on tools, Rigby and Bilodeau note that: "By tracking which tools companies are using, under what circumstances and how satisfied managers are with the results, we've been able to help them make better choices in selecting, implementing and integrating the tools to improve their performance" (2011: 9). In the 2011 survey results "benchmarking" takes the spot of most popular tool for the first time in a decade, leaving "strategic planning" second, while the results about usage and satisfaction of tools suggest that tried-and-true tools (benchmarking, strategic planning, and mission and vision statements) are highly rated and preferable even during a downturn. If we examine the Bain survey through a practice lens, a number of questions can be posed: for instance, does strategic planning represent a tool or a wider practice? Conceptually speaking, strategic planning can be seen as encompassing many other tools. This kind of critical reflection on many survey-based studies in the broader tools literature has led scholars to consider practice-inspired approaches on tool use, as we will see next.

A Snapshot of Two Traditional Strategy Tools: PESTLE and SWOT

The macro- and micro-environment analyses are traditionally the first steps of a strategic analysis; they are sometimes referred to as the PESTLE (or PEST) and SWOT analyses. The PESTLE (Political, Economic, Social, Technological, Legal, Environmental) framework is designed to identify macro-level influences on a firm or industry, while SWOT (Strengths, Weaknesses, Opportunities, and Threats) focuses on the external and internal environment of the particular organization.

Determining the influences by undertaking a PESTLE analysis in itself is not sufficient to determine the key strategic factors that affect a firm or industry; it is important to determine the relative strengths of these drivers and, more importantly, anticipate the changes in these drivers over time. For instance, the Environmental variable may not have been important several years ago, but may be of relative importance now. Given the time horizon of strategic planning, setting strategic direction on the current state rather than anticipating the changes that will take place over time can lead to a myopic strategy that is later rejected by consumers.

Ahmed et al. (2006) provide a SWOT analysis of Air China, the largest air carrier in China in terms of traffic volume and company assets, employing over 20,000 staff, including more than

2,300 pilots and 4,520 flight attendants at the time. According to these authors, Air China's strengths include: well-trained flight crew who are experienced in international operations and services; updated fleet and competent repair and maintenance expertise; advanced information systems; a good reputation in both international and domestic markets; and quality service and a number of rapidly increasing, loyal frequent flyers. On the other hand, Air China's weaknesses are: the unclear strategic direction largely diluting its capabilities and seriously confusing its brands; the fact that many quality service initiatives and practices are easily copied by its competitors; and finally the fact that the majority of resources, organizational concentrations, and management time are consumed on the domestic operation, resulting in weak offerings for the international market. Important strategy questions arising from these factors include the relative degrees of management focus and investment in addressing the weaknesses vs. investing to maintain and enhance the strengths, as well as questions of prioritization of the different issues.

USING STRATEGY TOOLS

7.2 Given the rapid changes in the business landscape and multiple customer targets, the work of strategy has become increasingly complex. Whittington (2004) calls for a deeper understanding about how new strategy tools (or what he terms *strategy technologies*) and concepts are developed, tested, and marketed and in particular how these tools are used in practice. He advocates that regardless of the connection between activities and firm outcomes, managers still need the right tools and skills to perform the real work of strategizing. As a result, a key question when practicing strategy is about the ways practitioners can influence other practitioners. Using the 3P framework, we can see in Figure 7.1 that there are two principal "pathways" of influence: the first occurs when practitioners use particular tools or methods

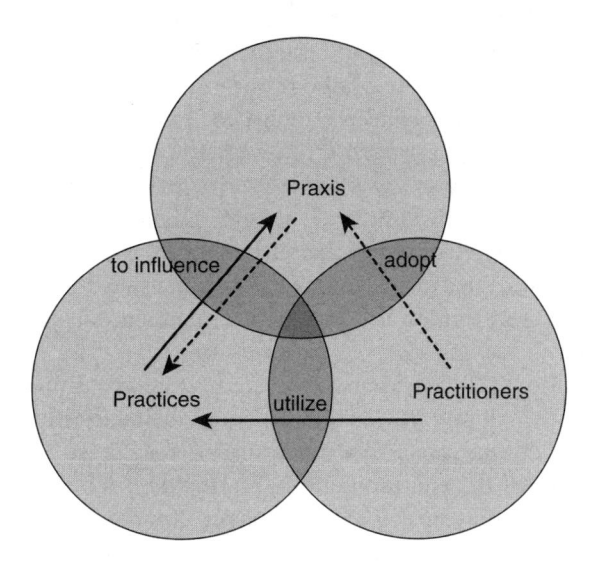

FIGURE 7.1 Understanding how practitioners influence praxis and practices

(practices) to influence the actions of other strategists; the second happens when practitioners use particular actions to alter the practices used by other practitioners. We can entitle the first path "artifact-oriented" and the second "action-oriented" based on their particular orientation. During the practicing of strategy, these pathways coexist as multiple strategic actors act and interact to create and execute strategy.

The first pathway is about the use of strategy tools. When practicing strategy, practitioners tend to resort to management tools and techniques to deal with and cope with uncertainty. The purpose of strategy tools is to aid and guide managerial decision making. They are a means to an end and when used appropriately can provide a powerful and persuasive medium of communicating directions for strategic action or inaction. But as Kaplan and Jarzabkowski (2006) note, even though business schools teach these strategy tools, we know very little about how they are actually used (if at all) in managers' day-to-day work of strategizing.

Knott argues that strategy tools need to be used differently according to the strategic problem needs and proposes five generic modes "to improve coherence in tools applications" (2006: 1093). The *analytical* mode allows prescriptions (e.g., real options analysis, Porter's Five Forces), whereas the *dynamic* mode looks for assumptions about future environment (e.g., dynamic capabilities framework or industry life cycle). The *metaphorical* mode is used for divergent thinking and experiential knowledge (e.g., analogical reasoning). The *facilitative* mode encourages creativity and communication and should be future oriented (e.g., SWOT, scenario planning). Lastly, the *interventionist* mode uses an approach as a blueprint (e.g., balanced scorecard). Knott notes that these modes highlight the centrality and importance of user adaptation of tools in practice.

Calori (1998) critiques the orthodox strategic management models because of their bias towards thinking to the detriment of other forms of reasoning, bias towards binary logic (either/or thinking) and a failure to recognize feeling as a source of reason. Given these concerns he advocates that there is an urgent need to renew our management models, recipes, and theories. Worren et al. (2002), similarly caution us that we need to be more pragmatic in our pursuits for more useful theories and models to help practicing managers. They argued that conceptual tools, while helping construct a more simplified frame of reality, might make it difficult for users to think outside that frame once it has been established. Jarratt and Stiles's (2010) more recent study using a strategy-as-practice approach on how methodologies and tools frame managers' strategizing practices found that there was a lot of criticism towards traditional strategy tools (e.g., SWOT, PEST, BCG...) due to their static nature in dealing with changing business environments (Jacobides, 2010). They outlined that although these tools guided formal strategizing through their uncomplicated, structured framework for analysis, they were also oversimplified and lacked explanatory power, reinforcing entrenched mental models that elaborate and extend on issues already known.

Jarzabkowski and Wilson (2006) discuss two contextual conditions that impact the way we can classify strategy theory and associated tools and artifacts: environmental velocity and knowledge intensity. *Environmental velocity* captures the increase in the speed, complexity, dynamism, and turbulence of the environment due to factors such as the knowledge economy, globalization, deregulation, and technological diffusion. *Knowledge intensity* is "the degree to which a firm is dependent upon the knowledge generation inherent in its activities and outputs, which may include both subjective and social knowledge bases as well as objective, codified and

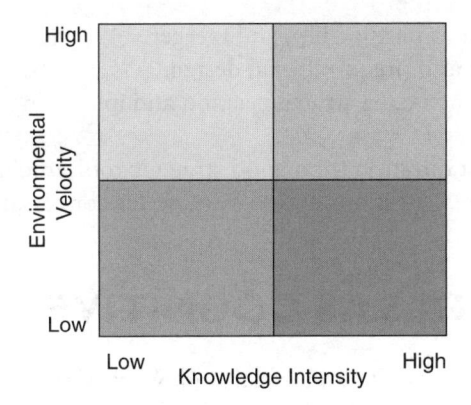

FIGURE 7.2 The environmental velocity-knowledge intensity matrix
Source: Adapted from Jarzabkowski and Wilson, 2006. Used with permission.

explicit knowledge bases" (p. 351). The resulting environmental velocity–knowledge intensity matrix (see Figure 7.2) could help classify strategy tools which managers find useful under different contextual conditions represented by the four quadrants. The authors then go on to argue that the use of strategy tools is more complex than direct application and goes beyond the original theoretical purpose for which the tools were created. Strategy tools in practice are appropriated and adapted by managers for particular purposes and outcomes; this "practical adaptation" of the tools is defined as *bricolage* (de Certeau, 1984).

Apart from consulting firms and in-house corporate universities, business schools are a fertile ground for teaching these tools to current and future strategy practitioners. Perhaps the most popular tools taught in strategy capstone courses, as evident in strategy textbooks and course outlines shared amongst Business Policy & Strategy members of the Academy of Management (refer to: http://www.bpsdiv.org/), are those that focus on Porter's 5 Force Model, Generic Strategies, SWOT, Resource Base View, Value Chain, BCG Matrix, McKinsey 7S, Balanced Scorecard, Strategy Clock, Strategic Group Maps, Strategic Factor Analysis Summary (SFAS), and Blue Ocean, *inter alia* (Kachra and Schnietz, 2008). Yet we know very little about how these tools are actually used (if at all) in managers' day-to-day work of strategizing (see Jarzabkowski, 2004; Jarzabkowski and Spee, 2009). Even more compelling is the view that we do not know enough about how users perceive these tools as they put them to practical use in a real organization.

At the institutional level, there is the expectation that strategy tools provide the basis for more enhanced strategy interactions, while at the individual level they improve the capabilities of the strategy practitioner operating within and across organizations. Nichols and Paroutis (2008) argue that strategy tools matter since, by understanding and using them, strategy practitioners are able to form communities of practice when dealing with complex strategic issues. They also recommend that managers develop a familiarity with the tools and models that offer help in the following areas:

- Understanding strategic context.
- Assessing markets and competitive dynamics.
- Undertaking competitor analysis.

- Exploring collaboration, partnership, and merger.
- Examining alignment and organizational design.
- Communicating and managing strategic action and measuring performance.

They also suggest that a test question for a good strategic tool, intelligently used, is: Does using this tool help us to ask better questions and to have better conversations?

STRATEGY TOOLS AS COGNITIVE ARTIFACTS

7.3 The seminal review of the Industrial and Work Organization Psychology field by Hodgkinson (2003) highlighted the great advances that have been made in the field of Human Computer Interaction (HCI) and how this body of work has informed the designs of artifacts in the workplace with particular attention to workers' cognitive capabilities and limitations. Viewing strategic tools as cognitive artifacts allows us to have a more fine-grained perspective to the power they impose on strategy practitioners in the performance of their strategic work, which incorporates as much the "thinking process" as that of the doing of strategy. In addition, as cognitions have such an influence on our subsequent behavior, it makes sense to view them as cognitive tools that help us make sense of our cognitively demanding environments.

Norman (1991) defines artifacts as devices that maintain, display, or function on information in order to serve as a representational form that affects human cognitive performance. They are man-made "things" that have the power to aid or enhance our cognitive abilities and hence our performance (Krippendorff, 1989). We call them cognitive artifacts because of the information-processing role played by these tools upon the cognitive thought processes of individuals when they engage in their use. Yet, as we noted earlier, strategy practitioners depend on the use of these strategic tools in order to carry out the important work of strategic analysis. However, we know little about the information processes played by these cognitive artifacts (such as strategy tools) and how they engage with information-processing activities of tool users. Yet there are numerous suggestions in the extant literature that these tools do have cognitive elements; Jarzabkowski (2004) for example referred to them as "psychological tools" and "conceptual schemas" that assisted strategists to generate meaning from their complex surroundings. Hence it seems that cognitive artifacts not only support human activity, but they also serve as tools to understanding human cognition (Nemeth et al., 2006; Pratt and Rafaeli, 2006; Shariq, 1998).

Using the above approach, Wright et al. (2013) examine whether the tools that are taught in business schools really help managers make better decisions. Complementing the increasing attention in the way strategy tools are used, this study used cognitive mapping techniques to uncover the dimensions of usefulness of 13 strategy tools as perceived by managers enrolled in a capstone strategy course. The authors show that contrary to current thinking about strategic tools, managers think in dualities (often paradoxically) and have a preference for multiple-tools-in-use, tools that provide different perspectives, peripheral vision, connected thinking, simultaneously help differentiate and integrate complex issues, and guide the thinking process. These findings highlight the need to understand the mental representations that practitioners have of their strategy tools. These representations can help us develop a micro-level and cognitive-oriented appreciation of how tool users interpret and make sense of strategy tools. These insights are also important for designing better tools and the nurturing of critical managerial competencies needed for a complicated world.

STRATEGY TOOLS AS MATERIAL ARTIFACTS

7.4 As we noted earlier in this chapter, strategy tools or material artifacts, such as Porter's five forces and SWOT, have become integral parts of the business reality for many organizations (Rigby and Bilodeau, 2007). Practice-based studies have examined how strategy making is mediated by particular artifacts, for example, PowerPoint (Kaplan, 2011), plans (Giraudeau, 2008), and numbers (Denis et al., 2006). In these studies, the artifacts created are imbued with knowledge properties by those using them, and are not static objects but continuously changing and acquiring new properties within a process of strategic knowledge production (Jarzabkowski and Spee, 2009; Jarzabkowski et al., 2013; Kaplan, 2011). Furthermore, provided they help negotiate and develop shared and new knowledge among those using them, strategic artifacts are said to act as boundary objects (Spee and Jarzabkowski, 2009).

Studies within the organization studies domain acknowledge the importance of objects, artifacts, and materiality (Carlile et al., 2013) as socio-material elements that shape social action (Dameron et al., 2015; Leonardi, 2015; Leonardi and Barley, 2010; Orlikowski and Scott, 2008) and hence strategizing (e.g., Balogun et al., 2014; Eppler and Platts, 2009; Heracleous and Jacobs, 2008; Kaplan, 2011; Stigliani and Ravasi, 2012). Artifacts assist organizational members in making sense of and ascribing new meanings to changing organizational circumstances, and rationalizing what they do. Kaplan (2011) showed that the use of PowerPoint facilitated the assembly, interpretation, representation, and sharing of information.

Researchers have also paid attention to the ways actors use a wide range of artifacts, such as drawings and prototypes (Bechky, 2003; Carlile, 2002; Sutton and Hargadon, 1996), slide presentations (Kaplan, 2011), visual maps (Doyle and Sims, 2002), concept development (Stigliani and Ravasi, 2012), and Lego bricks (Heracleous and Jacobs, 2008; Oliver and Roos, 2007). In their study, Stigliani and Ravasi (2012) argue that an understanding of how material artifacts and practices enable individuals and groups to construct new understandings is largely missing from theories of collective sensemaking. More recently, Werle and Seidl (2015) examine the different material artifacts, including PowerPoint slides, in a company that, in collaboration with other companies, examined the strategic topic of "flexible production." Their study took a practice-based approach to show how the use of a constellation of material artifacts can lead to a shift in the strategic topic. Paroutis et al. (2015) investigate the ways in which managers visually interact with strategy tools (a strategy map) to produce knowledge about strategic issues within workshops using a video-based micro-analysis and tracking the visual interactions between the participants and the tool. They showed that knowledge patterns vary depending on the patterns of visual interactions (shift, inertia, and assembly), and used the concept of affordances (properties related to the materiality of an artifact that enable or constrain its use) to show how the tool enables these patterns and brings change or reproduction of the status quo.

CONCLUSION

7.5 In this chapter we focused our attention on the strategic tools utilized by strategists. Instead of a descriptive account of strategy tools and their use, we have chosen to raise awareness of practice-based aspects of their use and how, through their use, they have potential to influence the practicing of strategy. We have also discussed two principal "pathways" of influence by strategists: an "artifact-oriented" and an "action-oriented" pathway. When applying such insight to the use of strategy tools, we realize that the way strategy tools are used goes beyond their direct application and is a more complicated, social, ongoing, and dynamic phenomenon. The key insight here is that in order to get a more complete picture of the practicing of strategy we need to appreciate the praxis behind the practices and vice versa (as we represent in Figure 7.1). In terms of strategy tools, such a practice-oriented approach means that less attention needs to be paid to the kinds of tools used and more to the actual ways these tools are used and adapted by practitioners when dealing with strategic issues. When considering the ways practitioners can use to influence tools (and other *practices*), we argue that the language and discourse around strategy are key (Barry and Elmes, 1997). Accordingly, in the two chapters that follow we first deal with the role of language in its ability to shape meanings and strategy processes, and in the second with an examination of the multidimensional nature of strategy workshops. These chapters are complementary in their effort to showcase the multidimensional nature of the methods (practices) employed in practicing strategy.

REVISION ACTIVITIES

In this chapter we have highlighted the importance of strategy tools in practicing strategy. Based on the arguments you have read about the use of tools, do you believe that strategy tools can also be misused, and, if so, how? What do you think could be the reasons for such misuse? Do these reasons have to do with incorrect application of the tool or unsuccessful adaptation of the tool to the particular context?

Find examples of organizations (private or public) where particular strategy tools have been used. Why do you think such tools have been used in the particular firms and to what effect? Develop some recommendations to improve the use of these tools.

FURTHER READINGS

- **Book:** McKeown, M. (2011) *The Strategy Book*. Financial Times/Prentice Hall. In Part 6, the reader can find analysis of a number of classic and more recent strategy tools, concepts, and models: from SWOT to Porter's value chain, and from Kotter's eight phases of change to Kaplan and Norton's balanced scorecard.

- **Papers:** For a comprehensive set of studies examining different aspects of the relationship between materiality and strategy, please refer to special issue by the *British Journal of Management*, 26(S1), 2015 and the associated editorial: Dameron, S., Le, J., and LeBaron, C. (2015) Materializing strategy and strategizing material: Why matter matters. *British Journal of Management*, 26(S1): S1–S12.

REFERENCES

Ahmed, A. M., Zairi, M., and Alwabel, S. A. (2006) Global benchmarking for internet and e-commerce applications. *Benchmarking: An International Journal*, 13(1/2): 68–80.

Balogun, J., Jacobs, C., Jarzabkowski, P., Mantere, S., and Vaara, E. (2014) Placing strategy discourse in context: Sociomateriality, sensemaking, and power. *Journal of Management Studies*, 51(2): 175–201.

Barry, D. and Elmes, M. (1997) Strategy retold: Toward a narrative view of strategic discourse. *Academy Management Review*, 22: 429–52.

Bechky, B. A. (2003) Object lessons: Workplace artifacts as representations of occupational jurisdiction. *American Journal of Sociology*, 109: 720–52.

Calori, R. (1998) Essai: Philosophizing on strategic management models. *Organization Studies*, 19: 281–306.

Carlile, R. P. (2002) A pragmatic view of knowledge and boundaries: Boundary objects in new product development. *Organization Science*, 13: 442–55.

Carlile, P. R., Nicolini, D., Langley, A., and Tsoukas, H. (2013) *How Matter Matters: Objects, Artifacts, And Materiality In Organization Studies. Perspectives on Process Organization Studies*. Oxford: Oxford University Press.

Clark, D. N. (1997) Strategic management tool usage: A comparative study. *Strategic Change*, 6(7): 417–27.

Dameron, S., Le, J., and LeBaron, C. (2015) Materializing strategy and strategizing material: Why matter matters. *British Journal of Management*, 26(S1): S1–S12.

de Certeau, M. (1984) *The Practice of Everyday Life*. Berkeley: University of California Press.

Denis, J. L., Langley, A. and Rouleau, L. (2006) The power of numbers in strategizing. *Strategic Organization*, 4(4): 349–77.

Doyle, J. and Sims, D. (2002) Enabling strategic metaphor in conversation: A technique of cognitive sculpting for explicating knowledge. In A. Huff and M. Jenkins (eds.), *Mapping Strategic Knowledge*. London: Sage, pp. 63–85.

Eppler, M. J. and Platts, K. W. (2009) Visual strategizing. The systematic use of visualization in the strategic-planning process. *Long Range Planning*, 42: 42–74.

Giraudeau, M. (2008) The drafts of strategy: Opening up plans and their uses. *Long Range Planning*, 41(3): 291–308.

Gunn, R. and Williams, W. (2007) Strategic tools: An empirical investigation into strategy in practice in the UK. *Strategic Change*, 16: 201–16.

Heracleous, L. and Jacobs, C. D. (2008) Crafting strategy: The role of embodied metaphors. *Long Range Planning*, 41: 309–25.

Hodgkinson, G. P. (2003) The interface of cognitive and industrial, work and organizational psychology. *Journal of Occupational and Organizational Psychology*, 76: 1–25.

Jacobides, M. G. (2010) Strategy tools for a shifting landscape. *Harvard Business Review*, 88: 76–85.

Jarratt, D. and Stiles, D. (2010) How are methodologies and tools framing managers' strategizing practice in competitive strategy development? *British Journal of Management*, 21: 28–43.

Jarzabkowski, P. (2004) Strategy as practice: Recursive, adaptive and practices-in-use. *Organization Studies*, 25: 529–60.

Jarzabkowski, P. and Spee, A. P. (2009) Strategy-as-practice: A review and future directions for the field. *International Journal of Management Review*, 11: 69–95.

Jarzabkowski, P. and Wilson, D. C. (2006) Actionable strategy knowledge: A practice perspective. *European Management Journal*, 24(5): 348–67.

Jarzabkowski, P., Spee, A. P., and Smets, M. (2013) Material artifacts: Practices for doing strategy with "stuff." *European Management Journal*, 31: 41–54.

Kachra, A. and Schnietz, K. (2008) The capstone strategy course: What might real integration look like? *Journal of Management Education*, 32: 476–508.

Kaplan, S. (2011) Strategy and PowerPoint: An inquiry into the epistemic culture and machinery of strategy making. *Organization Science*, 22: 320–46.

Kaplan, S. and Jarzabkowski, P. (2006) Using strategy tools in practice – how tools mediate strategizing and organizing. *Advanced Institute of Management Research Paper No. 047*.

Knott, P. (2006) A typology of strategy tool applications. *Management Decision*, 44(8): 1090–105.

Krippendorff, K. (1989) On the essential contexts of artifacts or on the proposition that "design is making sense (of things)." *Design Issues*, V: 9–39.

Leonardi, P. M. and Barley, S. R. (2008) Materiality and change: Challenges to building better theory about technology and organizing. *Information and Organization*, 18: 159–76.

Nemeth, C., O'Connor, M., Klock, P. A., and Cook, R. (2006) Discovering healthcare cognition: The use of cognitive artifacts to reveal cognitive work. *Organization Studies*, 27: 1011–35.

Nichols, C. and Paroutis, S. (2008) Engaged strategy participation: Going beyond "buy-in." *Critical Eye Review*. http://criticaleye.net/insights-detail.cfm?id=1409 (date accessed: February, 2012).

Norman, D. A. (1991) Cognitive artifacts. In J. M. Carroll (ed.), *Designing Interaction: Psychology at the Human-Computer Interface*. Cambridge: Cambridge University Press, pp. 17–38.

Oliver, D. and Roos, J. (2007) Beyond text: Constructing organizational identity multimodally. *British Journal of Management*, 18: 342–58.

Orlikowski, W. J. and Scott, S. V. (2008) Sociomateriality: Challenging the separation of technology, work and organization. *Academy of Management Annals*, 2: 433–74.

Paroutis, S., Franco, A., and Papadopoulos, T. (2015) Visual interactions with strategy tools: Producing strategic knowledge in workshops. *British Journal of Management. Special issue: Materializing Strategy and Strategizing Materials*. 26: S48–S66.

Pratt, M. and Rafaeli, A. (2006) Artifacts and organizations: Understanding our "objective" reality. In A. Rafaeli and M. Pratt (eds), *Artifacts and Organizations: Beyond Mere Symbolism*. Mahwah, NJ: Lawrence Erlbaum Associates, pp. 279–88.

Rigby, D. K. and Bilodeau, B. (2007) Bain's global 2007 management tools and trends survey. *Strategy & Leadership*, 35(5): 9–16.

Rigby, D. K. and Bilodeau, B. (2011) Management tools & trends 2011. Report by Bain & Company, May, 11. Available at: www.bain.com/publications/articles/Management-tools-trends-2011.aspx (date accessed: May 25, 2015).

Shariq, S. Z. (1998) Sense making and artifacts: An exploration into the role of tools in knowledge management. *Journal of Knowledge Management*, 2: 10–19.

Spee, A. P. and Jarzabkowski, P. (2009) Strategy tools as boundary objects. *Strategic Organization*, 7(2): 223–32.

Stigliani, I. and Ravasi, D. (2012) Organizing thoughts and connecting brains: Material practices and the transition from individual to group-level prospective sensemaking. *Academy of Management Journal*, 55: 1232–59.

Sutton, R. I. and Hargadon, A. (1996) Brainstorming groups in context: Effectiveness in a product design firm. *Administrative Science Quarterly*, 41: 685–718.

Werle, F. and Seidl, D. (2015) The layered materiality of strategizing: Epistemic objets and the interplay between material artefacts in the exploration of strategic topics. *British Journal of Management*, 26 (S1): S67–S89.

Whittington, R. (2004) Strategy after modernism: Recovering practice. *European Management Review*, 1: 62–8.

Worren, N., Moore, K., and Elliott, R. (2002) When theories become tools: Towards a framework for pragmatic validity. *Human Relations*, 55: 1227–50.

Wright, R., Paroutis, S., and Blettner, D. (2013) How useful are the strategic tools we teach in business schools? *Journal of Management Studies*, 50(1): 92–125.

INFLUENCING STRATEGY THROUGH DISCOURSE

8

Learning Objectives

- Appreciate the constructive nature of language and discourse and how discourse may shape various aspects of strategy.
- Understand the various ways in which discourse has been studied, especially with application to strategy and organization.
- Offer an additional interpretive lens for understanding the main dimensions of the strategy-as-practice framework (practitioners, practices, and praxis).

INTRODUCTION

8.1 In this chapter we discuss the fundamental role of language and discourse in its ability to shape meanings as well as strategy processes. We begin with a discussion of the constitutive role of language in organizations, and proceed with an elaboration of corresponding views of strategy and organization. We then discuss the different ways in which language and discourse have been studied, in terms of the functional, interpretive, structurational, and critical approaches. In addition to providing several brief examples, we also provide two brief cases that help to clarify the role of language in influencing practitioners, practices, and praxis.

LANGUAGE AND MEANING IN ORGANIZATIONS

8.2 A fundamental and inescapable part of organizations, as well as of the processes that comprise them (including the strategy process), is that language plays a key constitutive role (Heracleous, 2006a). This role is not just communicational, as classical understandings of strategy and a functional view of language as simply transmitting clear and unambiguous meanings, contained in words, from one person to another (e.g., the conduit metaphor of language as explicated by Reddy (1979) and further discussed by Axley (1984)) would hold. Developments in philosophy (Wittgenstein, 1968), linguistics (Lakoff and Johnson, 1980), and the sociology of knowledge (Berger and Luckmann, 1967) have shown us, however, that language is not simply functional, but rather constitutive, in a number of senses. First, and fundamentally, our mental maps are symbolic, constituted by linguistic labels. In this elemental sense, our mental maps are metaphorical, since they are representations of things, situations, or people (the target domains) through something else, linguistic labels, and other symbols (the source domains). We imbue environmental stimuli with meaning based on our mental maps, and the constitution of mental maps is via linguistic labels (see, e.g., Lakoff and Johnson, 1980; van Dijk, 1990). It is easy to see the fundamental potency of discourse in shaping understandings in organizations at all levels, including teams, corporations, societies, or nations.

Second, language helps to direct our attention in particular situations, and helps to frame (Scheff, 2005) how an issue should be looked at. Is a customer complaint a potential waste of time and a cost to address, a distraction from more important things, a useful insight, or a source of innovation? Is a competitor's price reduction an initiation of a price war, a sign that the competitor has become more efficient and can still maintain its margins while making a more competitive market offering, a sign that it is desperate and trying to raise its capacity utilization, or a sign that it has decided to compete at a lower market segment? It very much depends on how such issues are viewed in a particular organization, its dominant logic (Prahalad and Bettis, 1986), the framings fostered by the leadership of the organization that guide perceptions, and the values and operating processes that develop over time and are institutionalized, consistent with those framings (Smircich and Morgan, 1982). In this sense, discourse is at the basis of processes of enactment (Weick, 1977); agents act to realize the directions and responses that their cognitive maps and interpretations tell them are appropriate in a certain situation. This applies to strategy as much as other contexts; the dominant logic acts as a filter of information that directs attention to specific aspects of reality and guides appropriate responses (Bettis and Prahalad, 1995; Prahalad and Bettis, 1986).

The examples above, though about customer complaints and competitors' price changes, indicate that while meanings are attributed and constructed via the cognitive interface, this does not mean that everything is socially constructed. Some customer complaints may indeed be a waste of time and funds to address: for example, those initiated in bad faith to unfairly take advantage of liberal corporate policies relating to refunds or replacements. Some price reductions by competitors may be related to a variety of motives that may or may not be fully understood by other organizations. What matters from a competitive advantage point of view is that the discursive framings that constitute organizational values promote alignment with the strategy, as well as a productive organization culture that is customer oriented and embodies adaptability. Again from the perspective of competitive advantage and of strategy as an applied field, comparative performance (e.g., Devan et al., 2007), which could be multidimensional and incorporate stakeholder measures, offers a way to evaluate whether a strategy and associated processes and values are effective, and confirms that there are robust, pragmatic elements such as competitive intensity, sunk costs, and other strategy-related characteristics and resource deployments that cannot just be "wished away" (Child and Smith, 1987) by agents.

So, language matters, not only in a functional but also in a constitutive sense. How we talk about things directs our perceptions and evaluations, and guides our actions. What is the relationship between language and discourse? We employ the term **discourse** in this chapter to refer to collections or groups of texts (oral or written) that share certain common features. Since **language** makes up texts, it can be seen as the raw material of discourse, and individual texts can be seen as both manifestations and constitutive of broader discourses (Heracleous, 2006a; Heracleous and Hendry, 2000).

CORRESPONDING VIEWS OF STRATEGY AND ORGANIZATIONS

8.3 One view of strategy consistent with an understanding of the fundamental role of discourse is the interpretive view described by Chaffee (1985), at the time in comparison to the "linear" and "adaptive" views. Chaffee (1985), in an article that anticipated further developments in the interpretive approach to strategy, noted that such an approach could be defined as "orienting metaphors or frames of reference" (p. 93), intentionally using the plural to indicate the multiplicity of perspectives that could in practice apply to a strategic direction or statement. She went on to note that this view of strategy "depends heavily on symbols and norms" (p. 93) and "emphasizes attitudinal and cognitive complexity" (p. 94), where strategists would actively shape perceptions of various stakeholders relating to the strategy and to the organization. The narrative perspective of Barry and Elmes (1997) that strategy is a form of fiction, and strategists are authors of fiction, is consistent with Chaffee's interpretive view. In viewing strategy as fiction, Barry and Elmes (1997) highlight that strategies can be seen as stories or narratives, that are made up or constructed, and are employed to engage and persuade their audiences. Further, as Hendry (2000) argued, strategic decisions do not occur in a vacuum; they take place within particular discourses that operate both at a deeper, structural level as well as at the level of everyday communication and that shape strategic decisions.

One view of organization conducive to a focus on discourse was expressed by Pondy and Mitroff (1979) in their classic work building on Boulding's (1957) levels of complexity to suggest that organizations are multi-cephalous systems which possess "a sense of social order, a shared culture, a history and a future, a value system" (Pondy and Mitroff, 1979: 9). Such systems incorporate features of lower levels of complexity including symbol processing, internal representations, and generative mechanisms. This contrasted with other prominent views of organization at the time including more mechanistic approaches (Morgan, 1986).

Viewing language as implicated in the social construction of reality implies that our theories of organization (and all theories more broadly) are not necessarily objective truths but rather institutionally reinforced and paradigmatically mediated forms of linguistic representations

(Astley, 1985). This view of language was elaborated by Berger and Luckmann (1967) in their classic treatise on the social construction of reality where they suggested that linguistic labels objectify, typify, and ultimately institutionalize social and perceptual categories. This view does not deny the existence of more objective realities (from a strategic perspective, for example, things such as levels of investment to implement a strategic direction or indicators such as market share), but rather suggests that our understandings of such realities are mediated and (inter) subjectively constructed.

How does discourse relate to strategy-as-practice? The strategy-as-practice perspective refocused attention on the work of strategists and other relevant actors, consistent for example with the process tradition (e.g., Pettigrew, 1985) and with early work seeking to understand what managers actually do during their daily work (Mintzberg, 1971). A fundamental and constitutive aspect of daily interactions is the language used, which can itself be seen as a social practice in the sense for example of the recurrent rationalizations, patterns of arguments, and vocabularies that are used in specific contexts.

For example, Hirsch's (1986) study showed that the takeover process in the USA has been talked about and made sense of in terms of a group of genres such as "the western, in which the ambush and the shoot-out replace the offer made and actions taken; the love affair and/or marriage; warfare, replete with sieges, barricades, flak, and soldierly honor; mystery; and piracy on the high seas, with raiders and safe harbours" (p. 815), and that the intensity of the metaphorical framings reduced over time as takeovers were becoming an institutionalized corporate practice. He suggested that such linguistic, metaphorical framings fulfilled three functions: cognitive, in that they helped agents ascribe meaning to and make sense of the takeover process which was a relatively novel type of strategic action at the time; social–psychological functions in that these framings contributed toward legitimation of takeovers and therefore reduced the psychological strain and stigma of managers being involved in these activities; and, third, institutional functions, in that these framings helped to routinize and build shared understandings of the process, and therefore helped to integrate it in broader institutional systems.

By paying attention to the language employed by and in organizations, we can gain insights into why agents act as they do – insights which can also inform our understanding of organization-level actions. Fiol (1989) for example found that firms that talked about external boundaries (between themselves and other organizations) as strong, were less likely to engage in joint ventures, and vice versa for firms that talked about external boundaries as weak. Even at the level of single organizations therefore, there are specific linguistic frames that contribute to sense making and guide action. Smith and Eisenberg (1987) for example showed how the differing root metaphors of employees and management at Disneyland (drama and family), and the divergent interpretations of these metaphors by the two groups, led to widely different world-views about the nature of work and led to conflicts when management-implemented policies meant to increase organizational efficiency.

A discursive perspective, which has rich theoretical antecedents in a variety of fields such as sociology and linguistics (see Heracleous, 2006a), can inform (and has informed) understanding of strategy-as-practice. We cite several studies throughout this chapter which give a sense of how understanding discourse helps us understand such aspects as how communication can support strategy (Argenti et al., 2005), how metaphors and conversations can provide insights to and help accomplish strategic change processes (Liedtka and Rosenblum, 1996; Marshak, 1993), how linguistic labels shape discussions of organization design with strategic significance (Heracleous and Marshak, 2004), or how the seemingly neutral language of accounting systems can embody power considerations (Jacobs and Heracleous, 2001). Such studies can directly speak to the agenda of strategy-as-practice, as originally framed by Whittington (1996) for example, to help us understand "how strategists 'strategize'" (p. 732).

As is apparent from the examples discussed thus far, and as will be made clearer in the forthcoming discussion, from the perspective of the tripartite framework of the strategy-as-practice approach (e.g., Jarzabkowski and Spee, 2009), a discursive, processual focus can help us gain insights on who the actors involved are and what their role is in organizational processes (the "practitioners" dimension); what they do when they strategize (the "praxis" dimension); as well as the broader flow and patterns of the "practices" they engage in (institutionalized processes such as planning cycles or discursive practices).

APPLYING DISCURSIVE APPROACHES TO STRATEGY AND ORGANIZATION

8.4 Given the elemental understanding that our mental maps are linguistically constituted, and that different framings by different agents can lead to different interpretations of similar actions or situations, strategy and organization researchers have investigated a variety of questions. These investigations sometimes make explicit their assumptions on the constitutive role of language, but often these assumptions are implicit. Balogun et al. (2014) provide a useful review of the variety of perspectives through which strategy discourse (how strategy as a field has been framed), as well as the discourses involved in particular instances of strategizing, have been studied. Their review addresses poststructuralist discourse analysis, critical discourse analysis, narrative analysis, rhetorical analysis, conversation analysis, and analogy and metaphor analysis.

Discursive studies of strategy can be typologized in a number of ways. One proposed typology is between functional, interpretive, and critical studies (Heracleous and Barrett, 2001). Of course, the usual caveats apply: typologies are Weberian ideal types (Hekman, 1983), which help to analytically make sense of the variety of studies, but many studies are combinations of these types and some studies cannot be easily typologized, indicating the richness of theoretical antecedents, types of data, and research questions that may be explored.

Functional approaches are concerned with how language may be employed by organizational actors (such as strategists, organization development practitioners, or change agents) to achieve certain outcomes such as successful strategic change, cultural shifts, or higher commitment to a course of action. At least on the surface, the view of language here is a "representational" or "correspondence" one, emphasizing its communicative rather than constitutive role, consistent with the conduit metaphor noted above. Examples of such studies include Argenti et al. (2005), Cuno (2005), Ford and Ford (1995), Liedtka and Rosenblum (1996), and Price (2007). Cuno (2005) for example outlines how he employed identity-defining storytelling as the Director to foster the turnaround of the Harvard University Art Museums. Argenti et al. (2005) further argue that communication has to be viewed from a long-term perspective as a process that can facilitate strategy implementation and effective positioning of the company, through its alignment with the business strategy. They suggest that communication with different constituencies such as media, employees, or government using channels such as press releases, town hall meetings, and lobbying can contribute to a variety of objectives such as improved public relations, effective crisis management, building internal consensus, and meeting social expectations. The focus on these studies is on the functional aspects that could be achieved through using language, rather than on the processes through which language becomes constitutive.

Some studies explicitly recognize the constitutive role of language, but their key aim is still to understand and facilitate the functional effects of language use. These studies can be located between the functional and interpretive approaches. Examples of such studies include Barrett et al. (1995), Ford (1999), Heracleous and Jacobs (2005), and Marshak (1993). Within a view of organizations as socially constructed entities, Ford (1999) argues that organizations are constituted by conversations, and therefore having new and different conversations while downplaying or removing old conversations can accomplish organization change. Further, Marshak (1993) suggests that the metaphorical images of change that change agents hold have implications for how they view their role in managing the change, and on the actions that they and others take with respect to the change. For example, a view of change as a need to "fix and maintain" is a quite mechanistic one that contrasts with a more organic view of change as a need to "build and develop." In the former case the change agent would see themselves as a mechanic or repair person, whereas in the latter case as a coach or developer, undertaking different types of actions as a result (in this case for example short-term re-engineering type of actions vs. medium- and long-term capability development type of actions).

Heracleous and Klaering (2014) explored the rhetorical strategies employed by the late Steve Jobs, the legendary founder of Apple Inc., to understand whether charismatic leaders alter their rhetoric in different contexts, and if so, how. The authors found that Jobs did indeed customize his rhetoric to particular audiences and situations, but that he combined this customization with continuity in the central themes and root metaphors he employed. Further, they found that Jobs' *ethos* (the perceived credibility or character of the speaker in a particular situation) shaped the extent of *logos* (appeal to logic) and *pathos* (appeal to emotion) employed. The authors suggested that the ability to customize a leader's message to particular audiences while at the same time consistently emphasizing certain central messages may be a key aspect of the rhetorical competence of charismatic leaders.

Interpretive studies recognize more explicitly the constitutive role of language and seek to understand how this constitutive process takes place. Often such studies are informed by the concepts and methods of social theory, as well as sophisticated understandings of agency, action, and recursiveness in social systems. Often such studies track managerially relevant outcomes, but understanding how to effectively produce such outcomes is not as much the main aim or motivation of the study, as trying to understand the underlying discursive processes involved in the social construction of reality including the changing of perceptions. Studies from this perspective include Heracleous and Jacobs (2008), Heracleous and Marshak (2004), Jarzabkowski and Sillince (2007), Jarzabkowski et al. (2010), Sharma and Grant (2011), and Suddaby and Greenwood (2005).

Heracleous and Marshak (2004), for example, employed a perspective of discourse as situated symbolic action to show how a single label ("principal-led") referring to a change in the organization design, specifically how consulting teams would organize in their engagement with client projects, was loaded with layers of meaning that went beyond denotation to connotation. These connotative meanings had to be appreciated by organization development practitioners as well as other actors engaged in the organization design decision, in order to understand the politically charged decision process and the tense interactions that took place. For an expanded discussion of this example, see the mini case below.

MINI CASE: HOW A LABEL EMBODIES LAYERS OF MEANING THAT SHAPE STRATEGIC DECISIONS

The context of the analysis is a meeting of senior managers of Systech, a major IT organization, who met to debate a new business model for the organization's advanced consulting services division. The group president, who had recently joined the organization, wanted to implement a "principal-led" model of client engagement, where principals were in charge of multi-functional teams, made decisions pertaining to all aspects of this engagement, and in effect owned the client relationship. This was a substantial shift from the more traditional, functionally based, distributed model of client engagement that had been employed at the division. This shift had fundamental implications for the power base and status of the various functions and individuals within them, and not surprisingly was strongly opposed. The main representative of the principal-led model in the meeting at some point acknowledged that the Systech model had been different and perhaps the move to the principal-led model could involve retaining some shared responsibilities. After that point, discussion was more cooperative and a new integrated model was developed, which retained features of both the distributed and principal-led models, labeled the "Advanced Services Division Business Model." This, however, did not stop the group president from relabeling it as "principal-led" soon after the meeting.

A perspective of discourse as situated symbolic action can help us appreciate the different layers of meaning involved. First, the perspective of discourse as action focuses on what actors said and the possible intent of their communicative actions. As an example, at the locutionary level, the meeting was initiated without mentioning its purpose, and through posing "customers first" as a key goal. At the illocutionary level this may have been an attempt to find common ground, encourage productive discussion, and downplay the conflicting political interests and opinions lurking under the surface.

Second, discourse as situated action emphasizes an understanding of the nested contexts (e.g., situational, organizational, institutional) within which communicative actions take place and helps us interpret such actions in light of their context. In this case, the background of the group president as a former partner in a Big Four accounting firm that operated along the lines of the principal-led model helps us understand the level of his commitment to this model. An understanding of the backgrounds of the different meeting participants (whether from Systech or the acquired firm) helps us interpret their position and reactions with respect to the two potential models. The fact that the acquired firm had employed the principal-led model rather than the acquirer added a further layer of meaning which questioned the principal-led model.

(Continued)

(Continued)

Finally, discourse as situated symbolic action sensitizes us toward attention to how discourse can frame and represent issues in specific ways, as well as attention to the symbolism of interactional situations as a whole. Discursive interactions, appearing on the surface to be simply about information exchange, could involve issues of power, control, and dominance. This was manifested in the Systech case between the oldtimers, representing the distributed model, and the newcomers, representing the principal-led model. Further, the acknowledgment by the newcomer and advocate of the principal-led model that, given the Systech way of operating, some responsibilities could be shared, was not just an acknowledgment but a peace offering, a symbolic indication that he accepted the legitimacy of aspects of the distributed model.

The authors showed how each of the perspectives (discourse as action, as situated action, and as symbolic action) adds a piece of the puzzle to help us understand the finer points of what went on. The analysis showed that the denotational meaning of "principal-led" needs to be complemented with its context-dependent connotational meanings to gain a fuller appreciation of the socio-political issues involved in the debate, as well as the shape of the final decision on the mode of organization design that would be employed. The reinsertion of the label "principal-led" shows how power can be exercised through language and formal position.

To explicitly adopt a strategy-as-practice vocabulary, the practitioners at the meeting engaged in praxis (communicative actions) that could only be understood in some depth if the deeper discursive aspects of the main label and contentious issue in the meeting, "principal-led," were fully appreciated. The stakes in this case were specific practices, or how consultants would organize internally and engage with clients in the future. These practices were not simply about the most efficient way to organize, but encompassed underlying dimensions of politics, status, and power.

The *structurational* approach (Barrett et al., 2013; Giddens, 1984; Heracleous, 2006b; Heracleous and Barrett, 2001; Heracleous and Hendry, 2000; Jarzabkowski, 2008) can be seen as being a type of interpretive or hermeneutic approach. The emphasis here is on grasping the interplay and mutual constitution between agency and structure, and as far as language is concerned, how surface communicative actions are patterned by deeper discursive structures and changes to both over time. The assumption is that such structures are influential in the social construction of organizational reality and therefore to organizational outcomes.

For example, Jarzabkowski (2008) identified three types of strategic behaviors: interactive, relating to face-to-face interaction with others; procedural, relating to change in administrative processes; and integrative, an ongoing combination of interactive and procedural behaviors. She found that sequential behaviors that attend to either action or structure dimensions were successful in shaping strategy in only weakly institutionalized contexts, whereas integrative behaviors were successful in both weakly and strongly institutionalized contexts.

Heracleous and Barrett (2001) employed a discourse analysis approach based on hermeneutics and rhetoric, within a structurational meta-theoretical paradigm, to track communicative actions and deep structures of groups of stakeholders in the London Insurance Market, and how these influenced the implementation of electronic trading systems. They uncovered the main trends in the structuring process of the discourses of market leaders, brokers, and underwriters, and multinational brokers at both the communicative and deep structure levels, and linked these to their actions over time. The challenges of strategic change implementation in this case could be understood in terms of the discourses of the different groups involved, which were fragmented and largely conflicting, leading to actions that were unsupportive of the implementation process.

Finally, *critical* discourse studies assume that current social and organizational configurations and practices are fundamentally unequal and unfair, crystallizations of the outcomes of ongoing power struggles between social classes or groups of actors. These configurations are maintained by a variety of practices including discursive ones, where actors' identities and subject positions are discursively constructed to perpetuate the status quo in favor of the dominant groups or classes. The aim therefore is to unmask such discursive processes and foster change to the status quo. The assumptions of the interpretive approach inform critical discursive studies, with the added ingredients of fundamental unfairness that needs to be exposed, and a view of researchers as committed to social change toward what they regard as an improved social configuration. Critical discourse studies most often gain inspiration from Foucault's (1972, 1977) archaeological and genealogical approaches. In his work on the archaeology of knowledge (1972), Foucault sought to examine how underlying rules that are unknown or taken for granted by actors can regulate discourses, associated social practices, and subject positions. Drawing from a Foucauldian perspective, Hardy and Thomas (2014) show how particular strategy discourses can produce corresponding subject positions (e.g., a strategy of cost effectiveness producing the subject position of the cost-conscious employee), and can have power effects via what they call practices of intensification; which are in turn met by various modes of resistance.

Further, Jacobs and Heracleous (2001) employed an archaeological approach in their examination of German management accounting, or "Controlling Science." They found that Controlling Science, far from being a neutral accounting system, as presented on the surface through the discursive terms employed, in fact embodied the fundamental elements of Jeremy Bentham's Panopticon: hierarchical observation and normalizing sanction. These render its role to be more than an organizational function, in effect fulfilling the role of a technology of power or disciplinary regime. For an expanded discussion, see the mini case below.

MINI CASE: GERMAN MANAGEMENT ACCOUNTING AS A TECHNOLOGY OF POWER

Jacobs and Heracleous (2001) analyzed the conceptual foundations of Controlling Science, in particular its claim to decontextualized or universal rationality, and its chief goals of central coordination and control through planning. They found that its view of organization is mechanistic, a set of tools that can be rationally deployed to achieve certain goals. People are seen as cogs in the machine and have to meet the standards set by Controlling Science, which employs the rational, self-interested assumptions of agency theory to model human behavior.

(Continued)

(Continued)

The authors found close affinities with Taylor's Scientific Management in both assumptions on the nature of organization and role of individuals, and operationalization of these assumptions, finding that Taylorism could be seen as a conceptual ancestor of Controlling Science. They suggested that Panopticism could serve as a common unifying metaphor between the two approaches, through its cornerstones of hierarchical observation and normalizing sanction. In a Panoptical system agents could be watched and monitored at any time without knowing when this was taking place, and strict sanctions could be applied for deviation from the norms. The Taylorist task system and labor office could be seen as representations or operationalizations of these Panoptical cornerstones.

This similarity between Taylorism and Controlling Science, and the unifying metaphor of Panopticism, are not simply conceptually important, since they still shape organizational practices and lead actors both to conform to and try to subvert the controlling system in what Giddens (1984) termed the "dialectic of control." The authors examined how the system of Controlling Science, employed in a consulting organization, was associated with processes such as distortion of communication, manipulation of figures, reduction of behavioral options for agents, and application of self-discipline under the assumption of hierarchical observation. These can be seen as organizational costs of a control system characterized by Panoptical principles.

To employ a strategy-as-practice vocabulary, the practitioners in this case were under the control of a Panoptical system which was manifested as a specific accounting practice, limiting practitioners' options for praxis, and leading to praxis that not only perpetuated but also aimed to subvert and circumvent the accounting practice.

CONCLUSION

8.5 In conclusion, to gain a deeper understanding of strategy processes, why practitioners think and act as they do (their praxis), why certain practices become institutionalized and others do not, or why certain strategic changes fail and others succeed, it is helpful to employ a discursive focus. Such a focus can inform us of the patterns of meanings that shape such processes and how agents engage with these meanings in a mutually constitutive process.

REVISION ACTIVITIES

In this chapter we discussed the fundamental role of language and discourse in shaping our perceptions, practices, and praxis. Being reflexive about your own experience with language, can you think of any instances where you believe it shaped your own thinking? Which of the lenses of discourse we discussed in this chapter (functional, interpretive, structurational, critical) would be most appropriate to analyze these instances? Should more than one lens be used, and why?

CEOs are often capable rhetoricians and storytellers. Identify instances where you believe CEOs made effective or ineffective use of language. Explain which aspect of the language they used made these instances effective (or not, as the case may be), as well as which lenses of discourse you found useful in making this type of evaluation.

FURTHER READINGS

- **Book**: Berger, P. and Luckmann, T. (1967) *The Social Construction of Reality*. London: Penguin. An accessible discussion of the social construction of reality, with special reference to language and how linguistic labels help to objectify, typify, and over time institutionalize ideas.
- **Book**: Heracleous, L. (2006a) *Discourse, Interpretation, Organization*. Cambridge: Cambridge University Press. Offers an informed overview of the various conceptual approaches to discourse, and examples of empirical applications of some of these approaches.
- **Paper**: Heracleous, L. and Barrett, M. (2001) Organizational change as discourse: communicative actions and deep structures in the context of information technology implementation. *Academy of Management Journal*, 44: 755–78. An elaborate application of rhetoric and hermeneutics to the area of organization change; shows how discourse analysis offers a way to understand practitioners' points of view and actions or inactions in the context of change.
- **Paper:** Heracleous, L. and Klaering, A. (2014) Charismatic leadership and rhetorical competence: An analysis of Steve Jobs's rhetoric. *Group & Organization Management*, 39: 131–61. Shows how Steve Jobs, as an acknowledged great strategist, charismatic leader and persuader, employed rhetoric to position Apple Inc. in the eyes of stakeholders in particular ways consistent with the company strategy.
- **Paper**: Suddaby, R. and Greenwood, R. (2005) Rhetorical strategies of legitimacy. *Administrative Science Quarterly*, 50: 35–67. Shows how rhetorical strategies employed by agents, such as use of certain vocabularies and theorizations, can have institutional-level effects, showing the potency of discourse to influence its context.

REFERENCES

Argenti, P. A., Howell, R. A., and Beck, K. A. (2005) The strategic communication imperative. *MIT Sloan Management Review*, Spring: 83–9.
Astley, W. G. (1985) Administrative science as socially constructed truth. *Administrative Science Quarterly*, 30: 497–513.
Axley, S. R. (1984) Managerial and organizational communication in terms of the conduit metaphor. *Academy of Management Review*, 9: 428–37.
Balogun, J., Jacobs, C., Jarzabkowski, P., Mantere, S., and Vaara, E. (2014) Placing strategy discourse in context: Sociomateriality, sensemaking and power. *Journal of Management Studies*, 51: 175–201.
Barrett, F. J., Thomas, G. F., and Hocevar, S. P. (1995) The central role of discourse in large-scale change: A social construction perspective. *Journal of Applied Behavioral Science*, 31: 352–72.
Barrett, M., Heracleous, L., and Walsham, G. (2013) A rhetorical approach to IT diffusion: Reconceptualizing the ideology-framing relationship in computerization movements. *MIS Quarterly*, 37: 201–20.

Barry, D. and Elmes, M. (1997) Strategy retold: Toward a narrative view of strategic discourse. *Academy of Management Review*, 22: 429–52.
Berger, P. and Luckmann, T. (1967) *The Social Construction of Reality*. London: Penguin.
Bettis, R. A. and Prahalad, C. K. (1995) The dominant logic: Retrospective and extension. *Strategic Management Journal*, 16: 5–14.
Boulding, K. (1957) General systems theory – the skeleton of a science. *Management Science*, 2: 197–208.
Chaffee, E. E. (1985) Three models of strategy. *Academy of Management Review*, 10: 81–98.
Child, J. and Smith, C. (1987) The context and process of organizational transformation – Cadbury Limited in its sector. *Journal of Management Studies*, 24: 565–93.
Cuno, J. (2005) Telling stories: Rhetoric and leadership, a case study. *Leadership*, 1: 205–13.
Devan, J., Klusas, M. B., and Ruefli, T. W. (2007) The elusive goal of corporate outperformance. *McKinsey Quarterly*, Web exclusive, May: 1–3.
Fiol, M. (1989) A semiotic analysis of corporate language: Organizational boundaries and joint venturing. *Administrative Science Quarterly*, 34: 277–303.
Ford, J. D. (1999) Organizational change as shifting conversations. *Journal of Organizational Change Management*, 12: 480–500.
Ford, J. D. and Ford, L. W. (1995) The role of conversations in producing intentional change in organizations. *Academy of Management Review*, 20: 541–70.
Foucault, M. (1972) *The Archaeology of Knowledge*. London: Routledge.
Foucault, M. (1977) *Discipline and Punish*. London: Penguin.
Giddens, A. (1984) *The Constitution of Society*. Cambridge: Polity.
Hardy, C. and Thomas, R. (2014) Strategy, discourse and practice: The intensification of power. *Journal of Management Studies*, 51: 320–48.
Hekman, S. J. (1983) Weber's ideal type: a contemporary reassessment. *Polity*, 16: 119–37.
Hendry, J. (2000) Strategic decision making, discourse, and strategy as social practice. *Journal of Management Studies*, 37: 955–77.
Heracleous, L. (2006a) *Discourse, Interpretation, Organization*. Cambridge: Cambridge University Press.
Heracleous, L. (2006b) A tale of three discourses: The dominant, the strategic and the marginalized. *Journal of Management Studies*, 43(5): 1059–87.
Heracleous, L. and Barrett, M. (2001) Organizational change as discourse: Communicative actions and deep structures in the context of information technology implementation. *Academy of Management Journal*, 44: 755–78.
Heracleous, L. and Hendry, J. (2000) Discourse and the study of organization: Toward a structurational perspective. *Human Relations*, 53: 1251–86.
Heracleous, L. and Jacobs, C. (2005) The serious business of play. *MIT Sloan Management Review*, Fall: 19–20.
Heracleous, L. and Jacobs, C. (2008) Understanding organizations through embodied metaphors. *Organization Studies*, 29(1): 45–78.
Heracleous, L. and Klaering, A. (2014) Charismatic leadership and rhetorical competence: An analysis of Steve Jobs's rhetoric. *Group & Organization Management*, 39: 131–61.
Heracleous, L. and Marshak, R. (2004) Conceptualizing organizational discourse as situated symbolic action. *Human Relations*, 57(10): 1285–312.
Hirsch, P. M. (1986) From ambushes to golden parachutes: Corporate takeovers as an instance of cultural framing and institutional integration. *American Journal of Sociology*, 91: 800–37.
Jacobs, C. and Heracleous, L. (2001) Seeing without being seen: Toward an archaeology of controlling science. *International Studies of Management and Organization*, 31(3): 113–35.
Jarzabkowski, P. (2008) Shaping strategy as a structuration process. *Academy of Management Journal*, 51: 621–50.
Jarzabkowski, P. and Sillince, J. A. A. (2007) A rhetoric-in-context approach to building commitment to multiple strategic goals. *Organization Studies*, 28: 1639–65.

Jarzabkowski, P. and Spee, A. P. (2009) Strategy-as-practice: A review and future directions for the field. *International Journal of Management Reviews*, 11: 69–95.

Jarzabkowski, P., Sillince, J. A. A., and Shaw, D. (2010) Strategic ambiguity as a rhetorical resource for enabling multiple interests. *Human Relations*, 63: 219–48.

Lakoff, G. and Johnson, M. (1980) *Metaphors We Live By*. Chicago, IL: University of Chicago Press.

Liedtka, J. M. and Rosenblum, J. W. (1996) Shaping conversations: Making strategy, managing change. *California Management Review*, 39: 141–57.

Marshak, R. J. (1993) Managing the metaphors of change. *Organization Dynamics*, 22(1): 44–56.

Mintzberg, H. (1971) Managerial work: Analysis from observation. *Management Science*, 18: 97–110.

Morgan, G. (1986) *Images of Organization*. London: Sage.

Pettigrew, A. (1985) *The Awakening Giant: Continuity and Change in ICI*. Oxford: Basil Blackwell.

Pondy, L. R. and Mitroff, I. I. (1979) Beyond open systems models of organization. *Research in Organizational Behavior*, 1: 3–39.

Prahalad, C. K. and Bettis, R. A. (1986) The dominant logic: A new linkage between diversity and performance. *Strategic Management Journal*, 7: 485–501.

Price, I. (2007) Lean assets: New language for new workplaces. *California Management Review*, 49: 102–18.

Reddy, M. (1979) The conduit metaphor – a case of frame conflict in our language about language. In A. Ortony (ed.), *Metaphor and Thought*. Cambridge: Cambridge University Press, pp. 284–324.

Scheff, T. J. (2005) The structure of context: Deciphering frame analysis. *Sociological Theory*, 23: 368–85.

Sharma, A. and Grant, D. (2011) Narrative, drama and charismatic leadership: The case of Apple's Steve Jobs. *Leadership*, 7: 3–26.

Smircich, L. and Morgan, G. (1982) Leadership: The management of meaning. *Journal of Applied Behavioral Science*, 18: 257–73.

Smith, R. C. and Eisenberg, E. M. (1987) Conflict at Disneyland: A root-metaphor analysis. *Communication Monographs*, 54: 367–380.

Suddaby, R. and Greenwood, R. (2005) Rhetorical strategies of legitimacy. *Administrative Science Quarterly*, 50: 35–67.

van Dijk, T. A. (1990) Social cognition and discourse. In H. Giles and W. P. Robinson (eds.), *Handbook of Language and Social Psychology*. Chichester: Wiley, pp. 163–83.

Weick, K. (1977) Enactment processes in organizations. In B. M. Staw and G. R. Salancik (eds.), *New Directions in Organizational Behavior*. Chicago, IL: St. Clair Press, 267–300.

Whittington, R. (1996) Strategy as practice. *Long Range Planning*, 29: 731–5.

Wittgenstein, L. (1968) *Philosophical Investigations*. Oxford: Blackwell.

PRAXIS   C

The purpose of Section C is to examine aspects of praxis around the making and execution of strategy inside and across their firms. In Chapter 9 we examine the issue of strategic alignment, and discuss in detail the Environment-Strategy-Capabilities-Organization (ESCO) model. Our aim is to showcase the importance of finding a balance across these elements when practicing strategy. This is a key challenge for strategists, particularly when facing challenging, new environments. In Chapter 10, we showcase how strategy is practiced across multiple firms using insights from mergers and acquisitions (M&As). Such an inter-organizational perspective is increasingly important for strategy making, as firms increasingly rely on collaborations with other firms to support their strategy. In Chapter 11 we shed light on the concept of strategic ambidexterity and examine how such an approach could assist strategists in dealing with complex issues, and particularly with contradictory strategy demands. Taken together, these chapters provide insight into the nature and employment of activities that allow managers to: align their organization with their environment and strategy; find ways to collaborate with other firms; and deal with tensions by taking an ambidexterity perspective.

STRATEGIC ALIGNMENT: THE ESCO MODEL[1]

9

> **Learning Objectives**
>
> - Appreciate the nature of strategic alignment and how it influences organizational success or failure.
> - Explore the processes by which strategic misalignments can develop over time.
> - Understand the role of practitioners such as CEOs and boards of directors in fostering practices and taking actions (praxis) that can either enhance strategic alignment or increase misalignments, ultimately leading to failure.

INTRODUCTION

9.1 In this chapter we present the ESCO (environment, strategy, core competencies and organization) strategic alignment model. We bring the model to life by showing how strategic misalignments can develop and grow over time, ultimately leading to corporate failure, through exploring the trajectories of two once successful companies, Worldcom and Nortel Networks. In terms of the strategy-as-practice framework of practitioners, practices, and praxis, we illustrate a number of insights: first, how *practitioners* (strategists, including leaders and boards of directors) are central to processes of alignment and misalignment. Senior management has the authority to make resource allocation decisions and can over time build competencies of adaptability that can enable the organization to remain strategically aligned in the face of environmental change. The board of directors has the responsibility to both monitor as well as guide the strategy of the organization.

---

[1]This chapter is based on Heracleous, L. & Werres, K. 2015, On the road to disaster: Strategic misalignments and corporate failure, *Long Range Planning*, published ahead of print.

In the context of environmental uncertainty, it is the decisions, actions, and inactions (in other words the *praxis*) of practitioners such as the CEO, senior management, and the board of directors that influence whether the organization will develop the core competencies needed to remain competitive, or whether it will develop internal dysfunctions such as too high levels of complexity and fragmentation, or a demoralized workforce, that will ultimately lead to failure. We also show how *practices*, whether intended ones such as aggressive expansion via acquisition, and successive rounds of downsizing, or implicit ones such as weak internal controls and insufficient customer focus can precipitate strategic misalignments that ultimately lead to corporate failure.

STRATEGIC ALIGNMENT AND PERFORMANCE

9.2 Why does strategic alignment matter to strategists? The main reason is the link between alignment and performance, what Venkatraman (1989) refers to as normative fit. The assumption is that higher levels of alignment lead to higher performance, and conversely, significant misalignments foster low performance and can even lead to corporate failure. Performance is influenced by both external factors such as industry structure, industry change, and environmental uncertainty, as well as internal factors such as coordination and control, corporate culture, strategy and leadership (Anderson and Tushman, 2001; Fredrickson, 1986; Freeman et al., 1983; McGahan and Porter, 1997). An alignment perspective interrelates pertinent factors both internally within an organization, as well as between an organization and its environment. Research has acknowledged that internal organizational alignment or fit, as well as alignment with the external environment, are necessary conditions for organizational survival and success in the long run (Beer et al., 2005; Miles and Snow, 1984a; Porter, 1996).

Within strategic management, the alignment approach grounded in industrial economics or contingency theory is referred to as an "outside-in approach" (Voelpel et al., 2006). Strategy and structure are viewed as being a response to external factors that act as key determinants of the firm's performance (Ginsberg and Venkatraman, 1985; Porter, 1980; Venkatraman and Camillus, 1984). In contrast, the resource-based view, referred to as an "inside-out approach" (Voelpel et al., 2006) emphasizes internal elements such as resources and capabilities as routes to competitive advantage (Barney, 1991; Grant, 1991; Wernerfelt, 1984). Despite contrasting perspectives on directionality, both schools agree that strategic alignment can lead to competitive advantage, and conversely, that misalignment can lead to failure (Chabrak and Daidj, 2007; Miller, 1996; Porter, 1996; Powell, 1992).

Strategic alignment frameworks have incorporated several interrelated factors. One well-known example includes the classic McKinsey "7-S Framework" (Waterman et al., 1980). More recently, the ESCO framework has been proposed (Heracleous and Werres, 2015; Heracleous et al., 2009) that explicitly incorporates the external environment, as well as performance as an outcome. This occurs within a processual representation that begins from leadership, moves on to alignment, and results in performance consequences.

Four Domains: Environment, Strategy, Core Competencies, and Organization

The ESCO framework suggests that a company's *strategy* has to be aligned with its competitive *environment*; the strategy also has to be supported by appropriate *core competencies*, which can be delivered through suitable *organizational* configurations (including culture, structure, processes, and people). We outline these four domains in turn.

Firms are faced with discontinuity and rapid environmental changes caused by technological development, disruptive innovations, intense global competition, alterations in government regulations, and industry structures (Beer et al., 2005; Crossan et al., 2008; Ireland and Hitt, 2005). A firm's misalignment to drastic environmental changes represents one of the most common and dangerous sources of misalignment in organizations (Heracleous et al., 2009).

The second alignment element, strategy, relates to the classic classifications proposed by Porter (1985), Hannan and Freeman (1986), and Miles et al. (1978) who emphasize the need for a clear strategy as an essential strategic choice. Subsequently, dynamic views of strategy recognized that things change, competitive advantage is fleeting and that constant realignment between strategy and environment is needed (Ghemawat, 1991; Peteraf, 1993). From this perspective, managing change is the major strategic challenge faced by organizations (Brown and Eisenhardt, 1998). Strategic (re)alignment is here seen as a continuous process that requires the top management to balance emerging strategies with a deliberate and coherent strategic direction (Mintzberg, 1987).

The third domain of alignment in the ESCO framework is core competencies, which when aligned would support the strategy of the corporation. The development of core competencies represents one of the key concepts within the resource-based view of the firm (Barney, 1991; Prahalad and Hamel, 1990). This view suggests that when a firm's resource and capability configurations are valuable, rare and imperfectly imitable, and when the firm is organized to exploit these configurations, this can be a source of competitive advantage (Barney et al., 2001). Whereas established routines and structures provide stability and increase efficiency, in many cases they prevent firms from renewing their current resource base, or accomplishing ambidexterity, a balance between exploitation and exploration (March, 1991). As a result, core competencies may turn into core rigidities (Leonard-Barton, 1992). The concept of dynamic capabilities relates to the proactive process of developing a resource base that is most adequately suited to the rapidly changing environment (Eisenhardt and Martin, 2000; Teece et al., 1997) and emphasizes the significance of capabilities such as flexibility, innovation, and self-organization (Miles et al., 1997; Rindova and Kotha, 2001).

The final element, organization, deals with strategy implementation and is constituted by the four components of structure, processes, people, and culture. Structure and processes have seen much attention in the academic literature, particularly in relation to strategy and performance (Bartlett and Ghoshal, 1991; Miles et al., 1978). A firm's structure involves aspects such as the division of tasks, centralization, coordination, and formalization that are all closely linked to organizational processes. Structural choices have important consequences. For instance, a highly formalized organizational structure facilitates precise decision-making and can enhance reliability, but at the same time reduces the level of flexibility and increases the likelihood of path-dependent behavior (Miller, 1986). Structural dimensions are seen as essential to the implementation of a chosen strategy and hence, as important determinants of corporate performance (Fredrickson, 1986).

With regard to the people element, the key role of human resource management is seen as ensuring organizational fit with the environment while emphasizing a healthy degree of flexibility (Christiansen and Higgs, 2008; Milliman et al., 1991). This can be achieved through coherence of human resource management with business strategy (Bennett et al., 1998; Schuler and

TABLE 9.1 Key concepts of strategic alignment

	Categories	Relevant concepts	Key authors
Key distinctions in the literature	Conceptualizations of fit	Descriptive vs. Normative fit	Venkatraman, 1989
	Outside-in alignment approach	Industrial organization, Contingency theory	Ginsberg & Venkatraman, 1998; Porter, 1980
	Inside-out alignment approach	Resource-based view	Barney, 1991; Wernerfelt, 1984
Holistic strategic alignment frameworks	McKinsey 7-s	Alignment among seven hard and soft elements	Peters & Waterman, 1982
	ESCO	Alignment among four elements	Heracleous et al., 2009; Heracleous & Werres, 2015
Levels of strategic alignment	Environment	Dynamism, complexity uncertainty	Beer et al., 2005; Aragon-Correa & Sharma, 2003
	Strategy	Generic strategies, Dynamic models	Ghemawat, 1991; Miles et al., 1978; Peteraf, 1993; Porter, 1985
	Competencies	Resources capabilities, dynamic capabilities	Barney et al., 2001; Prahalad & Hamel, 1990; Teece et al., 1997
	Organization	Structure Process, People, Culture	Miles et al., 1978; Fredrickson, 1986; Milliman et al., 1991; Arogyaswamy & Byles., 1987
Driving force	Leadership	Leadership styles & skills; Strategic impact	Crossan et al., 2008; Powell., 1992

Jackson, 1987). This involves a fit between a firm's strategy and human resource elements such as recruitment, development, and incentives, that support specific employee skills and behaviors (Wirtz et al., 2008; Wright and Snell, 1998). Christiansen and Higgs (2008), in line with Miles and Snow (1984b), found that firms with a tightly aligned human resource and business strategies achieve superior performance in comparison to those that are misaligned.

With regard to the final element, culture, a distinction is made between internal and external cultural fit, whereby the former is concerned with consistency of culture within the organization, while external fit addresses the degree of alignment between a corporate culture and a firm's strategy and environment (Arogyaswamy and Byles, 1987). Culture can be a major organizational strength when it guides employees and positively shapes their behavior. However, sources of misalignment derived from culture are also multifaceted. For example, misalignment between culture and strategy can adversely influence implementation and therefore, the success of the strategy itself (Scholz, 1987). There is also a threat of a cultural clash and disruption of current norms when drastic changes in a firm's strategy or structure are made in response to environmental changes; this again can result in internal misalignment.

The driving force that bears responsibility, and has the authority to take decisions and make resource allocation choices that can align the above levels is leadership (Fiedler, 1996; Heracleous and Werres, 2015; Powell, 1992). Such decisions can shape the firm's culture, strategic direction, core competency development, and strategy execution (Beal and Yasai-Ardekani, 2000; Gerard et al., 1999; Ramaswamy et al., 1994). Crossan et al. (2008), following Gardiner (2006) discuss "transcendent leadership," a holistic approach that highlights a leader's boundary spanning task of acting within and across organizational levels to achieve alignment. Table 9.1 illustrates the key concepts and authors relevant to strategic alignment.

STRATEGIC MISALIGNMENT AND FAILURE

9.3 Numerous multinationals, once healthy and leading corporations such as General Motors, Enron, Conseco, American Airlines, and Chrysler have faced bankruptcy. Why do so many previously highly successful firms fail? Misalignments do not just appear fully formed, they develop over time, often in complex, subtle and surreptitious ways. Whereas the link between strategic alignment and performance has been recognized (Beer et al., 2005; Miles and Snow, 1984a; Powell, 1992) the processes of how strategic misalignments can develop over time and lead to corporate failure have hardly been explored.

Most studies on corporate failure have adopted a rather static orientation, neglecting to take a time-sensitive, stage perspective of how a corporation can move towards failure (Zajac et al., 2000). In light of environmental dynamism and the insights that can be afforded from a longer-term examination, scholars have called for research that examines fit and alignment "within a longitudinal perspective" (Venkatraman, 1989: 441).

Are there typical patterns of how misalignments develop? What are the processes that can lead to failure if left unchecked, and can we identify stages toward failure? This chapter explores these questions by applying a strategic alignment perspective that examines the interrelated levels of environment, strategy, competencies, and organization (Heracleous and Werres, 2015; Heracleous et al., 2009). We outline six interrelated stages of strategic misalignment, where the first three stages mark the most significant antecedent factors leading to corporate failure. Once strategic misalignments are established at one organizational level, in the following stages they expand from this level to various other areas inside the organization. Finally, significant gaps are created between the strategy and the demands of the competitive environment, as well as the strategy and the competencies that should support it, which lead to corporate failure.

UNDERSTANDING CORPORATE FAILURE

9.4 The deterministic view of corporate failure (Mellahi and Wilkinson, 2004) focuses on the external environment and is mainly constituted by industrial organization and organizational ecology studies. From this perspective, corporate failure results largely from the impact of industry factors rather than from a firm's internal factors (Barron, 2001). The industrial organization paradigm builds on initial work conducted by the economist Schumpeter who argued that drastic changes in the environment were responsible for extreme waves of industry entry and exit and hence represented the major cause of failure (Schumpeter, 2003 [1943]). Subsequent work by Porter (1980) found that industry factors such as rivalry, entry barriers, and growth rate were key determinants of organizational performance and hence possible failure. Other related work has emphasized demand turbulence and competition as the major causes of decline and failure (Ghemawat, 1991; Lippman and Rumelt, 1983).

The second school within the deterministic view, organizational ecology, is grounded in the natural selection model developed by Hannan and Freeman (1977). With respect to corporate failure, four key elements have been outlined: population density, industry life cycle, age, and size (Hamilton, 2006). In particular the concept of population density has received much empirical attention (Dobrev et al., 2001; Hannan and Carroll, 1992). The "density-dependence" logic is based on the assumption that higher density leads to increased legitimacy, as well as increased competition (Hannan and Freeman, 1988), leading to a U-shape relationship between density and failure (Agarwal et al., 2002). Further, the industry life cycle concept acknowledges the continuous transformations in an industry's structure and competitive environment which calls for a time-variant approach when assessing the relationship between external factors and organizational survival (Agarwal et al., 2002). Failure in this perspective is considered to be a natural phenomenon dependent on varying market efficiencies (Klepper, 1996).

Much industrial organization work has addressed the topic of organizational age and size in relation to failure (Baldwin and Gorecki, 1991; Lieberman, 1990) after Stichcombe's (1965) early study introduced the concept of liability of newness. Since then, numerous studies found an inverse relationship between age and failure, explained by a lack of experience, structure, and stability of young firms (Carroll, 1983; Freeman et al., 1983). Liability of newness and its high risk of failure can also be applied to established firms that have undergone drastic changes, because these changes often disrupt established routines (Amburgey et al., 1993; Hamilton, 2006); even though change can also increase survival chances if there is higher alignment between the firm and the environment (Haveman, 1992; Stoeberl et al., 1998). Finally, with respect to organizational size, and following from the concept of the liability of smallness, it is generally agreed that failure rate decreases with increased firm size (Freeman et al., 1983; Sutton, 1987). The industrial organization perspective has been useful in understanding industry dynamics as well as the impact of attributes such as firm age and size, but it does not address agents' behavioral motives or corporate internal factors, which have been persistent critiques of this perspective over the years (Mellahi and Wilkinson, 2004).

In contrast to the deterministic school, the voluntaristic perspective constituted by organization studies and organizational psychology emphasizes internal factors including strategy, resources and capabilities, leadership, managerial cognition, managerial decision-making and organizational inertia, as fundamental to success or failure (Argenti, 1976; D'Aveni and MacMillan, 1990). For example, it has been argued that boards of directors that are passive, lack strategic thinking competencies and that are not involved in strategic decision making contribute to organizational decline and failure (Finkelstein, 2006; Gilson, 1990; Mellahi, 2005).

So do narcissistic leaders who do not seek outside opinions and exhibit overreliance on past behaviors and strategies (Maccoby, 2000; Rosenthal and Pittinsk, 2006).

A prominent concept of organization studies, initially arising from population ecology, is inertia (Hannan and Freeman, 1984). Inertia is present when the speed of environmental change is higher than the changes made in core features of an organization, as reflected in strategies, structures, or behavioral capabilities (Hannan and Freeman, 1984). A highly formalized organizational structure established through high levels of standardized routines leads to increased corporate stability and reliability, but can also lead to structural and cognitive inertia and higher chances of failure if environmental dynamism and uncertainty increase (Kelly and Amburgey, 1991; van Witteloostuijn, 1998). Structural inertia increases with age and size, which makes this phenomenon a more prominent concern for large, established firms (Stichcombe, 1965).

Further, established institutional norms and constant conformity to certain long-established structural configurations may increase cognitive inertia, thus diminishing the appetite for change in the minds of top management (Barr and Huff, 1997). Hodgkinson and Wright (2002) for example describe cognitive inertia as a phenomenon that leads managers to become overly dependent on established mental models to the detriment of change. Table 9.2 outlines the key concepts and authors relevant to corporate failure.

TABLE 9.2 Perspectives on corporate failure

	Concepts	Key authors
Deterministic perspective-Industrial organization and organizational ecology	Industry change/Environmental uncertainty (IO)	Anderson & Tushman, 2001; Ghemawat, 1991; Lippman & Rumelt 1983; Porter 1980; Schumpeter & Schwedberg, 2003
	Influence of other organizations (OE)	Baum & Singh, 1994; Hannan & Freeman, 1977
	Population density (OE)	Hannan & Carroll, 1992; Hannan & Freeman, 1989; Zammuto & Cameron, 1985
	Industry life cycle (OE)	Agarwal et al., 2002
	Age & size (OE)	Carroll, 1983; Freeman et al., 1983; Stichcombe, 1965; Sutton, 1987
Voluntarist perspective-Organization Studies and organizational psychology	Top management strategic choices (OS)	Argenti, 1976; Child, 1972; Longenecker & Simonetti, 1999
	Structural inertia (OS)	Hannan & Freeman, 1984; van Witteloostuijn, 1998
	Cognitive inertia (OS/OP)	Barr & Huff, 1997; Hodgkinson & Wright, 2002

CASES IN POINT: STRATEGIC MISALIGNMENTS AND FAILURE AT WORLDCOM AND NORTEL NETWORKS

9.5 We take a longitudinal perspective to explore the processes through which two once-successful companies in the telecom industry, WorldCom and Nortel Networks, reached bankruptcy. In so doing, we identify a set of common stages that gradually created more and more significant misalignments which led to the decline of these firms. When assessing the reasons for the decline of WorldCom, one might claim that the firm's bankruptcy was simply a result of the fraudulent accounting practices that were employed within the company which precipitated a stock collapse. However, as Heracleous and Werres (2015) show, these accounting practices were only the tip of an iceberg that was composed of a multifaceted set of causes and several misalignments which grew bigger over time. Table 9.3 gives a chronology of key events at WorldCom.

An analysis of WorldCom's trajectory over time indicates three interrelated misalignments as paramount to its failure. First, a misalignment between strategy and organization due to insufficient integration of the multitude of acquired firms. Second, internal misalignment due to inappropriate corporate culture and human resource practices. Third, a misalignment rooted in ineffective leadership and corporate governance that affected all levels of the organization (see Table 9.4).

TABLE 9.3 WorldCom – Chronology of events

1983	Foundation of LDDC (Long Distance Discount Service)
1985	Bernie Ebbers becomes CEO and remains in this position for the next 17 years
1989	LDDC goes public
1994	International expansion through acquisition of IDB Communications
1995	LDDC becomes WorldCom (WC) and Sullivan takes on role as CFO
1985–1997	Continuous expansion through related diversification (numerous acquisitions which led to accumulated debt of $41 billion in 1997)
1997	Following the Telecom Act in 1996, drastic expansion especially in the internet segment and transformation into full-service provider
1998	Acquisition of MCI for $37 billion (combined market capitalization of $60 billion)
1999	Stock price reaches historical peak of $64.50
2000	Proposed merger with Sprint Communication is rejected by regulatory agencies
2001	Drastic decline of stock price and first wave of layoffs (6,000 employees)
2002 (Spring)	SEC commences investigations into WorldCom's accounting practices; further 4,000 jobs cut; Ebbers resigns
2002 (Summer)	Auditors reveal $4 billion of accounting fraud; Scott Sullivan, CFO, is held mainly responsible for these practices and laid off; Share price drops below $0.20
2003 (July)	WorldCom files for bankruptcy, listing assets of $103.8 billion

STRATEGIC ALIGNMENT: THE ESCO MODEL

TABLE 9.4 Main misalignments at WorldCom

Elements	Description
Strategy and Organization	Insufficient integration of acquisitions due to high complexity, volume, and speed, leading to:
	Inter-unit rivalry, incompatible systems, redundancies, deficient financial integration, cultural clashes
Corporate culture and People	Unhealthy work environment: lack of transparency, unclear responsibilities, low empowerment and people development, high staff turnover, rivalry
	Culture of passive acquiescence, unquestioned loyalty, autocracy, groupthink
Leadership and corporate governance	Top management focuses on numbers and neglects human factors
	Passive Board of Directors dominated by CEO, low levels of initiative and direction, lack of independence, low levels of control over key decisions

An analysis of Nortel's trajectory (see Table 9.5) shows a different story on the surface, but remarkably common stages of misalignment when the two cases are analyzed in comparison to each other.

Nortel Networks' immense size and global scope led to a high level of organizational complexity, where three main areas of misalignment can be identified as being most significant, ultimately leading to Nortel's downfall. First, a misalignment between strategy and core competencies; second, a misalignment between strategy and environment; and third, a misalignment rooted in ineffective leadership and corporate governance, and affecting all levels of the organization. Table 9.6 on p.119, outlines these misalignments.

Cross-case analysis of WorldCom and Nortel reveals both similarities and differences between them. With respect to differences, the age of the two organizations was markedly different; WorldCom was set up in 1983 and declared bankruptcy in 2002, whereas Nortel was founded in 1895 and declared bankruptcy in 2009. The timespan of decline as well as turnaround efforts were also markedly different. WorldCom's decline was swift, from the first signs in 1999 to 2002, during which CEO Ebbers initiated relatively incremental changes to the strategy. Decline at Nortel occurred over nine years (2000–9), during which time radical turnaround actions such as restructuring and turnaround actions were initiated. Finally, there were marked differences in the dominance of the CEO; since 1985, WorldCom had just one CEO, Ebbers; whereas Nortel had high levels of top management turnover, particularly during 2001 to 2006.

Despite the marked differences, there were some significant commonalities. Both firms operated in the US Telecoms industry, facing similar external forces including level of competition, technological developments, and government regulations. The telecom boom in the 1990s led to overvalued stock prices, and easy access to credit, enabling both to pursue aggressive acquisition and growth strategies. Both were hit hard when the telecom bubble burst, facing

TABLE 9.5 Nortel – Chronology of events

1895	Founding of Northern Electric and Manufacturing Company, spinoff from Bell Canada
1914	Renamed to Northern Electric Company following merger with Imperial Wire and Cable Company
1973	Northern Electric goes public; Bell Canada majority owner; core business is provision of telecom equipment
1980s	Exponential growth nationally and internationally; several acquisitions aimed to acquire needed technology
1995	100th birthday: Renamed to Nortel Networks and positioned as global integrated network solution provider
1997	CEO Roth initiates wave of acquisitions (17 in total; 11 just in 2000 worth $20bn) aiming to strengthen Nortell's focus and capabilities on high-speed networks, from telephone switches
2000	Peak of Telecom Boom; Nortel top telecom supplier, with over 95,000 employees; revenues triple in 5 years to $30bn; stock price rises to $124 and market capitalization reaches $350bn. But... Bell Canada drastically reduces its stake and CEO Roth cashes in stock options worth C$ 135m
1995–2000	Meanwhile, debt built up; passive board of directors did not question reckless expansion; weak audit and accounting control system; high levels of organizational complexity from weak post-merger integration
2001	Collapse of internet/Telecom boom: many clients go bankrupt or slash purchasing budget; price deflation; Nortel's revenues decline by 50%; 45,000 jobs cut; stock price in freefall; acquisition write-downs of $16bn
2002	Detection of accounting fraud; share price drops further; drastic restructuring, 10,000 further job losses
2004	Restatement of 2003 profits after further financial irregularities detected; top team fired for financial mismanagement
2005	New CEO Zafirovski initiates another radical restructuring program; downscoping by selling divisions; further reductions in headcount, additional outsourcing
2006–2008	Depressed revenues and fierce competition; layoffs reduce morale, many talented employees leave, creativity and innovation declines; stock price drops below $1 in 2008, company de-listed
2009	Nortel files for bankruptcy in January

STRATEGIC ALIGNMENT: THE ESCO MODEL

TABLE 9.6 Main misalignments at Nortel

Elements	Description
Strategy and core competencies	Aggressive acquisitions did not address problems of slow and infrequent innovations in late 1990s
	Radical downsizing in 2000; layoffs and reduced R&D expenditure, loss of former competitive advantage in terms of technology and innovations
Strategy and external environment	Aggressive acquisition strategy during telecom boom in late 1990s, involving overpriced acquisitions, leads to high levels of debt and risk
	Telecom market crash in 2000 leads to reduced growth and profitability rates
	Inward orientation of management following accounting scandal
	Missed opportunities to build strategic partnerships and failure to keep up with dynamic environment
Leadership and corporate governance	High levels of top management turnover
	Aggressive, uncontrolled expansion led by CEO Roth leads to large debt obligations
	Downsizing, numerous layoffs, financial mismanagement (led by CEO Dunn)
	Drastic restructuring led by CEO Zafirovski unsuccessful in revitalizing Nortel
	Board of directors ineffective as a control mechanism, allowing risky expansion and not detecting accounting fraud

difficulties in servicing their high levels of debt after 2000. Both exhibited fraudulent accounting practices during 2000.

Importantly, however, in both cases the leadership, strategy, and corporate governance systems played a very significant role in their process of demise. Both organizations pursued a strategy of aggressive expansion through acquisition. This was initiated by aggressive leadership, facilitated by a passive board of directors that did not provide the required controls, guidance, and stewardship of the company. Both firms witnessed a negative impact of this strategy at the organizational level where the extent and speed of acquisition activity led not only to ineffective post merger integration and high levels of debt, but subsequently to various types of organizational problems. These were most obvious at the level of people and processes, over time affecting negatively the culture, design, and core competencies of the organizations, and finally accentuating the misalignment between the strategy and the imperatives posed by the competitive environment, leading to failure. Table 9.7 displays this process.

Even though we noted the significant impact of environmental change and industry conditions on organizations' performance, these cases illustrate how internal organizational factors such as the quality of leadership and corporate governance, as well as the soundness of strategic decisions and of their execution are fundamental to success or failure. These findings are consistent with strategic management research on the relative effects of industry factors versus organizational factors on corporate performance (McGahan and Porter, 1997; Rumelt, 1991), as well as with

TABLE 9.7 Stages of corporate failure

Stages	Feature
Stage 1	Ineffective leadership and passive, dominated board of directors
Stage 2	Aggressive growth strategy (e.g., via acquisition), or over-ambitious investments, funded by easy credit and overvalued stock
Stage 3	Ineffective strategy execution (e.g., insufficient post merger integration). Which gradually becomes obvious through comparative performance
Stage 4	Misalignments at the organizational level (duplication of processes, inefficiency, downsizing leads to loss of talented people)
Stage 5	Further misalignments at organization level (culture becomes unproductive and inward looking, core competencies weaken). Within an unforgiving environment (e.g., industry hit by external shock)
Stage 6	Strategy and core competencies not aligned with requirements of competitive environment, leading to failure

the strategic choice perspective (Child, 1972, 1997) that highlights the role of managerial agency in addition to industry structure.

Specific environmental trends have differential impact on organizations rather than a deterministic one, depending on organizations' internal factors such as their design, competencies, and strategic choices. Consistent with the relevant literature (Crossan et al., 2008; Powell, 1992), the first antecedent factor of corporate failure relates to leadership and corporate governance, which act as driving factors of strategic alignment, as well as misalignments, as seen in the two case examples.

Figure 9.1 incorporates this insight of the fundamental role of leadership, as well as the relationship between alignment and performance. The framework offers an integrative perspective of the various factors relevant to both organizational performance, as well as failure.

Further, the stage model of corporate failure (Table 9.7), shows that corporate failure should not be understood as the result of a single factor such as accounting fraud, or a single strategic decision such as an ill-fated acquisition. Rather, the model sheds light on strategic misalignments and ultimate corporate failure, by highlighting that it is a process arrived at over time, through interrelated antecedents. The three initial stages, ineffective leadership and governance, followed by unduly risky strategic decisions and then by lax implementation, set the stage for failure since they precipitate various types of organizational misalignments that enlarge the gap between the strategy and competencies of the organization on the one hand, and the demands of the external environment on the other hand.

Figure 9.2 illustrates how the various misalignments discussed in the case examples can be positioned in the strategic alignment framework.

STRATEGIC ALIGNMENT: THE ESCO MODEL

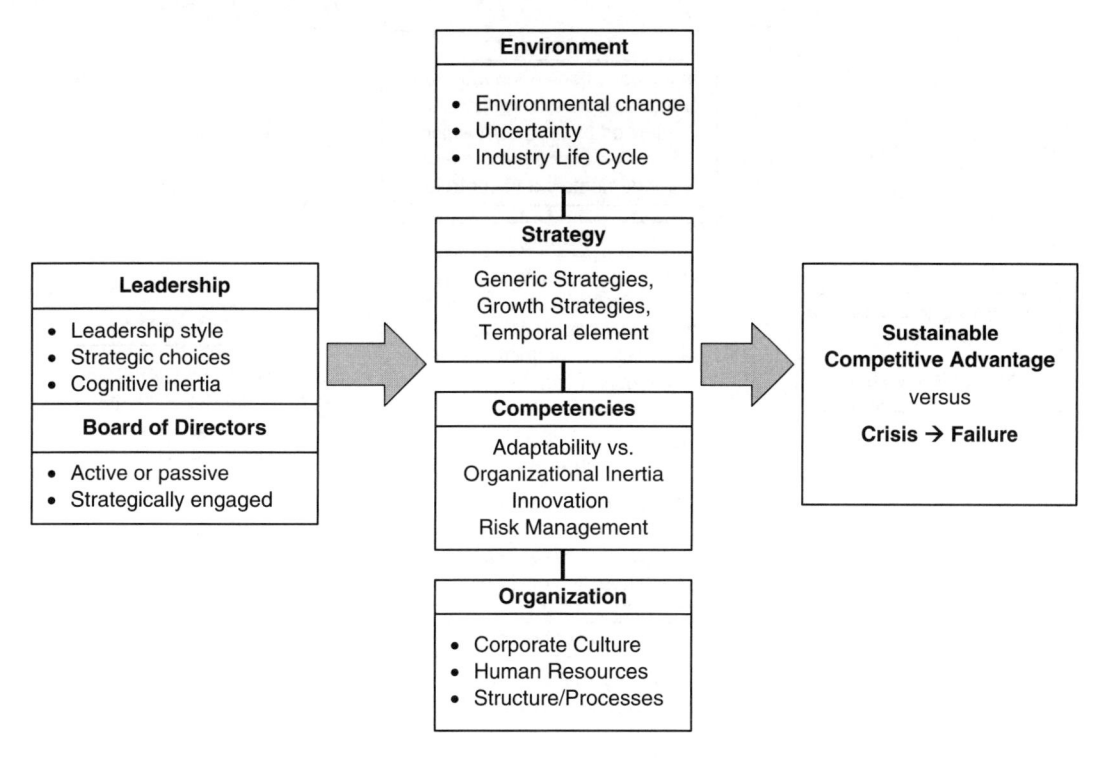

FIGURE 9.1 Strategic alignment model

The frameworks developed in this study (Table 9.7 and Figure 9.1) can be employed as important diagnostic tools by senior managers, strategic planners, or consultants to evaluate potential misalignments; and if appropriate, to gain advance warning of whether the organization is at risk of failure. Importantly, such an analysis would then allow a firm to take appropriate actions to arrest a process of decline, which would be crucial in order to achieve a successful turnaround. The stage model of failure can offer an early warning system of the development of strategic misalignments, raising awareness of important antecedents of strategic misalignments, potentially allowing a firm to take action at an early stage.

Further, we are reminded of the crucial role of leadership and governance (stage 1), the limits and dangers of risky and aggressive growth strategies (stage 2), and the vital importance of effective execution (stage 3). A dominant CEO/Chair combined with a passive board, can enable aggressive growth strategies to go unchecked until it's too late. Such strategies can become a stone around the neck of organizations if the environment turns sour and if they have built up substantial debt that they cannot then service once their performance and share prices decline. A risky strategy, badly executed, is a recipe for failure. It leads to organizational misalignments that gradually spread to put the organization in a highly compromising position, from which it is almost impossible to recover. Being aware of these risk factors and avoiding them, is essential for strategists.

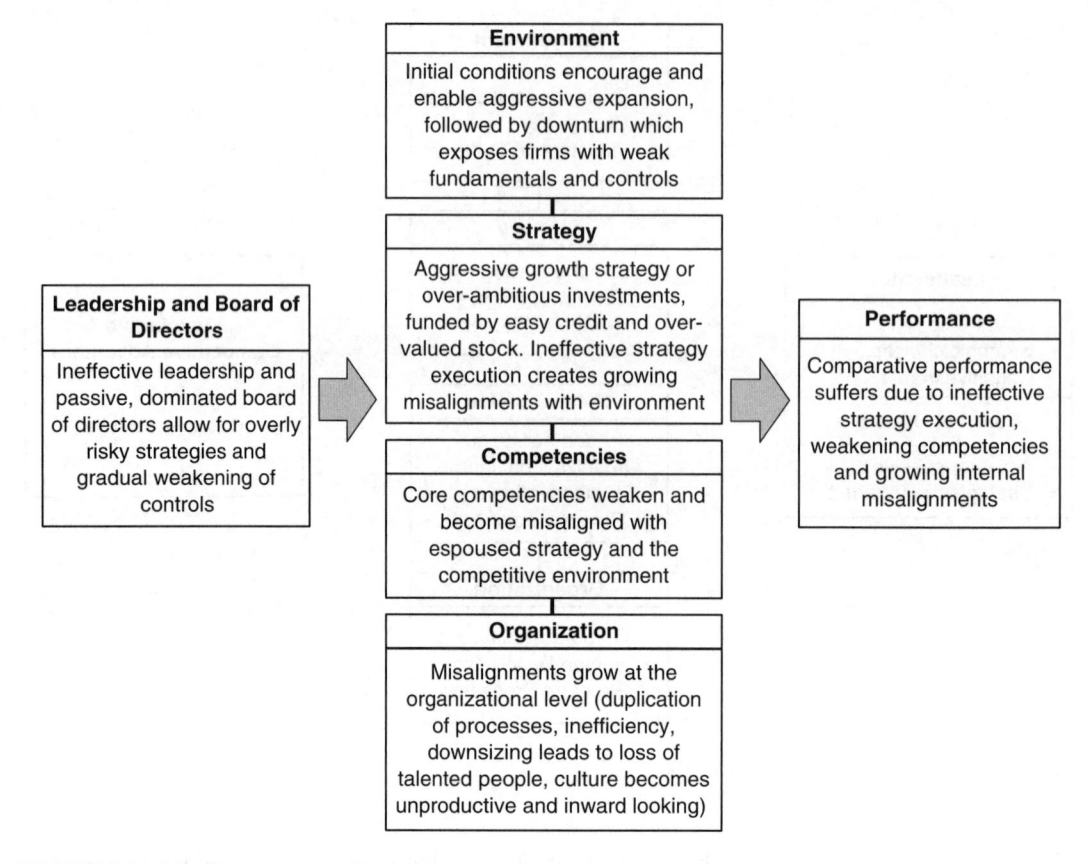

Environment
Initial conditions encourage and enable aggressive expansion, followed by downturn which exposes firms with weak fundamentals and controls

Strategy
Aggressive growth strategy or over-ambitious investments, funded by easy credit and over-valued stock. Ineffective strategy execution creates growing misalignments with environment

Leadership and Board of Directors
Ineffective leadership and passive, dominated board of directors allow for overly risky strategies and gradual weakening of controls

Competencies
Core competencies weaken and become misaligned with espoused strategy and the competitive environment

Performance
Comparative performance suffers due to ineffective strategy execution, weakening competencies and growing internal misalignments

Organization
Misalignments grow at the organizational level (duplication of processes, inefficiency, downsizing leads to loss of talented people, culture becomes unproductive and inward looking)

FIGURE 9.2 Misalignments positioned in the strategic alignment model

REVISION ACTIVITIES

Identify recent cases of corporate failure and try to understand why these companies failed through exploring their trajectory over time, as well as their strategy and organization. Map the main misalignments that led to failure on the ESCO framework, including the role of leadership, the strategy, core competencies and organization, as well as the role of environmental change.

Identify recent cases of corporate failure and write a brief narrative of their path towards failure. What was the role of practitioners, practices, and praxis in this path? What was the role of environmental change? What do you think was most significant in the particular cases you are analyzing, environmental change or internal factors, and why?

FURTHER READINGS

- **Paper:** Heracleous, L. and Werres, K. (2015) On the road to disaster: Strategic misalignments and corporate failure. Forthcoming, *Long Range Planning.* Offers further grounding of the strategic alignment framework described in this chapter in the literature, and also offers a more extensive discussion of the case studies described in this chapter, which can shed more light on practitioners, practices, and praxis as related to strategic alignment and misalignments.
- **Paper:** Beer, M., Voelpel, S., Leibold, M., and Tekie, E. (2005) Strategic management as organizational learning: Developing fit and alignment through a disciplined process. *Long Range Planning*, 38: 445–65. Describes an applied, practice-oriented process by which organizations can engage their employees to evaluate their levels of alignment and develop corrective actions.
- **Paper:** Mellahi, K. and Wilkinson, A. (2004) Organizational failure: A critique of recent research and a proposed integrative framework. *International Journal of Management Reviews*, 5/6: 21–41. Offers a review of literature on organizational failure, and the multitude of interrelated factors that can precipitate it.

REFERENCES

Agarwal, R., Echambadi, R., and Sarkar, M. B. (2002) The conditioning effect of time on firm survival: A life cycle approach. *Academy of Management Journal*, 45: 971–94.

Amburgey, T., Kelly, D., and Barnet, W. P. (1993) Resetting the clock: The dynamics of organizational change and failure. *Administrative Science Quarterly*, 38: 51–73.

Anderson, P. and Tushman, M. L. (2001) Organizational environments and industry exit: The effects of uncertainty, munificence and complexity. *Industrial & Corporate Change*, 10: 675–711.

Aragon-Correa, J. A. and Sharma, S. (2003) A contingent resource-based view of proactive corporate environmental strategy. *Academy of Management Review*, 28: 71–88.

Argenti, J. (1976) Corporate planning and corporate collapse. *Long Range Planning*, 9: 12–17.

Arogyaswamy, B. and Byles, C. M. (1987) Organizational culture: Internal and external fits. *Journal of Management*, 13: 647.

Barney, J. (1991) Firm resources and sustained competitive advantage. *Journal of Management*, 17: 99–120.

Barney, J., Wright, M., and Ketchen, D. (2001) The Resource-based view of the firm: Ten years after 1991. *Journal of Management*, 27: 625–41.

Barr, P. S. and Huff, A. S. (1997) Seeing isn't believing: Understanding diversity in the timing of strategic response. *Journal of Management Studies*, 34: 337–70.

Barron, N. B. (2001) Organizational ecology and industrial economics: A comment on Groski. *Industrial and Corporate Change*, 10: 541–8.

Bartlett, C. A. and Ghoshal, S. (1991) Global strategic management: Impact on the new frontiers of strategy research. *Strategic Management Journal*, 12: 5–16.

Beal, R. M. and Yasai-Ardekani, M. (2000) Performance implications of aligning CEO functional experiences with competitive strategies. *Journal of Management*, 26: 733–62.

Beer, M., Voelpel, S., Leibold, M., and Tekie, E. (2005) Strategic management as organizational learning: Developing fit and alignment through a disciplined process. *Long Range Planning*, 38: 445–65.

Bennett, N., Ketchen, D. J., and Schultz, E. B. (1998) An examination of factors associated with the integration of human resource management and strategic decision making. *Human Resource Management*, 37: 3–17.

Brown, S. L. and Eisenhardt, K. (1998) *Competing on the Edge: Strategy as Structured Chaos*. Boston, MA: Harvard Business School Press.

Carroll, G. R. (1983) A stochastic model of organizational mortality: Review and re-analysis. *Social Science Research*, 29: 303–29.

Chabrak, N. and Daidj, N. (2007) Enron: Widespread myopia. *Critical Perspectives on Accounting*, 18: 539–57.

Child, J. (1972) Organizational structure, environment and performance: The role of strategic choice. *Sociology*, 6: 1–22.

Child, J. (1997) Strategic choice in the analysis of action, structure, organizations and environment: Retrospect and prospect. *Organization Studies*, 18: 43–76.

Christiansen, L. C. and Higgs, M. (2008) How the alignment of business strategy and HR strategy can impact performance. *Journal of General Management*, 33: 13–33.

Crossan, M., Vera, D., and Nanjad, L. (2008) Transcendent leadership: Strategic leadership in dynamic environments. *Leadership Quarterly*, 19: 569–81.

D'Aveni, R. and MacMillan, I. (1990) Crisis and the content of managerial communications: A study of the focus of attention of top managers in surviving and failing firms. *Administrative Science Quarterly*, 35: 634–57.

Dobrev, D. S., Kim, T.-Y., and Hannan, M. T. (2001) Dynamics of niche width and resource partitioning. *American Journal of Sociology*, 10: 1299–337.

Eisenhardt, K. M. and Martin, J. A. (2000) Dynamic capabilities: What are they? *Strategic Management Journal*, 21: 1105–21.

Fiedler, F. E. (1996) Research on leadership selection and training: One view of the future. *Administrative Science Quarterly*, 41: 241–50.

Finkelstein, S. (2006) Why smart executives fail: Four case histories of how people learn the wrong lessons from history. *Business History*, 48: 153–70.

Fredrickson, J. W. (1986) The strategic decision process and organizational structure. *Academy of Management Review*, 11: 280–97.

Freeman, J., Carroll, G. R., and Hannan, M. T. (1983) The liability of newness: Age dependence in organizational death rates. *American Sociological Review*, 48: 692–710.

Gardiner, J. J. (2006) Transactional, transformational, and transcendent leadership: Metaphors mapping the evolution of the theory and practice of governance. *Leadership Review*, 6 (Spring): 62–76.

Gerard, G., Randall, G., and Sleeth, M. A. (1999) Organizing culture: Leader roles, behaviors, and reinforcement mechanisms. *Journal of Business and Psychology*, 13: 545–60.

Ghemawat, P. (1991) *Commitment: The Dynamic of Strategy*. New York: Free Press.

Gilson, S. C. (1990) Bankruptcy, Boards, Banks, and Blockholders. *Journal of Financial Economics*, 27: 355–87.

Ginsberg, A. and Venkatraman, N. (1985) Contingency perspectives of organizational strategy: A critical review of the empirical research. *Academy of Management Review*, 10: 421–34.

Grant, R. B. (1991) A resource based theory of competitive advantage: Implications for strategy formulation. *California Management Review*, 33: 114–35.

Hamilton, E. A. (2006) An exploration of the relationship between loss of legitimacy and the sudden death of organizations. *Group & Organization Management*, 31: 327–58.

Hannan, M. T. and Carroll, G. (1992) *Dynamics of Organizational Populations: Density, Legitimation, and Competition*. Oxford: University Press.

Hannan, M. T. and Freeman, J. (1977) The population ecology of organizations. *American Journal of Sociology*, 82: 929–64.

Hannan, M. T. and Freeman, J. (1984) Structural inertia and organizational change. *American Sociological Review*, 49: 149–64.

Hannan, M. T. and Freeman, J. (1986) Where do organizational forms come from? *Sociological Forum*, 1: 50–72.

Hannan, M. T. and Freeman, J. (1988) The ecology of organizational mortality: American labor unions. *American Journal of Sociology*, 94: 25–52.

Haveman, H. A. (1992) Between a rock and a hard place: organizational change and performance under conditions of fundamental environmental transformation. *Administrative Science Quarterly*, 37: 48–75.

Heracleous, L. and Werres, K. (2015) On the road to disaster: Strategic misalignments and corporate failure. *Long Range Planning* (forthcoming).

Heracleous, L., Wirtz, J., and Pangarkar, N. (2009) *Flying High in a Competitive Industry* (rev. edn.). Singapore: McGraw-Hill Asia.

Hodgkinson, G. and Wright, G. (2002) Confronting strategic inertia in a top management team: Learning from failure. *Organization Studies*, 23: 949–77.

Ireland, R. D. and Hitt, M. A. (2005) Achieving and maintaining strategic competitiveness in the 21st century. *Academy of Management Executive*, 19: 63–77.

Kelly, W. and Amburgey, T. (1991) Organizational inertia and momentum: A dynamic model of strategic change. *Academy of Management Journal*, 34: 591–612.

Klepper, S. (1996) Entry, exit, growth and innovation over the product life cycle. *American Economic Review*, 86: 560–81.

Leonard-Barton, D. (1992) Core capabilities and core rigidities: A paradox in managing new product development. *Strategic Management Journal*, 13: 111–25.

Lieberman, M. B. (1990) Exit from declining industries: "Shakeout" or "stakeout"? *RAND Journal of Economics*, 21: 538–54.

Lippman, S. A. and Rumelt, R. P. (1983) Uncertain imitability: An analysis of interfirm differences in efficiency under competition. *Bell Journal of Economics*, 13: 418–38.

Maccoby, M. (2000) Narcissistic leaders. *Harvard Business Review*, 78: 68–77.

March, J. G. (1991) Exploration and exploitation in organizational learning. *Organization Science*, 71–87.

McGahan, A. and Porter, M. (1997) How much does industry matter, really? *Strategic Management Journal*, 18: 15–30.

Mellahi, K. (2005) The dynamics of boards of directors in failing organizations. *Long Range Planning*, 38: 261–79.

Mellahi, K. and Wilkinson, A. (2004) Organizational failure: A critique of recent research and a proposed integrative framework. *International Journal of Management Reviews*, 5/6: 21–41.

Miles, R. E. and Snow, C. C. (1984a) Fit, failure and the hall of fame. *California Management Review*, 26: 10–28.

Miles, R. E. and Snow, C. C. (1984b) Designing strategic human resource systems. *Organizational Dynamics*, 13: 36–52.

Miles, R., Snow, C., Mathews, J., and Coleman, H. (1997) Organizing in the knowledge age: Anticipating the cellular form. *Academy of Management Executives*, 11: 7–20.

Miles, R. E., Snow, C., and Meyer, A. (1978) Organizational strategy, structure, and process. *Academy of Management Review*, 3: 456–62.

Miller, D. (1986) Configurations of strategy and structure: Towards a synthesis. *Strategic Management Journal*, 7: 223–40.

Miller, D. (1996) Configurations revisited. *Strategic Management Journal*, 17: 505–12.

Milliman, J., Von Glinow, M. A., and Nathan, M. (1991) Organizational life cycles and strategic international human resource management in multinational companies: Implications for congruence theory. *Academy of Management Review*, 16: 318–39.

Mintzberg, H. (1987) Crafting strategy. *Harvard Business Review*, 65: 66–75.

Peteraf, M. A. (1993) The cornerstones of competitive advantage. *Strategic Management Journal*, 14: 179–91.

Porter, M. E. (1980) *Competitive Strategy, Techniques for Analyzing Industries and Competitors*. New York: Free Press.

Porter, M. E. (1985) *Competitive Advantage: Creating and Sustaining Superior Performance*. New York: Free Press.

Porter, M. E. (1996) What is strategy? *Harvard Business Review*, 74: 61–78.
Powell, T. C. (1992) Organizational alignment as competitive advantage. *Strategic Management Journal*, 13: 119–34.
Prahalad, C. K. and Hamel, G. (1990) The core competence of the organization. *Harvard Business Review*, 48: 79–91.
Ramaswamy, K., Thomas, A. S., and Litchert, R. J. (1994) Organizational performance in a regulated environment: The role of strategic orientation. *Strategic Management Journal*, 15: 63–74.
Rindova, V. P. and Kotha, S. (2001) Continuous "morphing": Competing through dynamic capabilities, form, and function. *Academy of Management Journal*, 44: 1263–80.
Rosenthal, S. A. and Pittinsk, T. L. (2006) Narcissistic leadership. *Leadership Quarterly*, 17: 617–33.
Rumelt, R. P. (1991) How much does industry matter? *Strategic Management Journal*, 3: 167–85.
Scholz, C. (1987) Corporate culture and strategy: The problem of strategic fit. *Long Range Planning*, 20: 78–84.
Schuler, R. S. and Jackson, S. (1987) Linking competitive strategies with human resource management practices. *Academy of Management Executive*, 1: 207–19.
Schumpeter, J. A. (2003 [1943]) *Capitalism, Socialism and Democracy*. London: Routledge.
Stichcombe, A. L. (1965) *Social Structures and Organizations. Handbook of Organizations*. Chicago, IL: Rand McNally.
Stoeberl, P. A., Parker, G. E., and Joo, S. (1998) Relationship between organizational change and failure in the wine industry: An event history analysis. *Journal of Management Studies*, 35: 537–55.
Sutton, R. I. (1987) The process of organizational death: Disbanding and reconnecting. *Administrative Science Quarterly*, 32: 542–69.
Teece, D. J., Pisano, G., and Shuen, A. (1997) Dynamic capabilities and strategic management. *Strategic Management Journal*, 18: 509–33.
van Witteloostuijn, A. (1998) Bridging behavioral and economic theories of decline: Organizational inertia, strategic competition and failure. *Management Science*, 44: 501–21.
Venkatraman, N. (1989) The concept of fit in strategy research: Towards verbal and statistical correspondence. *Academy of Management Review*, 14: 423–44.
Venkatraman, N. and Camillus, J. (1984) Exploring the concept of fit in strategic management. *Academy of Management Review*, 9: 513–25.
Voelpel, S., Leibold, M., and Tekie, E. (2006) Managing purposeful organizational misfit: Exploring the nature of industry and organizational misfit to enable strategic change. *Journal of Change Management*, 6: 257–76.
Waterman, R. H., Peters, T. J., and Phillips, J. R. (1980) Strategy is not organization. *Business Horizons*, June: 14–26.
Wernerfelt, B. (1984) A resource-based view of the firm. *Strategic Management Journal*, 5: 171–80.
Wirtz, J., Heracleous, L. and Pangarkar, N. (2008) Managing human resources for service excellence and cost effectiveness at Singapore Airlines. *Managing Service Quality*, 18: 4–19.
Wright, P. M. and Snell, S. A. (1998) Toward a unifying framework for exploring fit and flexibility in strategic human resource management. *Academy of Management Review*, 23: 756–72.
Yin, R. K. (2008) *Case Study Research: Design and Methodology*. Thousand Oaks, CA: Sage Publications.
Zajac, E., Kraatz, S., and Bresser, R. (2000) Modelling the dynamics of strategic fit: A normative approach to strategic change. *Strategic Management Journal*, 21: 429–53.

PRACTICING STRATEGY ACROSS FIRMS: INSIGHTS FROM M&As

10

Learning Objectives

- Examine the application of practice-related concepts to the study of mergers and acquisitions.
- Demonstrate that mergers and acquisitions provide an interesting, although complex, context within which to study the practicing of strategy.
- Understand the stages through which mergers and acquisitions happen and how these stages can be examined through a practice perspective.
- Raise awareness that M&A practices involve a shifting web of strategy actors spanning many organizational and institutional boundaries.

INTRODUCTION

10.1 How to grow companies to protect and enhance their competitive position in an increasingly turbulent world is of key concern to management and company stakeholders. An array of growth options exists from organic expansion through hybrid arrangements such as strategic alliances to full ownership where mergers and acquisitions (M&A) is often the preferred strategy. Each strategic option has important implications for the way in which organizations engage with their contexts and have implications for the work of strategists. This chapter focuses on strategy practices for a particular growth strategy – M&A, as it is a strategy context of great importance to organizations, economies, industries, regions, and a wide range of stakeholders (Angwin, 2007). Although the following discussion is specific to M&A there are many resonances with other expansion strategies, such as joint ventures and other types of strategic alliance, as strategy practitioners need to engage with a number of evolving contexts. Through the discussion the chapter will show how strategy practice(s) occur within a coexistent and fluid interplay between contexts.

It is worth focusing upon M&A as a strategy practice context as over half a century of research has revealed its importance to a wide variety of stakeholders at different levels and geographies (Angwin, 2007). In dollar terms 2014 alone witnessed in excess of $3.5 trillion of M&A – an amount greater than the entire GDP of France in the same year, the worlds fifth largest economy. With M&A now a global phenomenon many new questions are being raised about how to select appropriate targets, transact deals and manage integration to enhance strategic advantage, but one core issue persists – why do 50% of all M&A fail? To constantly observe that M&A outcome is no better than a stochastic process is to undermine the value of top managers in this endeavor, investors and markets who support the activity, and raises significant questions about the value of research efforts to improve the situation. The burning question of why so many M&A take place, when 50% fail, has driven scholars from a wide range of disciplines, most notably finance, economics, strategy, organizational behavior, human resources, and psychology, to attempt to find answers to this problem. Each has focused on particular aspects of M&A, identifying important aspects from the perspective of a single discipline (Angwin, 2007). However, for the level of research effort expended, the amount of unequivocal findings remains disappointingly small (Grant, 2002) and many are so broad as to be of little value to practitioners. Indeed, despite half a century of research focusing upon M&A, the results are disappointing and there is even some empirical evidence that the failure rate of M&A is increasing.

Reasons for the lack of consistent findings include the practical difficulties involved in researching M&A and the complex nature of the phenomena themselves (see Angwin, 2007, 2012). Practical difficulties in researching M&A have too often resulted in convenience-led research (i.e., researching issues where secondary data are readily available rather than tackling questions that require engagement with primary data). The complexity of M&A as a process phenomenon, involving all aspects of business and multiple levels of organizations across many interfaces, has rarely been embraced. M&A research has tended to focus on a single disciplinary approach, just one level of analysis and a particular stage in the M&A process (Javidan et al., 2004). This has elicited some important insights but has also served to fragment understanding of M&A, resulting in large amounts of disparate unconnected information and, importantly, dividing M&A formation concerns from implementation. The failure of disciplines to interrogate other perspectives and the lack of interdisciplinary research may be a reason why so many "results" from M&A research are inconclusive or unhelpful (Angwin, 2007; Gomes et al., 2012a).

In addition to the need for a more integrative view of M&A academically we need to overcome fragmented and partial views of the M&A process at a practice level. A more holistic approach to the interactions between actors and levels of analysis can bring new insights and perspectives on core questions. A micro-level approach can reveal hitherto concealed aspects of M&A practice that may be confounding current findings on performance. In this chapter, the aim is to offer an integrative approach to understanding M&A, which links an overall perspective on M&A with micro activities and processes.

The chapter uses the strategy as practice approach, adopts a sociological view of M&A as a set of social practices, and examines the intimate connections between institutions, practitioners, practices, and processes (Whittington, 2002). The integrative and holistic nature of a strategy-as-practice approach provides a broad tapestry within which to explore micro aspects of M&A. In particular, a strategy-as-practice approach highlights, rather than ignores or downplays, the dynamic interconnections between layers of context.

A surprising feature of M&A literature is that it tells us very little about who the practitioners are in M&A, how they interact and what they do throughout the process. There is a great deal more to know about M&A practitioners and the skillfulness of their work. For this reason, perceiving M&A through a Strategy-as-Practice lens allows focus upon practitioners, who are key to the framework. Surfacing which practitioners are involved, what activities they engage in, and how these affect the course of M&A is critical for going beyond broad characterizations of M&A and getting closer to the ground (Bower, 2004) to produce more valuable and insightful research.

Overall, we have chosen M&A as a topic to include in our investigation of practicing strategy as: (a) M&A are one of the most significant corporate actions that companies can take and in the last five years $14.85 trillion of deals were transacted (2010–14 inclusive); (b) there is long-standing and continuing data to show that M&A are highly problematic phenomena which traditional research approaches have failed to fully understand; (c) traditional strategy research into M&A has tended to adopt cross-sectional quantitative approaches concerned with finance, performance, and policy issues rather than focusing upon the temporal practices of actors using qualitative longitudinal research. It is only fairly recently that strategy researchers have taken the process approach seriously and adopted a much broader range of methods (Angwin and Meadows, 2009) – indeed for several years there have been calls for methodological pluralism (Meglio and Risberg, 2010). A practice approach is therefore (a) needed (to more fully explain the well-documented problems of M&A) and (b) novel in this context. Next we outline such an approach.

A STRATEGY-AS-PRACTICE APPROACH TO M&A

10.2 This is a new take on key issues in the domain of strategic management that may affect firm outcomes. Its newness means that the "practice" approach is currently evolving with a number of frameworks in circulation attempting to crystallize the essence of what a practice approach might be (see www.strategy-as-practice.org). Central to the orientation of the "practice" group is a greater emphasis on vertical interactions, a downplaying of the organizational boundary across which these interactions take place, and an emphasis on the actual activities and actions of practitioners (see Johnson et al., 2003) which lead to strategic outcomes.

This book focuses upon a 3P's model of **practitioners; practices; praxis** and their interaction (Whittington, 2002) (refer to Section 1.6). The focus on **practitioners** is to identify who the key practitioners are in the strategic process in question. So often in M&A research these practitioners are assumed to be top management and often at one moment in time. However, from a practice perspective, practitioners may include an M&A director at head office, functional or divisional directors, middle managers and other employees in an organization as well as their opposite numbers in the other merging firm. In addition to practitioners within the focal firms, there are many other practitioners who are influential in the course of a deal, such as key customers and suppliers, institutional investors and professional advisers, including lawyers, investment bankers, accountants, and public relations advisors. A practice approach not only allows for interactions between actors across organizational boundaries, it also allows for a dynamic interpretation of M&A – to recognize process, and that the practitioners involved in the process may change in importance over time. To illustrate, Figure 10.1 shows a simplified M&A process identifying key external actors at different times in the flow of events. It is recognized that the actual process for a M&A may well be much more complex than the figure describes, with feedback loops, additional phases and omitted phases, (Angwin et al., 2015), but as a high-level overview it shows where external practitioners of different types may engage in the process.

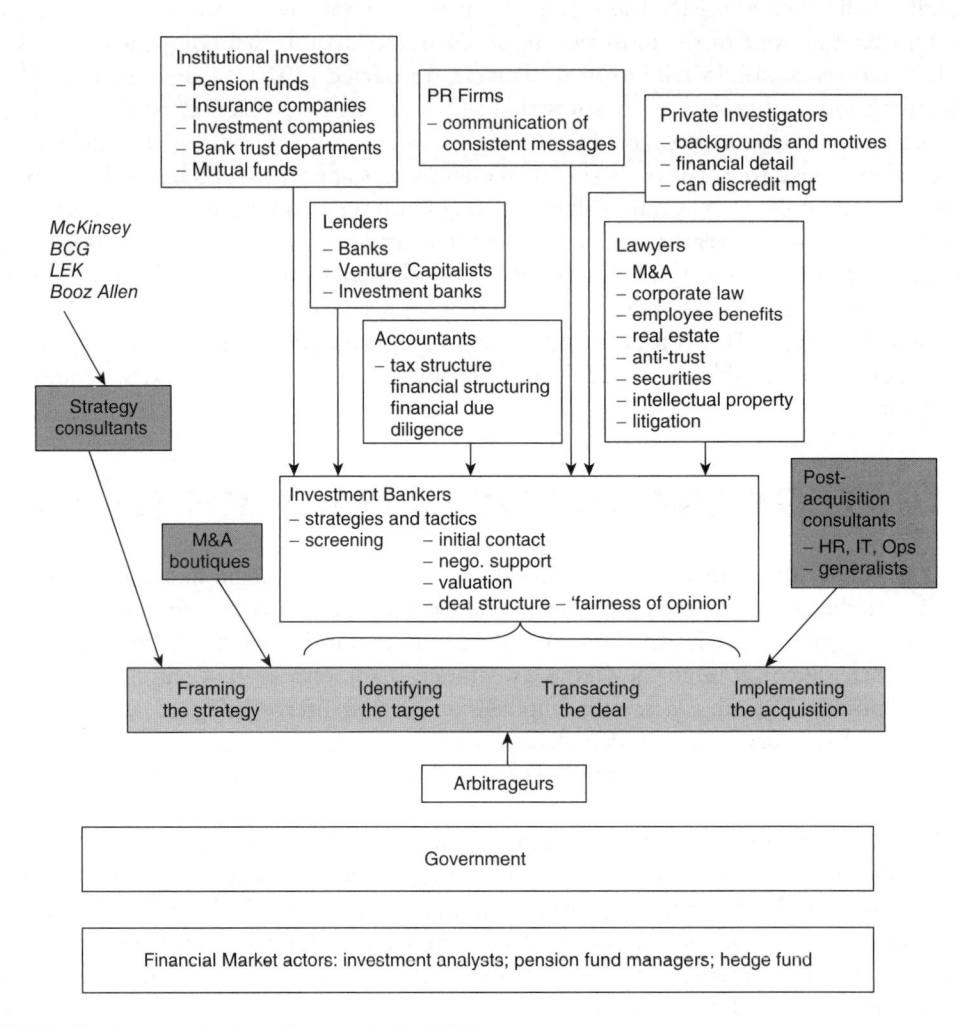

FIGURE 10.1 Important external actors in the M&A process

The **practices** focus is on tools and techniques "in use" by practitioners. These may range from highly codified models, susceptible to sophisticated quantitative analysis, to rules of thumb or heuristics. Practices may also be generic in nature or highly customized for specific contexts. "Practices-in-use" will show varying degrees of overlap between the practitioners involved. With such a large number of different actors within the M&A process there are a very large number of practices in use. However, certain practices have greater centrality to the process than others. For instance the contract for the purchase of the target company assumes center stage in the negotiation and purchase of a company and is contributed to directly by many different professional advisors as a living document. Linked to the contract will be rules and regulations from corporate law as well as best-practice guidance enshrined in a takeover code. Another key area of formalized practice is tools and techniques for company valuation. Although there is a profusion of different approaches to valuation, for most deals it is normal to find discounted cash-flow calculations of value based upon future earnings and synergy assumptions. In addition there are likely to be asset-based valuations and market-based methods of value calculation. Less formalized but no less important practices are due diligence methods that can range from prescriptive to exploratory. Bounded by concerns for secrecy and time (Angwin, 2004; Angwin et al., 2015), due diligence practices can vary enormously in scope of activities across M&A (Angwin, 2001) but they are widely perceived as a critical part of investigating value in a target organization (Gomes et al., 2012b). All of these practices serve an important role in framing understanding and perceptions of the M&A process.

Praxis focuses on what practitioners actually do – their "work." This would include how they spend their time, what actions and activities they engage in and how they prioritize them. In the early stages of the M&A process, the acquirer may wish to communicate informally with the potential target company. This may be handled through an intermediary or a CEO may engineer a "chance" encounter with his opposite number in order to sound them out regarding a possible deal. This opening approach may colour the nature of subsequent actions. Negotiations are another vital part of M&A transactions and occur between the protagonists, their advisors, and a wide range of stakeholders. A great deal of time is spent articulating and persuading parties with different interests to support or reject a proposed deal (Angwin et al., 2004). These meetings can have very different styles with some being friendly attempts to work towards a common goal and others being very confrontational to the point of open hostility.

While the 3Ps conceptualization is attractive in giving weight to the work of practitioners, it tends to downplay the role of institutional forces, which can have a very significant role in M&A. For this reason, a different version is used in this chapter, which highlights the constraining and facilitating role of the institutional context. In this model of strategy-as-practice, proposed by La Ville and Mounoud (2003), the practitioners involved are known and distributed around the framework. The focal practices are the result of institutional forces, tools, and techniques in use and actual practitioner activities. The framework is shown in Figure 10.2 and is organized around three components: **text; tools; talk**.

Text consists of structures/discourses of strategy as embodied in institutions, fads, and fashions. It is the institutional and social context within which M&A activity is conducted. This "text" dominates the M&A domain and drives "tools" used to operationalize the M&A process. The text also bounds the activities of practitioners by means of explicit legal requirements as well as less explicit social rules and norms. An example of "text" is the UK's City Code for Takeovers

```
                Text                   Production          Talk
        Societies, Institutions,   ←─────────────→    Actions, activities, narratives,
         Fashions, Fads, Gurus       Domination      routines e.g., interactions,
                                                              episodes

                                   M&A as Practice
   Operationalize/                 ⇨ Reconstituting        Constraining/
   conceptualize                   ⇨ Resisting             potentializing
                                   ⇨ Innovating

                                        Tools
                              Concepts, language, techniques,
                                        models
```

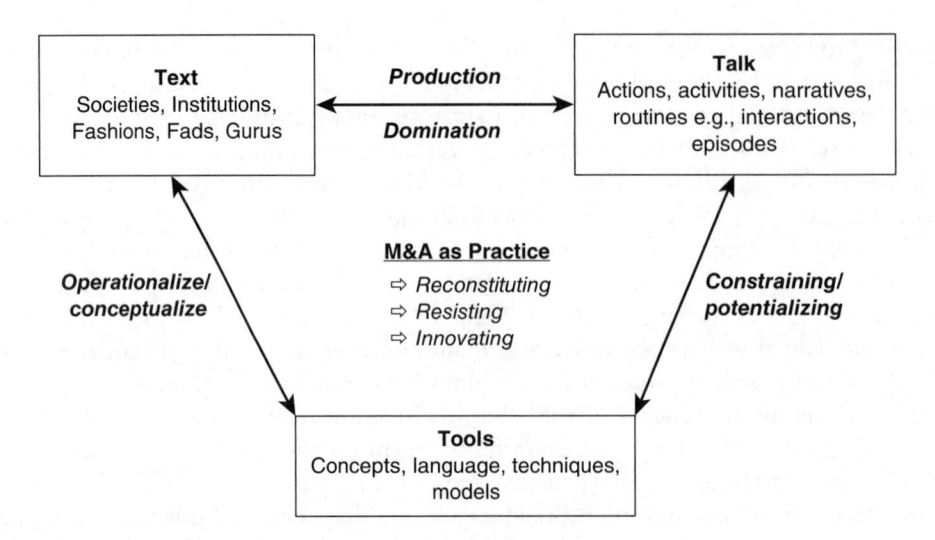

FIGURE 10.2 An integrative framework for M&A as practice

Adapted from La Ville and Mounoud (2003). Used with permission of John Benjamins Publishing Co.

and Mergers. The Code has been developed since 1968 to reflect the collective opinion of those professionally involved in the field of takeovers as to appropriate business standards and as to how fairness to shareholders and an orderly framework for takeovers can be achieved. The rules set out in the Code have a statutory basis in relation to the United Kingdom. Exhibit 1 is a summary of some of the most important Rules.

EXHIBIT 1: SUMMARY OF MAIN RULES IN THE TAKEOVER CODE

- When a person or group acquires interests in shares carrying 30% or more of the voting rights of a company, they must make a cash offer to all other shareholders at the highest price paid in the 12 months before the offer was announced (30% of the voting rights of a company is treated by the Code as the level at which effective control is obtained).

- When interests in shares carrying 10% or more of the voting rights of a class have been acquired by an offeror in the offer period and the previous 12 months, the offer must include a cash alternative for all shareholders of that class at the highest price paid by the offeror in that period. Further, if an offeror acquires for cash any interest in shares during the offer period, a cash alternative must be made available at that price at least.

- If the offeror acquires an interest in shares in a target company at a price higher than the value of the offer, the offer must be increased accordingly.

- The target company must appoint a competent independent adviser whose advice on the offer must be made known to all the shareholders, together with the opinion of the board.

PRACTICING STRATEGY ACROSS FIRMS: INSIGHTS FROM M&As

- Favorable deals for selected shareholders are banned.
- All shareholders must be given the same information.
- Those issuing takeover circulars must include statements taking responsibility for the contents.
- Profit forecasts and asset valuations must be made to specified standards and must be reported on by professional advisers.
- Misleading, inaccurate or unsubstantiated statements made in documents or to the media must be publicly corrected immediately.
- Actions during the course of an offer by the target company which might frustrate the offer are generally prohibited unless shareholders approve these plans.
- Stringent requirements are laid down for the disclosure of dealings in relevant securities during an offer.

Employees of both the offeror and the offeree must be informed about an offer and the employee representatives of the offeree have the right to have a separate opinion on the effects of the offer on employment appended to the offeree board's circular.

The Takeover Code must be followed to the letter and also observed in its intent. This "text" provides a framing context for tools and talk. The end-of-book case study on the hostile takeover of Blue Circle by Lafarge illustrates the important framing effects for the unfolding of the battle and the activities of the protagonists.

Tools consist of techniques, concepts, models and language. They are a primary means by which the demands of "text" are conceptualized and operationalized. Such "tools" serve to potentialize and constrain the actions and activities of practitioners. They may also cause aspects of the "text" to be revisited. A new financial technique, for instance, may require adjustments to legislation and monitoring procedures. There may also be circumstances where the "text" alters conditions to discourage the use of certain tools and techniques. "Tools" potentialize the ability of practitioners to act and craft a deal. They also limit their activities by framing the ways in which they perceive M&A.

MINI CASE: TOOLS INFLUENCING TEXT

In 1989 there was a very acrimonious takeover battle between the Swiss food giants, Jacob Suchard and Nestlé for control of the UK confectionery company, Rowntree. Before the first bid, Rowntree's shares were trading at £4.77 but by the end of the battle, Nestlé ultimately

(Continued)

(Continued)

paid £10.75 per share. It was widely suggested that the gap between Rowntree value in the UK equity market and what it was worth to Nestlé, was mainly the value of its brands that included Kit-Kat, Quality Street, After Eight, Polo, and Yorkie. These were undisclosed on Rowntree's balance sheet and so undervalued by stock market analysts. It was very evident in Rowntree's defence that it was aware of the great value of its brands but the conventions of the day meant they were not included in the balance sheet. In response to this deal, many other UK companies began to put a value for their brands on their balance sheets and put pressure upon the ASC to change its rules. The argument was that non-recognition of brands by UK companies meant these businesses were systematically undervalued and available "on the cheap" for overseas acquirers. In 1989 Rank Hovis McDougall managed to defend itself successfully from a hostile bid by carrying out an off-balance sheet brand evaluation exercise that greatly increased the perceived value of the company. Grand Metropolitan announced it would be recording the value of all brands it subsequently acquired in its balance beginning September 1988. It would also apply this retrospectively, for the previous three years, leading to £500m being added to the value of the balance sheet. These events made the issue of the valuation of intangibles on the balance sheet the major topic for the Accounting Standards Committee (ASC) to consider in December 1989 and, in the light of these developments, they began to change their position.

Source: Rutherford (2007).

Talk is about the actions, activities, and narratives involved as practitioners enact M&A. What practitioners talk about, and focus upon, is influenced by the tools they use. In facing unusual situations practitioners may need to be creative and adaptive or develop tools for their own purposes. Practitioner's "talk" is also influenced by the societal context in which they are located, which privileges some information and activities over others. However, practitioners through innovative activities may also influence the "text" and cause adjustment to what is legitimate and possible. Through practitioner actions and activities the strategic "text," and its "tools," may be subverted, mastered, or transformed.

MINI CASE: PRACTITIONERS' "TALK"

In 1998 Sir Richard Sykes of Glaxo Welcome and Jan Leschley of SmithKline Beecham disagreed over the merger of their two giant pharmaceutical companies. Although this was dressed up as a clash about cultures and structure, it was clear they could not agree on who would get the top jobs. Jan Leschley retired two years later and the merger was then concluded.

PRACTICING STRATEGY ACROSS FIRMS: INSIGHTS FROM M&As

> **MINI CASE: "TALK" INTERACTS WITH "TEXT"**
>
> In June 2004, Bill Harrison, CEO of JP Morgan Chase (JPM) and Jamie Dimon, CEO of Bank One celebrated the completion of their friendly $58bn merger. At that point Milberg Weiss, a leading class action law firm, served a lawsuit, claiming Harrison could have paid $7bn less if Dimon had been given the top job of the combined group immediately. It was suggested that Dimon was saying, "the sooner I get the job, the less you have to pay." Harrison, however, was determined to stay on, to steer the merger. The agreement for him to remain for two years led to JPM paying a premium of 14% to the market price – $7bn. Who gets the key job is a key issue in M&A negotiations and raises the question of who the companies are run for.

At the core of the model is *practice* as an intimate interplay between text, tools, and talk. This allows the practice of M&A to show routine as much as innovation, structure as much as restructuring, acceptance as much as resistance. In the consumption of M&A through practice there is potential for reconstitution, resistance or innovation at multiple levels of activity. The practitioner actively interprets, criticizes, learns, and experiments with the implications of M&A initiatives.

Although the La Ville and Mounoud (2003) orientation is toward middle managers embedded within a focal organization, this ignores the critical role of other practitioners in M&A, such as top managers. They are also enmeshed in a series of opposing forces, both internal and external to the firm, and are part of the unfolding of strategic initiatives forged by complex stakeholder pressures. "M&A as practice" focuses on the interaction between discourses of "grand-strategy" and "everyday actions." Top managers stand at a pivotal point between the macro-drivers of context and shifting coalitions of interests in organizations. The La Ville and Mounoud (2003) framework also focuses on just one organization. However, by definition in M&A, two organizations at a minimum are involved, which adds an additional layer of complexity to the "M&A as practice" approach.

MINI CASE

10.3 The merging companies are located in a very fragmented, declining European industry. Industry consolidation is attractive to address overcapacity in the industry and the growing strength of supplier and customer bargaining power.

The protagonists

The two merging companies are pure players in the same industry. Company A has a fully integrated process, with a strategic emphasis on cost efficiency: "We must continually improve our cost efficiency." "We aspire to achieve the best productivity in the world." Despite being able to increase capacity substantially, it was doubtful pre-merger whether Company A had sufficient marketing resources to fully utilize the new capacity. Company B has traditionally struggled against larger plants because its investment in efficiencies was inadequate and incremental cost reductions insufficient to keep its unit costs competitive. However, Company B did possess a number of attractive niche products and an extensive distribution network. Its approach to sales was to sell direct to users, which is people intensive. The business employed nearly three times the number of Company A.

The deal

The deal was planned during record levels of M&A activity. The strong stock market supported investor enthusiasm for consolidation mergers in industrial sectors and cross-border M&A. Working closely with investment banks, lawyers, and accounting firms, both companies had frequent meetings to hammer out the terms of the deal. Attention focused on the merger document as the primary means of addressing key issues necessary to win approval from institutions. From the announcement to the merger completion, both management teams also embarked on a communications campaign, arguing why the merger was a good deal: "The strategic and synergistic fit of the two companies is excellent, and our intention is to deliver to our shareholders the inherent value in a focused … company" (CEO, Company A). "The merger combines the cost leadership position of Company A with the wide product range and extensive distribution network of Company B to create further opportunities in the fast-growing markets" (CEO, Company B).

Anticipated benefits of the merger

The merger prospectus identified synergies of €100m+ per annum to be realized in two years. They included:

1 *Production economies of scale* – through volume consolidation.
2 *Market power* – by becoming the dominant producer in the market, potentially giving market control and higher margins.
3 *Administrative savings* – efficiencies in sales, distribution, purchasing and R&D.
4 *Financial savings* – capital investment sharing in this capital-intensive industry is helped by reducing duplicate investments.

Post-acquisition approach

The top management used the post-acquisition process framework by Angwin (2000) to identify their integration approach as *subjugation*, with consolidations across the group replacing business unit idiosyncrasies with centralized control. They aimed for "overnight" change in business identity through excellent communications to convey the strategic vision to internal and external stakeholders. Teams were set up immediately to plan and implement integration in depth in all major functional areas, as well as addressing cross-functional issues such as corporate and national cultural compatibility. High levels of meticulous planning would be necessary to cope with the complexity of this integration style and the speed with which changes would need to be made, but there was no evidence of any detailed post-merger plan at the beginning of the post-merger integration phase.

Post-merger activities

Very early attention was paid to the new identity of the business so that the first action of ownership would be the rolling out of the new image. A new logo was launched; videos were distributed; brochures, flags, stationery were all coordinated with launch-day presentations. This was a massive task and was achieved with military precision. The positive effect on employees was tangible. After this flurry of activity, communications quickly became a single medium, through the company intranet.

As a merger, implicit in the agreement was a balance in top management posts. The CEO and four top executives were from Company A and five top executives from Company B. On day seven of the merger, the senior executive in charge of sales and marketing, drawn from Company B, left unexpectedly and was replaced by a more junior non-commercial executive from Company A. The consequences were no commercial voice on the executive committee, despite being a key strategic area for the new group, a dramatic increase in workload for the new appointee, who was also keeping his other responsibilities, the loss of tacit knowledge about how Company B operated in this, their core area of expertise, and the altering of the balance of power at the executive level.

In the production area, executive management preferred appointing younger managers to production units. Two new managers of production units were appointed but both subsequently left along with another manager from a different unit. These changes hindered executive management in gaining control and being able to make any changes to these units.

Rationalizing sales/distribution required the amalgamation of sales offices across Europe. While early actions in this respect seemed coherent, implementation was more difficult in some geographic areas than others. In Sweden, amalgamation was accomplished in less than 70 days, and in Italy not at all. In Sweden, merging the offices proved straightforward, as Company A's presence had been small and its MD was happy to take a less prestigious position in a larger unit. In his view: "titles are meaningless and I am too old to worry about such things." He was able to maintain the motivation of his employees and the two business units had developed a good relationship over time and found working together straightforward.

In Germany, the largest market in Europe, Company B's unit being in the midst of substantial reorganization, complicated the merger. There was clear evidence the new approach was working but the manager was becoming frustrated as new management was questioning his reorganization. This led to significant uncertainty among employees. The support for the reorganization model had been from the senior executive who had left seven days after the merger. The German manager was now reporting to the senior executive appointment who was so busy that, in effect, he was reporting to a regional manager. This signified a loss of prestige and made the German manager more remote from a key decision maker. In addition, the regional manager style was from the power culture of Company A, where it was the norm to give instructions and expect them to be followed, whereas the German manager was from Company B, where there was a more person-oriented culture and dialogue was the norm. To add to his frustration, towards the end of the first 100 days, senior executives visited him to insist he find ways to reduce his costs by 30%. This had become an unexpected priority of top management, who realized that cost reduction in sales was easier than elsewhere in the group.

In Italy, with the second largest market in Europe, the two operations from both companies were of comparable size. The managers could see the advantages of combining their operations and simplifying their supply arrangement. However, they were told not to take any actions. Initially this was met with disappointment but after three months this disappointment turned to bitter criticism of top management. There had been poor communication and there was no clear information on plans for the future. There was considerable uncertainty amongst employees and key staffs were considering their positions.

In addition to rationalizing sales businesses, it was intended to streamline vertically through the production to sales process. This would reduce what was perceived as an unacceptable cost of administration. Wherever possible, standard product should be supplied direct to market. Additional processing and stockholding activities would have to focus on more value added activities and act as true profit centers. The model (shown in Figure 10.3) was presented on day 10 of the merger and issued as a formal document on day 31.

Large numbers of employees in the sales companies were worried, understandably, and many questioned the logic. One of the strengths brought by Company B to the merger was the market power provided by being close to the customer. This network allowed the company to penetrate most of the main markets and took away some of the power of large stockists. Moving towards the proposed model would mean greater reliance on independent stockists as well as losing proximity to customers. The model showed management intended to move towards Company A's "lean and simple" production-led approach. It sent the message that cost efficiency was king. The problem for Company B was that it was a complex organization of multiple production units, with local invoicing and credit controls. Managing directors in the countries understood the new model, but couldn't see how it could be implemented without very serious change, particularly in information technology.

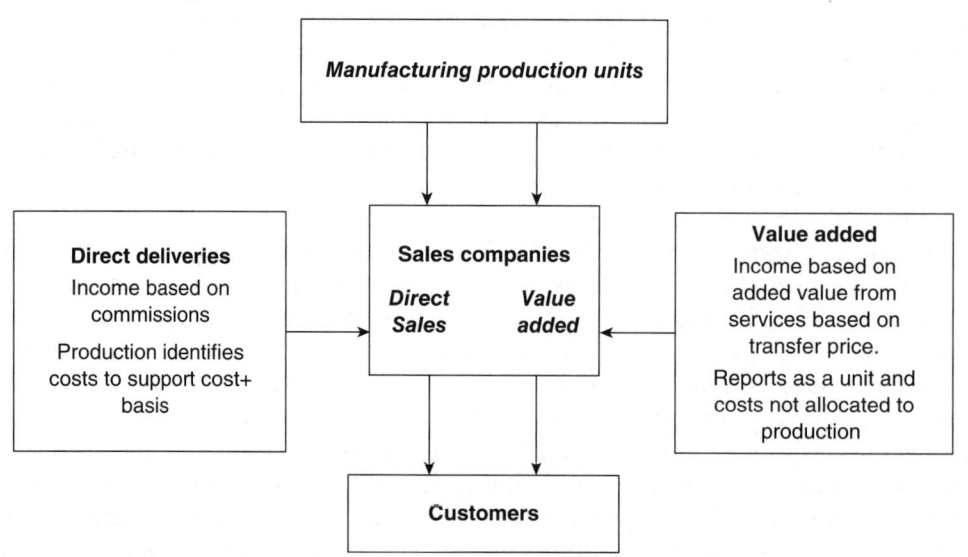

FIGURE 10.3 Path of actions for de-duplicating sales/distribution and presenting a unified face to market

Establishing financial control

Day 1 of the merger, the chief financial officer's message was to control finance while there was high capital spend on production. Fifty-two days into the merger, all unit managers were instructed to prepare and update the year's forecast as well as prepare a five-year plan within a month. This instruction was greeted differently around the group. The Italian managing director felt he couldn't see six months ahead, let alone five years, whereas his Swedish counterpart saw it as an opportunity to put forward his growth intentions. This request had a heavy impact on management time when significant changes were expected. In the words of one manager: "the 5-year plan work has detracted from the daily operational change and may have slowed the pace in the first 100 days." The wisdom of requesting such a plan has also to be questioned because it assumed autonomous units when the situation was for many units to move towards merging.

Integrating information technology (IT)

The most problematic area was integrating IT. Only two actions were taken to address this. One, a study detailing its complexity was presented after 55 days and revealed there were 450 different computer systems in operation, costing around €65m per annum. Senior management realized this was a large project, but underestimated significantly its complexity.

Local management was reluctant to authorize further expenditure on IT without being clear on the company vision for IT. Even the smallest changes met with strong resistance. For instance, throughout the 100-day period there were debates on which e-mail system to use and no agreement was reached. Getting information from this vast range of systems was also problematic and top management found it incredibly difficult to operate without coherent information in a common format.

Areas of inaction

Company A and B are in the same industry but are headquartered in different countries and are organized differently. They differ in national and corporate cultures and yet no actions were taken to manage culture shift. They were also organized very differently and had quite different values about how to operate in this industry. No actions were taken to make these differences explicit or to manage some form of transition.

While a great deal of information was transmitted to the employees over the 100 days, at the end of the period an internal review concluded that communications had not been very good. The dominant channel for disseminating information was the company intranet, but only 65% of employees had access on their own desks. In a group survey, 62% of employees felt the intranet was not good enough. In addition, information was not well controlled with any senior person apparently acting as editor. As a consequence, unit managers often found themselves unprepared for questions from staff. In one instance an analyst's report from a major bank had been included, which predicted the closure of a major manufacturing facility! The communication was also one-way with the exception of an interactive part of the website. Only six questions were registered from a workforce of 16,000! Having had their review, it is surprising that actions were not taken to improve communications.

Merger review

After one year, a formal update of merger synergies was presented. Expectations for the first year had been revised down 60%. Sales and marketing savings showed the biggest variance, being scaled down 70%. The sales operational model remained the favored way of operating but had still not been implemented 18 months post-merger. This simpler, lower cost method of operation was not achieved, computer systems had not been changed and there were important markets where management had still not addressed the issue of more than one channel to market. Nevertheless sizeable cost reductions were still demanded. This led to game playing among sales company managers in working with commodity-producing units for greater savings and neglecting non-commodity units. The non-commodity units were beginning to realize they could no longer expect the same level of market-based resources to sell their volumes or promote new products.

Lack of strategic direction for manufacturing unit product programmes continued. Eighteen months post-merger, managing directors of production plants presented their current and intended programmes to sales company executives. There was an obvious overlap of current programmes, with different plants targeting the same market segments. In the words of the group marketing manager: "I now see that I can get product A from at least two producers and I can get product B from everywhere!"

This continued lack of clarity, and top management not acting decisively, allowed production units to continue to develop their own programmes. This was contrary, and detrimental, to achieving better economies of scale.

IT continued to be a difficult issue post-merger. The complexities and the cost of changing major systems led to existing systems being maintained. In fact, some system changes intended prior to the merger were reviewed and a number of plans were either put on hold or scrapped. Management directed its attention to conserving cash. If there was no urgency to modify or change systems, they favored maintaining the status quo. This made it more difficult to integrate the company and left sales companies having to work in a number of different systems when they loaded orders remotely onto individual manufacturing centers.

Face-to-face communication between management and employees deteriorated as the cost pressures began to build. Travel restrictions were imposed and visits, between sites, reduced. The intranet continued to be the main distribution channel for information.

The macro-context had also deteriorated. At the merger, European consumption was forecast to grow at 5.5% but the reality was an unexpected fall of 6.3%. Variation in raw material prices also had the effect of reducing inclusive prices by 10%. This led to lower prices in the market and under-loading of plants during the summer months. Management was forced to issue a profit warning for third-quarter results and pressure for cost reduction throughout the business intensified.

The deteriorating business situation caused management to bring in a number of unintended measures, aimed at stemming cash flow from the business: "The Group is far away from the cash position in the original business plan." Initiatives to generate cash internally from reductions in work in progress or finished goods stocks became a priority. Large-scale investments were on hold for at least three years and there was increased possibility of plant closures and divestment of non-core activities. Forecasts for future synergies were optimistic but as the merger integration manager remarked: "Synergies are often forgotten after two years of a merger." The difficulties in realizing fundamental synergies raised serious questions about the shape of the future organization and the stock market down-rated their shares.

At this time the deputy CEO announced he was leaving, despite his insistence, at the merger launch seminar that he was "on board" for the long term. His replacement came from Company A, further swaying the balance of top executives. It then became known that the firm's largest two competitors were to merge and then, shortly afterwards, the company itself received a takeover bid, which was ultimately successful.

Questions

1 Using the "strategy-as-practice" framework outlined in this chapter, explain why this merger was able to take place.
2 Using the same framework, examine the post-acquisition integration phase and explain why this process failed to achieve its stated intentions.
3 What can be learned about the coherence of the "strategy-as-practice" framework throughout the M&A process in this case?

CONCLUSION

10.4 A strategy-as-practice approach to M&A has the advantages of allowing examination of interactions between actors across organizational and sub-organizational boundaries and allows for a dynamic interpretation of M&A – to recognize process. The mini case study illustrates disconnection between pre-merger intentions and post-merger actions, a classic divide in the study of M&A (Angwin, 2000; Gomes et al., 2012a), and this can be harmful to the merger process (Angwin and Vaara, 2005). This concept of "strategic disconnect" is more fully explored in Angwin et al. (2015). The strategy-as-practice framework, adopted in this chapter, goes some way to cross this divide and provide some explanation for process failure – in particular it highlights the failure of linkages between "text," "tools," and "talk" to accommodate tensions. It also raises important questions: if the majority of intended changes did not make sense on the ground, then why was the merger proposed, and accepted, on this basis? This focuses attention on how firms interface with institutions and the mechanisms of persuasion and argumentation that might be used. The tools employed to implement the merger were clearly too broad for purpose. How might these have been adjusted and customized? Indeed, there is clearly a need for new tools to handle more complex post-merger integrations. There is evidence of practitioner activities that were commercially sensible and innovative in avoiding the simplistic and, in some cases, erroneous prescriptions of "tools." Why were some of these activities not anticipated? Why was innovation ignored, with no feedback into post-merger plans and conceptualizations? In what ways can practitioners be involved in the production of text in such a way that alignment may be improved? If reconstitution of the strategic text is more the norm than the exception in mergers, why are there few mechanisms for this to feedback into "text?"

M&A as practice perspective, as articulated in this chapter, shows through the mini case how links between what practitioners do and multiple contexts over time can explain strategic outcome. Reflexivity is apparent as a continuous, fluid, interaction between multiple levels, between macro-environment and micro-contexts. This highlights the translation difficulties and tensions between universal high-level strategy and multifaceted micro-contexts. The advantage of the M&A as practice approach is to extend the insights of the process school from the organizational to the micro-levels as well as to reconnect with outcomes. A practice perspective can show how broad strategic intents for certain merger results can be mutated through the complexity and variance of micro-contexts to achieve different outcomes (Angwin, 2004). The more holistic approach of M&A as practice helps to cross the harmful divide between content and process (Pettigrew, 1992; Rumelt et al., 1994), between M&A formulation and integration, and can provide a richer explanation for merger outcome than is current in the literature. In particular, it draws attention to dynamic interconnections over time across multiple levels of analysis and these may connect, disconnect, and reconnect over time to shape strategic outcome. These insights also apply to other forms of strategic expansion such as strategic alliances including outsourcing, franchising, and joint ventures. The framework articulated in this chapter can help focus attention, in these others forms of strategic renewal, upon how strategy practice(s) occur in fluid interplay between contexts, affecting organizational outcomes.

REVISION ACTIVITIES

Identify a merger or acquisition in the news and identify the text, tools, and talk involved. Critically evaluate the extent to which you believe these elements interact positively or negatively with each other. Based on this analysis, what is your prognosis for the future of this deal?

FURTHER READINGS

- **Book**: Angwin, D. N. (2007) *Mergers and Acquisitions*. Oxford: Wiley/Blackwell. Offers an in-depth understanding of the M&A phenomenon using a multi-disciplinary approach.

    Papers:
- Angwin, D. N., Paroutis, S., and Connell, R. (2015) Why good things don't happen: The micro-foundations of routines in the M&A process. *Journal of Business Research*, 68(6): 1367–81.
- Angwin, D. N. and Meadows, M. (2014) New integration strategies for post acquisition management. *Long Range Planning*, 48(4), August: 235–51. DOI: 10.1016/j.lrp.2014.04.001.
- Angwin, D. N., Mellahi, K., Gomes, E., and Peters, E. (2014) How communication approaches impact mergers and acquisitions outcomes. *International Journal of Human Resource Management*, published online. Available at: http://dx.doi.org/10.1080/09585192.2014.985330.
- Teerikangas, S., Very, P., and Pisano, V. (2011) Integration managers' value-capturing roles and acquisition performance. *Human Resource Management*, 50(5): 651–83.

These papers provide further insights into the actors and their practices in the M&A process and their interplay with contextual pressures.

- **Paper**: Clark, S. M., Gioia, D. A., Ketchen, D. J., and Thomas, J. B. (2010) Transitional identity as a facilitator of organizational identity change during a merger. *Administrative Science Quarterly*, 55(3): 397–438. An elaborate investigation of how two top management teams' identities changed during the initial phases of a merger between two formerly rival healthcare organizations; identifies the emergence of a transitional identity by practitioners (an interim sense about what their organizations were becoming); and offers a process model of organizational identity change during a merger.

- **Paper**: Larsson, R. and Finkelstein, S. (1999) Integrating strategic, organizational, and human resource perspectives on mergers and acquisitions: a case survey of synergy realization. *Organization Science*, 10(1): 1–26. Offers a process model that describes how synergy realization is a function of the similarity and complementarity of the two merging businesses (combination potential), the extent of interaction and coordination during the organizational integration process, and the lack of employee resistance to the combined entity.

- **Paper**: Maguire, S. and Phillips, N. (2008) Citibankers at Citigroup: a study of the loss of institutional trust after a merger. *Journal of Management Studies*, 45: 372–401. Presents the loss of trust among a group of employees at Citigroup after its creation through the merger of Citicorp and Travelers, and shows how issues of organizational identity and identification processes can result in the loss of institutional trust in a post-merger context.

REFERENCES

Angwin, D. N. (2000) *Implementing Successful Post-Acquisition Management*. Harlow: Financial Times/Prentice Hall.

Angwin, D. N. (2001) Mergers and acquisitions across European borders: National perspectives on pre-acquisition due diligence and the use of professional advisers. *Journal of World Business*, 36(1): 32–57.

Angwin, D. N. (2004) Speed in M&A integration: The first 100 days. *European Management Journal*, 22(4): 418–30.

Angwin, D. N. (2007) *Mergers and Acquisitions*. Oxford: Blackwell/Wiley.

Angwin, D. N. (2012) Typologies in M&A research. In D. Faulkner, S. Teerikangas, and R. Joseph (eds.), *Oxford Handbook of Mergers and Acquisitions*. Oxford: Oxford University Press, Chapter 3.

Angwin, D. N. and Meadows, M. (2009) The choice of insider or outsider top executives in acquired companies. *Long Range Planning*, 37: 239–57.

Angwin, D. N. and Vaara, E. (eds.) (2005) Connectivity in merging organizations. *Organization Studies*, special issue, 26(10): 1447–635.

Angwin, D. N., Paroutis, S., and Connell, R. (2015) Why good things don't happen: The micro-foundations of routines in the M&A process. *Journal of Business Research*, 68(6): 1367–81.

Angwin, D. N., Stern, P., and Bradley, S. (2004) The target CEO in a hostile takeover: Agency or stewardship – can the condemned agent be redeemed? *Long Range Planning*, 37(3): 239–57.

Bower, J. L. (2004) When we study M&A, what are we learning? In A. Pablo and M. Javidan (eds.), *Mergers and Acquisitions: Creating Integrative Knowledge*. Oxford: Strategic Management Society/Blackwell, Chapter 13.

Gomes, E., Angwin, D.N., Weber, Y., and Tarba, S. (2012a) Critical success factors through the Mergers and Acquisitions process: Revealing pre- and post-M&A connections for improved performance. *Thunderbird International Business Review*. Wiley, 55(1), Jan/Feb: 13–35.

Gomes, E., Angwin, D.N., and Melahi, K. (2012b) HRM practices throughout the Mergers and Acquisition (M&A) process: A study of domestic deals in the Nigerian banking industry. *International Journal of Human Resource Management*, 23(14): 2874–900.

Grant, R. (2002) Corporate strategy: Managing scope and strategy content. In A. Pettigrew, H. Thomas, and R. Whittington (eds.), *Handbook of Strategy and Management*. London: Sage.

Javidan, M., Pablo, A., Singh, H., Hitt, M., and Jemison, D. (2004) Where we've been and where we're going. In A. Pablo and M. Javidan (eds.), *Mergers and Acquisitions: Creating Integrative Knowledge*. Oxford: Strategic Management Society/Blackwell, Chapter 14.

Johnson, G., Melin, L., and Whittington, R. (2003) Micro strategy and strategizing: Towards an activity-based view. *Journal of Management Studies*, 40(1): 1–22.

La Ville, V. and Mounoud, E. (2003) What do we mean by "Strategy as Practice?" In B. Czarniawska and P. Gagliardi (eds.), *Between Discourse and Narration: How Can Strategy Be a Practice?* Amsterdam: John Benjamins.

Meglio, O. and Risberg, A. (2010) Mergers and Acquisitions – Time for a methodological rejuvenation of the field? *Scandinavian Journal of Management*, 26(1): 87–95.

Pettigrew, A. M. (1992) The character and significance of strategy process research. *Strategic Management Journal*, 13: 5–16.

Rumelt, R., Schendel, D., and Teece, D. J. (1994) Fundamental issues in strategy. In R. Rumelt et al. (eds.), *Fundamental Issues in Strategy*. Boston, MA: Harvard Business School Press.

Rutherford, B. A. (2007) *Financial Reporting in the UK: A History of the Accounting Standards Committee, 1969–1990*. Routledge Historical Perspectives in Accounting. Abingdon: Routledge.

Whittington, R. (2002) Practice perspectives on strategy: Unifying and developing a field. *Academy of Management Best Paper Proceedings*, Denver, CO.

STRATEGIC AMBIDEXTERITY: DEALING WITH TENSIONS

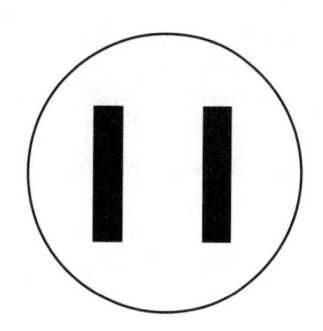

11

Learning Objectives

- Appreciate the nature of strategic ambidexterity and how it supports efforts of organizations and their managers to deal with contradictory tensions.
- Explore the processes through which strategic ambidexterity can be achieved.
- Understand the practices and actions that practitioners can adopt to enhance their firm's strategic ambidexterity.

ORGANIZATIONAL AMBIDEXTERITY

11.1 Given the tensions on strategy practitioners and their organizations to gain competitive advantage in increasingly turbulent and competitive markets, the concept of ambidexterity has been gaining ground (Birkinshaw and Gibson, 2004; Raisch and Birkinshaw, 2008; Simsek, 2009). Organizational ambidexterity as a term was first used by Duncan (1976), who proposed that dual structures should be formed within an organization so as to support the initiation and the execution phases of an innovation. These phases are sequential in accordance with the innovation cycle, a concept adopted in ambidexterity research as "temporal sequencing" (O'Reilly and Tushman, 2008). Wider interest in the concept of ambidexterity, however, is primarily due to March's (1991) seminal article on exploration and exploitation processes of organizational learning. March described exploration and exploitation as two fundamentally different activities, whereby exploitation refers to "refinement, efficiency, selection and implementation" and exploration refers to "search, variation, experimentation and innovation" (1991: 71).

The two processes are regarded as incompatible, leading to organizational tensions as both compete for scarce resources and entail different capabilities within the organization. Experimenting and exploring is more time consuming, entails uncertain results, and has a longer time horizon than refining current knowledge and extending current competencies; yet March (1991) underlines the need for a balance between the two, for superior organizational performance. Research on ambidextrous organizations has shown that the pursuit of both exploration and exploitation (through structural or temporal separation) is indeed both feasible and beneficial to organizational performance (He and Wong, 2004; O'Reilly and Tushman, 2004).

Firms overemphasizing exploration or exploitation, however, risk getting caught in failure traps or success traps respectively (Levinthal and March, 1993). Cameron and Quinn (1988) refer to this process of negatively reinforcing cycles as unproductive schismogenesis; a process of self-reinforcement where "one action or attribute perpetuates itself until it becomes extreme and therefore dysfunctional" (1988: 6).

Ambidexterity research has challenged established notions, for example the idea supported by traditional research in strategy, that attempting to pursue both differentiation and cost-leadership strategies results in firms being "stuck in the middle" (Porter, 1980), becoming mediocre in both exploration and exploitation (Ghemawat and Costa, 1993; O'Reilly and Tushman, 2008). Recent strategy research has advocated dual business models (Markides and Oyon, 2010) as a way for firms to simultaneously pursue different strategies, balance exploration and exploitation, and accomplish strategic ambidexterity (Judge and Blocker, 2008; Voss & Voss, 2013). The mini case below showcases some of the challenges faced by firms undertaking simultaneously exploration and exploitation activities. Twitter is based on a simple model that the firm needs to keep pushing into new markets and users – critically to also get current users to use their service even more (exploitation). At the same time, it needs to explore ways to keep updating/refreshing the service and to make their model more accessible to the advertising community in ways that taps into their userbase (exploration).

MINI CASE: TWITTER – SIMPLICITY AS A BUSINESS MODEL FOR USERS, AND THE MARKET TOO

In October 2013, a few days before Twitter's IPO, there are still question marks about the uniqueness of their business model. But the social media giant remains in a slightly odd position: its revenues in the first half of 2013 more than doubled that of the equivalent period last year, and yet its net losses have also increased.

What makes such a company so attractive? One of the key reasons is that markets and investors are more clued up about social media companies than even a year or two ago. Twitter may have a unique business model, but without the confidence of business investors, this IPO would be pointless. And the expected confidence in Twitter is only apparent, as investors have learned from its great rival: Facebook. Investors now also have more experience in dealing with business models released by social media companies. Gauging the future growth potential of any one social media brand was considered a lottery not so long ago; as the industry matures, it is becoming increasingly easier to predict.

Twitter describes its platform as "unique in its simplicity," This statement distills the fundamental business model of the firm and explains why analysts are still predicting further growth. Stemming from its roots as an SMS-based messaging system, the limit of 140 characters per tweet means that it is relatively easy to attract new users while keeping current users actively engaged. The relatively low-bandwidth, short messages also puts less pressure on internet and mobile phone networks, which allows for a more reliable and integrated experience for users across various platforms and geographical locations.

Fast forward to May 2015, and Twitter's share price took a US$8 billion tumble after their results were leaked early, prior to market closure – ironically through a tweet. The social networking site posted results showing revenue had risen 74% to US$436m but it missed analysts' expectations of US$456.2m. It has now lowered its 2015 full-year expectations.

Finally, the simplicity of the platform has allowed the firm to offer a set of reliable and non-complicated products for platform partners (twitter cards, twitter for websites, special development tools) and advertisers (promoted tweets, promoted accounts, and promoted trends). On one level, Twitter's business model is working. The social media platform is attracting more users than ever before. The number of monthly active users is up and breaking the 300m barrier for the first time. It also informs a large number of media reports. So there is room for optimism, in spite of its latest disappointing revenue figures.

But the company must convince advertisers and investors that its business model can deliver long-term value for them. This is done through a mix of keeping the active number of users high and finding ways to monetize its offering. To do so, Twitter has a strategy that is in the right direction: strengthening its core offering, reducing barriers to consumption, and delivering new apps and services. Advances across these three areas have helped Twitter deliver growth in its revenues and user-base: mobile, international, and ad engagements.

New services, acquisitions, and partnerships can take time to deliver results. And while they might keep users happy, the question is: are investors willing to give Twitter the time? The latest stock performance might suggest otherwise, but the company's strategy is one worth investing in.

Source: Paroutis (2013, 2015).

INDIVIDUAL-LEVEL AMBIDEXTERITY

11.2 Individual-level studies are based on the assumption that ambidextrous organizations need ambidextrous individuals who are able to understand and be sensitive to the demands of both exploration and exploitation practices (O'Reilly and Tushman, 2004). Lassen et al. (2009), for example, underline the key role of middle managers in pursuing both market exploitation and technological innovation through what they call "dual management" (p. 22); the ability to balance planned and emergent activities and reconcile market and technological understandings. As these activities demand constant social negotiation within the organization, the importance of incentives and opportunities for managers to engage in dual management is underlined, highlighting the need for both structural and sociocultural solutions.

Mom et al. (2007) also focus on the individual manager level of analysis to examine bottom-up, top-down, and horizontal knowledge inflows in relation to managers' exploration and exploitation activities. They find that exploration and exploitation activities are complementary as well as simultaneous; top-down knowledge inflows enhance exploitation activities whereas bottom-up and horizontal inflows enhance exploration activities. In a similar vein, Mom et al. (2009) define ambidextrous managers as multi-taskers, able to host contradictions, and refine and renew their knowledge, skills, and expertise. Eisenhardt et al. (2010) finally explore how leaders balance efficiency and flexibility through high-order thinking and expertise. They suggest that by the means of abstraction, cognitive variety, and work interruptions that are nevertheless inherently flexible and efficient, managers use simple, cognitive solutions to address the complex tensions of exploration and exploitation.

A PARADOX-BASED APPROACH

11.3 A paradox is literally a contention that is beyond belief, in the sense of being counter to ordinary expectations (Rescher, 2001: 3). Paradoxes are defined as "contradictory yet interrelated elements that seem logical in isolation but absurd and irrational when appearing simultaneously" (Lewis, 2000: 760). Paradox was introduced as a framework to deal with the inherent complexity of organizational life by Cameron and Quinn (1988). It is now recognized that organizations are constituted at the core by embedded paradoxes such as autonomy and control, collective action and individual interests, continuity and change, closed and open systems, and deliberate and emergent management (Bouchikhi, 1998; Lewis and Smith, 2014).

Using a paradox perspective, Smith and Lewis (2011) identify four categories of paradoxes within organizations: paradoxes of learning (based on the tensions created between the old and the new); paradoxes of organizing (based on the diverging forces for control and flexibility); paradoxes of belonging (stemming from the tension between the self and the other within an organizational context); and last, paradoxes of performing (stemming from the plurality of goals from internal and external stakeholders). The tensions arising represent core organizational activities (knowledge, interpersonal relationships, processes, and goals) and occur not only within each category, but also at their intersections and across organizational levels. Further research on organizational paradoxes has addressed a variety of themes including the tensions of continuity and change in the face of radical change (Huy, 2002), contradictions of collaboration and control in corporate governance (Sundaramurthy and Lewis, 2003), and tensions of committing to multiple strategic goals (Jarzabkowski and Sillince, 2007). The memo below by Stephen Elop, sent to his employees at Nokia from his post as CEO, highlights a number of tensions Nokia was facing internally and externally. The construction and consumption of the particular memo demonstrates how the particular CEO identified and communicated the challenging tensions his firm was dealing with, as a way to then mobilize his employees to face this reality and start developing appropriate initiatives and processes in response. These tensions internally materialized across the choices the firm had between being a volume leader (exploiting) and keep innovating (exploring). These are also evident in the internal tensions between the software and hardware division – each one of them was focusing on targets that were not always

STRATEGIC AMBIDEXTERITY

coordinated or compatible. Hence, the engineering capability that Nokia handsets were known for, generated by the hardware division, were indeed matched with the easy-to-follow layout of the menus, generated by the software division. As new players came into the market and as new mobile users became increasingly interested in content rather than functionality, Nokia was left behind as hardware capability was not enough to keep them competitive.

MINI CASE: NOKIA – THE BURNING PLATFORM MEMO

Stephen Elop was named the new President and CEO of Nokia on September 21, 2010. At the time Nokia was facing increasing competition from Samsung, Apple, HTC, and RIM and also declining market share in the smartphone and feature mobile (cell) phone segments. A few months after his appointment, Elop sent a memo to all Nokia employees. The following are some indicative extracts:

> There is a pertinent story about a man who was working on an oil platform in the North Sea. He woke up one night from a loud explosion, which suddenly set his entire oil platform on fire. In mere moments, he was surrounded by flames. Through the smoke and heat, he barely made his way out of the chaos to the platform's edge. When he looked down over the edge, all he could see were the dark, cold, foreboding North Sea waters. As the fire approached him, the man had mere seconds to react. He could stand on the platform, and inevitably be consumed by the burning flames. Or, he could plunge 30 meters in to the freezing waters. The man was standing upon a "burning platform," and he needed to make a choice. He decided to jump. It was unexpected. In ordinary circumstances, the man would never consider plunging into icy waters. But these were not ordinary times – his platform was on fire. The man survived the fall and the waters. After he was rescued, he noted that a "burning platform" caused a radical change in his behavior. We too, are standing on a "burning platform," and we must decide how we are going to change our behavior.
>
> In 2008, Apple's market share in the $300+ price range was 25%; by 2010 it escalated to 61%. They are enjoying a tremendous growth trajectory with a 78% earnings growth year over year in Q4 2010. Apple demonstrated that if designed well, consumers would buy a high-priced phone with a great experience and developers would build applications. They changed the game, and today, Apple owns the high-end range.
>
> And then, there is Android. In about two years, Android created a platform that attracts application developers, service providers and hardware manufacturers. Android came in at the high-end, they are now winning the mid-range, and quickly they are going downstream to phones under €100. Google has become a gravitational force, drawing much of the industry's innovation to its core. The first iPhone shipped in 2007, and we still don't have a product that is close to their experience. Android came on the scene just over 2 years ago, and this week they took our leadership position in smartphone volumes. Unbelievable.
>
> This is what I have been trying to understand. I believe at least some of it has been due to our attitude inside Nokia. We poured gasoline on our own burning platform. I believe we have lacked accountability and leadership to align and direct the company through these disruptive times. We had a series of misses. We haven't been delivering innovation fast enough. We're not collaborating internally. Nokia, our platform is burning.

(Continued)

(Continued)

We are working on a path forward – a path to rebuild our market leadership. When we share the new strategy on February 11, it will be a huge effort to transform our company. But, I believe that together, we can face the challenges ahead of us. Together, we can choose to define our future. The burning platform, upon which the man found himself, caused the man to shift his behavior, and take a bold and brave step into an uncertain future. He was able to tell his story. Now, we have a great opportunity to do the same.

Elop moved to Macromedia's Web/IT department in 1998 before gradually shifting to the sales side, eventually heading up worldwide sales and operations as chief operating officer. Elop became Macromedia's CEO in January 2005. "His nickname was the General," said Chris Swenson, a software analyst at NPD Group Inc., who was an employee at Macromedia during Elop's tenure. "With his military-style flat-top haircut, Elop stuck out among the young, green-haired and pierced employees" at the San Francisco company, Swenson said. "Stephen is one of the most hard-charging, energetic guys I've ever met," said Umesh Ramakrishnan, vice chairman at Centreville, Va., executive search firm CTPartners, who has worked with Elop on career moves in the past. "He works 24/7. And he has an uncanny knack for predicting where the software market is headed."

Sources: *Computerworld*, *BusinessWeek*, www.engadget.com. Used with permission of Engadget.

STRATEGIC AMBIDEXTERITY: MANAGING PARADOXICAL DEMANDS

11.4 Discussions of how organizations can achieve ambidexterity are very much dependent on how ambidexterity is conceptualized, the level of analysis, and most importantly whether exploration and exploitation are considered competing or complementary aspects of the organizational phenomena in question (Papachroni et al. 2016). Following a paradoxical view of organizational ambidexterity as a firm's ability to be equally dexterous in different and often conflicting areas, aiming to synthesize or transcend polarities, enables us to move beyond the dominant separation-oriented prescriptions of the structural, contextual, and temporal, ambidexterity literature. Viewing exploration and exploitation activities not as mutually exclusive but as interwoven polarities, shifts management thinking from an either/or to both/and mindset.

At the core of paradox theory lies the acceptance of dualities of coexisting tensions, where no compromise or singular choice between them has to be made (Eisenhardt, 2000; Westenholz, 1993). The effective management of these tensions by senior leaders is based therefore on finding creative ways to engage both poles; capitalizing on the inherent pluralism within the duality (Knight and Paroutis, 2016; Smith, 2014). This process of managing paradox by shifting rigid dualities into more workable entities has often been referred to in the literature as synthesis or transcendence (Chahrazad et al., 2011; Chen, 2002; Lewis, 2000; Poole and Van De Ven, 1989).

An alternative framework for managing organizational paradoxes is proposed by Lewis (2000) as a means for managers to not only understand but also benefit from tensions created within the organization. In this context, working through paradox is based on immersion and exploration of paradox rather than suppressing its underlying tensions and requires actors to actively learn to cope with tensions and ambiguity. The paradox framework proposed by Lewis (2000) identifies the root causes of paradox, its underlying tensions, and how these are reinforced by actors' defensive reactions, when they try to deal with paradox. Lewis proposes three ways to identify paradoxes: the narrative way through the analysis of discourse (e.g., see Luscher et al., 2006); the psychodynamic way that involves working with actors to help both actors and researchers to recognize conflicts; and the multi-paradigm approach where different conceptual lenses are employed as sensitizing devices.

Andriopoulos and Lewis (2009) explore the exploration–exploitation innovation tensions in five product design companies. Through their study, the authors identify three innovation paradoxes: strategic intent (related to the tensions of profitability and creativity); customer orientation (related to the tensions of tight and loose relationship with the clients); and personal drivers (related to the tensions of discipline and passion). Consistent with the pursuit of synthesis as a way to deal with paradox, these tensions are addressed within these organizations through concepts and practices that combine these polarities; such as paradoxical vision, diversity in product portfolio, and a view of the employees as practical artists.

Recent research on how CEOs view and handle paradoxes (Fredberg, 2014) is consistent with the synthesis approach; CEOs recognize paradoxical goals and tensions as simultaneous, ongoing features of organizations, and find applied, ongoing solutions to them. Smith et al. (2010) also found that managing successfully a complex business model such as an ambidextrous organization, depends on leaders' ability to make dynamic decisions, build commitment to both overarching visions and agenda-specific goals, learn actively at multiple levels, and engage in conflict management.

In a similar vein, Beech et al. (2004) explore the approach of holding the paradox open in a study of an organization undergoing radical change. They use the theory of serious play as means to action that can enable actors to deal with paradoxes through expressing emotions, exploiting ambiguity, challenging rules, and experimenting with boundaries. In this study, the actors transcended the paradox created by the demands of organizational change that called for both centralized and decentralized services in the NHS, only to discover that new paradoxes emerged; pointing to paradox as an inherent feature of organizational life that is both the outcome and driver of change.

Table 11.1 below outlines the main approaches in the ambidexterity literature, their main assumptions with respect to the two types of activities involved, and their propositions for accomplishing ambidexterity. Paradox theory extends our conceptual arsenal by offering the assumption that the poles can be complementary and dynamically interrelated over time, and assuming that they are in a state of duality rather than a dualism, preserving the option of integration. Paradox theory also proposes that synthesis of the poles, or transcendence via reframing can take place and fosters the pursuit of organizational processes that can contribute to both poles of the paradox.

Achieving strategic ambidexterity requires an understanding of the pressures and tensions that practitioners face, which come in sharp relief at times, such as when organizational change is planned or implemented – for example, when dealing with the tension between top-down versus bottom-up change, internal organizational versus external strategic alignment, or between empowerment versus control. In such conditions, effective change agents know that the answer is not either/or, but both/and, with the goal of building up organizational and individual capacity

TABLE 11.1 Dominant approaches to ambidexterity and paradox theory.

Dominant approach	Fundamental assumption	How to manage tensions	Key proposition
Structural ambidexterity	Contradictory poles, dualisms	Spatial separation	Institute separate business units with different designs, cultures, and processes focused on exploration or exploitation
Contextual ambidexterity	Independent poles, dualisms	Temporal separation	A supportive organizational context can enable individuals to choose between alignment and adaptability activities at different times
Temporal ambidexterity	Contradictory poles, dualisms	Temporal separation	Alternate temporally and sequentially between longer periods of exploitation with shorter periods of exploration
Paradox theory	Complementary or interrelated poles, dualities rather than dualisms	Moving beyond temporal or spatial separation to synthesis or transcendence	Paradoxical thinking can enable managers to simultaneously and longitudinally work through tensions of exploration and exploitation; encourages reframing situations to enable transcendence of paradoxes; and fosters the institution of organizational processes that can simultaneously support pursuit of both paradoxical poles

Adapted by Papachroni, et al., 2015

for actualizing both poles of the paradox. Organizations that exhibit these competencies, such as Apple Inc. (Heracleous, 2013a) and Singapore Airlines (Heracleous and Wirtz, 2010, 2014), are able to develop capabilities, organizational designs and processes, and leadership thinking that enable the transcendence (Bednarek et al., 2014) and synthesis of tensions (refer to the mini case box below).

Often the development of ambidextrous capabilities takes place over time. For example, Apple Inc. moved from its early days of intense exploration (but low exploitation) in the late 1970s and 1980s, to the early to mid-1990s when both exploration and exploitation were low, until Steve Jobs returned in 1997 and focused on returning Apple to its former creative glory (exploration), as well as hiring the current CEO, Timothy Cook in 1998 with an explicit mandate to enhance efficiency (exploitation). Perhaps, influenced by his practice of Zen Buddhism and interest in transcendental experiences, Jobs saw that exploration and exploitation were not necessarily conflicting and incompatible. Several of Apple's organizational choices (Heracleous, 2013a) can be understood from a paradoxical perspective (e.g., flat, empowering but also centralized organization design; high levels of concurrent engineering involving cross-functional inputs, accompanied by high levels of secrecy).

MINI CASE: QUANTUM STRATEGY: WHAT APPLE AND SINGAPORE AIRLINES HAVE IN COMMON

For over three decades, Michael Porter's seminal work on corporate strategy has dominated management thinking, dictating that companies make clear choices among generic strategies: cost leadership vs. differentiation, or broad appeal vs. niche market. To align resources, organizations then design, staff, and create policies to support their chosen strategy. The idea that a company could achieve differentiation through innovation, service excellence, or other value-adding features, as well as cost leadership (compared with the company's peer group), has been alien to this thinking.

Yet some leading companies have developed capabilities and strategic positions that would normally be considered contradictory. For example, Singapore Airlines delivers exceptional service, supported by continuous innovation, while maintaining a leaner cost structure than its peers, at a level of efficiency only found in the budget airline segment. Apple offers popular, innovative products that redefine whole industries, while at the same time its efficiency levels are higher than those of the traditional cost leader, Dell.

Heracleous (2013a and 2013b) calls such a configuration of capabilities and positions Quantum Strategy, after the idea that at the quantum level of reality, the same electron can be two places at the same time, and two different electrons can occupy the very same physical space. While such a situation seems impossible, it is real and can serve as a fruitful analogy for companies and leaders that wish to develop a strategy that is hard to imitate and can deliver a competitive advantage. What are some principles that can help a company implement Quantum Strategy?

Focus and simplicity

Focus and simplicity can help you deliver high levels of value as well as do so efficiently – focus in terms of product and markets, avoiding unrelated diversification and overpopulated, complex product lines. Simplify your organization, remove unproductive processes, and make a concerted effort to gain synergies among your related businesses.

Strategic investment

When you make technology, people development, or other investments, keep the above goals in mind and invest only if both are satisfied. The right investments to accomplish dual goals cannot always be justified by conventional, short-term financial measures. They have to be made based on strategic principles and courageous leadership, willing to be different and to break from the "me too" mentality, which results only in average performance or mediocrity.

Role model

Instill the appreciation for dual capabilities in the organization's culture by serving as a role model, consciously and consistently making decisions and taking actions that symbolize the

(Continued)

(Continued)

strategic values you wish the organization to develop. Steve Jobs, for example, was the embodiment of innovative, groundbreaking thinking as well as Zen-like levels of simplicity and focus.

Business systems

Think in terms of business systems rather than value chains and engage these systems globally in a way that strengthens the dual capabilities that underlie your strategy. Value chains encourage linear, input-process-output thinking with a view to optimizing operations. Business systems, on the other hand, are interorganizational networks that involve competition as well as collaboration to achieve synergies beyond the boundaries of a single company. Thinking in terms of business systems fosters the pursuit of differentiation in the most efficient way, rather than simply the goal of operational optimization.

Corporate strategies that blend positions and capabilities traditionally considered distinct are difficult to accomplish; which is what makes them valuable. The choices that courageous leaders have to make are not between generic strategies as conventionally thought, but are rather tough organizational and investment choices that can lead to effective development and integration of apparently conflicting capabilities.

Sources: Heracleous (2013a, 2013b).

CONCLUSION

11.5

Modern organizations and their strategy practitioners often face contradictory demands, for example: exploitation and exploration. In this chapter we highlighted the importance of strategic ambidexterity when strategy practitioners deal with such contradictory goals. We also showed that a paradox-based approach allows viewing exploration and exploitation activities not as mutually exclusive but as interwoven polarities shifts management thinking from an either/or to both/and mindset. In such a context, strategy practitioners can consider how to advance their ambidextrous capabilities by adopting tools and technologies (practices) or particular actions (praxis) that can allow them to balance the contradictory goals they manage.

REVISION ACTIVITIES

How would you characterize Stephen Elop's "burning platform" memo? What is he trying to achieve by releasing it to all his employees? Which of the four dimensions of strategy discourse do you see in this memo? Do you think Elop will be successful and why or why not?

Find communications related to strategic issues from a CEO. You can search for communications in the form of blogs, Twitter posts, YouTube clips, or media from investor relations websites.

What can you learn from these communications? What do you learn about the meaning of strategy for the particular firm that you did not know before? Do you find any surprising findings? Why do you think this is so?

Note: Parts of this chapter were based on Papachroni et al. (2015).

FURTHER READINGS

- **Paper**: Heracleous, L. (2013a) Quantum strategy at Apple Inc. *Organizational Dynamics*, 42: 92–9. Provides a detailed account of the ways Apple has been able to balance seemingly contradictory tensions over time. This way of managing such contradictions is termed as Quantum strategy and has allowed Apple to gain a leading position in multiple markets and product categories.

- **Paper**: Bednarek, R., Paroutis, S., and Sillince, J. (2014) Practicing Transcendence: Rhetorical Strategies and Constructing a Response to Paradox. *Academy of Management Best Paper Proceedings*. Offers an examination of the kinds of rhetorical strategies employed in response to paradoxical conditions.

REFERENCES

Andriopoulos, C. and Lewis, M. W. (2009) Exploitation-exploration tensions and organizational ambidexterity: Managing paradoxes of innovation. *Organization Science*, 20: 696–717.

Bednarek, R., Paroutis, S., and Sillince, J. (2014) Practicing Transcendence: Rhetorical Strategies and Constructing a Response to Paradox. *Academy of Management Best Paper Proceedings*, 2014 Strategizing, Activities and Practices (SAP) IG Best Paper Award.

Beech, N., Burns, H., De Caestecker, L., Macintosh, R., and Maclean, D. (2004) Paradox as invitation to act in problematic change situations. *Human Relations*, 57: 1313–32.

Birkinshaw, J. and Gibson, C. (2004) Building ambidexterity into an organization. *MIT Sloan Management Review*, 45: 47–55.

Bouchikhi, H. (1998) Living with and building on complexity: A constructivist perspective on organizations. *Organization*, 5: 217–32.

Cameron, K. S. and Quinn, R. E. (1988) Organizational paradox and transformation. In R. E. Quinn and K. S. Cameron (eds.), *Paradox and Transformation: Toward a Theory of Change in Organization and Management*. Cambridge, MA: Ballinger, pp. 1–18.

Chahrazad, A., Denis, J.-L., and Langley, A. (2011) Having your cake and eating it too: Discourses of transcendence and their role in organizational change dynamics. *Journal of Organizational Change Management*, 24: 333–48.

Chen, M-J. (2002) Transcending paradox: The Chinese "middle way" perspective. *Asia Pacific Journal of Management*, 19: 179–99.

Duncan, R. B. (1976) The ambidextrous organization: Designing dual structures for innovation. In R. H. Kilmann, L. R. Pondy, and D. Slevin (eds.), *The Management of Organization Design: Strategies and Implementation*. New York: North Holland, pp. 167–88.

Eisenhardt, K. M. (2000) Paradox, spirals, ambivalence: The new language of change and pluralism. *Academy of Management Review*, 25: 703–5.

Eisenhardt, K. M., Furr, N. R., and Bingham, C. B. (2010) Microfoundations of performance: Balancing efficiency and flexibility in dynamic environments. *Organization Science*, 21: 1263–73.

Fredberg, T. (2014) If I say it's complex, it bloody well will be. CEO strategies for managing paradox. *Journal of Applied Behavioral Science*, 50: 171–88. doi:10.1177/0021886314522859.

Ghemawat, P. and Costa, J. E. (1993) The organizational tension between static and dynamic efficiency. *Strategic Management Journal*, 14: 59–73.

He, Z-L. and Wong, P-K. (2004) Exploration vs. exploitation: An empirical test of the ambidexterity hypothesis. *Organization Science*, 15: 481–94.

Heracleous, L. (2013a) Quantum strategy at Apple Inc. *Organizational Dynamics*, 42: 92–9.

Heracleous, L. (2013b) What Do Apple and Singapore Airlines have in common? Quantum Strategy. *Business Week*, the management blog, available at: www.bloomberg.com/bw/articles/2013-07-31/what-do-apple-and-singapore-airlines-have-in-common-quantum-strategy (date accessed: March, 2015).

Heracleous, L. and Wirtz, J. (2010) Singapore Airlines' balancing act. *Harvard Business Review*, July–August: 145–9.

Heracleous, L. and Wirtz, J. (2014) Singapore Airlines: Achieving sustainable advantage through mastering paradox. *Journal of Applied Behavioral Science*, 50: 150–70. doi:10.1177/0021886314522323.

Huy, Q. N. (2002) Emotional balancing of organizational continuity and radical change: The contribution of middle managers. *Administrative Science Quarterly*, 47: 31–69.

Jarzabkowski, P. and Sillince, J. (2007) A rhetoric-in-context approach to building commitment to multiple strategic goals. *Organization Studies*, 28: 1639–65.

Judge, W. Q. and Blocker, C. P. (2008) Organizational capacity for change and strategic ambidexterity. Flying the plane while rewiring it. *European Journal of Marketing*, 42: 915–26.

Knigt, E. and Paroutis, S. (2016) Becoming salient: The TME leader's role in shaping the interpretive context of paradoxical tensions, *Organization Studies*, forthcoming.

Lassen, A. H., Waehrens, B. V., and Boer, H. (2009) Re-orienting the corporate entrepreneurial journey: Exploring the role of middle management. *Creativity and Innovation Management*, 18: 16–23.

Levinthal, D. A. and March, J. G. (1993) The myopia of learning. *Strategic Management Journal*, 14: 95–112.

Lewis, M. W. (2000) Exploring paradox: Toward a more comprehensive guide. *Academy of Management Review*, 25: 760–76.

Lewis, M. W. and Smith, W. K. (2014) Paradox as a metatheoretical perspective: Sharpening the focus and widening the scope. *Journal of Applied Behavioral Science*, 50: 127–49. doi:10.1177/0021886314522322.

Luscher, L. S., Lewis, M., and Ingram, A. (2006) The social construction of organizational change paradoxes. *Journal of Organizational Change Management*, 19: 491–502.

March, J. G. (1991) Exploration and exploitation in organizational learning. *Organization Science*, 2: 71–87.

Markides, C. and Oyon, D. (2010) What to do against disruptive business models (when and how to play two games at once). *Sloan Management Review*, 51(4): 25–32.

Mom, T. J. M., Van Den Bosch, F. a. J., and Volberda, H. W. (2007) Investigating managers' exploration and exploitation activities: The influence of top-down, bottom-up, and horizontal knowledge inflows. *Journal of Management Studies*, 44: 910–31.

Mom, T. J. M., Van Den Bosch, F. a. J., and Volberda, H. W. (2009) Understanding variation in managers' ambidexterity: Investigating direct and interaction effects of formal structural and personal coordination mechanisms. *Organization Science*, 20: 812–28.

O'Reilly, C. A. and Tushman, M. L. (2004) The ambidextrous organization. *Harvard Business Review*, 82: 74–81.

O'Reilly, C. A. and Tushman, M. L. (2008) Ambidexterity as a dynamic capability: Resolving the innovator's dilemma. *Research in Organizational Behavior*, 28: 185–206.

Papachroni, A., Heracleous, L., and Paroutis, S. (2015) Organizational ambidexterity through the lens of paradox theory: Building a novel research agenda. *Journal of Advanced Behavioral Science*, 51: 71–93.

Papachroni, A., Heracleous, L. and Paroutis, S. (2016) In pursuit of ambidexterity: Managerial reactions to innvoation-efficiency tensions. *Human Relations*. Forthcoming.

Paroutis, S. (2013) Facebook paves the way for investor confidence in Twitter. The Conversation. Available at: https://theconversation.com/facebook-paves-the-way-for-investor-confidence-in-twitter-18973 (date accessed: October 8, 2013).

Paroutis, S. (2015) Twitter gets stung by an errant tweet but investors shouldn't write the company off. *The Conversation*. Available at: https://theconversation.com/twitter-gets-stung-by-an-errant-tweet-but-investors-shouldnt-write-the-company-off-41066 (date accessed: May 1, 2015).

Poole, M. S. and Van De Ven, A. H. (1989) Using paradox to build management and organization theories. *Academy of Management Review*, 14: 562–78.

Porter, M. (1980) *Competitive Strategy*. New York: Free Press.

Raisch, S. and Birkinshaw, J. (2008) Organizational ambidexterity: Antecedents, outcomes, and moderators. *Journal of Management*, 34: 375–409.

Rescher, N. (2001) *Paradoxes, their Roots, Range and Resolution*. Chicago, IL: Open Court.

Simsek, Z. (2009) Organizational ambidexterity: Towards a multilevel understanding. *Journal of Management Studies*, 46: 597–624.

Smith, W. (2014) Dynamic decision making: A model of senior leaders managing strategy paradoxes. *Academy of Management Journal*, 57, 1592–1623.

Smith, W. K. and Lewis, M. W. (2011) Toward a theory of paradox: A dynamic equilibrium model of organizing. *Academy of Management Review*, 36: 381–403.

Smith, W. K., Binns, A., and Tushman, M. L. (2010) Complex business models: Managing strategic paradoxes simultaneously. *Long Range Planning*, 43: 448–61.

Sundaramurthy, C. and Lewis, M. (2003) Control and collaboration: Paradoxes of governance. *Academy of Management Review*, 28: 397–415.

Voss, G. B. and Voss, Z. G. (2013) Strategic ambidexterity in small and medium-sized enterprises: Implementing exploration and exploitation in product and market domains. *Organization Science*, 24: 1459–77.

Westenholz, A. (1993) Paradoxical thinking and change in the frames of reference. *Organization Studies*, 14: 37–58.

CASE STUDIES

D

As portrayed in the previous chapters, there are a number of ways that a practice approach to strategy can help us appreciate the way strategy is made and executed. In Section D we turn our attention on strategy educators who use practice-based approaches to inform their teaching. In Chapter 12 we outline a practice-led approach to learning and teaching, which we hope will guide educators using the concepts outlined in the previous three parts of the book in their classrooms. We are also offering a set of eight case studies that can be used in sessions about practicing strategy.

TEACHING STRATEGY USING THE STRATEGY-AS-PRACTICE APPROACH

12

TOWARD A PRACTICE-LED APPROACH TO LEARNING AND TEACHING

In this section, using insights and frameworks from studies on research-led teaching, we outline aspects of a practice-led approach to learning and teaching. Many studies have highlighted the importance of designing learning activities that explicitly promote the links between the activities of research and teaching, a process broadly known as research-led teaching (Boyer, 1990; Elton, 2001; Jenkins et al., 2003; Rowland, 1996; Trigwell et al., 2000). However, there is no simple answer to the research–teaching relationship. Studies have, for example, suggested that this relationship is shaped by disciplinary contexts and their views about research (Brew, 2003). Other studies highlight the importance of the particular stakeholders involved in the process and suggest that the focus should be on what students, academics, and other members of the university understand and experience as research-led teaching and learning (Zamorski, 2002). Lindsay et al. (2002) studied undergraduate and postgraduate students drawn from eight different disciplines at a UK university. Their findings indicate that, in both groups, the frequency of positive comments about lecturer research activity increased as the quantity and quality of research in their discipline increased (as measured by their Research Assessment Exercise (RAE) ratings). Both groups showed consistency in articulating the benefits of lecturer research, including enhanced knowledge currency, credibility, competence in supervision, and enthusiasm/motivation. On the other hand, both groups were also consistent in identifying reduced availability of lecturers, competition with teaching, and curriculum distortion as negative effects of lecturer research activity. Similar results were reached by Jenkins et al. (1998). A recent study by Wei et al. (2007), based on undergraduate ratings of 2,364 teachers lecturing in different courses during four semesters in Beijing Normal University, demonstrates that teaching effectiveness and research productivity are positively correlated. Robertson and Bond (2001) have also demonstrated the importance of investigating how academics experience teaching and research and their interrelation. Their qualitative study suggests that there is substantial variation in academics' experiences of the meaning of the relation between teaching and research. Further, they argue that such variation requires more exploration using methods that differ from those that have been associated with past research in this area. The study of economics faculty by Noser et al. (1996) indicates a very weak relationship between research output and teaching effectiveness. Importantly, this study highlights that faculty opinions on the research–teaching relationship seem to be influenced by both institutional and individual characteristics.

At the same time, a number of studies have supported the importance of embracing elements of research-led teaching in curriculum design and delivery (Hattie and Marsh, 1996). In the discipline of geography, for instance, Jenkins (2000) argues that a research-based curriculum enables students to develop both their research skills and their future capacity to make a contribution to discipline-based research. In their study Holbrook and Devonshire (2005) demonstrate the integration of a research-led teaching approach in an online context, using an ocean (climate) model simulation activity in two undergraduate units as a case study. Their findings also demonstrate how a research-led module could draw upon disciplinary research as the underpinning content and stimulus for learning, while at the same time incorporate tasks designed to simulate scientific thinking. Elton (2001) argues that a positive link between research and teaching might exist due primarily to the processes – rather than the outcomes – underpinning research and teaching. In more detail, student-centered teaching and learning processes are intrinsically favorable toward a positive link, while more traditional teaching methods may at best lead to a positive link for the most able students, who in the perception of traditional academics are considered as the "future university teachers."

In light of the above-mentioned debates, scholars have developed approaches to research-led teaching that recognize the multiple layers of the concept. Brew (2003) classifies research-led teaching into three broad categories: (a) teaching that draws on discipline-based research; (b) teaching that develops student research skills; and (c) teaching research that investigates the effectiveness of learning activities and student learning. Holbrook and Devonshire (2005) propose labeling these three categories as: (a) research-informed teaching; (b) research-skills teaching; and (c) research-inquiry teaching.

We now turn our attention to adjusting this research-led approach to the perspective and concepts of strategy-as-practice. In other words, having established the multi-layered features of the notion of research-led teaching, the question that we aim to answer is: how could a practice-led teaching approach be actually developed and realized? Addressing a similar line of inquiry, Jarzabkowski and Whittington propose a strategy-as-practice-based approach to bring strategy research and education closer to practice and note that:

> A strategy-as-practice approach would entail cases based on the real-time unfolding of strategy to illustrate how and why the actions and interactions of multiple actors shape strategy ... such cases would aim to provide deep understanding of how strategic practitioners actually work and the implications that this holds for shaping strategy. (2008: 285)

They conclude that: "strategy-as-practice offers a different solution to the tangled problem of the relationship between strategy research and practice. In place of the gap *between* strategy research and practice, it proposes research *on* practice. The work, workers, and tools of strategy are center stage" (p. 285).

Building on the research-led classification by Brew (2003) and Holbrook and Devonshire (2005), and the suggestions by Jarzabkowski and Whittington (2008), we develop below three interrelated aspects of a practice-led teaching approach (see Figure 12.1). The combined effect of all three aspects can lead to learning and teaching efforts that are practice-led in the spirit of the approach outlined by Jarzabkowski and Whittington (2008).

Practice-informed teaching: the first angle of the practice-led teaching approach is based on using practice-based research to inform the content of strategy modules. While the knowledge base of strategy-as-practice has been on sociological theories of practice, which provide deep insights into management practice (Jarzabkowski and Whittington, 2008), there have been a number of studies providing us with practice-oriented concepts and frameworks (for instance, the environmental velocity/knowledge intensity matrix developed by Jarzabkowski and Wilson, 2006). This textbook has also provided practice-oriented frameworks (for instance, the ESCO model in Chapter 1). The strategy educator can encourage their students to search for further practice-oriented concepts and frameworks that can act as devices to aid reflection and discussion of particular strategy actions in cases or other media. However, the key benefit from utilizing practice-informed research is to develop awareness in students about concepts closer to the daily practice of strategists (for instance, the concept of discourse as developed in Chapter 5), concepts that can help them appreciate and decode the actions and interactions of key actors in the making and execution of strategy.

Practice-skills teaching: another part of a practice-led teaching approach concerns the development of practice skills in students. This means that students develop the ability to better

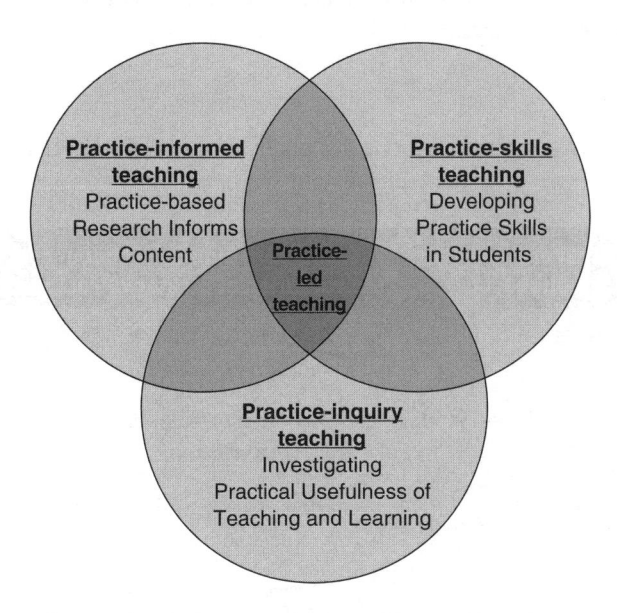

FIGURE 12.1 Elements of a practice-led approach to teaching and learning.

understand the work, workers, and tools of strategy. Such skills can be developed by using: (a) role-plays related to the module material; (b) company projects where students have to engage with multiple strategy stakeholders to appreciate the problem and develop a solution; (c) assignments that focus on questions related to practice (we have provided examples of such assignment questions in Chapter 1 under "Revision activities"); (d) course design that is co-developed with students who can propose appropriate exercises or illustrations of strategy practice for classroom discussion.

Practice-inquiry teaching: the third angle is related to investigating the practical usefulness of teaching and learning. At this point, it has to be noted that authors in the field of "critical management studies" (Alvesson and Willmott, 1992; Mintzberg, 1989; Reed and Anthony, 1992) call for managerial education that develops understanding through questioning of ideas, concepts, and assumptions, leading to more creative and effective solutions to problems. According to Reynolds, "Unless management educators apply a critical perspective to all aspects of a course, informing the design of both content and process, it could be that they encourage a reflexivity in their students that they have not applied to their own practice" (1997: 318). Using this critical approach, we argue for a classroom approach that encourages students to think critically about the ways managers practice strategy. For this kind of discussion, the educator can use questions that require: first, divergent and imaginative thinking about the case material, in order to conceive of different patterns, or create "what if?" scenarios; and, second, assessment of a range of possible outcomes and future probabilities, i.e., possible developments different from those in the case's narrative or outside its timeframe. Following on from Jarzabkowski and Whittington (2008), the focus of these questions would be on the work, workers, and tools of strategy. In the right column of Table 12.1, we present examples of these kinds of questions that encourage synthesis and evaluation of strategy practice. This type of classroom questioning can be particularly useful during plenary analysis of practice-oriented strategy cases.

TABLE 12.1 Contrasting classroom questions that encourage analysis with ones that encourage synthesis and evaluation.

Classroom questions that encourage Analysis of Strategy Situations	Classroom questions that encourage Synthesis and Evaluation of Strategy Practice
– "How did the firm organize its operations…?"	– "How did the top management team reach the decision to…?"
– "How were the firm's changes designed…"	– "How would you evaluate the actions of the key strategists in the case…?"
– "Analyse the issues facing the firm."	
– "What are the firm's core competencies?"	– "How would you characterize the interaction of X and Y strategic actors in the case…?"
	– "Did they utilize the right tools when…?"

Adapted by: Paroutis and Palmer, 2007

ANALYSIS OF PRACTICE IN CASE STUDIES

In this final section, we first start with the traditional approach to teaching strategy cases and then present features in analyzing practice in case studies. In the strategy domain, the emergence and popularity of journals such as the *Academy of Management Learning & Education* are indicators of the increasing trend among strategy scholars to focus on the content and process related to management education. Yet, within most business schools, the traditional and well-established way of teaching by strategy academics has not changed significantly since the 1980s in the reliance principally on the use of case studies. There are a number of studies about strategy-based teaching and the use of the case method. For instance, in their review of US strategy teaching, Greiner et al. (2003) synthesize some of these elements in a "strategic mind-set" which they characterize as comprehensive/integrative, needing a range of skills, and working dynamically in uncertain conditions. To these they add spontaneity, dynamic change, and individuality. Significantly for MBA teaching, their skills set emphasizes behavioral alongside analytical, i.e., the how/execution as well as the what/content. Argyris (1980) also applied his framework of "Theories Espoused/In Use" in his critical review of his Ivy League peers teaching executives with cases. By contrasting observations in strategy classrooms and actual strategizing practice, Paroutis and Palmer (2007) found an emphasis on the use of the cases in the classroom upon analysis, i.e., deconstructing, whereas in strategizing practice in firms the emphasis is on interpretation, reconstructing, and synthesizing the corporate story or paradigm. Accordingly, the kinds of capabilities developed to "prepare" the classroom participants *for* strategy practice using the case method could potentially represent only a limited subset of the actual capabilities required *in* strategy practice. In order to deal with this gap, we propose using the practice-led teaching approach we outlined earlier. For the analysis of practice-oriented strategy cases, eight of which are included in this book, it is useful to use the 3P framework (refer to Section 1.6 and Figure 12.2).

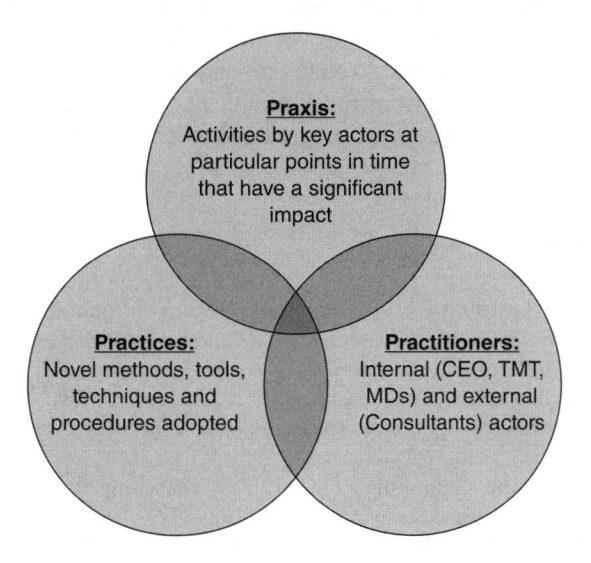

FIGURE 12.2 Analyzing strategy case studies through the 3P framework

Case analysis of strategy praxis requires a focus on the actual activities of particular strategists that have led to particular strategic decisions adopted by the organization. This can be achieved by isolating the precise actions of the key actors in the case and also by classifying these actions in particular periods in time. Furthermore, comparisons can be made across the actions taken in different time periods and alternative scenarios of future actions can be developed. It has to be noted that while in some cases such detailed activities might be articulated clearly, in others these activities can be revealed only through further investigation and data collection by the students.

Analyzing the practices in a strategy case entails detailed investigation of the methods, tools, and procedures followed when taking strategic actions. For instance, strategy cases often mention the particular strategy tools or processes that were followed to inform the strategic decisions taken by the top team or CEO when deciding on a complex strategic issue. Some cases also focus on the failed use of strategy methods, and then it is useful to consider the reasons and context of such failed use and ways such use could have been more successful.

Finally, focusing on the practitioners in a strategy case means focusing on the role and impact of internal (CEO, TMT, MDs, managers, teams) or external (consultants, government agents) actors. An important aspect of this analysis is to examine how particular actors interact with other actors (e.g., the frequency and quality of interactions) and the outcomes these interactions have in taking strategic decisions. Overall, understanding and analyzing the practitioners, practices, and praxis in a strategy case can be achieved with careful analysis and by using the concepts, frameworks, and ideas we have provided in this book.

We next present eight diverse strategy cases that can be analyzed using a practice approach. Each one of them can be linked with and analyzed using the themes we developed in Parts I to III. We are focusing on cases of firms both established (Apple, Centrica) as well as entrepreneurial (Wikipedia), of various sizes and from different industries, both experiencing success (Apple) and failure (Marconi). We also examine innovation and entrepreneurship-based case settings (Narayana hospital, Oxford Brookes University, and Wikimedia). In choosing, researching, and writing such diverse cases we were inspired by the call by Kaplan who notes that for the practice lens on strategy to be established in the strategic management field it must gain: "access to the upper echelons of for profit corporations (both established firms and entrepreneurial start-ups) in order to further develop the strategy-as-practice view" (2007: 989).

REFERENCES

Alvesson, M. and Willmott, H. (1992) *Critical Management Studies*. London: Sage.
Argyris, C. (1980) Some limitations on the case method. *Academy of Management Review*, 8(2): 291–8.
Boyer, E. (1990) *Scholarship Reconsidered: Priorities of the Professoriate*. San Francisco: Jossey-Bass.
Brew, A. (2003) Understanding research-led teaching. *HERDSA News*, 25(1): 3–5.
Elton, L. (2001) Research and teaching: conditions for a positive link. *Teaching in Higher Education*, 6(1): 43–56.
Greiner, L. E., Bhambri, A., and Cummings, T. G. (2003) Searching for a strategy to teach strategy. *Academy of Management Learning & Education*, 2(4): 402–21.
Hattie, J. and Marsh, H. W. (1996) The relationship between research and teaching: A meta-analysis (in Reviews). *Review of Educational Research*, 66(4): 507–42.

Holbrook, N. J. and Devonshire, E. (2005) Simulating scientific thinking online: An example of research-led teaching. *Higher Education Research & Development*, 24(3): 201–13.

Jarzabkowski, P. and Whittington, R. (2008) A strategy-as-practice approach to strategy research and education. *Journal of Management Inquiry*, 17(4): 282–6.

Jarzabkowski, P. and Wilson, D. C. (2006) Actionable strategy knowledge: A practice perspective. *European Management Journal*, 24(5): 348–67.

Jenkins, A. (2000) The relationship between teaching and research: Where does geography stand and deliver? *Journal of Geography in Higher Education*, 24(3): 325–51.

Jenkins, A., Blackman, T., Lindsay, R., and Paton-Saltzberg, R. (1998) Teaching and research: Student perspectives and policy implications. *Studies in Higher Education*, 23(2): 127–41.

Jenkins, A., Breen, R., Lindsay, R., and Brew, A. (2003) *Reshaping Teaching in Higher Education: Linking Teaching with Research*. London: Kogan Page.

Kaplan, S. (2007) *Strategy as Practice: An Activity-Based Approach* (book review). *Academy of Management Review*, 32(3): 986–90.

Lindsay, R., Breen, R., and Jenkins, A. (2002) Academic research and teaching quality: The views of undergraduate and postgraduate students. *Studies in Higher Education*, 27(3): 309–27.

Mintzberg, H. (1989) *Mintzberg on Management – Inside Our Strange World of Organizations*. New York: Free Press.

Noser, T. C., Manakyan, H., and Tanner, J. R. (1996) Research productivity and perceived teaching effectiveness: A survey of economics faculty. *Research in Higher Education*, 37(3): 199–221.

Paroutis, S. and Palmer, G. (2007) Developing capabilities for practice: Do we really teach MBAs how to be effective strategists? Paper presented at the Third Organizational Studies Summer Workshop, June, Crete, Greece.

Reed, M. and Anthony, P. (1992) Professionalizing management and managing professionalization: British management in the 1980s. *Journal of Management Studies*, 29(5): 591–613.

Reynolds, M. (1997) Towards a critical management pedagogy. In J. Burgoyne and M. Reynolds (eds.), *Management Learning*. London: Sage, pp. 312–28.

Robertson, J. and Bond, C. H. (2001) Experiences of the relation between teaching and research: What do academics value? *Higher Education Research & Development*, 20(1): 5–19.

Rowland, S. (1996) Relationships between teaching and research. *Teaching in Higher Education*, 1(1): 7–20.

Trigwell, K., Martin, E., Benjamin, J., and Prosser, M. (2000) Scholarship of teaching: A model. *Higher Education Research and Development*, 19(2): 155–68.

Wei, H., Cheng, X., and Zhao, K. (2007) On the relationship between research productivity and teaching effectiveness at research universities. *Frontiers of Education in China*, 2(2): 298–306.

Zamorski, B. (2002) Research-led teaching and learning in higher education: A case. *Teaching in Higher Education*, 7(4): 411–27.

STRATEGIC LEADERSHIP AND INNOVATION AT APPLE INC.[1]

> Apple, Inc. is actually four diverse and thriving companies all wrapped up into one. It's a hardware company, a software company, a services company, and a retail company. Most technology companies in the world can manage one or two of these disciplines, but only Apple has all four entities working in harmony. (Bajarin, 2011)

Back in 1997 few would have thought that Apple Computers would one day be recognized as one of the most innovative companies in the world, transcending the barriers of the computer industry to compete in the consumer electronics, telecommunications, and music industries (see Figure 13.1 for an outline of Apple's product and service portfolio). Since the return of Steve Jobs to the company, Apple rose from a $2 billion company in 1997 to nearly $417 billion in 2011, overtaking Exxon Mobil to become the world's most valuable company by market capitalization in August 2011 (*Economist*, 2011a). In 2010 Apple surpassed Microsoft in market capitalization, which was regarded as an important milestone in the technology industry (Rusche, 2011). By the end of March 2012, Apple's market capitalization rose to $573bn, more than twice that of Microsoft at $273bn; and it accounted for 4.5% of the S&P 500, and 1.1% of the global equity market (*Economist*, 2012). The company's upward trajectory continued, and by March 2015 Apple Inc. was still the most valuable company in the world, worth over $719bn. In comparison, Google was worth $380bn, Exxon Mobil $351bn, and Microsoft $336bn.

Building on innovative products that have redefined their markets (such as the iPod, the iPhone, and the iPad), a consumer base as loyal as a fan club, and a business model characterized by integration of products and services, lean operations, and operational synergies that no

---

[1]This case was prepared by Professor Loizos Heracleous and Angeliki Papachroni for the purposes of class discussion and is not meant to illustrate effective or ineffective handling of administrative situations.

Apple Inc. Key Product and Service Portfolio

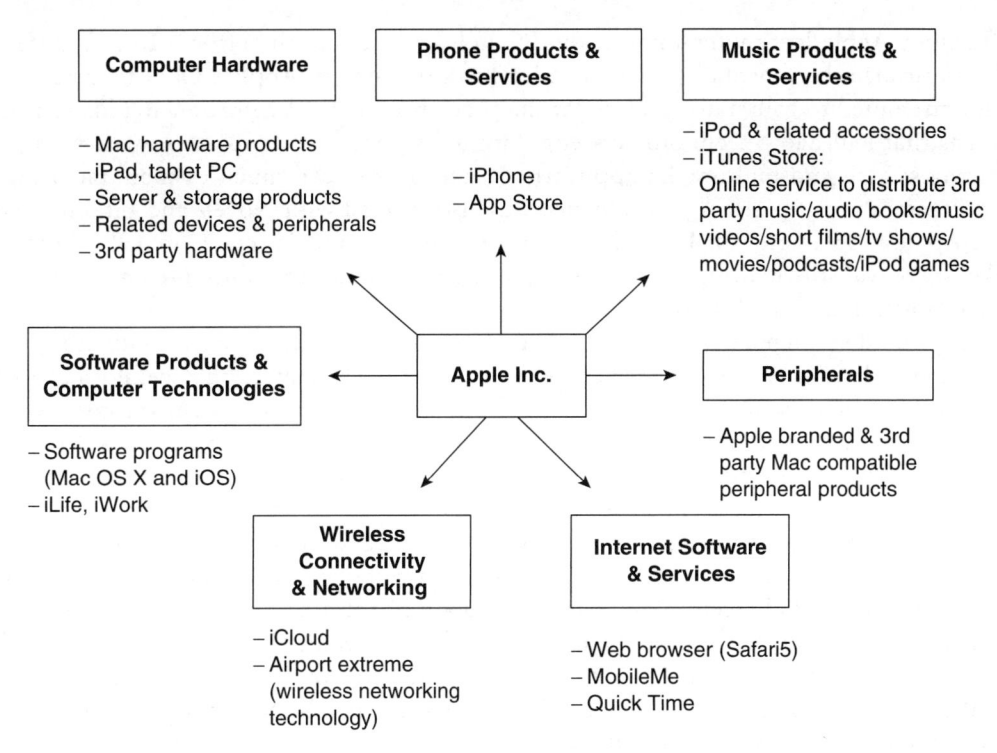

Computer Hardware
- Mac hardware products
- iPad, tablet PC
- Server & storage products
- Related devices & peripherals
- 3rd party hardware

Phone Products & Services
- iPhone
- App Store

Music Products & Services
- iPod & related accessories
- iTunes Store:
  Online service to distribute 3rd party music/audio books/music videos/short films/tv shows/movies/podcasts/iPod games

Software Products & Computer Technologies
- Software programs (Mac OS X and iOS)
- iLife, iWork

Peripherals
- Apple branded & 3rd party Mac compatible peripheral products

Wireless Connectivity & Networking
- iCloud
- Airport extreme (wireless networking technology)

Internet Software & Services
- Web browser (Safari5)
- MobileMe
- Quick Time

FIGURE 13.1 Apple Inc. Key Product and Service Portfolio

Source: Authors.

competitor could easily imitate, Apple outperformed its competitors and the market. In 2011, the year that Steve Jobs died, Apple reported $108bn in revenues – up from $65bn in 2010 – and $26bn net income and nearly $82bn in cash reserves (Nuttall, 2011). By the year ending September 2014, Apple had revenues of $182bn and cash reserves of $155bn. Operating income stood at 28.7%, and net income at 21.6% (Annual Report, 2014). See investor.apple.com for Apple's financial performance.

JOBS' TURNAROUND AND REBUILDING AN INNOVATIVE ORGANIZATION

Things haven't always been that rosy for the company once known as the underdog of the computer industry. During the time when Steve Jobs was away from the organization (1985–97) Apple progressively degenerated to the point of struggling for survival. Apple charged premium prices and operated through a closed proprietary system, at a time when more economical, IBM-compatible PCs gained mass appeal. Its cost base was high compared to its major competitors. This combination of factors led to shrinking market share and lower profitability. Apple lost momentum in the PC industry, despite the effort of three different CEOs to reverse the downfall (see Table 13.3 for a timeline of Apple's CEO tenures). John Sculley attempted to gain market share (at the time around 7%) by introducing lower priced products that still had a technological edge, forged alliances with IBM to work on a joint operating system and multimedia applications, and outsourced much of manufacturing to subcontractors to cut costs. A joint alliance was also formed with Novell and Intel to reconfigure Apple's OS to run on Intel chips. By the end of Sculley's tenure in 1993 however, market share was still at around 8%, and Apple's gross profits had reduced from around 50% to 34% (Yoffie and Slind, 2008).

During Spindler's tenure, the alliances with Intel and Novell, as well as with IBM, were exited, and a decision was taken to license Apple's OS to companies that would make Mac clones (a decision subsequently reversed by Jobs in 1997). There was focus on international growth, and more cost-cutting efforts. With performance remaining flat, Spindler was replaced by Gil Amelio. In 1996, under Amelio, Apple went through three successive restructurings and further cost cutting. At the same time, Amelio aimed to return Apple to its premium price, differentiation strategy (Yoffie and Slind, 2008). The biggest challenge at the time was the release of Apple's new-generation operating system in response to the release of Microsoft's Windows 95, which had received great attention upon its release one year earlier. Apple's OS system named Copland, on the other hand, was so behind schedule that the company decided to turn to external help. Ironically, Apple turned to NeXT, a software company founded by Steve Jobs after his departure from Apple in 1985. Meanwhile, Apple's market share fell to 3% and Amelio was forced out by the board of directors.

After NeXT's help with the new version of Apple's operating system, Apple's executive board resolved to buy the company. A year later, in July 1997, Jobs was offered the title of Apple's CEO, after spending a few months as a consultant at Apple. This was a crucial time in the company's history. Apple's stock had sunk to $3.30 and the company reported a net loss of $708 million in its second quarter that year, flirting with bankruptcy. At the same time competitors such as Dell and Microsoft were thriving, following the tech boom of the late 1990s. Jobs took on the role of Interim CEO in 1997 and then became CEO during 2000.

The return of Steve Jobs to Apple in 1997 marked the beginning of a new era for the company. Jobs worked for a salary of $1 per year for 30 months (and plenty of stock options), leading to Apple's successful turnaround. His priority was to revitalize Apple's innovation capability. "Apple had forgotten who Apple was," as he noted in an interview (Burrows, 2004), stressing that it was time for Apple to return to its core values and build on them. At the time, Michael Dell was asked at an investor conference what Jobs should do with Apple. He replied "I'd shut it down and give the money back to the shareholders" (Burrows and Grover, 2006).

According to a former Apple executive who participated in Jobs' first meeting with the top brass on his return to Apple, Jobs went in with shorts, sneakers, and a few days' beard, sat on a swivel chair, spun slowly, and asked them what was wrong with Apple. Jobs then exclaimed that it was the products, and that there was no sex in them anymore (Burrows and Grover, 2006). Upon taking charge, Jobs announced that Microsoft would invest $150m in Apple, reaffirming its commitment to producing Microsoft Office and other products for the Mac, and soon scrapped the Mac OS licensing program, that he believed was cannibalizing Mac sales (Yoffie and Slind, 2008). He axed 70% of new products in development, kept 30% that he believed were "gems," and added some new projects that he believed could offer breakthrough potential. He also revamped the marketing message to take advantage of the maverick, creative Apple brand, and re-priced stock options to retain talent (Booth, 1997).

In January 2000, when Apple became profitable with a healthy share price, Apple announced that it would buy Jobs a Gulfstream V jet, at a cost of $88m, fulfilling Jobs' request for an aeroplane so he could take his family on vacation to Hawaii and fly to the East coast. Larry Ellison, Oracle CEO and a board member at Apple, said at the time, "with what he's done, we ought to give him five airplanes!" (Elkind, 2008). Between 2003 and 2008 Apple's sales tripled to $24 billion and profits increased to $3.5 billion, up from a mere $24 million. Apple topped the list of Fortune 500 companies for total return to shareholders both over 2003–8 (94% return) as well as over 1998–2008 (51% return) (Morris, 2008: 68), a remarkable achievement.

In January 2007, Apple Computer changed its name to Apple Inc. (Yahoo finance, 2008), signifying a shift away from its computer vendor roots. Since 2006, revenues from desktop and portable computers were accounting for less than half of Apple's total revenues; and by 2011, just one fifth. By early 2007, Apple had come a long way: it had produced the world's fastest personal computer, introduced a series of attractive new Macintosh models with a reliable, competitive operating system known for its astonishing backward compatibility, created a cult following of iPod users, and begun its inroads into the mobile phone industry with the iPhone.

REDEFINING THE PC INDUSTRY

Upholding the value of user friendliness, Steve Jobs led the launch of the first iMac in 1998, his first project after his return to the company. The iMac, or "the computer for the rest of us," its slogan when it was launched, revolutionized desktop computing by combining technological advancements and unique design. The combination of a CPU, a CD ROM drive and a modem all packed in a translucent case, that could support all "plug and play" peripherals that were designed for Windows-based machines, for the compelling price of $1,299, marked Apple's dynamic comeback. Even though the iMac was the fastest selling Macintosh model ever, Apple refused to rest on its laurels, continually updating its hardware and operating system, and launching newer models and software almost every four months. Most importantly the iMac was the first Apple product with wide consumer acceptance, since 70% of sales were Apple converts, adding to the Macs already in use, helping Apple double its worldwide market share to 6% by the end of 1998 (Linzmayer, 2004).

In parallel, Steve Jobs proceeded to simplify Apple's product mix in terms of four lines of desktop and portable computers designed for both the professional and consumer markets. Following the iMac's success, the iBook was launched in 1999. This consumer portable computer featured an optional AirPort wireless networking hub that allowed up to ten Macs to share an Internet connection. Just six weeks after the iBook's unveiling, Apple had received more than 140,000 advance orders, making it a success equal to the iMac (Linzmayer, 2004).

After the introduction of the iMac and the iBook, Apple's figures looked a lot healthier. In October 1999 Apple announced its eighth consecutive profitable quarter and closed that fiscal year with revenues of $6.1 billion and net earnings of $601 million. Whereas most of Apple's innovations led to an even more closed Apple archipelagos (software and hardware integration), at the same time Jobs decided to loosen control in other areas, for example the use of standard interfaces, such as the USB port. This change made the Mac a more open system since users of a Mac Mini for example could use a non-Mac keyboard (Yoffie and Slind, 2008). In the years to follow, a variety of innovative proprietary applications, developed in-house, supported the Macintosh product lines. These include programs such as Apple's own Web browser, Safari, developed in 2003, as well as those in the iLife package (iDVD, iMovie, iPhoto,) that offered editing and creative opportunities to users.

GROWING THE APPLE ECOSYSTEM: BREAKTHROUGH INNOVATION IN THE CONSUMER ELECTRONICS AND ENTERTAINMENT INDUSTRIES

In 2001 Apple introduced its first iPod, launching a new era for the company as it entered the consumer electronics industry. Capitalizing on the emerging trend of MP3 music, Apple introduced a breakthrough product that soon became synonymous with the MP3 music player category. With impeccable design and easy to use menu, the iPod could load 1,000 songs in just 10 minutes and play music for 10 hours. The integration with the iTunes 2.0 software also enabled easy synchronization of music libraries. A year later, in 2002 Apple released iPods with larger memory that were compatible with Windows, a move that further pushed iPod sales. By the end of 2003 more than one million iPods were sold, marking the first substantial stream of revenues apart from the Macintosh. Since then the iPod product range has been renewed every three to five months and the company announced in 2007 that it sold the 100-millionth iPod. These numbers made the iPod the fastest selling music player in history (Apple, 2007).

One the most important innovations for Apple has been the launch of the iTunes Music store in 2003, a revolutionary service through which consumers could access and purchase online music for only $0.99 per song. The iTunes Music Store was compatible with all iPods (running both on Macs as well as Windows-based computers) and served as Apple's Trojan horse to what Jobs had envisioned as the digital hub where digital content and Apple devices would be seamlessly interconnected. The downloaded songs had royalty protection and could only be played by iPods, bringing the interoperability between Apple's hardware, software, and content to a new level and creating higher barriers to entry into this ecosystem. iPods had the capacity to display videos and through them Apple became a significant distributor of movies and TV shows. Five years after entering the music business, Apple surpassed Walmart to become the largest music retailer in the USA (McCracken, 2011a).

Apple's next groundbreaking innovation was the iPhone, a device combining a phone, a music player, and a personal computer that redefined the mobile phone industry in the same way iPod and iTunes revolutionized the music industry. According to Jobs, "It was a great challenge: Let's make a great phone that we fall in love with. Nobody had thought about putting operating systems as sophisticated as an OS X inside a phone, so that was a real question" (quoted in Morris, 2008: 69). iPhone's success has been attributed not only to its technological capacity but also to its design: "We had a different enclosure design for this iPhone until way too close to the introduction to ever change it. And it came one Monday morning and I said: I just don't love it. And we pushed the reset button. That happens more than you think because it is not just engineering and science. There is art too." (Jobs quoted in Morris, 2008: 70). According to Burrows and Grover (2006), "Jobs' true secret weapon is his ability to meld technical vision with a gut feel of what regular consumers want and then market it in ways that make regular consumers want to be part of tech's cool club." The success of the iPhone has been phenomenal. In 2011 alone, iPhone handset sales reached 72.3 million units, up from nearly 40 million in 2010.

In 2008 Apple launched the App Store, the only authorized service for loading programs onto the iPhone. The App Store was based on the same principle of seamless integration between hardware and software, giving Apple 30% of third-party developers' revenues along the way. Although Apple followed a particularly strict policy regarding the authorizing of applications, the App Store still gave the iPhone a vast selection of desirable applications, adding precious content to the iPhone offering (McCracken, 2011a).

The Apple ecosystem was further reinforced in 2010, with the introduction of the iPad, a tablet computer that aimed at revitalizing a niche and up till then commercially risky product category. Whereas the iPad was initially received with some skepticism, Jobs' intuition proved correct. Within its first year of release, Apple sold 14.8 million iPads (McCracken, 2011a) and with the launch of the iPad 2 sales rose further to an astonishing 32 million in 2011, giving Apple two-thirds of the tablet computer market. Spurred by the iPad's success, the tablet computer market grew to approximately $35bn in 2012 (*Economist*, 2011b). At the same time, the traditional PC market experienced stagnation, marking what was seen as the first signs of the post-PC era (Forbes, 2012a).

During the launch presentation of the iPad Jobs revealed that the company was already in agreement with top publishers such as Penguin and Simon & Schuster for the creation of specially made books to be purchased online at the new iBooks store. Applications were also available for the electronic version of major newspapers such as the *New York Times*. Further, the iPad was designed so that most of the 140,000 gaming applications already available at the App Store, could run on it straight away, turning it into a key gaming platform. In order to ensure that the iPad was seen as more than an entertainment gadget, the iWork software (including word-processing, spreadsheet, and presentation software) was also updated. The iPad was priced at $499 for the basic version and $829 for one with larger memory and a 3G wireless connection, making it premium priced but approachable for consumers (*Economist*, 2010).

In October 2011, Apple introduced iCloud, a cloud service for storing music, photos, applications, calendars, and documents that can be wirelessly transferred to multiple iOS devices, Macs, and Windows-based computers. During its first three months of release 85 million customers had signed up (Elmer-DeWitt, 2012). iCloud came with 5GB of free space while additional space could be purchased from Apple. By providing a means of integrating the use of multiple Apple devices iCloud marked a key strategic move towards a mobile Apple ecosystem (Satariano and Burrows, 2011).

In early 2015 the market was eagerly awaiting the commercialization of the Apple Watch, a re-invention of the watch as a lifestyle gadget which could exploit Apple's enviable cache of apps including health, financial, travel, and entertainment. Apple billed the watch as "the most personal product we've ever made, because it's the first one designed to be worn"

(Apple Inc., 2015) and would introduce three editions at different price points; a regular model, a sports model, and a luxury model.

THE COMPETITIVE LANDSCAPE

Given Apple's diversified product portfolio, competition includes companies from various industries; from computer hardware and software to mobile communications and internet. In that context apart from traditional competition from PC manufacturers who have struggled to keep up in the mobile, what some have called post-PC era, Apple's increasing role in content distribution has brought the company a new set of competitors such as Amazon and Google (Bajarin, 2011).

The giants: IBM and Microsoft

By 2015, the computer technology industry had undergone some profound changes that shaped the competitive context within which Apple operated. IBM, the once undisputed leader in PC manufacturing, had gradually moved away from its traditional territory of computer hardware and with a focus on computer technology, research, and service consulting became a very different company from what it used to be in the 1990s. In 2014 IBM had sales of $92.8 billion in services, software, and hardware to businesses and governments. Its market capitalization in March 2014 was $162bn, and its profitability was healthy, with an operating margin of 21.4% and a net margin of nearly 13%.

IBM's acquisition of PwC Consulting in 2002 marked the company's serious entry into the business services sector (Doz and Kosonen, 2008: 38). After selling its PC and laptop business to Chinese company Lenovo in 2005 (a segment it had itself created) to allow a higher strategic focus on services, and higher end servers, IBM's strategy also moved to encompass open business approaches. IBM was a significant contributor to open source movements such as Linux by investing in the program's development, growth, and distribution (Linux is supported on all modern IBM Systems) and in 2005 the company gave away approximately 500 software patents (valued over $10 million) with the aim of enhancing global innovation and profiting from newly created business opportunities. Through these actions, IBM aimed to enlarge the global market for IT products and services and to benefit by responding to this demand. IBM made over 50 acquisitions during 2002–7, building a portfolio around "networked, modularized and embedded technologies, including service-oriented architecture (SOA), information on demand, virtualization and open, modular systems for businesses of all sizes" (IBM Annual Report, 2007: 2). With IBM exiting the PC manufacturing industry the competitive environment in this front included HP, Dell, Acer, and Lenovo.

Following the launch of the IBM PC, Microsoft dominated the PC operating system market mostly because it offered an open standard that multiple PC makers could incorporate into their products. Windows OS became the dominant operating system in the industry with more than 85% of all PCs in the world running on some Windows version (Yoffie and Slind, 2008). By 2009 Microsoft faced increased competition in the software front from Apple, HP, IBM, and Sun Microsystems, as well as Linux OS derived from UNIX. Microsoft's portfolio also included the online search and advertising business (MSN portals, Live Search, etc.) in which the company sought to invest further. In 2009 after a long period of speculation Microsoft and Yahoo joined forces in the internet-search business in an effort to respond to Google's market domination (BBC, 2009). Microsoft's position in the entertainment industry was holding strong with the Xbox 360 console selling 13.7 million units in 2011 (Microsoft Annual Report, 2011). Microsoft's revenue reached $93.5 billion in fiscal year 2014, with an operating profit margin of 30.6% and net margin of 22.1%. By 2014 Microsoft was facing new challenges stemming from stagnating growth of the PC industry due to increased interest in mobile devices such as smartphones and tablet PCs, leading to a gradual decline in its Windows revenues. As a competitive response Microsoft released its Mobile Operating System, Windows Phone in 2011 as part of a partnership with Nokia; and announced an update of its Windows OS for tablet PCs (*New York Times*, 2012a).

The computer vendors: Hewlett-Packard, Dell, and Lenovo

After the acquisition of Compaq in 2002, which brought significant scale in its desktop and laptop product lines, HP became the world's largest PC vendor, surpassing rival Dell in 2007 with a 3.9% market share lead. By 2011 the company's revenue was $125 billion, making it the world's largest technology company in terms of revenues; even though its profitability was relatively thin, at 8.4% operating profit margin, and 4.75% net profit margin (and market capitalization of $48.2bn in mid-March 2012); reflecting the intense levels of competition in the computer hardware industry. By the fiscal year 2014, HP's revenues declined to $110bn, with operating profits remaining at 8% and net profits at 4.5%; with a market capitalization of $60bn in March 2015. HP's portfolio included personal computing, imaging and printing-related products and services, as well as enterprise information technology infrastructure, including enterprise storage and servers, technology support and maintenance, consulting and integration and outsourcing services. After experiencing a turbulent period due to an unsuccessful effort to enter the mobile business, in 2011 HP was the largest PC manufacturer in the world with 17.6% share of worldwide PC shipments in the first quarter of 2011 (Shukla, 2011). If tablet PCs, however, are included in the global PC market, HP has been overtaken by Apple as market leader due to the stellar success of the iPad from 2011 onwards (Mellow, 2012).

Dell Inc. offered a range of product categories including desktop personal computers, servers and networking products, storage, mobility products, software and peripherals, and services. It was the first computer company to sell customized PCs directly to consumers without using intermediaries. Once the leading PC vendor in terms of both profitability and market share, Dell faced increased competition in the desktop and notebook business that made it difficult to sustain its earlier growth and profitability rates.

Although Dell had based its success in its distinctive business model of direct sales and built to order manufacturing, in 2011 the company was surpassed by China-based Lenovo, which rose to second place in the PC market after HP with sales of more than 12 million units, growing by more than 25% over the previous year. Dell had $62bn of revenues in 2011, with relatively thin profitability of 7.2% operating margin and 5.6% net margin, with a market value in March 2012 of $30.6bn. By 2012 Lenovo announced its very own cloud strategy to integrate its line of personal computing, smartphones and tablets marking its aspired transformation from a hardware manufacturer to a "solutions provider" (*New York Times*, 2012b). In October 2013 Dell went private, acquired by its founder Michael Dell and technology investment company Silver Lake Partners, in a $25bn deal.

Emerging competition: Google, Amazon, and Samsung

Apple's ecosystem of products topped with the iCloud strategy, was faced with several competitors including Amazon, Google, and Samsung. Apart from being the biggest online retailer with $89bn revenues in 2014, Amazon also offered its own cloud service. With products and services that span digital music, movies, books, TV shows, and consumer electronics, Amazon was a leading competitor in the digital content market (Bajarin, 2011). Amazon's tablet proposition, the Kindle Fire challenged the iPad due to its low entry price: $199 versus $499 for the iPad 2 (Forbes, 2012b); even though its aesthetics and functionality were below those of the iPad, but improving. Reflecting the challenging nature of Amazon's markets, its profit margins were razor thin or negative. In 2014, its operating margin was 0.2% and net margin was –0.27%, with a market value of $174bn in March 2015.

At the same time, Google with its Chrome browser and its Android operating system that run on both tablets and smartphones was a credible challenger in these product-markets. Contrary to Apple's ecosystem approach, Google made its Android system available to be installed on a variety of different handsets by Sony, Motorola, Samsung, LG, and others. Android's code was open for manufacturers and developers whose applications were available at the Android Market. By fiscal year 2014, Google had revenues of $66bn, operating profits of 25.6%, net profits of 21.9% and market value of $380.9% in March 2015. Samsung, a South Korean conglomerate operating in the mobile telecommunications, consumer electronics, information technology, healthcare, and other sectors, became a leading competitor in mobile phone and tablet devices through offering high quality, keenly priced hardware based on the Android operating system. As a corporation, Samsung had revenues of $186.6bn, with operating margin of 12.1% and net margin of 11.2%, and a market value of $192bn in March 2015.

PLAYING WITH DIFFERENT RULES

Deep Collaboration

Long before it was voted as the world's most innovative company, Apple had placed its trademark on a long list of technological breakthroughs including the mouse, the graphical user interface, color graphics, built-in sound, networking and wireless LAN, FireWire, and many more (some of which, such as the mouse and graphical user interface were inspired from Steve Jobs' visit to Xerox Parc in 1979). Apple's approach over the years had been to make use of a personal computer as easy and intuitive as possible through developing a highly responsive operating system, establishing standard specifications to which all applications' software packages were expected to conform, strict control of outside developers, and delivering computers with high performance (Cruikshank, 2006).

Apple's innovations enhanced the consistency across applications, which translated to ease of use, an attribute that helped to explain to some extent Apple's loyal consumer base.

Another significant characteristic of Apple's approach to innovation was the diffusion of innovation across the value chain (Cruikshank, 2006) with both high-end and mid-market products that appealed to a wide audience ranging from amateurs to professionals. According to Jobs, "Apple's DNA has always been to try to democratize technology. If you make something great then everybody will want to use it" (quoted in Morris, 2008: 69).

Many of the disruptive innovations Apple has introduced are based on what employees call "deep collaboration," "cross pollination," or "concurrent engineering." This refers to products not developed in discrete stages but by "all departments at once – design, hardware, software – in endless rounds of interdisciplinary design reviews" (Grossman, 2005). In an interview about how innovation is fostered in the company, Jobs noted that the system for innovation is that there is no system: "The reason a lot of us are at Apple is to make the best computers in the world and make the best software in the world. We know that we've got some stuff that (is) the best right now. But it can be so much better. ... That's what's driving us ... And we'll sleep well when we do that" (quoted in Cruikshank, 2006: 25).

Although Apple has been envied for its ability to catch the wave in new technology fronts earlier than competitors (such as in the case of iTunes and the iPhone) Jobs describes it as a rather slow process:

> Things happen fairly slowly, you know. They do. These waves of technology, you can see them way before they happen, and you just have to choose wisely which ones you are going to surf. If you choose unwisely, then you can waste a lot of energy, but if you choose wisely, it actually unfolds fairly slowly. (Jobs, quoted in Morris, 2008: 70)

Sticking with a Proprietary Ecosystem

> In a world filled with junky devices, clunky software, inscrutable error messages and annoying interfaces, Jobs' insistence on a simple, integrated approach led to astonishing products marked by delightful user experiences. Using an Apple product could be as sublime as walking in one of the Zen gardens of Kyoto that Jobs loved. ... Sometimes it's nice to be in the hands of a control freak. (Isaacson, 2011)

Apple's innovations have redefined existing product categories such as music players and mobile phones, and helped the company successfully enter hotly contested new markets such as the entertainment industry. Key to these achievements have been the focus on design, the consumer experience, and the seamless integration of hardware and software and content. The tight integration of its own operating system, hardware and applications, has been a strategy followed diligently by Apple. As Steve Jobs says: "One of our biggest insights [years ago] was that we didn't want to get into any business we didn't own or control the primary technology, because you'll get your head handed to you. We realized that for almost all future consumer electronics, the primary technology was going to be software. And we were pretty good at software" (Morris, 2008: 70).

Apple is nearly unique among contemporary technology companies in doing all of its own design in-house, at its Cupertino campus. Other companies have outsourced most or all of their product design function, relying on outsourced design manufacturers (ODMs) to develop the products that with minor adaptations will fit into their product lines. Apple, however, believes that having all the experts in one place – the mechanical, electrical, software, and industrial engineers, as well as the product designers, leads to a more holistic perspective on product development; and that a critical mass of talent makes existing products better and opens the door to entirely new products. According to Jobs:

> ... you can't do what you can do at Apple anywhere else. The engineering is long gone in the PC companies. In the consumer electronics companies they don't understand the software parts of it. There's no other company that could make a MacBook Air and the reason is that not only do we control the hardware, but we control the operating system. And it is the intimate interaction between the operating system and the hardware that allows us to do that. There is no intimate interaction between Windows and a Dell computer.
> (quoted in Morris, 2008)

The company's tightly knit proprietary system has been frequently seen as the reason for Apple's loss of initial momentum in the PC industry and increasing isolation until the mid 90s. According to Kahney, "When Jobs returned to Apple in 1997, he ignored everyone's advice and tied his company's proprietary software to its proprietary hardware" (Kahney, 2008: 142). He has persisted in following this strategy over the years even as other Silicon Valley firms were turning towards openness and interoperability. Tony Fadell, Vice President of engineering in the iPod division, notes that Apple aims to develop a self-reinforcing, synergistic system of products rather than a series of individual products: "The product now is the iTunes Music Store and iTunes and the iPod and the software that goes on the iPod. A lot of companies don't really have control, or they can't really work in a collaborative way to truly make a system. We're really about a system" (quoted in Grossman, 2005).

Over the years, there have been some notable exceptions to this proprietary approach. In order to reach a broader consumer base, in late 2003 Apple offered a Windows compatible version of iTunes allowing not only Windows users to use the iPod but more importantly to familiarize them with Apple products. Another milestone came with the company's switch from PowerPC processors made by IBM to Intel chips, a decision announced in mid-2005. This decision allowed Macs to run Windows software, implied lower switching costs for new Mac consumers and also allowed software developers to adapt more easily their programs for Apple. A previous alliance with Microsoft occurred in 1997 when Microsoft agreed to invest $150 million in Apple, reaffirming its commitment to develop core products such as Microsoft Office for the Mac.

Other Strategic Moves

Apple has developed a series of strategic alliances in the course of its efforts to become the center of the digital hub, where digital content would be easily created and transferred to any Apple device. Development of the iPod, iTunes, and iPhone have necessitated this collaborative approach, since entry in the entertainment and consumer electronics markets would not have been as successful without some key strategic partners (for example the big record labels such as EMI, Sony BMG, Universal and Warner Brothers for iTunes, or YouTube for the iPhone). In this process of building systems, Apple has been very selective about its strategic partners. Rather than aiming for the most partners, Apple focuses on engaging with the best companies for a specific purpose (for example the partnership with Google in developing mapping and video applications for the iPhone).

At the same time Apple has proceeded with a number of acquisitions intended to strengthen its core competencies. For example, in 2002 it acquired the German specialist in music software, Emagic, as well as Prismo Graphics, Silicon Grail, and Nothing Real, three small companies involved in professional-level video creation and production. In April 2008 Apple also announced the acquisition of the boutique microprocessor company PA Semi, known for its highly sophisticated and low priced chips. With that acquisition Apple is said to be building the capability to bring its chip design in-house, reinforcing an ever more tightly knit ecosystem that helps to prevent copycat designs from rivals and offers the ability to design chips for supporting specific new products or applications. According to CEO Tim Cook (said at the time he was COO): "One traditional management philosophy that's taught in many business schools is diversification. Well, that's not us. We are the antibusiness school" (Burrows, 2004).

In 2001, Apple created a retail division to enable it to sell its products directly to the public. By 2012 there were 357 retail stores in 11 countries (245 in the USA) accounting for almost 20% of total revenues (Apple's retail stores rose to 437 by 2014). In 2006 Apple entered into an alliance with Best Buy, and by the end of 2007 Apple products could be purchased in over 270 Best Buy stores (Yoffie and Slind, 2008). Being engaged at all parts of the value chain, including retail outlets, enabled Apple to shape the whole customer experience.

CORPORATE CULTURE AND ORGANIZATION DESIGN AT APPLE

> Among the many amazing things about Apple is how scrutinized it is. Rarely have a company, its products, and its top executive – the late Steve Jobs – been so thoroughly examined. And yet, for a corporation so frequently discussed, Apple is poorly understood. Its products are ubiquitous, but information about the institution is scarce – which is exactly how Apple wants it. (Lashinsky, 2012)

Along with being one of the most innovative companies in the world Apple has also gained a reputation of being among the most secretive as well. A T-shirt for sale at the company shop said: "I visited the Apple campus. But that's all I'm allowed to say." Few people know what happens behind closed doors; Apple employees are bound with strict confidentiality agreements and it seems that only one person authorized to ever talk about Apple was Steve Jobs. His keynote speeches where he presented Apple's newest products were kept under wraps until the last moment and were eagerly anticipated by consumers and media all over the world. The media coverage benefits were estimated at millions of dollars. Jobs' keynotes diligently followed a set sequence: first astonishing growth figures for each target market, presented through clear and simple slices, and then Jobs would present Apple's new product just by saying "oh and one more thing," followed by "cool, eh?!" The focus was on the product's usability, design, and simplicity.

Secrecy in terms of product launches was deemed necessary not only for generating hype but also for ensuring that the expectation of a new version of a product wouldn't cannibalize sales of the current version too much; and for keeping competitors guessing for as long as possible.

New recruits were not only warned that the penalty for revealing Apple secrets would be swift termination, but were also hired in so-called dummy positions, roles that remained unspecified until the hiring was complete. As a former employee describes:

> There were just these things that were kept very, very secret. There was a project we were working on where we put in special locks on one of the floors and put up a couple of extra doors to hide away a team that was working on stuff. You had to sign extra-special agreements acknowledging that you were working on a super-secret project and you wouldn't talk about it to anyone – not your wife, not your kids. (Lashinsky, 2012)

Before discussing a topic at a meeting all members would need to verify that they were "disclosed" on it, meaning they had been granted the permission to discuss it. The whole organization was thus comprised of smaller pieces of a bigger puzzle, which was in turn only known to the highest levels. This secretive approach was compared by analysts to terrorist organizations' cellular structure, which protects the organization from potential vulnerability if its individual members or groups are compromised (Lashinsky, 2012).

Apart from ensuring confidentiality, other aspects of Apple's organizational design provide the necessary agility and focus. Small teams bear responsibility for crucial projects, a characteristic that is reminiscent of startup companies. For example, only two engineers were said to have written the code for converting Apple's Safari browser for the iPad, a big and painstaking project (Lashinsky, 2011). Committees are not prevalent at Apple. As Jobs (2010) mentioned:

> We are organized as a startup. One person is in charge of iPhone Os software, one person is in charge of Mac hardware, one person is in charge of iPhone hardware engineering, another is in charge of worldwide marketing, another person is in charge of operations. We are organized like a startup. We are the biggest startup on the planet. And we all meet for three hours once a week and we talk about everything we are doing, the whole business. ... Every Monday we review the whole business. We look at every single product under development. I put out an agenda. Eighty percent is the same as it was the last week, and we just walk down it every single week. We don't have a lot of process at Apple, but that's one of the few things we do just to all stay on the same page. (Lashinsky, 2011)

Every Wednesday there would also be a marketing and communications meeting. Meetings would involve an action list next to which there was the name of the DRI, or directly responsible individual. In this meeting there are frank discussions between Apple employees at various levels. As a former Apple designer mentioned, "on a regular basis you either get positive feedback or are told to stop doing stupid shit" (Lashinsky, 2011).

The Top 100 team was a group of the 100 most influential employees from all ranks that would meet annually and discuss key strategic issues regarding the present and future of the company. The three-day intensive strategy session took place in a secret location, outside the company and even its existence was a well-kept secret for Apple. Members of the Top 100 team were not allowed to put the date down on their calendars, nor drive themselves to the meeting. Instead a company bus, leaving from Cupertino headquarters would take the team to places like the Chaminade Resort and Spa in Santa Cruz, which met two of Jobs prerequisites: good food and no golf. During the course of the event, the Top 100 team would discuss Apple's next steps and new products under development. Position in the hierarchy did not guarantee attendance;

as Jobs said, "that doesn't mean they're all vice presidents. Some of them are just key individual contributors. So when a good idea comes ... part of my job is to move it around ... get ideas moving among that group of 100 people" (Lashinsky, 2011).

In addition to secrecy and a start-up mentality, Apple's culture focused on intense work, creativity, and perfectionism, combined with a rebel spirit. For many years, Jobs stimulated thinking out of the box and encouraged employees to experiment and share with others "the coolest new thing" they had thought of. It may not be accidental that Apple's emblem of corporate culture is a pirate flag with an Apple rainbow colored eye patch, designed after a famous Jobs quote: "It's better to be a pirate than join the navy." This flag was hanging over the Macintosh building as Apple's team was working on the first iMac, to act as a reminder of their mission (Grossman, 2005).

Along with the rebel spirit, Apple had a tradition of long working hours and relentless pursuit of perfection. Each manufacturing and software detail was worked and reworked until a product was considered perfect, aiming for seamless integration of software and hardware. Apple's engineers spent so much time on each product that they were able to foresee and respond to any possible difficulties a consumer might encounter when using it:

> It's because when you buy our products, and three months later you get stuck on something, you quickly figure out [how to get past it]. And you think, "Wow, someone over there at Apple actually thought of this!" And then six months later it happens again. There's almost no product in the world that you have that experience with, but you have it with a Mac. And you have it with an iPod. (Jobs, quoted in Burrows, 2004)

Apple's employees were not paid astronomically. They were not pampered, nor did they enjoy unique privileges beyond what most large companies offered. They were talented people with passion for excellence, proud to be part of the Apple community. This pride stemmed from a corporate culture that fostered innovation and a sense of Apple's superiority against competitors, as a company that could shape the future of technology. Apple recruited talent of the highest caliber, and Jobs often approached and recruited people known as the best in their fields. Specialization and clear specification of responsibilities at Apple was a way of employing the best people for particular roles, reflecting Jobs' aversion towards a general management approach (Lashinsky, 2011).

During their first day at Apple, new employees did not get instructions on how to connect their computer to the network. The assumption was that having been hired at a technology company they would know how to do it themselves; and in the process would get a chance to meet others and blend into Apple. An informal iBuddy program provided support in the early stages of a new employees' entry into the company (Lashinsky, 2012). According to Gus Mueller, founder of a software development firm that develops software for Apple, "Apple only hires top-notch folks. I know a number of people there, and they are all super smart and creative. I don't know a single person who shouldn't be there" (*Guardian*, 2008). Debate is an important aspect of how great products get developed. As Jobs noted, "we have wonderful arguments. If you want to hire great people and having them stay working for you, you have to let them make a lot of decisions and you have to be run by ideas. Not hierarchy. The best ideas have to win. Otherwise good people don't stay" (Jobs, 2010).

For Apple employees this experience was both daunting and fascinating: "If you're a die-hard Apple geek, it's magical. It's also a really tough place to work" (Lashinsky, 2012). Contrary to

Google's infamous relaxed atmosphere, Apple is known for being tough and perfectionist. If any product release does not meet expectations, Apple can be a "brutal and unforgiving place, where accountability is strictly enforced" (Lashinsky, 2011).

Apple's Organization Design

Apple's organization design was flat and simple. Even though Apple did not have an official organization chart, one interpretation of its design was that the organization radiated around Jobs, with 15 Senior Vice Presidents and 31 Vice Presidents overseeing the main functions (Lashinsky 2011). In terms of this structure, Jobs would only be two levels away from any key part of the company; and financial management was centralized, with the only executive responsible for costs and expenses being the Chief Financial Officer. Jobs aimed for simplicity in the company structure as an enabler of the ability to be agile and successfully engage in the "deep collaboration" model. As an observer said: "Processes lead according to Jobs to efficiency, not innovation nor new ideas. These come from people meeting up in the hallways, calling each other in the middle of the night to share a new idea or the solution to a long thought as unsolved problem" (Grossman, 2005).

Jobs described this structure as one based on teamwork and trust:

> There is tremendous team work at the top of the company, which filters down to tremendous team work throughout the company. And teamwork is depended on trusting the other folks to come through with their part, without watching them all the time ... and that's what we do really well. And we are great at figuring out how to divide things up into these great teams that we have, all work on the same thing, touch bases frequently, and bring it all together into a product. We do that really well. And so what I do all day is meet with teams of people. And work on ideas and solve problems to make new products, new marketing programs or whatever.... (Jobs, 2010)

Despite advantages of flexibility and focus, the tight, CEO-centric organization structure built around Jobs' leadership raised concerns in terms of whether it could remain as successful under a different CEO (Waters, 2012).

STEVE JOBS' LEADERSHIP

> Some leaders push innovations by being good at the big picture. Others do so by mastering details. Jobs did both, relentlessly. (Isaacson, 2011)

When Jobs returned to Apple in 1997 after an absence of 12 years, he arrived with much historical baggage. He was Apple's co-founder at the age of 21, and was worth $200 million by the age of 25. He was then forced to resign by the age of 30, in 1985, after a battle over control with CEO John Sculley, which ended with Jobs losing all operational responsibilities. Jobs (who had been executive VP and General Manager of the Macintosh division) was considered a threat to the company, accused of trying to "play manager" and control areas over which he had no jurisdiction. He was considered "a temperamental micromanager whose insistence on total control and stylish innovation had doomed his company to irrelevance" (Burrows and Grover, 2006).

Twenty-three years later, however, Jobs was voted as one of the greatest entrepreneurs of all time by *Business Week* (Tozzi, 2007), and the World's Best CEO by *Harvard Business Review* in 2010 (Hansen et al., 2010). His leadership style and values left a mark on Apple in a way that only a few leaders had achieved, making his name synonymous with the company, its remarkable turnaround, and its groundbreaking innovations. Described by his colleagues as brilliant, powerful, and charismatic, he could also be a demanding and impulsive perfectionist. As Jobs puts it: "My job is not to be easy on people. My job is to take these great people we have and to push them and make them even better. How? Just by coming up with more aggressive visions of how it could be" (quoted in Morris, 2008: 70).

Jobs' control-orientation was reflected in the tight integration of hardware and software. According to insiders, he was opposed to using any sort of unauthorised applications or external software in Apple products. Everything was to be designed by and follow Apple's standards of user-friendliness, excellence and simplicity. As Jobs explained, "We do these things not because we are control freaks … We do them because we want to make great products, because we care about the user and because we like to take responsibility for the entire experience rather than turn out the crap that other people make." (Isaacson, 2011).

Many believe that Jobs' achievement of being regarded as one of the greatest technology entrepreneurs is not based so much on his knowledge of technology (he was not an engineer or a programmer, neither did he have an MBA or college degree) but on his innate instinct for design, the ability to choose the most talented team and "the willingness to be a pain in the neck for what matters for him most" (Grossman, 2005). With regard to the iMac, for example, a product concept he and Jonathan Ive, Head of Design had envisioned, the engineers were initially sceptical: "Sure enough, when we took it to the engineers, they said, 'Oh.' And they came up with 38 reasons. And I said, 'No, no, we're doing this.' And they said, 'Well, why?' And I said, 'Because I'm the CEO, and I think it can be done.' And so they kind of begrudgingly did it. But then it was a big hit." (Grossman, 2005). Jobs was cited as "co-inventor" on 103 Apple patents (Elkind, 2008).

Jobs could be both inspirational, but also experienced by employees as scary. According to Guy Kawasaki, former chief evangelist at Apple:

> Working for Steve was a terrifying and addictive experience. He would tell you that your work, your ideas, and sometimes your existence were worthless right to your face, right in front of everyone. Watching him crucify someone scared you into working incredibly long hours. … Working for Steve was also ecstasy. Once in a while he would tell you that you were great and that made it all worth it. (Cruikshank, 2006: 147)

Apart from displaying such behaviors as parking his car in handicapped places and publicly losing his temper, Jobs often made his employees burst into tears through direct and personal criticism. Robert Sutton, management professor at Stanford, discussed Steve Jobs in his book *The No Asshole Rule*, in the chapter on the virtues of assholes (Sutton, 2007). Sutton then reflected further on his discussion of Steve Jobs in his blog, suggesting that Jobs might be mellowing as he got older (Sutton, 2008). Yet, according to Palo Alto venture capitalist Jean-Louis Gasse, a former Apple executive who once worked with Jobs, "Democracies don't make great products. You need a competent tyrant" (Gasse, quoted in Elkind, 2008).

The high praise as well as high criticism made people try harder, jump higher, and work later into the night. Jobs is credited with imposing discipline on Apple, a quality that the company had lacked for years. The company that used to be known as the "ship that leaks from the top" (Linzmayer, 2004) due to its relaxed management style and corporate culture was soon transformed into a tightly controlled and integrated machine after Jobs' arrival. At Pixar, things were seen differently than at Apple, however. Reportedly Jobs spent less than a day per week there, and was hands off, particularly on the creative front. According to a Pixar employee, "Steve doesn't tell us what to do … Steve's our benevolent benefactor" (quoted in Burrows and Grover, 2006).

Jobs' charisma was depicted in the way he briefed his team concerning a new product: "Even though Steve didn't draw any of the lines, his ideas and inspiration made the design what it is. To be honest, we didn't know what it meant for a computer to be 'friendly' until Jobs told us" (Terry Oyama, quoted in Cruikshank, 2006: 30). As author Scott Kelby put it:

> There is one thing I am certain of: Steve's the right man to lead Apple. There's never been anyone at Apple who has had the impact that Steve has since his return. He may be a tyrant, demanding, unforgiving and the worst boss ever. But he is also a visionary. A genius. A man who gets things done. And the man who kept Apple afloat when a host of other nice guys couldn't. (Cruikshank, 2006: 175)

Jobs brought his own brand of strategic thinking to Apple; based on personal intuition and understanding of technology trends:

> The clearest example was when we were pressured for years to do a PDA, and I realized one day that 90% of the people who use a PDA only take information out of it on the road. Pretty soon cell phones are going to do that so the PDA market's going to get reduced to a fraction of its current size. So we decided not to get into it. If we had gotten into it we wouldn't have the resources to do the iPod. (quoted in Morris, 2008: 69)

Jobs understood that to be different as a company, you have to make tough choices; in Apple's case, this was clearly reflected in the product-markets it decided to pursue, as compared for example to large competitors. Referring to Apple's focus, he noted "I'm as proud of what we don't do as I am of what we do" (quoted in Burrows and Grover, 2006).

Preparing Apple for the post-Jobs era

Jobs' immense influence on Apple had given pause for skepticism regarding Apple's future without him. As *Fortune* magazine's editor Elkind noted: "In the 26 years that Fortune has been ranking America's Most Admired Companies never has the corporation at the head of the list so closely resembled a one-man show" (Elkind, 2008). After the onset of pancreatic cancer in 2003 and an operation to address it in 2004, by 2009 Jobs' health was again deteriorating. In January 2009 he announced that he was taking leave of absence from Apple until June, due to health issues relating to a "hormone imbalance." COO Tim Cook would handle day-to-day operations, and Jobs would stay involved in major strategic decisions.

Commentators disagreed on the degree of impact Jobs' absence would have. Some said that the new products Apple would introduce over the following 18 months had already been developed, and that Cook would manage Apple effectively in Jobs' absence. Others, however, believed that Jobs' motivational role, negotiation skills, and creative vision were crucial for Apple and therefore Jobs' absence would adversely affect the company (Macworld, 2009). Another medical leave followed in 2011, and in August 2011 Jobs resigned from his position as CEO, and Tim Cook, former COO, was appointed as CEO. In his letter of resignation he wrote: "I have always said if there ever came a day when I could no longer meet my duties and expectations as Apple's CEO, I would be the first to let you know. Unfortunately, that day has come" (Primack, 2011). He remained at Apple as Chairman, until his passing in October 2011. Cook's leadership role in Apple's operations since 1998 had given him a deep understanding of the company and a prominent position, being the only person to have a vast area of responsibility apart from Jobs and the one who replaced him during his medical absences.

During his last few years in the company Jobs wanted to make sure that the company's core values (the relentless perfectionism, the focus on design, the close cross-functional collaboration, and constant feedback loops), for which he so passionately fought, would guide Apple in his absence. In 2008, Jobs created the Apple University and personally hired Joel Podolny, then Dean of the Yale School of Management, who led a team of business professors to create a series of case studies on Apple's critical points in its history. These cases described strategic issues such as Apple's retail strategy and its iPhone supply chain strategy; and how Apple executives took decisions at these points. The cases aimed at training and preparing the next generation of Apple executives; as well as inculcating Apple's values and DNA to future executives (Lashinsky, 2011).

Many agreed that Jobs had built around him a team of competent, high-performing individuals who shared the same values and working style and could continue along the same lines in his absence (Snell, 2009). According to observers, Jobs' most important achievement was to make an entire company act and think like himself (McCracken, 2011b): "You can ask anyone in the company what Steve wants and you'll get an answer, even if 90% of them have never met Steve" (Lashinsky, 2011). In the end, Jobs' greatest achievement may not have been the design of the iMac, the iPod, the iPhone, or the iPad, but the design of Apple Inc. itself.

ENTERING A NEW APPLE ERA

Upon becoming Apple's CEO, Tim Cook maintained a low profile and focused on managing the transition to the post-Jobs era as smoothly as possible. He sent the following email to Apple employees to reassure them that he would remain faithful to Apple's DNA:

> I want you to be confident that Apple is not going to change. I cherish and celebrate Apple's unique principles and values. Steve built a company and culture that is unlike any other in the world and we are going to stay true to that — it is in our DNA. We are going to continue to make the best products in the world that delight our customers and make our employees incredibly proud of what they do. (in Cheng, 2011)

Apart from being a known workaholic who would begin emailing his colleagues at 4:30am or arrange meetings at any time of the day, little was known about the man who stood behind Jobs for almost 14 years. Observers noted, however, that Cook appeared to be more collegial than Jobs, giving much air time during his first keynote speech to his team: "the one thing about Apple that will change going forward is that we are not going to see one person representing himself as the physical manifestation of all Apple" (Menn and Dembosky, 2011). Contrary to the flamboyant personality of his predecessor, Cook was characterized as a "quiet, soft-spoken, low-key executive" and "the yin to Jobs' yang" (Friedman, 2011); but also as demanding and unemotional (Lashinsky, 2008).

Cook was recognized for his unprecedented discipline and focus on raising efficiency and market reach at Apple, having made some drastic decisions including closing down most of Apple's manufacturing plans, streamlining logistics, and pushing sales towards high-end retail outlets (Johnson, 2011). He was a strong believer in maintaining minimum inventory: "You kind of want to manage it like you're in the dairy business, if it gets past its freshness date, you have a problem" (quoted in Lashinsky, 2008).

During his first few months as CEO Cook announced the company's highest quarterly revenue in Apple's history for the first quarter of fiscal year 2012. With record quarterly revenues of $46.3bn and record sales of 37 million iPhone units and 15.4 million iPad units (Apple, 2012), Apple showed that its momentum was not only going strong, but also increasing. By March 2012, Apple's cash and liquid assets exceeded $100bn; a third of which was held in the USA, and two thirds overseas, managed by an Apple subsidiary, Braeburn Capital, based in Nevada. For the first time in 17 years, Apple announced in early 2012 that it would return money to shareholders through dividends and share buybacks amounting to $45bn. Even so, it was estimated that its cash hoard would rise to over $200bn by the end of 2014 (Duke, 2012). Apple's cash and liquid assets stood at $155bn in September 2014.

Despite record profits, by 2014 Apple was facing new challenges: one was the effects of leadership transition, with many observers wondering whether Apple could retain its distinct culture and set of capabilities after Jobs, particularly its ability to redefine markets with groundbreaking offerings. Further, in the smartphone market Apple was facing a strong alternative technology in terms of Google's Android system. High-quality hardware, which many believed were as good as the iPhone, were available from Samsung, such as the Samsung Galaxy. Amazon's Kindle was improving with subsequent releases.

Apple was competing in a technology industry where many companies, inspired by Apple's own model, started to move away from single devices and specialization towards mobile connectivity and interconnected service offerings. The benefits of the ecosystem approach were obvious, but there were also potential costs, that customers however seemed to not care too much about. According to an observer, Apple offers "beautiful hardware and intuitive software that, most of the time, is even more of a joy to use than it is to look at. The downside, … is that you are utterly in its hands: if you change your mind, there is no easy way out of Apple's system." (Greene, 2010).

After Jobs' passing, Apple continued to have outstanding financial performance. By early 2015, however, it had not introduced another groundbreaking product along the lines of the iPod, iPhone, or iPad. The Apple Watch was about to be launched, but there were several question marks about its ability to reach the kind of revenue figures that would make a difference to Apple's total revenues of $182bn in 2014. Analysts were wondering whether Apple would be able to sustain its innovation magic now that its chief architect had gone? Was Apple's operating model better understood by competitors and in danger of imitation? Was Apple making the best use of its enviable cash hoard? Could it keep delivering blockbuster products, which would result in the level of growth and profit performance that markets expected? Was Apple's huge size becoming a liability? What should Apple do differently, if anything, to address its strategic challenges and sustain its exceptional performance to date?

TABLE 13.1 Timeline of Apple's Chief Executive Officers

1977–1981	Michael Scott
1981–1985	Mike Markkula
1985–1993	John Sculley
1993–1996	Michael Spindler
1996–1997	Gil Amelio
1997–2000	Steve Jobs (Interim CEO)
2000–2011	Steve Jobs
2011–	Timothy Cook

REFERENCES

Apple Inc. (2007) 100 million ipods sold. April 9. Available at: www.apple.com/pr/library/2007/04/09ipod.html (date accessed: December 23, 2008).
Apple Inc. (2011) Annual Report.
Apple Inc. (2012) Apple reports first quarter results. January 24. Available at: www.apple.com/pr/library/2012/01/24Apple-Reports-First-Quarter-Results.html (date accessed: February 2, 2012).
Apple Inc. (2014) Annual Report.
Apple Inc. (2015) Watch. Available at: www.apple.com/uk/watch/ (date accessed: March 27, 2015).
Bajarin, B. (2011) Why competing with Apple is so difficult. *Time*, July 1. Available at: http://techland.time.com/2011/07/01/why-competing-with-apple-is-so-difficult/#ixzz1kZGeJkLX (date accessed: February 2, 2012).
BBC (2009) Microsoft and Yahoo seal web deal. July 29. Available at: http://news.bbc.co.uk/2/hi/8174763.stm (date accessed: February 2, 2012).
Booth, C. (1997) Steve's job: Restart Apple. *Time*, August 18. Available at: www.time.com/time/magazine/article/0,9171,986849,00.html (date accessed: December 23, 2008).
Burrows, P. (2004) The seed of Apple's innovation. Interview with Steve Jobs, *Business Week*, October 12. Available at: www.businessweek.com/bwdaily/dnflash/oct2004/nf20041012_4018_db083.htm (date accessed: December 1, 2008).
Burrows, P. and Grover, R. (2006) Steve Jobs' magic kingdom. *Business Week*, February 6. Available at: www.businessweek.com/magazine/content/06_06/b3970001.htm (date accessed: December 23, 2008).

Cheng, J. (2011) Tim Cook says "Apple is not going to change." *Wired*, August 25. Available at: www.wired.com/epicenter/2011/08/tim-cook-says-apple-is-not-going-to-change/ (date accessed: February 2, 2012).

Cruikshank, J. (2006) *The Apple Way*. New York: McGraw Hill.

Doz, Y. and Kosonen, M. (2008) *Fast Strategy*. Harlow: Wharton School Publishing, Pearson Education.

Duke, S. (2012) Apple's $100bn headache. *Sunday Times*, March 25, Business, p. 7.

Economist (2010) Steve Jobs and the tablet of hope. January 28. Available at: www.economist.com/node/15394190 (date accessed: February 2, 2012).

Economist (2011a) Largest non-financial companies. August 20. Available at: www.economist.com/node/21526381 (date accessed: February 2, 2012).

Economist (2011b) Information technology. November 17. Available at: www.economist.com/node/21537946 (date accessed: February 2, 2012).

Economist (2012) iRational? March 24, pp. 79–81.

Elkind, P. (2008) The trouble with Steve Jobs. *Fortune*, March 5. Available at: http://money.cnn.com/2008/03/02/news/companies/elkind_jobs.fortune/index.htm (date accessed: December 1, 2008).

Elmer-DeWitt, P. (2012) Apple blows past expectations in first post-Steve Jobs report. *Fortune*, January 24. Available at: http://tech.fortune.cnn.com/2012/01/24/click-here-for-apples-earnings/ (date accessed: February 2, 2012).

Forbes (2012a) Apple dominates PC market by destroying it. February 2. Available at: www.forbes.com/sites/greatspeculations/2012/02/01/apple-dominates-pc-market-by-destroying-it/ (date accessed: February 2, 2012).

Forbes (2012b) Amazon plays catch up with kindle fire, braces for iPad 3. January 24. Available at: www.forbes.com/sites/greatspeculations/2012/01/24/amazon-plays-catch-up-with-kindle-fire-braces-for-ipad-3/ (date accessed: February 2, 2012).

Friedman, L. (2011) Apple turns to Tim Cook to replace Steve Jobs. *Macworld.com*, August 25. Available at: www.macworld.com/article/161929/2011/08/apple_turns_to_tim_cook_to_replace_steve_jobs.html (date accessed: February 2, 2012).

Greene, R. (2010) Apple V Google. *Intelligent Life*, Winter. Available at: http://moreintelligentlife.com/content/ideas/robert-lane-greene/apple-v-google (date accessed: February 2, 2012).

Grossman, L. (2005) How Apple does it. *Time*, October 16. Available at: www.time.com/time/magazine/article/0,9171,1118384,00.html (date accessed: December 1, 2008).

Guardian (2008) Reading the runes for Apple. January 10. Available at: www.guardian.co.uk/technology/2008/jan/10/apple.steve.jobs (date accessed: December 11, 2008).

Hansen, M., Ibarra, H., and Peyer, U. (2010) The best performing CEOs in the world. *Harvard Business Review*, 88(1/2): 104–13.

HP Annual Report (2007) 162 pp.

IBM Annual Report (2007) 124 pp.

Intel Annual Report (2007) 115 pp.

Isaacson, W. (2011) American icon. *Time*, October 17. Available at: www.time.com/time/magazine/article/0,9171,2096327,00.html#ixzz1kZBq5m00 (date accessed: February 2, 2012).

Jobs, S. (2010) Interview at D8 Conference. Available at: http://allthingsd.com/20100607/steve-jobs-at-d8-the-full-uncut-interview/ (date accessed: October 30, 2015).

Johnson, B. (2011) Apple shares fall as Jobs quits. BBC News, August 24. Available at: www.bbc.co.uk/news/business-14661845 (date accessed: February 2, 2012).

Kahney, L. (2008) How Apple got everything right by doing everything wrong. *Wired*, April: 137–42.

Lashinsky, A. (2008) The genius behind Steve. *Fortune*, November 10. Available at: http://money.cnn.com/2008/11/09/technology/cook_apple.fortune/index.htm (date accessed: February 2, 2012).

Lashinsky, A. (2011) How Apple works: Inside the world's biggest startup. *Fortune*, August 25. Available at: http://tech.fortune.cnn.com/2011/08/25/how-apple-works-inside-the-worlds-biggest-startup/ (date accessed: February 2, 2012).

Lashinsky, A. (2012) The secrets Apple keeps. *Fortune*, January 18. Available at: http://tech.fortune.cnn.com/2012/01/18/inside-apple-adam-lashinsky/ (date accessed: February 2, 2012).

Linzmayer, O. W. (2004) *Apple Confidential 2.0: The Definitive History of the World's Most Colorful Company*. San Francisco: No Starch Press.

Macworld (2009) Jobs to take leave of absence until June. January 14. Available at: www.macworld.com/article/138215/2009/01/jobs.html?t=201 (date accessed: January 24, 2009).

McCracken, H. (2011a) Steve Jobs, 1955–2011: Mourning technology's great reinventor. *Time*, October 5. Available at: www.time.com/time/business/article/0,8599,2096251,00.html#ixzz1kxgHRRtE (date accessed: February 2, 2012).

McCracken, H. (2011b) The Beginning of the Post-Steve Jobs Era. *Time*, August 25. Available at: www.time.com/time/business/article/0,8599,2090322,00.html#ixzz1kZKmJHSA (date accessed: February 2, 2012).

Mellow, J. (2012) Apple passes HP in PC Shipments – or did it? *PC World*, January 31. Available at: www.pcworld.com/article/249054/apple_passes_hp_in_pc_sales_or_did_it_.html (date accessed: February 2, 2012).

Menn, J. and Dembosky, A. (2011) Apple's mystery men line up to fill the void. *Financial Times*, October 6. Available at: www.ft.com/cms/s/2/76aa0be6-f03d-11e0-96d2-00144feab49a.html#axzz1lD8qauF8 (date accessed: February 2, 2012).

Microsoft (2008) Annual Report. Available at: www.microsoft.com/investor/reports/ar11/index.html (date accessed: March 20, 2012).

Morris, B. (2008) What makes Apple golden. *Fortune*, March 17, 157(5): 68–71.

New York Times (2012a) Microsoft Corporation. February 2. Available at: http://topics.nytimes.com/top/news/business/companies/microsoft_corporation/index.html (date accessed: February 2, 2012).

New York Times (2012b) Four Screens Are Better than One with Lenovo's New "Personal Cloud" Vision. January 9. Available at: http://markets.on.nytimes.com/research/stocks/news/press_release.asp?docTag=201201081900BIZWIRE_USPRX_BW5060&feedID=600&press_symbol=185010 (date accessed: February 2, 2012).

Nuttall, C. (2011) Apple in race to keep ahead in 2012. *Financial Times*, December 19. Available at: www.ft.com/intl/cms/s/2/6a7cac22-31db-11e1-9be2-00144feabdc0.html#axzz1lD8qauF8 (date accessed: February 2, 2012).

Primack, D. (2011) Fallen Apple: Steve Jobs resigns. *Fortune*, August 24. http://finance.fortune.cnn.com/2011/08/24/fallen-apple-steve-jobs-resigns/ (date accessed: February 2, 2012).

Rusche, D. (2011) Apple pips Exxon as world's biggest company. *Guardian*, August 9. www.guardian.co.uk/business/2011/aug/09/apple-pips-exxon-as-worlds-biggest-company (date accessed: February 2, 2012).

Satariano, A. and Burrows, P. (2011) Steve Jobs uses iCloud to pick apart industry he helped form. Bloomberg, June 7. Available at: www.bloomberg.com/news/2011-06-07/apple-s-jobs-using-icloud-to-dismantle-the-pc-industry-he-helped-build.html (date accessed: February 2, 2012).

Shukla, A. (2011) Worldwide PC shipments slip in 2011. *PC World*, April 17. Available at: www.pcworld.com/article/225386/worldwide_pc_shipments_slip_in_2011.html (date accessed: February 2, 2012).

Snell, J. (2009) Apple: We're not a one-man show. Macworld.com. January 22. Available at: www.macworld.com/article/138370/2009/01/jobs_cook.html (date accessed: February 2, 2012).

Sutton, R. I. (2007) *The No Asshole Rule: Building a Civilized Workplace and Surviving One That Isn't*. New York: Business Plus.

Sutton, R. I. (2008) Fortune story on the trouble with Steve Jobs: Asshole, genius, or both? March 6. Available at: http://bobsutton.typepad.com/my_weblog/2008/03/fortune-story-o.html (date accessed: December 23, 2008).

Tozzi, J. (2007) The greatest entrepreneurs of all time. *Business Week*, June 27. http://www.businessweek.com/smallbiz/content/jun2007/sb20070627_564139.htm (date accessed: December 1, 2008).

Waters, R. (2012) Looking behind the curtain at Apple. *Los Angeles Times*, January 29. Available at: http://www.latimes.com/business/la-fi-books-20120129,0,4885088.story (date accessed: February 2, 2012).

Yahoo Finance (2008) Apple Inc. profile. Available at: http://finance.yahoo.com/q/pr?s=AAPL (date accessed: December 23, 2008).

Yoffie, D. B. and Slind, M. (2008) *Apple Inc., 2008*. Harvard Business School, Case 9-708-480, 32pp.

CENTRICA: STRATEGIZING IN A MULTI-UTILITY[1]

14

> My company, Centrica, is well experienced at facing change. In a way we were lucky because it was forced on us. We simply had to adapt to stay alive. But today, change is woven into the fabric of our business … By any stretch of the imagination the Centrica story is an extraordinary one. We've lived through the most intense period of upheaval and have changed beyond recognition. Roy Gardner, CEO

This case presents the events leading to the creation of Centrica, a unique multi-business firm, and covers the period 1997–2001. It also reflects on the main issues that Centrica's leadership was facing in the early stages of the company's life. The case invites the reader to consider the challenges of developing strategy in firms with multiple business units, as well as the challenges of executing strategy under an uncertain and competitive environment.

A CHANGING INDUSTRY

Deregulation of Electricity

The UK electricity and gas markets underwent a complete transformation during the privatization process in the 1990s. Before this process, the Central Electricity Generation Board (CEGB) was responsible for the generation and transmission of electricity in the UK, while the regional electricity boards were responsible for the distribution and supply of electricity. Following the privatization of the telecommunications sector in 1984, the gas industry in 1986, and the water industry in 1989, the UK government initiated the privatization of the electricity industry on March 31, 1990 (named Vesting Day). The main reasons for the privatization of the electricity

---

[1]This case was prepared by Sotirios Paroutis for the purposes of class discussion; it deals with a particular snapshot in the company's history and is not meant to illustrate effective or ineffective handling of administration situations.

market were the need to improve the efficiency of the sector and to offer increased value for customers. As a result, the industry was divided into four components: generation, transmission, distribution, and supply. PowerGen and National Power joined the private sector and took over the responsibility for non-nuclear electricity generation within England and Wales. Nuclear generation became the responsibility of Nuclear Electric, which remained in public ownership.

The infrastructure required for electricity transmission across England and Wales became the responsibility of the National Grid Company (NGC), while the distribution and supply was handed over to the regional electricity companies (RECs) (formerly known as the regional electricity boards). In Scotland, electricity generation, transmission, distribution, and supply were handed over to two vertically integrated companies, ScottishPower and Scottish Hydro. In 1990 competition in generation began when the electricity industry was privatized and since then a number of independent power producers have entered the market. Competition in supply also began in 1990 when customers with a demand in excess of 1MW were able to choose their supplier. Customers in the 100kW to 1MW market were able to choose their supplier in 1994. Total liberalization entered its final stage with the opening of the domestic electricity market in September 1998. This process was completed in July 1999 (see Figure 14.1).

Deregulation of Natural Gas

In 1982 the Oil and Gas (Enterprise) Act set the basis for competition into the gas supply market by enabling independent gas suppliers to sell gas to users who consumed 25,000 therms per annum or more. British Gas was the main player in this market. Before its privatization in 1986, British Gas was a nationalized company, handling all related activities in the midstream and downstream markets, from the purchase of gas, to storage, transportation, and the supply of gas to industrial, commercial, and domestic users.

As the monopoly supplier of gas in the UK, British Gas was the only source of custom for companies involved in production in the UK gas fields. It therefore decided to sign extensive

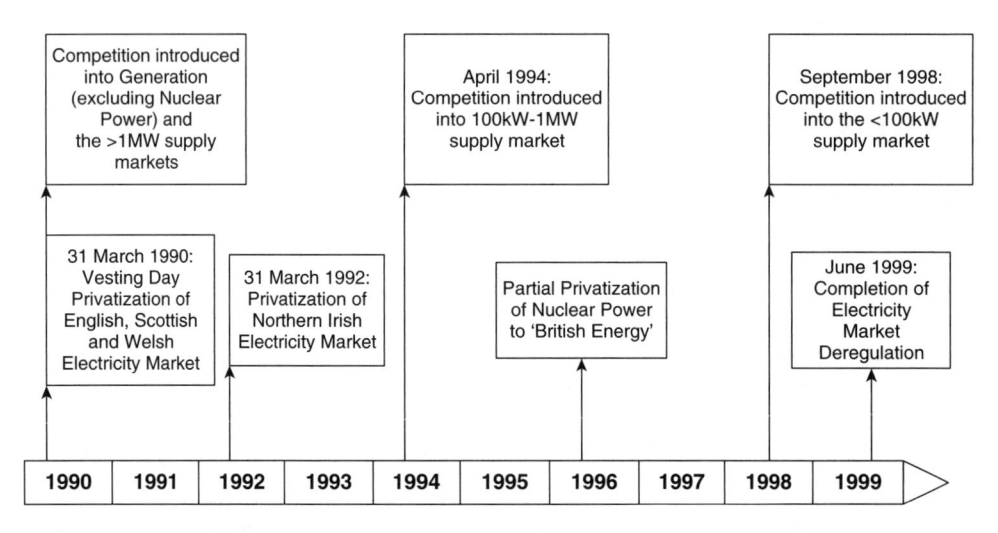

FIGURE 14.1 The deregulation timeline of electricity in the UK

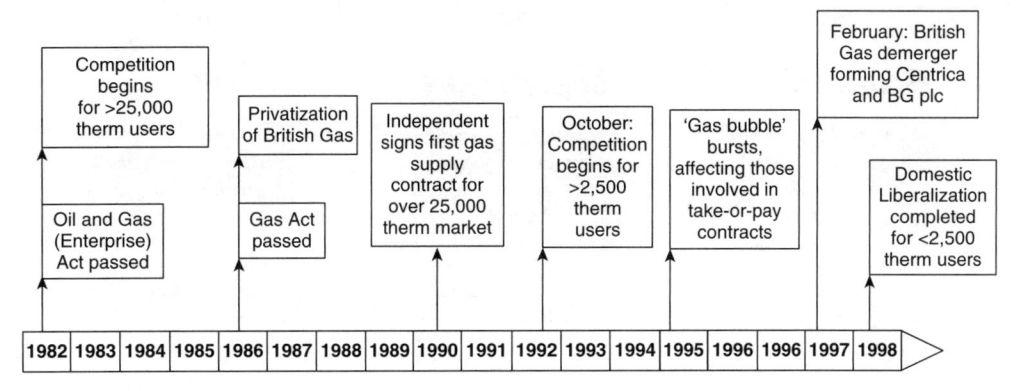

FIGURE 14.2 The deregulation timeline of natural gas in the UK

long-term (take or pay) contracts with producers, guaranteeing it would take all of the gas it produced or recompense those companies by paying the difference between its stated contract purchases and the amount actually purchased. British Gas declared that contracts were introduced in an effort to meet the obligations in its license, to maintain supply to all of its customers in the UK and to motivate upstream producers towards exploring and developing new gas fields. However, Ofgas, the industry regulator, decided that from March 1992 British Gas would firstly have to sell gas on the basis of a published and non-discriminatory schedule and secondly that it would have to lose a pre-determined percentage of its 100% dominance of the gas supply market. As a result, British Gas lost 60% of its market share in the 25,000 therm market and 45% in the 2,500 therm market, which was opened to competition in October 1992. The introduction of competition into the domestic market started in April 1996. The final stage of full deregulation of the domestic gas market was completed in May 1998, when all domestic customers were able to choose their supplier (see Figure 14.2).

SURVIVING THE EARLY YEARS

From British Gas to Centrica

Centrica was originally formed as part of the restructuring program for British Gas, when British Gas was demerged into two separate companies, BG and Centrica. The process began the previous decade, in 1986, with the privatization of the state-held gas monopoly, British Gas. British Gas was the sole natural gas supplier until 1990, when deregulation provided the opportunity for commercial competition. It was a vertically integrated firm and it was a classic example of the utility that extracted the gas out of the ground and then supplied it to homes and businesses. Hence, it was asset dominated and its focus was engineering excellence. Customer service was not a priority and the culture was dominated by a public sector ethos.

> It had been a successful company. And the old business model had worked. But its world was changing; specifically, competition in its core market was coming. And frankly it wasn't in any fit shape to compete. (Sir Roy Gardner, CEO)

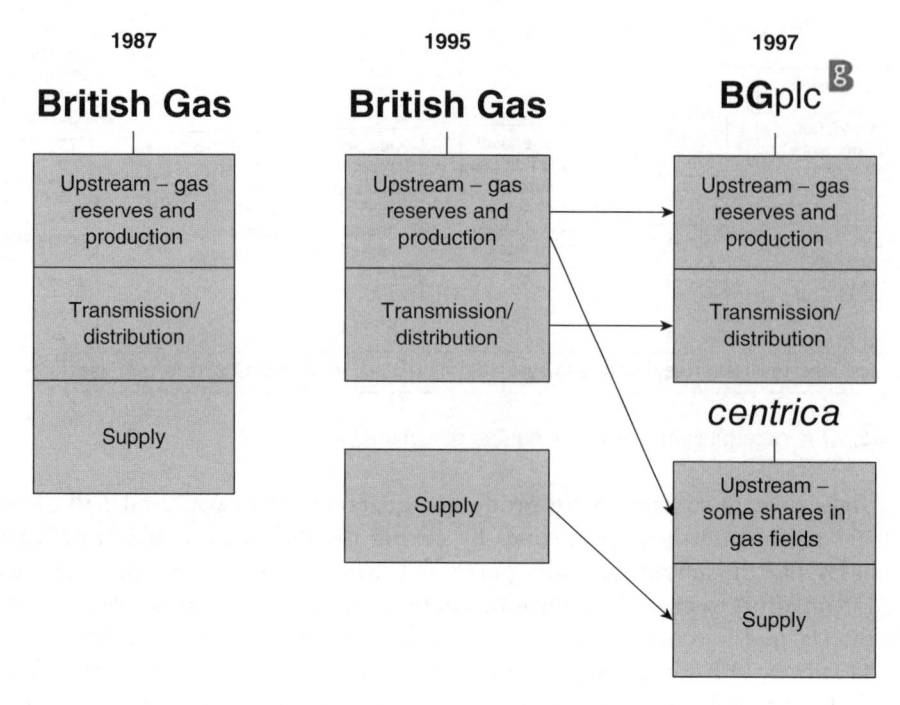

FIGURE 14.3 The principal stages in the demerger of British Gas

Despite its past success, British Gas was at the end of the 1990s facing a number of problems. First of all it had a seriously uncompetitive cost base. The main problem was the amount it was paying for its gas because of its historical take-or-pay contracts. And despite some cost-cutting it still suffered from significant over-manning. Customer service was suffering to the extent that some of the media were referring to British Gas as the most loathed company in Britain. And it had some businesses that were making substantial losses, as much as £1million a day.

In February 1997 British Gas plc, was demerged into Centrica plc and BG plc. The main reason for the demerger was that it was considered necessary to formally separate the gas supply and trading business from the monopoly transportation business. Even before 1997, these units of the company had already been forced by the regulator to adopt a policy of "Chinese walls" (see Figure 14.3) between operations to ensure equity in dealings between the transportation and supply arms. Pressure from competitors and the regulator finally led to the division of the two arms. The separation of the businesses focused the specialization needs for the different activities to function in a competitive market.

The demerger split the company into Centrica plc and BG plc (see Figure 14.4). BG plc comprised the gas transportation and storage business of Transco, along with British Gas's exploration and production (less the Morecambe power site, which was given to Centrica), international downstream, research, technology, and property activities. In October 2000 a demerger from BG plc resulted in Transco becoming a part of the Lattice Group plc. Centrica plc comprised the supply and trading business of former British Gas plc and earned the right to trade using the brands: "British Gas" within England, "Nwy Prydain" and "British Gas" in Wales, and "Scottish Gas" in Scotland:

When I joined the old British Gas it was clear to me that the changes required to turn the business around wouldn't happen within the existing structure and culture. A new business model was required. One in which the value chain was broken up ... Managing such diverse activities as engineering and customer service requires different skills, different cultures and different mindsets. This was what the demerger was all about. (Sir Roy Gardner, CEO)

Renegotiating Contracts

The first challenge for Centrica was survival. The speed of the deregulation in the industry drove forward competition in supply. At the same time the drop in the wholesale cost of gas rendered all of the take-or-pay contracts that British Gas had negotiated economically unsound. The combination of these two factors meant that as competition developed and companies accessed gas from different suppliers, British Gas was left with large amounts of gas for which it had contracted but was unable to pass on even some of the cost, as it was losing its industrial client base. With the 1997 demerger, Centrica inherited this economic burden of the take-or-pay contracts. Dealing with these contracts was considered as an important stepping stone for the future of the company. These contracts were the first big challenge for Centrica's management team after the demerger:

> Our first priority was survival ... So we set about renegotiating the gas contracts. We were locked into buying too much gas at prices well above the market – a potential exposure of around £4billion. The contracts had been signed before competition had even been considered. (Sir Roy Gardner, CEO)

> Management in the first phase was set on just surviving, renegotiating all those contracts, turning around the loss making businesses and services and so forth, which it did very successfully. (Jonathan Good, Manager Corporate Centre)

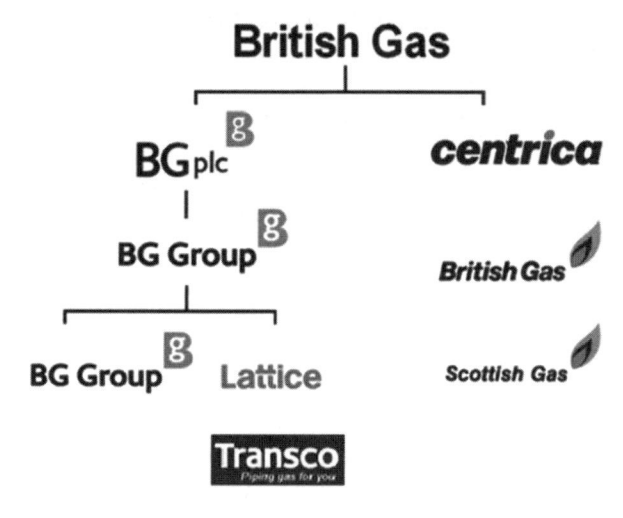

FIGURE 14.4 The companies and brands created after the split of British Gas

Source: www.bgplc.com

By the end of 1998 Centrica had successfully renegotiated most of its take-or-pay contracts with its Chevron contract being terminated in October 1998 and compensation paid to end the deal. The contracts with Conoco, Elf, Total, Phillips, Total Oil Marine, Fina, and Agip were renegotiated with lower volumes supplied and compensation paid accordingly. As a result, Centrica's exposure to the higher prices fixed in previous contracts was significantly reduced. Another important decision was to turn round or shut down the loss-making businesses. Hence 240 British Gas showrooms were closed.

THE CEO

Sir Roy Gardner has been Chief Executive of Centrica plc since it was formed on the demerger of the supply, services, and retail businesses of the former British Gas plc in February 1997. Prior to the demerger, Sir Roy was the Executive Director responsible for the trading businesses of British Gas having joined in November 1994 as Executive Director, Finance.

Before joining British Gas, he was Managing Director of GEC Marconi Limited and was appointed to the Board of GEC in 1994. He was Chief Operating Officer of Northern Telecom Europe Limited following their take-over of STC plc, previous to which he was Managing Director of STC Communications Systems and a member of the Board of STC plc. He joined STC in January 1986 as Finance Director from the Marconi Company Limited where he was Group Finance Director between 1979 and 1985. Sir Roy began his career at the British Aircraft Corporation where he worked in the Commercial Aircraft Division. On January 1, 2000, Sir Roy was appointed as a Non-Executive Director of Manchester United plc, and became Non-Executive Chairman on March 31, 2002. He was a Non-Executive Director of Laporte plc from December 1996 until the company's takeover in April 2001.

In February 1998 he was appointed President of the Carers National Association, now Carers UK. He is also a Trustee of the Development Trust (for the Mentally Handicapped) and was appointed as Chairman of the Employers' Forum on Disability at the beginning of February 2000. Sir Roy is a Fellow of the Chartered Association of Certified Accountants, the Royal Aeronautical Society and the Royal Society of Arts. He is also a Member of the Advisory Council of the Prince's Youth Business Trust and a Companion of the Institute of Management.

He is married with one son and two daughters. He lives in Hertfordshire and is a keen golfer and runner. He has raised money for a number of charities by completing the London Marathon in 1987, 1991, and 1992, the New York Marathon in 1996, and by climbing Mount Kilimanjaro in October 1999.

Source: Centrica Annual Reports; www.centrica.co.uk

Alongside the renegotiation of the take-or-pay contracts, the company also set the task of substantially improving its operational performance. The result was the success of British Gas Services in improving its operating performance, where a loss before exceptional charges of £196 million in 1996 was reduced to a loss of £49 million in 1997. Across the group as a whole a 13% reduction in operating costs before exceptional charges was achieved in 1997 compared with 1996. Finally, in 1998, British Gas Services posted its first profit of £9 million. Since then the services business has steadily recovered and has become a strong contributor in the group's earnings.

The new name

At the time of the demerger from British Gas plc, besides renegotiating the old contracts, it was considered important to come up with a new name. "Centrica" was chosen as the corporate name. This name was selected because of its ease of use internationally. In many languages the word Centrica is meaningless and therefore cannot conflict with overseas language translations. In general practice, Centrica is not positioned as a customer-facing brand, although internationally it is used alongside the local brand name to enable its new businesses to demonstrate a link with some of the core business values and scale of operation in Great Britain. The new name was another indication of a "fresh start" from the heavy legacy of British Gas.

The early organizational structure

In 1997 the Centrica group had four main business segments supplying products and services under both the British Gas and Scottish Gas brands: British Gas trading, British Gas services, Energy Centres, and Centrica Energy Management Group. In addition a number of complementary services, including financial services, in conjunction with joint venture partners, were under development under a fourth segment: British Gas financial services.

British Gas Trading was responsible for the supply of gas and electricity to domestic, industrial, and commercial customers. Domestic customers were supplied under the British Gas Home Energy and Scottish Gas brands. The company also sold to industrial and commercial customers primarily as Business Gas. Customers outside the reach of the mains network were supplied by the liquefied petroleum gas business. Centrica Energy Management Group was responsible for managing all the gas production activities, gas and electricity purchases, and wholesale energy trading of the group. British Gas Services specialized in the installation and servicing of domestic heating and security alarm systems and was aiming towards broadening its range of services provided to the home. Energy Centres were high-street retailers of gas and electric household products with over 240 outlets. British Gas Financial Services involved the Goldfish brand, notably the Goldfish credit card and Goldfish Guides. Centrica's home insurance package was offered under both the British Gas and Goldfish brands.

DEVELOPING AND EXPANDING

Building the "Centrica model"

With resolution of the British Gas legacy problems in sight, the focus of the Centrica management shifted towards implementing a "new business model and getting in shape for the future" (Sir Roy Gardner, CEO). During the early 1980s, vertical integration characterized most energy markets around the world. This enabled countries to build an infrastructure, to protect government strategic assets, and also to provide incentives for people to invest. In most situations, vertically integrated businesses existed and gas, electricity, and water were separate, under state control, and had boundaries set by strict regulations. Over the last 20 years, these vertically integrated businesses have been privatized and their markets liberalized. The value chains have been fragmented as those parts of the value chain that could be subject to competition have been opened up.

Overall, the main contextual changes in the broad UK electricity and gas industry concerned its regulatory status and the introduction of new technologies. The deregulation and liberalization process broke up the main segments that make up the electricity value chain (generation-transmission/distribution-supply). Hence utilities have been forced by the regulator to separate their businesses and the traditional model of vertically integrated monolithic utilities seems no longer to be justified since there is no longer room for considerable economies of scale. Alongside deregulation, new generation technologies have consistently reduced the minimum thresholds of efficient entry into a market, because of their lower costs compared to old-style nuclear or fossil-fuelled generation. Therefore, investment on a massive scale is no longer needed to enter the electricity market. As a result, many utilities from being a nationalized vertically integrated have moved to a situation where their management is making choices about the elements of the value chain on which they should concentrate. At the same time the lift of public protection has made utilities more sensitive to competition and customer-related issues.

In these new conditions, Centrica's CEO and other key executives sought to replace the old utility model that they inherited from British Gas. At the same time, it was widely accepted that customer acquisition and retention was gradually becoming very expensive, cutting margins to almost nothing. One way to deal with this issue was to sell a wide range of products and services to each customer, increasing individual customer value. To achieve this, the top management decided to develop a new business model where customer satisfaction and retention would be central. The new design would be powered by the drive to gain as much value from each customer as possible but at the same time reward loyal customers. However, this bold decision not to build Centrica around the established utility model where assets were a central priority raised a number of doubts regarding the future financial stability of the company. Investors and analysts were among the ones who expressed their worries:

> In the utility sector our split was ground-breaking. It was the first time that a utility customer base had been separated from the physical assets that supplied it. At demerger some commentators didn't give Centrica much hope. They called us "duff gas plc"! Little wonder that many of my colleagues thought I was mad to become its Chief Executive! (Sir Roy Gardner, CEO)

Despite these initial doubts, Centrica's management saw the demerger as a prime chance to build a new business model where the customer would have a prime position together with a strong asset base and retailing/supply capabilities. In contrast to the other business models dominating the utilities sector, namely the "pure independent power producer," "integrated independent power producer," "pure retail reseller," and "traditional utility" models, the new model would focus on gaining the maximum value per customer by exploiting synergies across multiple areas of expertise (see Table 14.1).

TABLE 14.1 The priorities of the Centrica model

	Areas of Expertise				
Model	Customers	Assets	Energy	Retailing	Outcome
Pure Independent Power Producer	×	√	√	×	total exposure to wholesale volatility
Integrated Independent Power Producer	√	×	×	√	inability to manage wholesale volatility and procurement
Pure Retail Reseller	√	√	√	×	Wholesale market focus; retail customers are a hedge
Traditional Utility	√	√	√	×	primary focus on asset mgmt; regulated return limits innovation
Centrica	√	√	√	√	Primary focus on customer; asset hedge to mitigate volatility

Source: Strategy presentation at the Global Power and Gas Leaders Conference, New York 18 September 2002 from: www.centrica.com

> With demerger we had the chance to start afresh. To determine what business we wanted to be in. What structure we needed. Build a new culture. Get rid of many of the old processes and develop new ways of working. And build new relationships without the baggage of the old ones. (Sir Roy Gardner, CEO)

It is noteworthy that the energy customer was already high in the list of priorities for the Centrica management team since the demerger effectively placed Centrica responsible for the customer-orientated British Gas businesses; providing gas, electricity and energy-related products and services to homes and businesses in the UK. Further than that, the demerger enabled the top management team to focus on the customer service issue in a way that was considered almost impossible under the old British Gas structure. Hence, Centrica became the first utility to make customer satisfaction an integral part of executive pay packages and the management team invested heavily on improving the company's customer support systems and training its staff.

Assets were also central in the new model and were considered important for the future of the company. Hence, since the demerger Centrica moved towards acquiring a number of smaller assets to increase its offshore gas resources. In October 1998 it acquired its first upstream operation for £248 million, PowerGen's North Sea (PGNS) division, which was renamed Centrica Resources. Two agreements to purchase offshore gas assets in the Southern North Sea and East Irish Sea from Dana Petroleum and British Borneo Oil & Gas were announced in February 1999. Centrica Resources purchased further offshore gas assets in the Southern North Sea in

October 1999. In the same month the company also announced an agreement with Veba Oil and Gas UK to purchase its 4.6% in the Hewett area fields and the associated Bacton Phillips terminal and 10% interest in the Thames area field. This increased Centrica's Hewett holding to 13.1%. To further expand its operations in the home market Centrica purchased Shells LPG (liquid petroleum gas) business.

The impact of these moves soon became evident in the company's share price and its main division of energy supply, gas supply and related services. In this segment the company became the largest supplier of residential gas. It also supplied a quarter of the UK's industrial gas and became the UK's largest heating installation and servicing company, through British Gas and Scottish Gas.

The Acquisition of the AA

Of paramount importance to the Centrica model was also the notion of growing the business by entering new markets; developing or acquiring new products, services, and brands. After the initial period of surviving and sorting out the "household," the top management team started considering new growth alternatives in an effort to sustain the growth momentum of the group and reduce the impact of the increasingly stiff competition in the energy market:

> If we changed nothing Centrica would be a shrinking business. Competition would take away market share and squeeze margins. But I wouldn't have agreed to become Chief Executive if I hadn't seen that there would be opportunities to grow the business. By entering new markets. Selling other products or services which would earn margins beyond those achievable in just gas. (Sir Roy Gardner, CEO)

This approach led the top management team towards a new potential area of growth previously not considered by other utilities, i.e., road services:

> A couple of years ago we were holding on strongly to our gas market share. We'd successfully entered the electricity market. Things were going well. But our opportunities for growth were limited. It was time to take a fresh look at what other parts of the household purse we could compete for. Essentially that's the story behind our purchase of the Automobile Association. (Sir Roy Gardner, CEO)

It occurred to the Centrica top management that after the home, the car is the next biggest source of expense and hassle to most households. So they looked at how the company could capitalize on that, using its skills and experience in the road services market:

> In terms of '99 it was probably that was really sort of saying okay well Centrica's survived that, we've done a mixture of defensive actions, like going into electricity, creating Goldfish, solving the take or pay contract issue we had. And now sort of saying well what are we going to do with these earnings and wanting to be a growth company. And sort of you know trying to make sure "well what is Centrica?" It's not a traditional utility … so it was looking to say "well what do we think are our core strengths?" In and around energy supply "well yes we're already big into that in the UK" but to find out opportunities in North America and Europe because those markets are being opened. And of course we had products and things being sold around the home like the central heating and those sorts of things, so trying to expand out of that. And the AA, whilst it is about the car, was seen as being a good fit with that. (Jack Foster, Energy Manager)

CENTRICA: STRATEGIZING IN A MULTI-UTILITY

Historically, the AA (Automobile Association) can be considered as a unique organization. Founded in 1905 by a group of motoring enthusiasts to initially help motorists avoid police speed traps, it is one of the most well-recognized and respected brands in the UK. It also provides a range of services from insurance, finance, vehicle inspections, driving tuition, AA publications through to up-to-the-minute traffic and travel information to assist the motoring public at large. The AA has also been the long-established voice of the motorist – respected by members, the public, safety experts, and government – on transport issues. With 9.4 million members in 1999, the AA was by far the largest motoring organization with some 3,600 highly trained patrols:

> the AA I think was seen from Centrica's side as having a lot of ... congruity with British Gas, the same kind of position in the national psyche, being around a lot of time, trust, you let British Gas engineers into your home and you trust the AA patrol man, running large fleets of vehicles, call-centres etc. And I think that was the first step to show that Centrica could ... move outside its historical energy footprint. And, it was well received by the city as moving Centrica forward. (Jonathan Good, Manager Corporate Centre)

The strong customer base of the AA and the potential synergies with British Gas (see Figure 14.5) drew the attention of the Centrica management. In July 1999 Centrica performed its largest corporate decision to date with the acquisition of the AA for £1.1 billion.

> Well – it fitted with our vision of taking care of the essentials. And there were huge operational synergies. We already had a fleet of mobile engineers who fixed things in customers' homes. The AA had a fleet of mobile engineers who fixed things at the roadside. The skills, processes and mindsets involved in managing these two fleets were closely aligned. Most importantly the acquisition gave us more customer relationships that we could learn from and leverage. (Sir Roy Gardner, CEO)

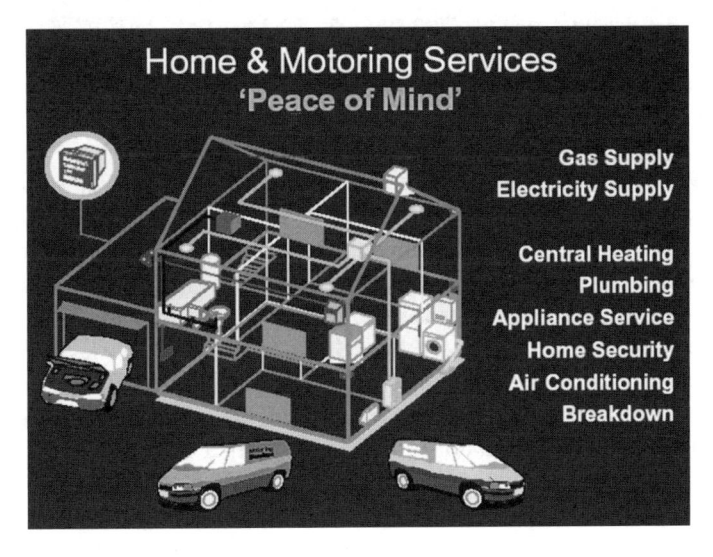

FIGURE 14.5 The AA motoring services complement the British Gas home services

Source: 'AA Acquisition' investor presentation from www.centrica.com

The AA reached its milestone customer level in October 2000 at the Motor Show in Birmingham, when the company signed up its 10 millionth subscriber. Overall, in four years AA membership grew from 9.4 million to more than 12 million and the AA started playing a growing part in Centrica's business. Also the AA brand has expanded in other areas. More specifically, Centrica offers home and motor insurance through the AA, with over 1.6 million policies in force, making the AA the number one insurance intermediary in Britain. AA Publishing also became the largest travel publisher in Britain, with AA guides and maps the leading products. Finally, the AA website grew into a well-regarded source of consumer information.

Further Acquisitions and Expansion

Following the acquisition of the AA, Centrica's management decided on a number of acquisitions aimed at supporting the Centrica model. The objective was to develop the existing British services further to gain a larger share in related markets, to increase international operations, especially in the USA and Canada, and at the same time to diversify further by securing more partnerships in newer customer segments and markets. The following three sections expose the most important of these acquisitions.

Financial Services – Goldfish

Goldfish was initially launched in September 1996 as the name of an innovative new credit card. The brand was created to allow British Gas to diversify into new commercial areas such as financial services, and was its first product in partnership with HFC Bank plc. The credit card proved a considerable success:

> The introduction of Goldfish credit card ... was [used] ... as a "defensive measure" to help retain gas customers because the more you spend on your Goldfish card, the more money you get off your gas bill and plus other products and services ... So Goldfish, sort of, arrived on the scene "by accident", used as a defensive measure, a new brand which has big recognition and personality of its own. (Jonathan Good, Manager Corporate Centre)

In just over four years, Goldfish grew to become the UK's seventh largest credit card (Source: HPI Research credit card tracking study 1996–2000). The rate of growth to over 1,000,000 cardholders has been extraordinary and unprecedented in the UK. A key reason for this success was the introduction of an innovative rewards program that allowed customers to save money on a range of home essentials. The rewards scheme offered vouchers for use in a range of shops, including the John Lewis Partnership, Dixons, Boots, Asda, and Marks and Spencer. Savings could also be made on British Gas bills and on a TV licence. In June 1998, Goldfish took its first step outside the financial services sector. Goldfish Guide is a set of tailor-made buying guides to help consumers make decisions on major purchases. Goldfish Guide covers different categories of cars, computers, domestic appliances, and home entertainment products. It was a response to the widespread frustrations of time-harried consumers having to plough through a mass of information when trying to decide on a major purchase. Goldfish Guide was initially published in printed form, and more than a million consumers requested a Guide to help simplify normally difficult buying decisions. In Fall 2000 Goldfish Guide was developed into an online service, with customers able to access up-to-date product information on the Goldfish website. Goldfish also developed a variety of financial services offerings for its customers, building on the ISA launched in 2000. It also entered the e-commerce world with the launch of the e-Tail Price Index in October 2000. This closely replicates the Retail Price Index (RPI) for online purchases and receives significant press, political, and economic interest.

Telecommunications – One.Tel

Centrica launched a telecommunications service, British Gas Communications, in September 2000 after reaching alliance agreements with Cable & Wireless, Vodafone, and Torch Telecom. This service quickly attracted around 340,000 active customers. To enable targeting of further customer segments, Centrica acquired the UK operation of One.Tel in July 2001. In that way Centrica extended not only its customer base but also the range of fixed mobile and internet (narrowband and broadband) services it could offer to potential customers.

International Expansion – Luminus, Energy America and Direct Energy

Growth continued in 2000 when Centrica moved into the US energy market. In July 2000 Centrica purchased Direct Energy Marketing Ltd, a Canadian energy supply business that had a 27.5% interest in Energy America. Direct Energy serves Canada and it is known for offering "peace of mind" through five-year fixed-price gas and electricity contracts to customers. Centrica acquired the remaining 72.5% of Energy America in December 2000. Energy America is not yet a developed and established brand within its markets; however, it provides a powerful name to be developed alongside the energy services business in the region. This international diversification continued in 2000 with the purchase of Luminus, a Belgian energy supplier.

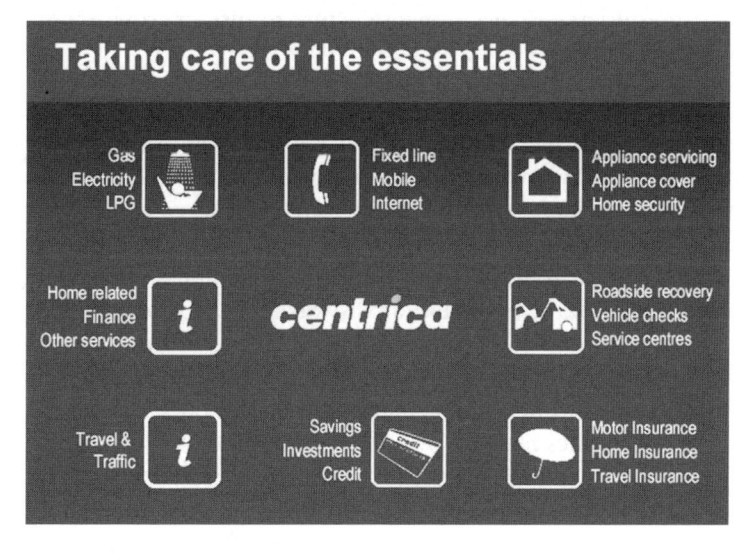

FIGURE 14.6 The AA motoring services complement the British Gas home services

Source: 'Strategy & Business Profiles year end 2001' investor presentation from www.centrica.com

> [We started] to look internationally and saying "well where are their markets that exhibit similar characteristics to what we've seen in the UK?" And out of that I guess came North America and I guess to a lesser extent Europe. I think North America is a region where we see the opportunities, now that liberalisation is happening. (Brian Austin, Director Telecommunications)

In March 2000, a corporate strap-line was introduced, "taking care of the essentials" to reflect the wider activities of the group (see Figure 14.6). The introduction of this new corporate identity, which does not obviously connect the parent company with the core activities of its major brands, enabled the Centrica management team to move into new areas of growth outside the boundaries of the traditional utility business model, such as road-services, financial services, and telecommunications.

The Emerging Challenges

In July 2001, Centrica was a totally different company compared to the company that demerged from British Gas in 1997. It had moved away from its traditional-utility past to a situation where assets, skills, and cultures are grouped together as competencies. It had become a multi-product, multi-brand organization with operations across different markets and continents:

> From inheriting a gas company, today I'm Chief Executive of a very different company. We're no longer single product, single brand. We now ... look after our customers in and around their homes. We have the established strong consumer brands ... We have relationships with 18 million households in the UK that together take somewhere around 40 million products from us. (Sir Roy Gardner, CEO)

This reality poses new challenges for Centrica in terms of managing an increasing number of employees, creating and developing its business model, making and executing corporate strategy, and introducing an appropriate organizational structure to sustain growth in the future.

Challenging the People

The people dimension is particularly important in Centrica's transformation. In just four years, Centrica had almost doubled the number of its employees (see Table 14.2). The core skill that the company inherited at demerger was the ability to manage large-volume transactions, essentially sending bills to customers and collecting money from them. The top management thought that this skill was simply not enough for the company to compete effectively in the local and global markets. Hence, a wide range of initiatives was launched towards developing a whole new skill set, for example around marketing and sales. The acquisitions also added a number of skills to the group in the areas of marketing, operations, sales and IT infrastructure. Furthermore, a new process was developed to help the management team expose what kind of skills existed in the businesses and which ones need to be added or acquired.

The company's management also realized that in order to deliver world class customer service, all the employees at every level and in every part of the organization should share the same values about customer service and customer focus. If they did not then the back office would not be able to give the front line the support they needed, resulting in decisions that were not fully focused on the customer.

TABLE 14.2 The number of Centrica employees 1998–2001

Business Areas	1998	1999	2000	2001
UK energy supply	6,595	7,285	8,800	9,524
British Gas home services	8,148	8,386	8,759	9,681
Telecommunications	–	–	111	800
North America energy supply	–	–	83	438
AA road services	–	2,145	7,730	7,904
AA personal finance	–	–	1,934	2,007
Goldfish financial services	36	567	27	59
Other businesses	1,648	1,217	861	1,137
Total number	16,427	19,600	28,305	31,550
Geographical Areas	**1998**	**1999**	**2000**	**2001**
Great Britain	16,427	19,532	27,936	30,832
North America	–	–	83	438
Rest of Europe	–	68	286	280
Total number	16,427	19,600	28,305	31,550

Source: Centrica annual reports.

Centrica's expansion into new products, services, and markets also meant a challenging shift in the culture of the company, from the heavy heritage of the traditional utility of the past towards a marketing oriented organization with strong growth potentials for the future:

> Within something like the old British Gas, there were a lot of people who'd worked there for a very long period of time, so that their whole culture and motivation was historic in the sense of what they knew. The change to selling electricity was controversial in some areas, let alone cross-selling across the whole brand. That was, still is, not a completely seamless process ... And I think, there is clearly value to be created through cross-selling and better service delivery and low-cost service delivery and all the rest of it, but actually often making that operationally happen with such a large scale, when you've historically not done it that way, is quite challenging. (Paul Cook, Manager Corporate Centre)

Challenging the Centrica Model

For both analysts and investors one of Centrica's great attractions has been the low capital intensity of its customer-focused strategy and its business model that focused on a strong asset base as well as energy production and retail capabilities (see Table 14.1). By 2001, Centrica's model had delivered significant results both in terms of growth and share performance:

> Our market capitalization has more than trebled since demerger and we've outperformed the FTSE 100 index by over 200%. (Sir Roy Gardner, CEO)

Despite this success, some were expressing their doubts about the model. Their main criticisms pointed toward the diverse portfolio of businesses under the Centrica group. Hence, some could see limited benefits in having the road services of the AA under the same roof with the home services of the British Gas or the fast-paced telecoms businesses developing alongside the traditional gas and energy businesses. Also, the growth potential of the model was under scrutiny. Despite the fact that the core UK energy business was continuing to deliver good economic results, supporting the newly acquired businesses and reaching the high growth targets of the past would require significant injections of capital. Clearly, after the period of expansion and acquisitions there were expectations for more organic growth by taking advantage of group-wide processes and synergies across the existing platform of businesses:

> To some, Centrica's strategy of massive diversification seemed initially to lack focus. Its aim was to offer a one-stop shop for all household needs – gas, electricity, telecoms, plumbing, insurance, you name it. On top of that the group went on to buy the AA, confounding the existing classification of its business. It was clearly no longer a standard utility. Skeptics worried that its expertise would wear thin when stretched over such a large area and that the multi-utility strategy would come to grief because inertia would grip much of the market. (Christine Buckley, Corporate profile No. 31: Centrica, *The Times*, September 9, 2002)

> It's still difficult for them [investors] to see how we are going to create the value ... so they're looking to see "is this extra margin really going to come through as a consequence of putting all these businesses together?" "Have they really re-invested this cash wisely and is it going to generate enough returns to hit directly the higher earnings expectations?" And that's quite a difficult piece, because I think nobody disagrees with the strategy, they just worry about how we're going to execute it effectively. (Paul Cook, Manager Corporate Centre)

For Centrica the rationale behind its portfolio of businesses stems from the multiple customer relationships this portfolio can achieve. This is possible not only through cross-selling, but through a more effective management of dealings with customers. More specifically, the customer value is based both on today's relationship and what the customer is potentially worth in the future. By selling over 40m products to 18m UK households, Centrica has the size to manage 400 million customer contacts every year – 400m opportunities for developing and broadening its customer relationships.

There are two basic drivers of customer value in the Centrica model (see Figure 14.7). The solid line shows as product holdings are added under the brand umbrella, the second and third products generally have a higher margin. The dotted line shows churn rates fall by nearly half when a customer buys more than one product. Put together, the increased margin and reduced churn of increased product holdings drive real value creation. The performance of the Centrica model can be evaluated using this approach. Hence, the model is considered successful if Centrica can sell multiple products per customer and achieve an increased margin.

> If all we end up doing is you know selling more products because we've bought more companies, and we buy another AA and we don't increase the profit margins, then actually the model isn't working, all we're doing is just becoming a bigger shop with more stuff on the shelves. But that's not what the Centrica model is really. It's very much about saying given the infrastructure, the call centers, the billing systems, the men in vans, we ought to be able to sell lots more products for relatively low cost...So the margins should go up, and the products per household should go up, and then you'll know that the model's working. (Jonathan Good, Manager Corporate Centre)

CENTRICA: STRATEGIZING IN A MULTI-UTILITY

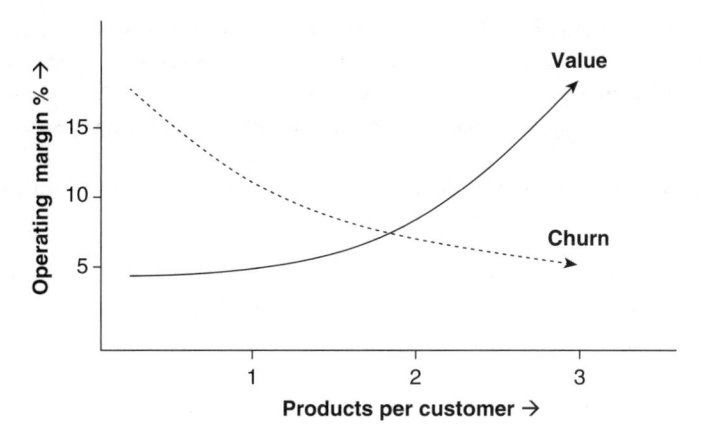

FIGURE 14.7 Drivers of customer value

Source: 'Strategy & Business Profiles year end 2001' investor presentation from www.centrica.com

> If you're going to create value you need to understand how you create value it's no good just saying you need to have x number of customers, you need to make sure that ultimately they're generating an economic profit in some way or other. (Paul Cook, Manager Corporate Centre)

Challenging the Strategy Process

The early strategic decisions of renegotiating the take-or-pay contracts, improving the economic performance of businesses, acquiring new businesses and expanding in new markets were based on the Centrica model. The goal of these opportunistic and defensive actions was to build a marketing-oriented organization with strong customer-management capabilities:

> I would describe a lot of what was done in the latter part of the 90's as being defensive ... the defensive things were very much trying to spread the risk. Electricity was one of those, Goldfish was one of those ... The AA was very much an opportunity to expand the type of home service products that we were providing. And of course the other areas, being international, so expansions into North America in particular. (Jack Foster, Energy Manager)

The principal values and priorities of the Centrica model were outlined soon after the demerger by the top executive team and the Chief Executive, Sir Roy Gardner:

> Well I think the core of what we do has always been, in a sense, Roy's, because it's his vision, the fact that we've got to where we've got to is very much down to his vision of where we need to be. But a lot of people, sort of historically, have said "no no no, let's stick with boring old British Gas" or whatever it might be, "lets not try and do anything clever here because there's lots of issues to sort out." So Roy always had this: "actually there's more to us than just British Gas." The difficulty is the creation of that and the mechanism. I think as we've grown as a company we've acquired, you know, new individuals around the executive table with different insights, with a different experience. (Paul Cook, Manager Corporate Centre)

Changes were made across the management teams at the corporate center and the businesses to support the new Centrica business model. The new managers brought valuable new marketing and strategic skills:

> When I was appointed Chief Executive I took very few of the old British Gas managers with me at the most senior level. They simply didn't have the focus or the mindset needed for the new competitive world. Today my Executive team is 100% new blood. And below the Executive, the senior management of the company is almost evenly split between old and new. This gives a good balance between experience and freshness of approach. (Sir Roy Gardner, CEO)

Clearly this meant that a number of managers from the old British Gas had to adapt in order to gain a place in Centrica's management:

> Those who remain from the old company are those who've demonstrated that they can adapt. They've shown that they can embrace the new world we're in. And they don't keep talking about "the old days" – I'm generally an even-tempered person but that's a sure way to get on my nerves! (Sir Roy Gardner, CEO)

This new executive team, the CEO, and the Board initiated and developed many of the early strategic decisions. They were also the primary actors in the company's strategic planning process. However, the growth of the company with new businesses (see Figure 14.8) introduced some new challenges for Centrica's strategy process. During the period 1997–2001, the strategy-making process had been based on an annual budgetary process while the principal strategic directions were decided centrally. This top-down approach, up to this point, had proved highly successful in terms of business and market performance. The acquisition of new businesses, however, placed considerable strain on the process. Having a plethora of businesses means different products, resources, markets, competitors, and cycle times. As a result, these businesses have different ways of spotting issues, setting priorities, and developing strategic initiatives. Furthermore, they are most likely to employ particular strategy-making processes reflecting different market dynamics and customized ways of implementing and evaluating strategic objectives.

> You clearly have different cultures in all of these businesses … you also have different relationships with the centre between these types of businesses, you know, so businesses that are on the defensive because they are feeling as though they are under-performing are clearly going to have a different relationship with the centre than businesses who know they are performing and are very sure of their position and you also have different levels of ability within these environments. (Mary Spender, Manager Corporate Centre)

> Different types of business do and should have different "personalities." But Centrica's chief strength lies in the extent to which its activities are pulled together at the centre. A strong overall vision. Sharing of experience. Achievement of synergies. To maintain this strength we believe that we do need to have an overall Centrica culture. A Centrica way of doing things. (Sir Roy Gardner, CEO)

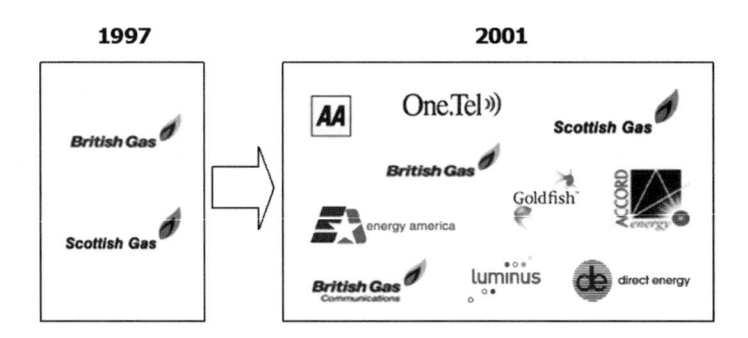

FIGURE 14.8 The growing portfolio of Centrica businesses 1997–2001

This need for a new Centrica culture and the increase in the company's portfolio of businesses led the executive team in 2001 to reconsider the group's strategy process:

> [As Centrica] got bigger you know, and whereas before we'd been able to run with comparatively thin processes because the directors knew the business very well, suddenly we were in different countries, we had different businesses, and the organization was crying out for more process. You know, without getting bureaucratic it needed a strategic planning process to decide where it should be investing. (Jonathan Good, Manager Corporate Centre)

Challenging the Organization

Alongside the challenges in the strategy process, the group in 2001 was facing new organizational challenges. The recently acquired companies and assets were grouped into business units according to the kind of service they provided to customers. This structure reflected the diverse portfolio of products and services that Centrica could offer:

> The AA, road side services, the patrol men that you see were put together with the British Gas engineers to create "Home and Road Services" because the feeling was that there were ... a lot operating synergies that you ought to ... put those two things together in the business unit. And then AA Insurance was very big insurance program, everything personalized was put together with Goldfish, because they are both financial services to create "Centrica Financial Services." (Jonathan Good, Manager Corporate Centre)

In July 2001, the group had a number of businesses: British gas trading, home and road services, Centrica financial services, business development, Centrica energy management group (CEMG), Centrica telecommunications and North America (see Figure 14.9). However, there were some issues regarding this particular way of organizing the group.

> Can a financial services business really have the same culture as a telecoms or a car breakdown business? Should we try to compromise? Are we really trying to create a completely uniform business? (Sir Roy Gardner, CEO)

> And at that stage ... we were saying ok "we're taking care of the essentials" but to be honest it wasn't a lot more to the strategy than that, I mean "taking care of the essentials" doesn't tell you really what you're doing, what you should try to organize yourself to do it, it just describes the products you happened to have, and you could say "well, what is the link between these?" ... we really needed to look harder into the organization, if this is the customer vision that we want, what kind of organization is going to deliver that? ... let's try and get the organization all sorted out here because otherwise we're just adding on bits and it's not coherent. (Jonathan Good, Manager Corporate Centre)

The challenge in this case was that the group's organizational structure was based on the structure of a gas company. However, the portfolio of businesses was reflecting the Centrica model and a new structure was required at that time away from the traditional forms adopted by utilities in the past:

> The question then was how do we organize the group ...? Because the structure was still very much the structure of a gas company. But the businesses we were operating were now much broader than that. So there was a need to sort of rebalance the focus on the organization ... If we are to be a Group who is, if you like, more than the sum of its parts, then we've got to really be very focused on the synergies which make it sensible to have the AA and British Gas and Goldfish all in one group. (Brian Austin, Director Telecommunications)

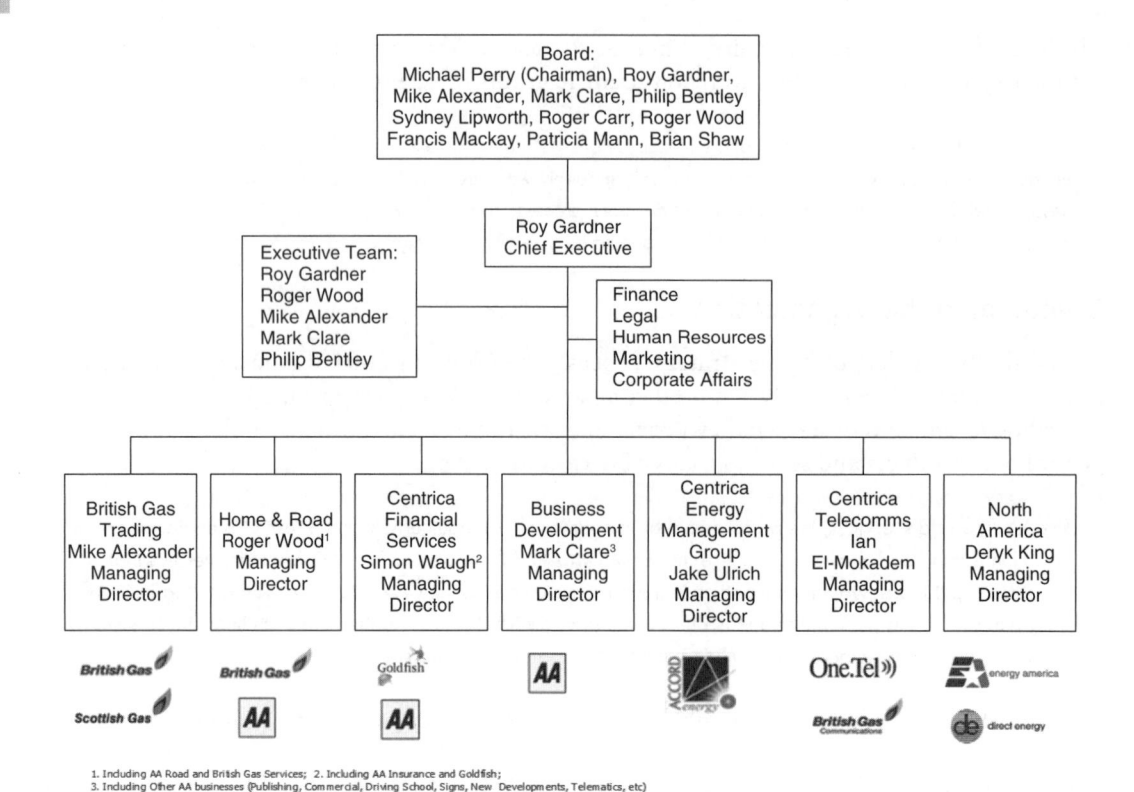

FIGURE 14.9 Centrica's organizational structure and brands (July 2001)

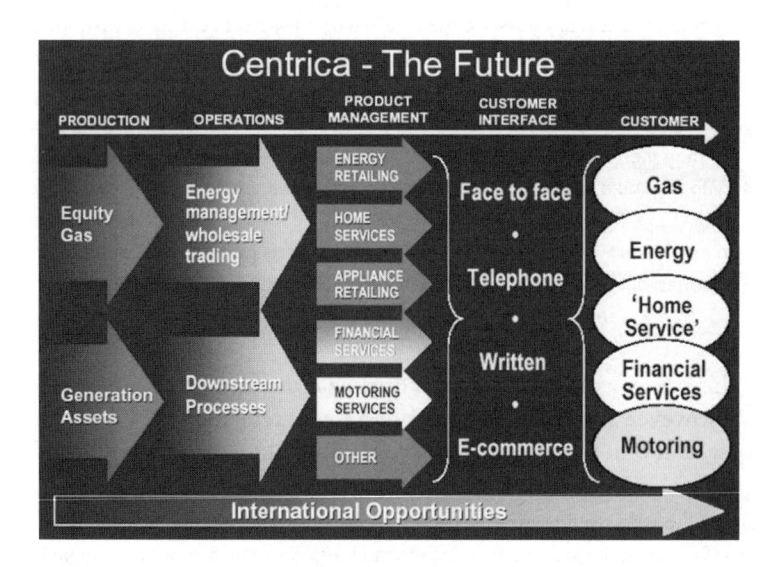

FIGURE 14.10 The future of the Centrica model (July 2001)

Source: www.centrica.com

In order to develop the Centrica of the future (see Figure 14.10) the executive team began in 2001 to examine alternative ways of reconfiguring Centrica's organizational structure to achieve synergies across the group and improve the company's operations. These strategic and organizational challenges were the prime topics during the Centrica Annual Planning Board Conference in July 2001.

CASE STUDY QUESTIONS

1 What do you think would be the principal challenges in implementing the new Centrica business model?
2 Is the Centrica model "aligned" with the environment that firm is operating in? Use the ESCO model to help you answer the question.
3 What are the principal actors involved in the Centrica strategy process? What might be some of the issues these actors face while Centrica is growing?
4 Assume you are consultants hired by the Centrica executive team. Design and propose a new strategy process for Centrica to be presented at the annual planning board conference in July 2001.
5 Examine the current businesses and structure of Centrica. What have been the key moments in the company's evolution since 2001?

REFERENCES

Strategy Presentation at the Global Power and Gas Leaders Conference, New York, September 18, 2002, Phil Bentley, Finance Director.
http://amadeus.bvdep.com and www.centrica.co.uk.
"Pan-European Utilities," report by HSBC, May 2002.
Corporate profile No. 31: Centrica, Christine Buckley, *The Times*, September 9, 2002.
Various Speeches of Roy Gardner from www.centrica.co.uk.
Interviews with Centrica Managers conducted by Sotirios Paroutis.

NARAYANA HEALTH: BRINGING QUALITY HEALTHCARE TO THE MASSES[1]

While on his early morning commute to his heart hospital, Dr. Devi Shetty, cardiac surgeon, founder and Chairman of Narayana Health, dresses into his surgical scrubs for a long day of back-to-back cardiac surgeries and patient consultations. He is well aware that he will not retire out of his scrubs until much later that night but this thought does not consume him through Bangalore's rush hour traffic. What does consume Dr. Shetty these days is how to take his successful business model outside of India. His mind is at work figuring out how to deliver affordable, quality healthcare to the rest of the world. He thinks back to the words of a friend who had said, "The most profitable hospital in the world is the one which is built on a ship and parked outside US waters because it gets to serve American patients, and yet stays away from its jurisdiction" (Ghosh, 2015). Dr. Shetty knows that to be relevant to the global healthcare industry, he has to grab the attention of the US market. How can he do that without having to set up shop in the heavily regulated US healthcare market? Can he replicate his business model in other parts of the world, especially in the West?

REDEFINING THE HEALTHCARE INDUSTRY

Narayana Health Group's (NH) flagship center with 300 beds was founded in 2001 and situated in the outskirts of the south Indian city of Bangalore. It aimed to make a positive contribution to Indian healthcare by serving everyone including the poor and underprivileged. NH founder, Chairman, and cardiac surgeon, Dr. Devi Shetty, is the heart of NH's success (Ramamurti, 2014). NH was inspired by one of Dr. Shetty's high-profile cardiac patients,

---

[1] This case was prepared by Karina Bruce and Professor Loizos Heracleous as a basis for class discussion and not to indicate effective or ineffective handling of an administrative situation.

NARAYANA HEALTH: BRINGING QUALITY HEALTHCARE TO THE MASSES

Mother Teresa, the founder of the Missionaries of Charity and a Nobel Peace Prize winner for her work with the poor. A lesson that she taught him and that had a profound impact on him is that "hands that serve are holier than lips that pray." During this time, Dr. Shetty was working for another hospital and constantly watching too many parents lose hope for their children after hearing how much surgery would cost. He decided to build a hospital with his father-in-law financially supporting his new venture. He decided to adopt a unique approach with a mission to provide quality cardiac healthcare to the masses.

NH combines "compassion, high-quality medical knowledge and skills, and an astute sense of making the business work for the poor" (Kothandaraman and Mookerjee, 2008). NH has lower costs than any other hospital in the world; the cost of open-heart surgery at NH for example is 95,000 rupees (US$1,583), much lower than in any other Indian hospital (US$5,000 to US$7,000) and in the USA, where Ohio's Cleveland Clinic for example charges around US$105,000 (*Economist*, 2015; Gokhale, 2013). NH's ultimate goal is to offer heart surgery at a cost of $800 (Shetty, 2013). Table 15.1 gives some comparative figures.

Yet while costs and prices charged are the lowest in the world, NH also delivers world-class quality. The 30-day post-surgery mortality rate for a coronary bypass procedure at NH's Bangalore hospital for example is 1.4%, below the average rate of 1.9% in the USA (Anand, 2009). And though it primarily serves the poor, NH generates healthier profit margins than most private hospitals in the USA (in 2010, NH reported 7.7% profit after taxes compared to an average of 6.9% in the USA) (*Economist*, 2010). Despite around 80% of NH's patients receiving some form of discount, it has achieved double-digit revenue growth year on year (Narayana Health, 2014). NH's revenue grew by over 200% from 2009 to 2014 and its EBITDA margin was 13% in 2013 (Madhavan, 2014).

In over 13 years, the flagship center has grown to become a 3,000-bed fully fledged multi-specialty "Health City" hospital comparable with the 3,200-bed Chris Hani Baragwanath Hospital in Johannesburg, South Africa, considered the world's largest hospital, and the 2,200-bed Florida Hospital, the largest community hospital in the USA (Khanna and Bijlani, 2012). NH opened 26 hospitals in 16 cities in India (see Appendix 15.A) with a total of 6,900 beds, employing 13,000 people including 1,500 doctors (Madhavan, 2014). With a goal to expand to 30,000 beds by 2020, its growth ambitions are comparable with the Hospital Corporation of America, the largest for-profit hospital chain in the USA with approximately 31,000 beds across 140 hospitals (Khanna and Bijlani, 2012).

NH houses India's largest bone marrow transplant unit; has one of the world's largest heart hospitals conducting the world's largest number of successful paediatric heart surgeries; and has

TABLE 15.1 Comparison of open-heart surgery prices

Hospital	Price of open-heart surgery (US$)
Typical United States research hospital	More than $100,000
Fortis Hospital (Indian private hospital)	$6,000
Care Hospital (Indian private hospital)	Slightly less than $6,000
Narayana Health (Indian private hospital)	$1,583

one of the largest telemedicine networks in the world. NH's success has been recognized with a number of awards in India and worldwide (see Appendix 15.B). Concurrently, India's most celebrated physician, Dr. Shetty, has won numerous awards including the 2013 Entrepreneur of the Year Award (see Appendix 15.C). NH has also gained academic and media attention, including case studies written at the Harvard Business School and a five-series television documentary on Aljazeera News (see Appendix 15.D).

The Global and Indian Healthcare Industry

Global Healthcare

The global healthcare industry[2] is worth US$7.2 trillion and is one of the most rapidly growing industries in the global economy (Deloitte, 2015). Global healthcare spending as a percentage of the world's gross domestic product (GDP) was 10.6% in 2014 and was projected to increase by 5.2% a year in 2014 to 2018, to US$9.3 trillion (Deloitte, 2015). Although the healthcare industry is growing, it is considered to be "in-crisis" because for the most part the quality of care has not shown improvement, and healthcare is inaccessible with costs unaffordable for a large part of the population (PwC, 2014).

The cost of healthcare has risen over the years but the struggle to maintain adequate levels of service to patients remains (Lim, 2014). The USA, the highest spender on healthcare, spends US$8,508 per person annually, yet 23% of adults either had serious problems paying medical bills or were unable to pay them (Deloitte, 2014). It was also reported that between 5% and 10% of hospitalized patients in developed countries acquired infections while in developing countries, patients affected can exceed 25% (World Health Organization, 2005). In the USA, 1.7 million patients develop infections while in a US hospital each year, resulting in 99,000 deaths (Deloitte, 2014), the sixth commonest cause of death in the USA (Kung et al., 2008). Other global concerns are the insufficient access of a healthcare system to around one billion people worldwide (Deloitte, 2014) and a shortage of medical staff estimated at 7.2 million worldwide (World Health Organization, 2013). Healthcare technologies such as telemedicine and electronic medical prescriptions do not have widespread adoption yet since they are expensive for most public healthcare systems already struggling to fund basic services (Deloitte, 2015). Notably, although treatments for many ailments including chronic diseases[3] do exist, the delivery of healthcare within a healthcare system is the highlighted problem.

India's Healthcare

India's healthcare industry is estimated at US$20 billion (compared to US$2.3 trillion in the USA), despite India having a population of around four times that of the USA. India's

---

[2]The healthcare industry consists of hospitals, medical and dental practices, medical equipment, and drug manufacturing; diagnostic laboratories, and healthcare delivery (Shetty, 2013). It is defined as "the collection of institutions and actors who provide healthcare (e.g., doctors, nurses, hospitals, pharmacies, etc.), the organizations that provide [other services] (e.g., insurers, government agencies, regulatory bodies), the organizations that offer preventive services; and the financial flows that finance the provision of healthcare" (Burns, 2014:7).

[3]Chronic diseases are the most common and costly type of diseases representing 63% of all deaths worldwide (Deloitte, 2014).

government spending on healthcare as a proportion of GDP is around 1%, one of the lowest in the world even compared to other Asian nations[4] (Richman et al., 2008). In 2002, the Indian government's share of spending on healthcare was 20% of the total of 5.1% of the GDP that was spent on healthcare[5] (Kothandaraman and Mookerjee, 2008). The rest of the spending (80%) was from private individuals and employers. Of India's 15,393 hospitals, 75% were privately owned, 30% of which cater to secondary[6] and tertiary[7] healthcare (Kothandaraman and Mookerjee, 2008).

Most Indian hospitals have achieved international accreditations from organizations such as Joint Commission International, and combined with their low cost have helped to turn India into a destination for medical tourism (Kothari, 2009). In 2014, India had a national per capita GDP of US$1,596 (compared to the US national per capita GDP of US$54,629) (World Bank, 2014). Specialist doctors such as cardiothoracic surgeons, nephrologists and oncologists in India earn anywhere from 20% to 74% of what their US counterparts earn (Govindarajan and Ramamurti, 2013). For instance, NH's cardiothoracic surgeons gross between US$150,000 and US$300,000, whereas the median income for their US colleagues is US$408,000. Salaries of nurses, medical staff, and hospital administrators in India are dramatically lower; some earn only 2% to 5% of what a US hospital would pay (Govindarajan and Ramamurti, 2013). Even when higher wages are to be factored in by adjusting the salaries of NH's doctors and other staff required for an open-heart surgery at NH to match US levels, the cost would still be only 4% to 18% of a comparable procedure in a US hospital (Govindarajan and Ramamurti, 2013). Moreover, other costs in India are higher than in the US. Equipment, such as MRI machines, and supplies, such as stents, are more expensive, and so is urban land (Govindarajan and Ramamurti, 2013). The rise of the middle-class in India has seen this segment reach upwards of 300 million. The private sector caters to these cash-paying, middle-class families' health needs (Richman et al., 2008). Even if major surgeries (such as open-heart surgery) are significantly cheaper in India, for most of the population (1.252 billion total population in 2013), where two-thirds of the population live on less than US$2 a day, it continues to be unaffordable (Gokhale, 2013). India's population distribution is 30% urban and 70% rural (areas with population of less than 9,000) according to the 2011 census (*Economic Times*, 2011). Those living in rural India have limited access to health services and are struggling to even receive basic primary care[8] (Munavalli et al., 2014). The major problem with the Indian healthcare system is accessibility, affordability, and quality care for two-thirds of India's poor population (Munavalli et al., 2014). Also, their quality of healthcare depends heavily on their ability to pay (Kazmin, 2013).

---

[4]Government spending on healthcare as a proportion of GDP is 1.8% in Sri Lanka, 2.3% in China, and 3.3% in Thailand (Richman et al., 2008).

[5]Spending included creating infrastructure, paying doctors' salaries, maintaining hospitals, and dispensing drugs.

[6]Patients from primary healthcare are referred to specialists in district hospitals and Community Health Centres.

[7]Specialized consultative care is provided usually on referral from primary and secondary medical care. Services include Intensive Care Units (ICUs), and diagnostic support services.

[8]Essential healthcare that rely on lay and professional care practitioners to provide education and prevention of health challenges, treatment of common diseases, immunization again infectious disease family planning and so on.

Although communicable disease is the major underlying cause for mortality and morbidity in India, non-communicable diseases have emerged as the second largest cause for morbidity with the number of cases set to reach 61 million coronary heart disease cases and 46 million diabetes cases by 2015 (Saligram et al., 2014). A study published in 2008 in the journal *Vascular Health and Risk Management* found that "the mortality rate from coronary artery disease among South Asians is two to three times higher than that of Caucasians" (Gokhale, 2013). In India, one in four people die of a heart attack and its per-capita health spending is less than US$60 a year:

> Congenital heart disease is of a particular concern. Around 24,000 newborns in India are affected every year and the rural population is particularly susceptible due to its poverty. Given that less than 20% of the population are supported by health insurance, treatment [is] only an option for the rich or those able to borrow to pay for the bill. (Hartigan, 2014)

Indian hospitals perform a total of 100,000 to 120,000 heart surgeries a year, well short of the estimated 2 million heart surgeries India needs (Gokhale, 2013). Dr. Devi Shetty recalls working in Kolkata at the Birla Heart Foundation in the 1990s seeing over 100 heart patients daily. Although most needed heart surgery, many never came back for it because they couldn't afford it (Kazmin, 2013).

The limited access to health services due to limited purchasing power, residence in underserved areas, and inadequate health literacy produces significant gaps in healthcare delivery among a population that have a disproportionately large burden of disease (Bhattacharyya et al., 2008). India's public hospitals where the poorer population seeks medical treatment, remain in shackles with "a shortage of doctors, lack of basic supplies, overcrowding and crumbling, dirty facilities. This forces many families to go deep into debt, often borrowing from informal moneylenders at high rates, to obtain private medical care" (Kazmin, 2013). Actual gaps in public health services have resulted in an estimated 47% of rural and 37% of the urban population either borrowing money or selling assets to pay for medical expenses (Madhavan, 2014) while the rest do not pursue treatment or resort to informal healers (Kazmin, 2013).

The gap in the delivery of healthcare to two-thirds of India's population has created entrepreneurs who have responded to social needs through innovative health service delivery models or "social enterprises" (Bhattacharyya et al., 2008). NH, a network of hospitals in India has developed a novel approach to increase the availability, affordability, and quality of healthcare service to the poor.

Narayana Health's Vision and Organization

NH's vision had been described as "bold" (Madhavan, 2014), "creative" (Ramamurti, 2014) and "fundamentally different" (Mahajan-Bansal, 2009). NH began during a time when the demand for cardiac surgeries in India was underserved. NH's vision "inspires its employees to achieve the impossible, attracting doctors, nurses and staff who buy into this vision that they must provide high tech, high quality care to all, irrespective of means" (Madhavan, 2014). NH prides itself as being a hospital that will never deny treatment due to a person's lack of funds.

Despite the pressures posed by its social mission, NH has managed to operate profitably, due to a business model that optimizes both efficiency and quality. Dr. Shetty outlines NH's thinking about profitability:

> We [NH] believe in making profits but not super profits – enough money to pay good salaries to employees, to maintain our infrastructure and remain attractive to investors ... We definitely want to keep our noses above water. If you don't make a profit, no bank will lend to you and no donor will give you money. (Kazmin, 2013)

Before NH, affordable high-quality cardiac care did not exist in India or anywhere in the world, unless provided by governments or paid for by insurance companies. NH has combined world-class quality, affordability, and scale simultaneously to create a fundamentally different economic model. "It shows that costs can be substantially contained," said Srinath Reddy, president of the Geneva-based World Heart Foundation, of Shetty's approach. Dr. Shetty is confident that India will soon become the first country in the world to disassociate health care from affluence: "The wealth of the nation has little to do with quality of health care its citizens can enjoy" (Madhavan, 2014).

Drive for efficiency

NH's business model partly relies on volume to benefit from economies of scale. NH conducts 150 major surgeries daily and approximately 12% of cardiac surgeries in India are performed at NH hospitals (Madhavan, 2014). NH's multi-specialty Health City is self-sufficient within each specialty (e.g., has its own operating theatres and intensive care units) to perform a high volume of surgeries while drawing on common facilities such as diagnostic equipment, sterilization department, blood bank and so on. For instance, NH managed to reduce the cost of bone marrow transplants from the Indian national average of US$27,000 to US$8,900 by leveraging the hospital's existing infrastructure. The blood bank had previously discarded used blood after 10 days as it was unsuitable for cardiac surgery but could now utilize blood for up to 26 days after collection in transplant procedures. Because of the high volume of patients NH can accommodate, its medical equipment has high levels of use. NH pays equipment suppliers a monthly rent for parking their machines and buys the reagents needed. Unit costs for each test remain low since NH facilities work 14 hours a day, 7 days a week (Knowledge@Wharton, 2010). To keep the cost of materials as low as possible, the NH network in India set up a central buying unit that handles up to 80% of all purchases of consumables and devices. NH does not advocate long-term contracts but negotiates contracts on a weekly basis to bring down purchasing prices and inventory carrying costs. When NH does purchase equipment, it chooses the most optimal rather than the latest model, without compromising on clinical care and outcomes. For instance, NH collaborated with Texas Instruments to develop a digital x-ray plate that was based on technology going off-patent. The cost of the original product was US$82,000 while the product NH and Texas Instrument developed based on the expired patent cost just US$3,000.

Through bringing up scale, NH can offer cheaper dialysis treatment, performs the highest amount of bone marrow transplants in India for cancer patients, and the highest number of surgeries for children in the world. Dr. Bhattacharyya, who researched innovative business models in the private sector within health systems in low- and middle-income countries including India, adds:

[S]o the volume thing, it is not unique but they are doing it at a higher level than anyone else. And applying it to things of greater complexity. Cataract surgery is very simple, it's a very simple procedure but paediatric surgery is crazy hard and the more complex the procedure, the more variability and surgical time, outcomes, and all these things. So, that's remarkable that they [NH] are able to – you know, apply these lean and simple processes to some complex areas of medicine." (2014)

Fixed salary model and capability development for doctors

NH spends 22% of its revenue on fixed salaries compared to 60%, the proportion commonly found in Western hospitals (Khanna et al., 2005). This does not mean that NH doctors are paid poorly. NH doctors are paid a fixed, industry-leading monthly salary, unlike other Indian hospitals where doctors receive a percentage of the revenues they generate. NH doctors work an average of 12 to 16 hours, undertake 70 to 100 consultations, and operate on four patients a day on average (Kavlekar, 2013; *South China Morning Post*, 2013). The fixed-salary model means that cost to the hospital decreases per procedure, as the number of procedures increases. To make the operating theatres conducive to working long hours, the design is spacious with large windows for natural light to come in and classical music playing in the background. Dr. Shetty views surgeons as artists who need a relaxing place to work; unlike when he was working as a surgeon in London where operating theatres were located in cramped basements with hardly any natural light.

Dr. Shetty also believes that it is only through performing as many operations as possible that doctors get the training they need to become better doctors: "A surgeon doing three or four operations a day does much better work than one doing three or four in a week," since repeatedly performing a medical procedure produces highly trained specialists and reduces error (Madhavan, 2014). At the same time, higher volumes cut per-unit cost of surgeries. NH surgeons who are in their 30s have done more than 3,000 surgeries whereas in the USA, the average cardiac surgeon does about 2,000 surgeries in their entire career. Since 2013, more than 93,000 cardiac surgeries have been performed across the NH network. Given the scale of activities, NH doctors have better opportunities to specialize in areas such as cardiac care, neurology, orthopaedics and so on. They also have opportunities to conduct research on a multitude of areas such as pathogenic infections, oncology, metabolic disorders, and maternal and child health, to advance therapeutics and diagnostics. Hospital administrators monitor the outputs and outcomes for each surgeon, such as waiting times and operation outcomes, which are transparent and available to all surgeons to see (Private Sector Innovation Programme for Health, 2014: 10).

Cross-subsidized pricing model

At NH, a regular surgery package costs the patient US$3,000. NH offers upgraded packages such as staying in a semi-private or private room, priced around US$4,000 to US$5,000. The upgraded rooms comprise around 20% of the total number of beds at the hospital, and approximately 20% of beds are used to serve non-paying patients, who nevertheless receive similar quality of care.

NH attracts a high volume of limited-income patients and follows a cross-subsidized pricing model to make healthcare affordable by charging according to the patient's ability to pay.

Wealthier patients pay the full price, which cross-subsidizes the services for lower income patients. Around 80% of NH's patients receive some form of discount and come to NH through a referral from NH mobile outreach vans, the telemedicine program, rural and town clinics, micro-insurance schemes, or through an overseas outreach program. Surgery costs less than $3,000 at NH, irrespective of complexity or length of hospitalization, 45% of NH patients pay considerably less. About 30% of patients are covered under a micro-insurance scheme that reimburses NH roughly US$1,200 per surgery (Knowledge@Wharton, 2010). Patients who can't afford to pay and have no medical insurance coverage receive discounted rates that are funded by NH's charitable trust, individual donors, or the hospital itself.

Full-paying patients include international medical tourists from 76 countries (primarily from Bangladesh, Middle East, Africa, and Malaysia) and wealthier Indian patients coming into NH attracted by its brand as a world-class healthcare facility. Nearly 15% to 20% of the patients treated at the Health City in Bangalore are medical tourists, averaging about 500 patients per month. NH began to be known worldwide for its paediatric cardiology, housing the largest paediatric intensive care unit in the world. The facility has an in-house travel agency, translation services, provides concierge services, and has its own accommodation facilities; in addition to this it has ties with hotels and airlines. A centralized international division, based in Bangalore, distributes patient cases to units depending on the required treatment.

Tracking the Financials Daily

The mission that includes the provision of below-cost care required careful planning and internal financial controls, so NH employed an innovative daily accounting system. Across its hospitals in India, NH ensures that every day in the afternoon doctors and senior administrators receive an SMS on their mobile phone with the previous day's revenues, expenses, and other financial indicators for all locations (Appendix 15.E). As Dr. Shetty explains:

> For us, looking at the profit and loss account at the end of the month of a hospital is like reading a post-mortem report. Whereas having the profit-and-loss account on a daily basis is a diagnostic tool which will help you to reduce cost. (Ted Talks, 2013)

Dr. Raghuvanshi, vice chairman, Medical Director and group CEO of NH adds, "Just the knowledge and information on the cost of their procedures will make the doctor more careful and sensitive to costs" (Bhattacharyya et al., 2008).

Ramamurti also adds, as he recalls a conversation with Dr. Shetty:

> Dr. Shetty had an interesting point. He asked me, "What do you think is the most expensive instrument device in the hospital – in any hospital?" Of course I thought about, you know, MRI machine, so on. And he said, "No, it is the doctor's pen. The most expensive." Because they [doctors] could just with a stroke of the pen, do that test, do this test, and so on. And, they are not required, not necessary tests. Then you are really adding a lot to the cost, so he says, "We really tell our doctors to stop and think about the value of every procedure, or every test that they prescribe. By getting this SMS everyday, they are reminded that they are doctors but also have to mind the cost that's completely lacking in the US, the doctors really don't know what things cost. (2014)

As a result, doctors are able to assess how many below-cost surgeries can be performed on any given day without adversely impacting profits. While at the same time, NH mines real-time data on 30 different parameters such as clinical outcomes, consumables used during surgery, time patients spend in ICU, and duration of stay in the hospital (Madhavan, 2014). Clinical outcomes and major clinical procedures are then discussed weekly among doctors where best practices are shared.

Process Improvement and Standardization

NH has streamlined its operations to clearly defined systems, processes, and protocols that the hospital calls "The NH Way." In Dr. Shetty's conference room, a quote reads: "Healthcare is all about process, protocol, and price." Determined to be more efficient through standardization and specialization, NH has created a digitized document akin to a constitution that defines how it should function, which includes clinical protocols such as how patients are received and transferred from one department to the next, and how medicines are administered. This documentation of operations is seen as a guideline rather than a set of rules to be strictly followed. It is a learning system from which anyone can deviate if they can show they can get a better outcome. Deviations are fed back and reviewed so that where an advantage is shown the standard protocol can be changed. Continuous improvement is an institutionalized value, according to Ramamurti:

> So this [improvement] is hanging over everybody's [head]. Everybody's aware that this is something that they try to achieve. And, when they are already working quite efficiently, how do you become more efficient? … led by Dr. Shetty … he does open heart surgery … and does, one or two surgeries himself [every day]. So, he has a chance to constantly ask himself, "Why am I doing it like this? Do I have to do all these things? Why can't I take a regular doctor and do all this? Why can't I have the nurse to do more of the work of some of the things I'm doing? Why can't I get someone else to do more of the work the nurse is doing?" So, these kinds of questions [are] constantly being asked. (2014)

NH's processes include the conduct of regular meetings and video conferences where NH doctors share experiences and best practices and review actual medical cases across NH hospitals (Ramamurti, 2014). In non-surgical processes, NH's consumable purchases are continuously evaluated to get the best cost without compromising quality. For instance, in 2010 NH switched to disposable drapes from linen ones because linen was time-consuming to clean after every surgery, which has reduced this cost significantly. At times, new approaches do not work, such as the introduction of the concept of zero inventory, because of problems with reliability of supplies; so NH went back to having an in-house store. As noted by Dr. Raghuvanshi, "An important element of innovation is to accept failure and take corrective measures" (Madhavan, 2014).

Using process manufacturing principles, NH deconstructs its surgeries to multiple discrete steps, seeking to standardize these steps and allocate them to suitably trained staff to be performed in the most efficient way. For instance, a bypass cardiac surgery typically takes five hours. The critical part takes up an hour and is performed by a specialist. The harvesting of the veins or arteries, opening and closing of the chest, suturing, and other less critical procedures are done by junior doctors. Nurses and paramedical staff prepare the patient. Other non-surgical tasks are also shifted to the larger NH facility such as claims processing and discharge summary preparation. Some activities requiring special skill sets such as tele-radiology are centralized to NH's Bangalore hospital to ensure optimal utilization of specialists.

NH specialists can perform four surgeries daily, six days a week, which not only enhances their specialization in a particular area, but also reduces error as well as costs. The majority of NH senior doctors specialize on 3 to 4 types of operations, while younger, generalist surgeons do about 10 to 15 types of operations (Bhattacharyya, 2014).

Ensuring constant supply of qualified personnel

NH invests heavily to train the next generation of specialists, nurses, and medical staff. By 2015, NH run 56 postgraduate programs for doctors and para-medical professionals, and 55 NH certified training programs with a total of around 1,945 students and trainees. In 2005, NH initiated its own training program and was the first in India to offer a diploma in cardiology, in collaboration with the Indira Gandhi National Open University (IGNOU). GPs are taught the skills to handle emergency and non-intervention cardiology. With a higher supply of cardiologists, the program enables a higher proportion of the population to have access to cardiac care with the aim aimed to decrease the costs of such care. Further, the lack of trained nephrologists to operate the dialysis machines was partly the reason for which the cost of treatment was expensive. NH offers a diploma in nephrology and other specialties to allow trained technicians rather than just doctors to operate the machines as is the case in the USA. This enables more doctors to offer treatment to patients by reducing the cost of provision, thus in turn lowering the cost of access to treatment.

Beyond training doctors and technicians, NH focuses on skill development for nurses and nursing assistants such as its pilot skills training program for 1,700 individuals across 20 NH hospitals in partnership with the Wadhwani Foundation. The content of the training program is a carefully designed job-competency curriculum, providing skills that are often missing from formal and informal nursing education programs in India. The curriculum includes typical medical procedures, functional English, life and workplace skills, basic IT skills, occupational safety, health and environment training, and medical math. All courses are deployed using an easily accessible online technology platform, reducing the dependence on and workload of teachers, while providing flexibility for students to study at their own pace and location.

A major challenge at NH is staff retention and recruitment, with nursing staff in particular having a high turnover rate. NH has instituted a nursing college to ensure a constant supply of qualified nurses and to keep labour costs in control. To ensure that its core group of nurses can be retained, NH adopted a policy of paying much higher wages to these nurses, with the remaining positions being filled by the continuous flow of incoming batches from its own college. Nursing students from poorer communities and remote areas are encouraged to apply since the college provides financial help in the form of access to bank loans from banks and government subsidies. NH provides the assurance of job opportunities once training is complete.

In partnership with Stanford University, NH has developed an audio-video-based curriculum to train spouses or other family members to be caregivers for patients so that there would be continuity of care when the patients return home. The person accompanying the patient in hospital is involved in the entire process of caring, together with the nurse, during the patient's hospital stay. As Dr. Shetty explains:

Traditionally, the spouse or the family member has no role to play in the patient care. A typical heart patient on the fifth day is ready to go home, family was not involved in the care, on the fifth day we call the wife, give her one plastic bag filled with medicines and tell her, ask her to take care of the husband. She's lost, she doesn't know what to do with him. Whereas if she's involved with the entire process of caring in the hospital ... there would be the continuity of the care when the patient goes home. (2013)

Getting the most out of technology

NH uses technology to optimize processes as well as to enable continuous improvement. For instance, NH piloted India's first online training course for clinical staff; and developed cloud capabilities to send out daily profit and loss statements. Dr. Bhattacharyya notes:

He [Dr. Shetty] jump to digital radiology at a time when that wasn't standard, the investment into cutting edge IT systems certainly suggests an appetite for innovation. And, the embedding of those systems – the just-in-time financial data, that's crazy stuff, right? Nobody does that. Like in my hospital it takes me – like I'm a researcher, I can get financial data that's 3 months old, that's what they give me. And I have to look at my bills, my secretary has to count up my expenses based on what I'm billing to figure out what my current budget is on the project I'm running. And these guys are saying that on a daily basis they know. So that is remarkable ... Just-in-time supply chains, those have been done ... But just-in-time financial data is crazy – it's great, it's brilliant but certainly not common. So, you know some bright mind who was thinking out of the box came up with that. (2015)

Further, current software in the healthcare industry enables hospital management to deal with accounting, billing, insurance claims, and inventory management, but not patient management. Even in the safest hospitals in the USA, one in 200 patients dies if they spend a night in the hospital, due to medical errors and not following protocols. In other words, getting admitted to the best hospital in the world is 10 times riskier than sky diving (Mahalakshmi, 2015). NH wants to embrace technology that has the potential to make patients safer. As Dr. Shetty says:

We have to bring health care down to process and protocols, like what they have done in the aviation industry. The aviation industry was exactly like this 30 to 40 years ago, when there were so many accidents. Today the aviation industry is safe, because pilots are not allowed to think! Health care is the last industry to embrace the power of technology. Information technology has changed the financial sector completely. It has changed the retail sector completely. It has changed the manufacturing sector. But in health care, it is not used at all. We have used technology only inside machines, and in hospitals to produce the bills and chart summaries. We are essentially using IT as a glorified typewriter. (Militzer, 2013)

Together with Cognizant Technologies, NH has begun an initiative to introduce a user-friendly software called "iCare," a clinical diagnostic support system which in 2014 was undergoing trials in Bangalore in the post-operation cardiac intensive care unit (Appendix 15.F). Every interaction between the doctor and the patient, or the nurse and the patient is written in the software based on NH's processes and protocols, which is aimed to reduce doctor and nurse errors. Traditionally, when a patient's oxygen saturation declines from 100% to 50%, the nurse first enters it on the hard-copy chart and then calls the doctor. This process from when the nurse looks for the number until the doctor picks up the call takes approximately 10 minutes. Meanwhile, the nurse's eyes are off the patient's monitor. However, with the iCare system, the nurse is given clear instructions on what they can do at that moment and if these actions do not help, then the nurse informs the doctor. NH plans to equip all its hospitals with iPads at every patient's bedside, containing real-time patient information, and wirelessly connected to a central server.

Strategic Innovation of Low-Cost Model

NH constantly questions standard practices and processes aiming to improve quality and reduce costs. For instance, NH tested the use of iPads with its iCare patient management system and its hospital is a testing ground for vendors. If the vendor can show that their equipment can cope with the patient volumes at NH, then the equipment can work in any other hospital. NH's high-quality healthcare at low cost model has been replicated in largely dense and populated areas, for example in various state capitals in India such as Kolkota and Ahmedabad. However, many of India's smaller and underdeveloped districts cannot sustain a Health City because it is not economically viable. Wanting to further reduce the cost of healthcare, NH investigated how to make a low-cost hospital that is economically viable for smaller cities with populations of 500,000 to 1,000,000.

NH designed a 300-bed small super-specialty hospital occupying a 150,000 square foot area, making an investment of US$6 million (Appendix 15.G). The cost is 25% of what this type of facility normally costs to build in India and was completed in eight months, compared to the usual time period of completion in three years. The first low-cost hospital was built in Mysore in partnership with the government of Karnataka which has 26% stake in the hospital (Kavlekar, 2013).

It was designed and built at a cost of a little over US$29,000 per bed while a similar hospital would have cost around US$82,000 to US$160,000 per bed. The design of the hospital was kept compact, with reduced empty spaces, and used prefabricated structures to save costs on expensive foundations and steel reinforcements, rather than building a conventional multi-story model. The use of natural light and restricting air-conditioning only to ICUs and OTs to save energy resulted in further savings. NH's tight control of its construction costs allowed it to pass on those savings to patients. Viren Shetty, senior vice-president for strategy and planning at NH said, "This is the lowest that is humanly possible; we have cut every bit of flab in the system" (Abrar, 2012). Dr. Shetty adds:

> In New York, there are hospitals coming up costing $600 million ... So first of all, we should ask ourselves, do we really need to build a complex structure? We live in houses without central air conditioning, why do we need hospitals with central air conditioning in the patient rooms? (Militzer, 2013)

The Mysore hospital has 9 operating theatres, 23 doctors, and about 40 nurses. The lack of central air conditioning in a hospital not only reduces costs but also enhances hygiene since poor indoor air quality is a source of infection. Shetty says, "The best sanitizer for a hospital is fresh air and sunlight. And modern hospital design does not allow both of them to come in" (Mukherji and Swaminathan, 2013: 34).

Learning from other industries & healthcare systems

Dr. Shetty has studied numerous industries, searching for applicable ideas that could help to improve access to care for poorer populations. His pursuit of economies of scale is not radical in the context of other industries; even he describes his process innovation as the "Walmart approach." In terms of cost, NH not only negotiates hard with suppliers for low prices and the right level of quality, but it has also gained operational efficiencies typically associated with factory assembly lines by applying Henry Ford's management principles. NH has deconstructed cardiac surgery into discrete steps that are standardized and repeated for each case so that overall quality and outcome improves, while overall cost is reduced by avoiding variation. NH's mastery of process innovation was recognized by the *Wall Street Journal*, which described Dr. Shetty as the "Henry Ford of heart surgery." NH has been further inspired by low-cost airlines that utilize their planes as much as possible to reduce average costs, given the heavy asset base and sunk costs. NH runs its operating theatres from early morning until late at night, six days a week. Most airlines lease their planes to reduce capital expenditure and gain higher operation flexibility. NH also leases most of its expensive medical equipment and maintains equipment it purchases very well to ensure good operational status and avoid costs that would arise from standstill. Inspired by how a trained elephant in Thailand painted a beautiful painting, Dr. Shetty pushes the importance of standardized systems in healthcare wherein clinical staff can be trained at a high level to perform any one skill reliably.

Dr. Shetty and his NH team also select best practices from other healthcare systems worldwide. NH doctors visit the best hospitals and then implement new, applicable ideas within NH (Singh, 2014). For example, with regard to health practitioners outside India, Dr. Shetty says:

> All over the world, there are two levels of health practitioners below the doctor, with various degrees and titles, who can take care of primary healthcare. This is something that should be implemented in India also. (Shetty et al., 2011)

Following Western healthcare systems, NH has expanded its training programs to include nurse intensivists, a registered nurse who has had additional education and training in a specialty area, and other medical technicians with the appropriate skills.

Extending Healthcare to the Masses via Micro-insurance Schemes

Following its vision, NH seeks to make healthcare universally affordable. Dr. Shetty notes that: "The world needs a mechanism to deliver what's already developed to 90% of the deprived population" (Shetty, 2013). In the cooperative societies of Karnataka, Dr. Shetty created Yeshaswini insurance, an innovative insurance scheme revolutionizing the provision of healthcare of the masses. It was launched as a state government scheme with the government contributing US$0.04 for every US$0.08 paid by the farmers. Prior to the Yeshaswini scheme, it was estimated that the average occupancy of hospitals in Karnataka was only 35%; although the state had 30, 500-bed private medical colleges, actual occupancy was low, reflecting the lack of affordability rather than a lack of infrastructure.

The Karnataka government provided infrastructure such as making its post offices available to collect the premium, track monthly payments, and issue a membership card (Narayana Health, 2014). At the end of the first year of operation in 2004, 9,039 surgeries had been performed and 35,814 patients had received outpatient consulting services. The Yeshaswini scheme was mostly used for low-cost treatments (around US$30) people would otherwise have forsaken given the lack of funds.

This scheme is arguably the world's largest health insurance scheme for the rural poor. The program comprises about 10% of NH's patient load. In 2011 the scheme insured 4 million farmers who paid a slightly higher premium of 18 rupees (US$0.20) a month, the only self-funding scheme in India today. Since 2013, 500,000 farmers have had different types of surgeries under the scheme, of which 50,000 were heart surgeries. Given its remarkable success the scheme has been replicated and extended across India, and is already becoming an important model of health insurance for disadvantaged populations around the world. The Yeshaswini scheme inspired the Andhra Pradesh and Tamil Nadu governments to start the similarly structured Arogyasri and Kalaignar healthcare insurance schemes.

NH is also trying to convince India's policy makers that the country's 850 million mobile phone subscribers who are spending US$2.45 per month could pay an extra US$0.33 to cover their healthcare. Dr. Shetty also wants to extend the provision of healthcare to a few million domestic helpers whose employers can pay in cash when they fall sick. But, if there is a scheme where the employee pays US$0.41 per month for healthcare, he believes every employer would contribute as well.

Telemedicine and mobile outreach clinics

Of the total number of Yeshaswini insurance holders, only 1% of patients needed surgical intervention. So, with the help of the Indian Space Research Organisation (ISRO), NH has established telemedicine, to provide consultations with patients based at remote locations. NH's telemedicine center is linked to a clinic in Kuala Lumpur, Malaysia, 52 cities in Africa and 450 telemedicine centers worldwide. Accessing patient data via satellite saves time and enables the provision of medical expertise to more patients more efficiently.

NH has three main networks: Coronary Care Unit Network; consultation at government hospitals; and the Family Physicians Network. If needed, patients are then referred to NH for surgical procedure. The Coronary Care Unit Network consists of government- and charitable-run hospitals in semi-urban and rural areas in India, where NH has trained and places doctors and other staff, to provide cardiac care and treat cardiac emergencies. NH also equipped each hospital with beds, electrocardiography machines, defibrillators, echocardiogram machines, and video conferencing equipment for telemedicine. The Karnataka state government linked up its remote state hospitals with NH cardiologists via tele-consultation. Also, NH established a Family Physicians Network wherein private independent general practitioners pay a nominal fee for the electrocardiography device and free software from NH that runs on standard personal computers. Patients' electrocardiographs are transmitted via the internet to NH from the doctors' offices and, within 10 minutes, a cardiologist report is provided to the general practitioner free of cost.

NH has set up mobile outreach clinics for cardiac diagnosis at no cost to the patient. Each bus carries the necessary equipment including electrocardiography and echocardiography equipment, defibrillators, and other essential cardiac care equipment. One experienced cardiologist and two technicians capable of performing echocardiograms ride in each mobile health van. The vans also carry a generator to deal with the challenge of unreliable power supply. Any patient needing further treatment is advised to go to the main NH hospital, where necessary surgical procedures are often provided at a lower cost than normal or with help from the charity trust of NH.

The NH Culture

NH has a team of around 100 world-class surgeons and cardiologists, led by Dr. Shetty, who are motivated by the shared vision of serving the needy and underprivileged. NH doctors become better surgeons with the high volume of patients that NH accommodates and, at the same time, they feel that their talents and skills are being applied in a way that helps society. NH's mission to help the poor and deep commitment to serve are embedded in its culture; and its staff are willing to go the extra mile. Doctors' dedication to the mission is evident by the long hours and shift work they put in to enhance productivity. Dr. Shetty, who by 2014 had performed over 15,000 surgeries, observes, "doctors at the pinnacle of their careers work 16–18 hours a day at our hospital. I can manage such eccentric people as I count myself as one amongst them. I understand them" (*Economic Times*, 2012). Dr. Bhattacharyya points out:

> Productivity in volume terms, for sure they are highly productive ... so they work more hours, paid on salary; that can only be culture. Right? To make a system like that work ... Sometimes you look at processes, some elements of Narayana Hrudayalaya that make perfect sense and that are easily replicated but when you unpack it, you realise, oh yeah, this is related to the culture where people are willing to go the extra distance. (2014)

Even though it is a for-profit hospital, NH is also a "spiritual do-gooder" as well as operationally excellent; a combination of tangible and intangible elements that is very difficult to copy in another organization (Bhattacharyya, 2014). NH doctors do not just want to treat the patient but often want to add value to their lives. For instance, an NH eye doctor who performed a cornea transplant to one of their handicapped patients, arranged an automated wheelchair for him and helped him find a job where he could work from home (Bhattacharyya, 2014). NH aims to never turn away any patient. As Singh, director of the NH television documentary series *Indian Hospital* for Aljazeera News puts it:

> And there [at NH], you have a hospital which doesn't consider the money part as the most important thing ... treatment is the main thing over there. (2014)

Though Dr. Shetty remains the public face of NH and a charismatic presence, he prefers to focus on performing surgeries rather than administrative duties. He says:

> I am essentially a heart surgeon who loves operating for the whole day if given a choice. I do spend about ten percent of my time every day in strategies, and day-to-day management of all our organization is left to the professionals. We do have senior doctors at key roles in the administration; however they too spend most of their time in patient care and have associates who do the day-to-day management. (Kothandaraman and Mookerjee, 2008: 6)

Narayana Health's Lean Management

NH is a family-owned private limited company with Dr. Shetty serving as the chairman. Leading the management team is vice-chairman, managing director, and group CEO Dr. Raghuvanshi, a paediatric heart surgeon who gave up surgery to focus on managing the fast-growing organization. Between 2011 and 2012, he had been recruiting a team of professionals from outside NH, which had traditionally been a doctor-run organization (*India Times*, 2013). "Doctors tend to have a uni-dimensional view of healthcare. We find it hard to go beyond the patient care part, ignoring other elements like the financial implications," he notes (Ganguly, 2013).

NH's management has a functional structure with the medical and finance department each headed by a director overseen by the Chief Operations Officer (COO). NH also has another level of administration that supports the senior management. Narayana's administrative team is kept extremely lean and flexible. This helps to avoid corruption especially in the way they handle organizational activities such as procurement of medical supplies and reagents. NH leadership are conscious of the need for a succession plan and advocate promotion from within. Dr. Shetty says:

> About the succession plan we have an institution, which is an academic institution, which trains every aspect of professional, involved in healthcare starting from top-level heart surgeons to the administrators. At every level we have people at various expertise and knowledge to replace the people on top as the time passes. Our aim is not to encourage lateral entry from outside, instead to nurture talent from within us, so that the culture of the institution perpetuates. (Kothandaraman and Mookerjee, 2008: 5–6)

The pool of doctors is still relatively small therefore doctors, like those in Bangalore, are under the direct leadership of Dr. Shetty. He says, "I have been lucky with my team. We have barely seen attrition. As they say, birds of the same feather flock together" (Singh, 2014).

Can the Low-cost, High-quality Business Model work outside India?

In 2013, NH had a stated objective of growing four times its size from 2013 to 2017 (Ganguly, 2013). To help fund its aggressive growth, two private-equity (PE) firms invested US$100 million for a 25% stake in the company in 2008 and would be looking at a partial or full exit around 2015. NH has expanded its footprint out of India aiming to bring its low-cost, high-quality healthcare service to North America to show that its model works in different contexts (Appendix 15.H). NH's Health City has been met with resistance especially in Western health systems since NH is bringing competition to their doorstep. In North America, NH has a joint venture with US-based Ascension Health Alliance, which in early 2014 was in the first phase of building a Health City in the Cayman Islands and was planning to gradually expand to a total of 2,000 beds. The Health City served the Caribbean region where many patients from this area currently go to the USA for their treatment. The Cayman Islands have recognized Indian medical degrees, a necessary condition of NH before it set up shop. NH controls the operations of the hospitals and had sent teams of people from its Bangalore Health City to its Health City in the Cayman Islands. Doctors from the flagship Health City in Bangalore and other support staff who are familiar with the NH system and culture go there to seed the next hospital with organizational competencies, and efficient processes, while Ascension's strength lies in its supply chain management.

Dr. Shetty has been committed to trying new approaches to provide affordable healthcare and to re-define healthcare standards in India and worldwide. Can NH's business model be successfully replicated in other parts of the world? How much longer can NH sustain a growth orientation while maintaining high-quality healthcare provision?

APPENDICES

APPENDIX 15.A Narayana Health's Existing and Upcoming Locations (Narayana Health, 2014)

APPENDIX 15.B Narayana Health's List of Awards (Narayana Health, 2014)

Year	NH Awards
2013	• Financial Times Arcelor Mittall Boldness in Business Awards in Corporate Responsibility/Environment category • Porter Prize for Industry Architectural Shift, by the Institute of Competitiveness • Philanthropy Award, Forbes India • Winner of Inc. India Innovative 100 Awards
2012	• Ranked 36th among World's 50 most innovative companies by Fast Company • Frost & Sullivan India Healthcare Excellence for healthcare service provider company of the year • FICCI Health Care Excellence Award for addressing industry issues • Finalist in Namma Bengaluru Awards in corporate social responsibility category
2011	• India Shining Star CSR Award for the exceptional CSR work done
2010	• CNBC & ICICI Lombard Award for best hospital

APPENDIX 15.C   NH Chairman, Dr. Devi Shetty List of Awards (Narayana Health, 2014)

Year	NH Chairman, Dr. Devi Shetty Awards
2013	• Ernst & Young – Entrepreneur of the Year Award, Life Sciences and Healthcare category
2012	• Indian of the Year by CNN-IBN • Lifetime Achievement Award by FICCI • The Economic Times Entrepreneur of the Year • Padma Bhushan Award for medicine, the third highest civilian award given by the Indian government
2011	• The Economist's Innovation Awards
2010	• Indian of the Year by NDTV
2005	• Social Entrepreneurship Award, Schwab Foundation
2004	• Citizen Extraordinaire, Rotary • Dr. B. C. Roy Award
2003	• Padma Shri, the fourth highest civilian award given by the Indian government • Ernst & Young – Entrepreneur of the Year • Sir M. Visvesvaraya Memorial Award
2003	• Rajyotsava Award, the second highest civilian award given by the Karnataka state government

APPENDIX 15.D   Narayana Health List of Selected Recognition (Narayana Health, 2014)

Media Communication	NH Selected Recognition
Articles, Case Studies & Books	• The Wall Street Journal • BBC News • Harvard Business School Case Study • The Guardian Weekly • Reader's Digest • India today • Wharton Business School, University of Pennsylvania • The Week: Health • Forbes • New Scientist • Geo Wissen
Television Media	• Discovery Channel • ABC • Bio • CNBC • Aljazeera • Hard Talk, BBC

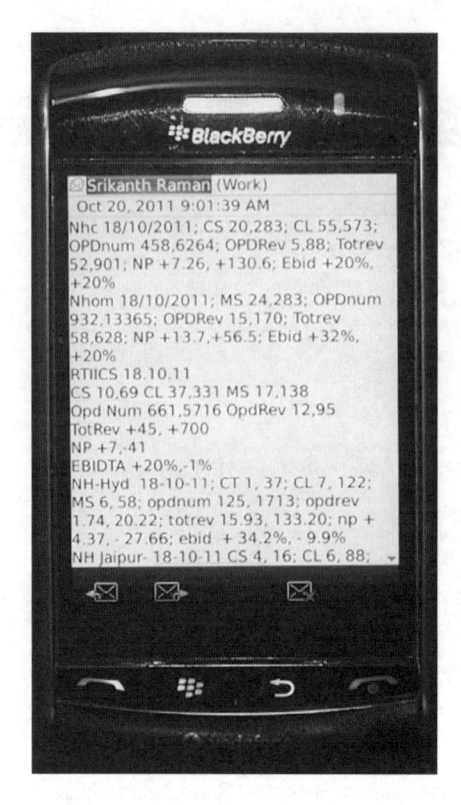

APPENDIX 15.E Daily Profit and Loss Statement via SMS

Source: Shetty, D. (2013) Available from: http://www.slideshare.net/amitkapoor/dr-devi-shetty-presentation

Used with permission of Dr Devi Shetty

APPENDIX 15.F ICARE System

Source: Shetty, D. (2013) Available from: http://www.slideshare.net/amitkapoor/dr-devi-shetty-presentation

Used with permission of Dr Devi Shetty

APPENDIX 15.G Low-cost, 300-bed hospital model

Source: Shetty, D. (2013) Available from: http://www.slideshare.net/amitkapoor/dr-devi-shetty-presentation
Used with permission of Dr Devi Shetty

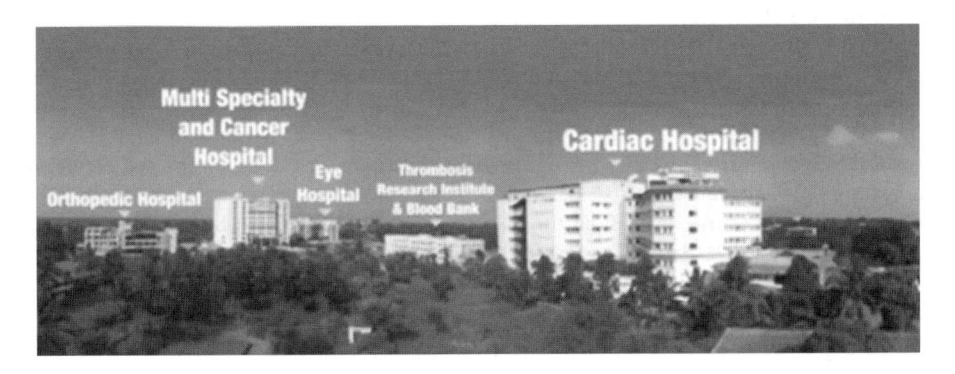

APPENDIX 15.H Narayana Health "Health City" in Bangalore

Source: Shetty, D. (2013) Available from: http://www.slideshare.net/amitkapoor/dr-devi-shetty-presentation
Used with permission of Dr Devi Shetty

REFERENCES

Abrar, P. (2012) Frugal innovation: Devi Shetty's Narayana Hrudayalaya to conduct heart surgeries at world's cheapest rates. Available at: http://articles.economictimes.indiatimes.com/2012-12-26/news/36008056_1_narayana-hrudayalaya-heart-surgeries-devi-prasad-shetty (date accessed: April 21, 2015).

Anand, Geeta (2009) The Henry Ford of heart surgery: In India, a factory model for hospitals is cutting costs and yielding profits. Available at: http://www.wsj.com/articles/SB125875892887958111 (date accessed: April 14, 2015).

Bhattacharyya, O. (2014) Interview on Narayana Health with Dr. Onil Bhattacharyya, conducted by Karina Bruce on June 6, 2014.

Bhattacharyya, O., McGahan, A., Dunne, D., Singer, P. A., and Daar, A. (2008) Innovative health service delivery models for low and middle income countries. Available at: http://www.rockefellerfoundation.org/uploads/files/406b65b8-f729-4fb6-8c62-f987b1c49a62-5.pdf (date accessed: 2013).

Burns, L. R. (2014) *India's Healthcare Industry: Innovation in Delivery, Financing, and Manufacturing.* New York: Cambridge University Press.

Deloitte (2014) Global health care outlook: Share challenges, shared opportunities. Available at: https://www2.deloitte.com/content/dam/Deloitte/global/Documents/Life-Sciences-Health-Care/dttl-lshc-2014-global-health-care-sector-report.pdf (date accessed: July 1, 2014).

Deloitte (2015) 2015 Global health care outlook: Common goals, competing priorities. Available at: http://www2.deloitte.com/content/dam/Deloitte/pl/Documents/Reports/pl_2015-health-care-outlook-global.pdf (date accessed: April 16, 2015).

Economic Times (2011) Almost 70% Indians live in rural areas: Census report. Available at: http://articles.economictimes.indiatimes.com/2011-07-15/news/29777954_1_rural-areas-urban-areas-census-report (date accessed: April 16, 2015).

Economic Times (2012) ET Awards 2012: Devi Prasad Shetty is entrepreneur of the year. Available at: http://articles.economictimes.indiatimes.com/2012-09-19/news/33952757_1_hospital-chain-narayana-hrudayalaya-cardiac-surgery (date accessed: November 5, 2015).

Economist (2010) First break all the rules. Available at: http://www.economist.com/node/15879359 (date accessed: April 16, 2015).

Economist (2015) Making the most of little: India explores new models. Available at: http://www.economist insights.com/healthcare/analysis/broadening-healthcare-access-brazil-through-innovation/casestudies (date accessed: April 16, 2015).

Ganguly, D. (2013) How can Dr Devi Shetty quadruple Narayana Hrudayalaya in five years? Available at: http://articles.economictimes.indiatimes.com/2013-05-24/news/39476325_1_heart-surgeon-elderly-patient-dr-devi-shetty (date accessed: July 1, 2014).

Ghosh, D. (2015) Devi Shetty's affordable health care services now in Cayman Islands. Available at: http://forbesindia.com/article/work-in-progress/devi-shettys-affordable-health-care-services-now-in-cayman-islands/39383/1 (date accessed: March 18, 2015).

Gokhale, K. (2013) Heart surgery in India for $1,583 Costs $106,385 in US. Available at: http://www.businessweek.com/news/2013-07-28/heart-surgery-in-india-for-1-583-costs-106-385-in-u-dot-s-dot-health (date accessed: July 1, 2014).

Govindarajan, V. and Ramamurti, R. (2013) Delivering world-class health care, affordably. *Harvard Business Review*. Available at: https://hbr.org/2013/11/delivering-world-class-health-care-affordably (date accessed: July 1, 2014).

Hartigan, P. (2014) Businesses for 21st century: new leaf paper / Dr Devi Shetty's business model. Available at: https://www.youtube.com/watch?v=73AMLjSZTVE (date accessed: May 1, 2015).

India Times (2013) Devi Shetty's Narayana Healthcare: Men behind success of his low-cost hospitals. Available at: http://economictimes.indiatimes.com/slideshows/corporate-industry/devi-shettys-narayana-healthcare-men-behind-success-of-his-low-cost-hospitals/ashutosh-raghuvanshi-group-ceo/slideshow_v1/20240859.cms (date accessed: April 22, 2015).

Kavlekar, P. (2013) Narayana Health's ten-year plan. Available at: http://www.thesmartceo.in/cover-story/narayana-healths-ten-year-plan.html (date accessed: July 5, 2014).

Kazmin, A. (2013) Corporate responsibility: From the heart. Available at: http://www.ft.com/cms/s/0/6a049988-85ba-11e2-bed4-00144feabdc0.html#axzz36EC4ngVp (date accessed: July 1, 2014).

Khanna, T. and Bijlani, T. (2012) Narayana Hrudayalaya Heart Hospital: Cardiac care for the poor (B). Harvard Business School Supplement, 712–402.

Khanna, T., Rangan K., and Manocaran, M. (2005) Narayana Hrudayalaya heart hospital: Cardiac care for the poor (A). Harvard Business School Case, 505–078.

Knowledge@Wharton (2010) Narayana Hrudayalaya: A model for accessible, affordable health care? Available at: http://knowledge.wharton.upenn.edu/article/narayana-hrudayalaya-a-model-for-accessible-affordable-health-care/ (date accessed: April 20, 2015).

Kothandaraman, P. and Mookerjee, S. (2008) Healthcare for all: Narayana Hrudayalaya, Bangalore. Available at: http://growinginclusivemarkets.org/media/cases/India_Narayana_Summary.pdf (date accessed: April 20, 2015).

Kothari, S. S. (2009) Pediatric cardiac care for the economically disadvantaged in India: Problems and prospects. *Annals of Pediatric* Cardiology, 2(1): 95–8.

Kung, H. C., Hoyert, D. L., Xu, J., and Murphy, S. L. (2008) Deaths: Final data for 2005. *National Vital Statistics Reports*, 56: 1–120.

Lim, K. K. (2014) Innovation in healthcare service delivery. Available at: http://www.oxbridgebiotech.com/review/business-development/innovation-health-care-service-delivery/ (date accessed: July 1, 2014).

Madhavan, N. (2014) Compassionate heart, business mind. Available at: http://businesstoday.intoday.in/story/biggest-india-innovation-narayana-health/1/205823.html (date accessed: July 7, 2014).

Mahajan-Bansal, N. (2009) CK Prahalad: A unique combination of strategic vision and financial acumen. Available at: http://forbesindia.com/interview/magazine-extra/ck-prahalad-a-unique-combination-of-strategic-vision-and-financial-acumen/1912/1 (date accessed: July 1, 2014).

Mahalakshmi, N. (2015) Big heart, better mind. Available at: http://www.outlookbusiness.com/the-big-story/lead-story/big-heart-better-mind-614 (date accessed: April 20, 2015).

Militzer, J. (2013) Cracking the code on affordable health care – Part 2. Available at: http://nextbillion.net/blogpost.aspx?blogid=3339 (date accessed: April 20, 2015).

Mukherji, A. and Swaminathan, H. (2013) The role of Right to Health in health care management and delivery in India: In conversation with Dr Devi Prasad Shetty, Chariman, Narayana Hrudayalaya. *IIMB Management Review*, 25(1): 28–35.

Munavalli, J. R., van Merode, F., Rao, S. V., and Srinivas, A. (2014) Healthcare of India: Today and tomorrow. *International Journal of Innovative Research & Development*, 3(2): 350–6.

Narayana Health (2014) What makes NH a global healthcare case study. Available at: http://www.narayanahealth.org/corporate-presentation.pdf (date accessed: July 1, 2014).

Private Sector Innovation Programme for Health (PSP4H) (2014) Understanding the India low cost model of healthcare delivery: A review of the literature. Nairobi, Kenya: PSP4H. Available at: http://www.psp4h.com/wp-content/uploads/2014/05/Understanding-the-India-Low-Cost-Model-of-Healthcare-Delivery-3.pdf (date accessed: November 5, 2015).

PwC (2014) Emerging trends in healthcare. Available at: http://www.pwc.com/gx/en/healthcare/emerging-trends-pwc-healthcare.jhtml (date accessed: July 1, 2014).

Ramamurti, R. (2014) Interview on Narayana Health, conducted by Karina Bruce on May 23, 2014.

Richman, B. D., Udayakumar, K., Mitchell, W., and Schulman, K. A. (2008) Lessons from India in organizational innovation: A tale of two heart hospitals. *Health Aff (Millwood)*, 27(5): 1260–70. Available at: http://content.healthaffairs.org/content/27/5/1260.full (date accessed: July 1, 2014).

Saligram, P., Bhattacharjee, A., Crooks, V., Schram, A., and Snyder, J. (2014) An overview of the medical tourism industry in Bangalore, India – Version 1.0. Department of Geography, Simon Fraser University, British Columbia, Canada.

Shetty, D. (2013) Heart surgery for $800. Available at: http://www.slideshare.net/amitkapoor/dr-devi-shetty-presentation (date accessed: May 14, 2015). Dr. Devi Shetty shall not be liable for any legal or monetary liabilities, if any, arising out of publication of this presentation material. The current data may be different than the one depicted at the time of presentation.

Shetty, D., Sammut, S. M., and Burns, L. R. (2011) Doing more with less – lessons from a doctor. Available from: http://isbinsight.isb.edu/less-lessons-doctor/ (date accessed: July 2, 2014).

Singh, G. (2014) Interview on Narayana Health with Gautam Singh, director of the NH television documentary series, Indian Hospital for Aljazeera News, conducted by Karina Bruce on May 30, 2014.

South China Morning Post (2013) Devi Shetty's Narayana Hrudayalaya can perform heart surgery for US$800. Available at: http://www.scmp.com/news/asia/article/1220078/devi-shettys-narayana-hrudayalaya-can-perform-heart-surgery-us800 (date accessed: April 20, 2015).

Ted Talks (2013) It's not a solution if it's not affordable: Dr. Devi Prasad Shetty at TedxGateway 2013. Available at: https://www.youtube.com/watch?v=C3CXhwJjnk4 (date accessed: May 14, 2014).

World Bank (2014) GDP per capita (current US$). Available at: http://data.worldbank.org/indicator/NY.GDP.PCAP.CD (date accessed: November 5, 2015).

World Health Organization (2005) WHO launches global patient safety challenge; issues guidelines on hand hygiene in health care. Available at: http://www.who.int/mediacentre/news/releases/2005/pr50/en/ (date accessed: May 14, 2015).

World Health Organization (2013) Global health workforce shortage to reach 12.9 million in coming decades. Available at: http://www.who.int/mediacentre/news/releases/2013/health-workforce-shortage/en/ (date accessed: April 16, 2015).

A "RELIABLE" RECOVERY? THE TURNAROUND OF THE RELIANT GROUP

16

OVERVIEW

At one time Reliant cars were a familiar sight on British roads. Famous for its three wheels, and loved by many, Reliant Cars Ltd was the second largest car company in the UK from the 1960s to the 1990s, producing 1/2m vehicles. However, in the early 1990s an economic recession affected its business and that of its major stakeholders, and with a rising cost base, the company went bust three times in five years. In 1996 an ex-engineer from Jaguar cars, Jonathan Haynes arrived with a new backer to buy the company out of administration. The question was whether he could turn around Reliant Cars Ltd and put it on a path to sustainable recovery.

HISTORY

The Reliant Car Company was formed in 1934 as a result of the Raleigh Cycle Company making the decision to discontinue production of their three-wheeled vehicles. The man in charge of that section of the Raleigh Company, Mr T. L. Williams, was made redundant but saw a future for the development of the three-wheeler, and set up a company and workshop in the garden of his home in Tamworth, Staffordshire. Reliant Cars Ltd was born the following year.

In the early years the Reliant was a 356kg van powered by a 750cc engine driving the rear wheels through 3-speed gearbox and shaft drive. The body was hardwood frame with aluminum panels attached to it. Williams was always enthusiastic about Reliant being as self-reliant as possible and so the company made its own engine. Reliant's engine was Europe's first mass-produced lightweight overhead-valve aluminum alloy engine. Post war the rising cost of aluminum for the car body led the company to turn to fiberglass to make first the body and, by 1964, the floor of the cars. The process employed consisted of building up layers of fiberglass and resin by hand to achieve a uniform thickness – although some components were produced by using matched dies and hot press moldings. The rolls of fiberglass arrived from suppliers and were cut, 60 layers at a time, into patterns. At least two layers of mat were used in a body molding and each three-wheeler was composed of some 160 mat patterns. By the mid 1970s, Reliant employed nearly 450 people in 106,000 square feet of floor space and the vehicles remained largely built by hand.

The Reliant Robin three-wheeled car was regarded to have a good design, small and narrow, at an affordable price with low insurance costs. It could do approximately 70 miles per gallon (when many 4-wheel cars at the time were averaging around 25 miles per gallon) and had a top speed of around 85 miles per hour. It was described in the 1970s as the most practical small car in Britain. The fiberglass body was surprisingly resilient and did not corrode like metal cars. Reliant cars also had the added advantage that unskilled owners could repair them. Indeed the relatively low level of sophistication of the car made it very popular with those owners who liked to maintain their own vehicles and the company did well in the sale of spare parts. In the broader context the 1970s oil crisis also was of great benefit to Reliant Cars as rapidly rising petrol prices spurred orders for their lightweight fuel-efficient cars.

Later, Reliant bought a prototype design for a four-wheeled sports car that subsequently became the best-selling sporting estate, the Scimitar GTE. Motoring enthusiasts at the time regarded the Scimitar as superior to its direct competitor, the Aston Martin and it was even favored by a member of the Royal family, Princess Anne. At the same time the company innovated with sporty three-wheelers, creating the "head turning" Bond Bug. During the 1980s the company created a utility/pickup vehicle and also a small three-wheeled commercial vehicle with a chassis and cab onto which a custom rear body could be added for any commercial use, such as a road sweeper, a flat back, a milk float, a hydraulic lifting rear bed. It was very attractive to public utility companies and councils due to its ability to negotiate narrow alleyways.

FIGURE 16.1 The Reliant Robin

© User Charles01 at Wikimedia Commons 2013 (https://commons.wikimedia.org/wiki/File:Reliant_Robin_registered_July_1975_748cc_at_Knebworth_2013.JPG)

FIGURE 16.2 The Reliant Scimitar

© User USX II at Wikimedia Commons 2012 (https://commons.wikimedia.org/wiki/File:1973_Reliant_Scimitar_GTE_overdrive_(8071885527).jpg)

The car was also desirable to would-be motorcyclists as it did not require the user to pass the full car license test. However, the firm failed to invest further in the Scimitar and its production was later discontinued.

By the 1990s Reliant Reliant was one of the last car companies to do it all themselves with their fiberglass bodies and 850cc aluminum engines. However, the owner of Reliant in the early 1990s, a major housing developer, collapsed with the economic recession in 1992. The company was sold to auto component manufacturers Bean Engineering but government interference in the UK car industry as a whole caused a severe crisis for these new owners. They were forced to sell and then the general economic recession pushed Reliant Cars Ltd. into administration.[1]

TAKING CHARGE

While in administration, Jonathan Haynes, an ex-Jaguar engineer decided to attempt a rescue of the ailing firm. Haynes's father had been famous for designing the E-type Jaguar, an iconic racing car, and the son, like his father, also had a passion for sports cars. He was attracted by Reliant's illustrious past even though sports cars hadn't been made since the early 1990s. Just before Reliant Cars Ltd went into administration the firm was only producing the Reliant Robin. The administrator let the workforce go and was selling off assets in order to pay back

---

[1]Administration is a rescue mechanism for insolvent entities and allows them to carry on running their business. It is an alternative to liquidation, which is the sale of all assets. A company in administration is operated by an administrator as a going concern in order to protect creditors, while options other than liquidation are sought. These may include re-capitalizing the business, selling the business to new owners, or demerging it into elements that can be sold and closing the remainder.

creditors. It was then an offer was received from Jonathan Haynes, backed by institutional funds, to buy all the remaining assets of the business. This was accepted and so Haynes was now faced with the challenge of how to restart the Reliant Motor Company in order to create a sustainable business?

It was raining on the day Haynes arrived at the Reliant Factory to take physical possession of the company. The cold wet weather only seemed to make the premises seem gloomier. The factory was in total disarray as the administrators had left the site in a mess. Machines had lain idle for months, they had seized up and rusted. Walking around the factory Haynes thought the machines were a good collection a museum would be proud of. There were leaks through the roof and buckets had to be put down to collect the water. There was dust and debris on all surfaces and bits and pieces of cars left everywhere. Calendars on the wall were out of date and pictures faded and broken. In one part of the factory there lay 14 partly assembled Reliant Robin cars. The first task though was to clean the offices, which Haynes did with the help of his young family. His wife, an accountant, could then begin to start making sense of the records, files, and systems.

Haynes' first task was to get production restarted. With antiquated machinery and unique fiberglass molding processes the only people able to repair and use the machines and begin making new car bodies were the original engineers that had been laid off, unpaid, many months earlier. It was a testimony to their loyalty to the Reliant Robin car, and their faith in the engineering skill of Haynes, that they even considered returning to this very uncertain future. In order to find these employees and choose which ones to reengage, as in the early days the main task was to get the factory working again, Haynes brought back some members of the original management team – the works manager, sales manager, mold shop manager, and the car parts buyers. As Haynes remarked "I had to build a team around me as it would have been impossible to do it on my own." This team selectively recruited back employees.

It would take the engineers many months to get the machines working again and the production line running. In the meantime procurement employees started work on re-engaging car part suppliers so they could get in all the parts needed to make cars once the line was fully functional. This proved very awkward indeed. The suppliers had lost many thousands of pounds when Reliant went into administration as it had failed to pay its debts. Not surprisingly they were absolutely unwilling to trust the new Reliant management with even the smallest items on credit. Even for bulbs costing 10p each they wouldn't supply until Reliant's cheque was cashed. This meant that Reliant could only operate with cash and not credit. There were other demands on working capital as well. Employees needed to be paid and, in order to get production moving as soon as possible, Haynes had to pay for large amounts of overtime.

To Haynes one of the most important employees in the company was Bruce – a salesman he appointed to sell spare parts. At the factory Haynes repeatedly asked Bruce to sell off spare parts and anything else he could find to generate £2,000 of cash per day.

Robin Reliant customers are passionate about their cars. Around 44,000 were registered at the time of Haynes taking control. Many had bought seven or eight cars over a sustained period of time and were extremely loyal. They were also regarded as the safest motorists on UK roads. The Reliant Robin had a strong image as it featured in a favourite BBC comedy *Only Fools and Horses* and was also the object of many jokes by the comedian Jasper Carrott. Although laughed at for its quirkiness, and downmarket image, many also regarded the Robin Reliant fondly – indeed the jokes were seen as free advertising. Part of the attraction may have been the unusualness of a three-wheeled car, and the camaraderie of an ownership club, which Haynes engaged with at Reliant car meetings, showing pictures to loyal owners of spruced-up Reliant models he intended to deliver. The car was certainly popular among market traders and farmers. It also had an advantage over other cars in that an owner only needed a motorcycle licence to drive it, rather than a driving licence. The former could be obtained by a 17-year-old whereas one had to be 18 for the latter. Also the Reliant Robin was often used as a car for the disabled, as the speed could be limited to 55mph. There were also no other three-wheeled cars on the market from competitors. The loyalty of the customers meant a continuous demand for spare parts and updates although many alternative suppliers had been meeting this demand when Reliant went into receivership. Haynes recognized this side of the business had been neglected and pushed parts sales employees to win the business back, even by undercutting if necessary.

One of Haynes early priorities was to meet with the car dealers to hear their views on what the customers wanted. He quickly learned that not only were customers loyal but there was also still a latent demand for the cars that dealers had struggled to fill. Indeed one of the dealers said, "I have customers backed up to buy the cars but I haven't received any stock." The dealers also had ideas about what Haynes might do to increase the attractiveness of the Reliant Robin to increase demand. Throughout the first year Haynes spent significant time meeting up with the dealers, to be responsive to their needs but he also demanded quick and prompt payment from them. However, dealer attitudes were cautious. As one commented, "we've seen it all before to be honest with you. We went through this last year and we hope these people have got it right this time – listen to what is wanted." Haynes said, "we now have around 150 orders in the system so now its just a question of getting the labour back in and getting production moving. The whole key was to hold off bringing people back until I had the parts and once I had the parts I could start bringing people back."

Haynes forecasted that the firm had to build 50 cars per month to pay his rehired 60-strong workforce and to balance the books. Fortunately when he took charge, he had discovered 14 Robins in nearly complete form that could be sold for quick money. They needed wheels and steering wheels and other parts, but these could be procured fairly easily for a few hundred pounds. Within a couple of months of taking charge of the factory and with relatively little effort these cars were finished and sold for cash. However, in the factory things were not going well. One of the key machines needed to make the crankshaft was broken and the engineers could not fix it.

DOING THINGS DIFFERENTLY

Haynes was conscious that traditional attitudes in the company had to change. Many employees had lived through the previous three collapses and were very cynical that anything would really change. In order to win back business in the spare parts market Haynes realized they had to undercut competitors and, crucially, offer a better service. He detected the attitude in Reliant of, "the answer's no, but perhaps we can do it, or perhaps we can but the answer's no!" In response Haynes would quote John Neil, CEO of Unipart "the answer's yes – now what's the question?" As Haynes remarked – "we have to change attitudes."

The fiberglass body of a Reliant Robin is made entirely by hand. For Haynes this was very inefficient as it meant he had to employ 20 employees just to make car bodies. This seemed overly labor intensive and outdated, as chopper guns existed that sprayed on fiberglass and could do the task more quickly. This technology would require fewer employees. Things came to a head in an argument between Haynes and the production foreman with Haynes arguing that he could save £250,000 in wages and make cars more quickly while the foreman, Bryan, said, "chopper guns cannot make car bodies like you want car bodies to be made." In order to resolve the dispute Haynes said, "go out and buy a chopper gun Bryan and we'll resolve this once and for all. I am not going to have a wage bill of £250,000 that I don't need. No – go out and borrow a chopper gun from our supplier and show me a body panel in chopper gun and one by hand and we'll sort this out."

Casting around for new ideas and innovations to draw in new customers Haynes decided to spend time discussing three prototypes he had inherited from the previous owners. These included the three-wheel pick-up and a brightly coloured yellow Bond Bug three-wheeler. In a meeting with his management team they discussed these prototypes. In particular Haynes felt the three-wheel pick-up should be a top priority for a new model and that the bug three-wheeler would turn heads. In asking for opinions some of the team remarked, "I think the bug is bloody horrible – perhaps it's my age!" Haynes responded, "it sold well in large numbers once," to which the operations manager said, "yes, but that was 25 years ago and times have moved on." To which Haynes said, "I know, I know – but we haven't got much else to sell off the shelf for which we have tools." The manager replied, "but we haven't got the tools for it, it doesn't meet current legislation and needs quite a lot of development work. What worries me is who is going to do all this development work? I can see a lot of cost. I am trying hard not to be desperately cynical but some of us have sat around this table and had more or less this conversation twice in the last two or three years and we have seen a lot of money wasted. I don't want to see that happen again."

FIGURE 16.3   Reliant Bond Bug

© User Rept0n1x at Wikimedia Commons 2011 (https://commons.wikimedia.org/wiki/File:Reliant_Bond_Bug_at_the_2011_Birkenhead_Park_Festival_of_Transport.jpg)

Meanwhile, there continued to be problems on the production line. A shortage of a few bits meant they were having problems finishing a few of the cars. This was causing aggravation from the shop floor to the management asking why haven't we got parts? So cars sat in the car park unsold waiting for parts.

In order to relax from the pressures at work, Haynes would spend some time on the family farm where he could often be seen sharing a beer with farm employees. Just before taking control of Reliant, Haynes had recently come through a severe crisis on the farm with managing the BSE contagion, which decimated British cattle. Now that the farm was on an even keel and with the current demands of Reliant he decided that year to starve the farm of investment.

CRISIS

Haynes then set a tough target – by August 5 they needed to produce 50 cars per month to balance the books and pay everyone. As Haynes said – it would be touch and go. He had tried to keep calm to inspire people and to stabilize people – to make sure there was a cohesive plan. He had had to count to 10 a couple of times to stop himself losing his temper. Sitting with the management team in one of their regular catch-up meetings, around a table littered with schedules and lever arch files of product and parts schedules and sales plans, in a meeting room with pictures of sports cars on the walls, Haynes told the assembled: "What I am going to say now ain't going to come easy – but we are dead unless we produce 50 cars with our own new engines in August. We are going to have a serious cash problem."

Although spurred on by demand the body manufacture had started going well, it was a different matter regarding making the engines. The machines had been standing idle and no maintenance had taken place – "no spanner had been put onto them." A vital machine for producing crankshafts was still broken and before that could be resolved they couldn't progress any further. As Haynes remarked: "I am wetting myself with anxiety about this crankshaft. Is it going to work? I reckon we have 48 hours left to make up our minds whether we are going to produce crankshafts here or whether we outsource to a supplier – we cannot afford to make a muck up of it." The production manager looked a little surprised and said, "Well they are going through." Haynes responded, "What about the transverse machine [for making crankshafts]?" The production manager responded, "We bypassed that – we're not using it." Haynes' concern for production was clear: "We are safe aren't we? This is a mountain we have to climb and if we don't climb it I am not so sure we will succeed – and I can't say it with a more friendly, smiling, un-nervous face than I have now, but we have got, got, got, to produce these cars. No short cuts, other than overtime, overtime, overtime. Keep the lads back to 6 o'clock, 7 o'clock [sales manager rubs his eyes from fatigue]. Two full weekends." Speaking directly to Bruce the sales manager, Haynes said:

> I cannot emphasize enough the load on your shoulders. You are now the single most crucial person in this company to provide me with £2,000 a day. You've got to do it – I don't care what you sell. If you see something in the car park that will sell, sell it! If you see someone wants to buy a disabled car down there, sell it! If you see someone who wants to buy out of that yard of scrap, sell it. Sell, Sell, Sell Bruce. You are the most crucial person we've got. We have to have £2,000 a day coming in off spare parts.

The raw materials to make engines had to be ordered weeks in advance. If just one item was missing the production line would stop. So the orders for thousands of bits were checked daily at the shortages meeting. The buyers were really struggling to get steel valve seat inserts having spent eight weeks trying to order them, so they were feeling under great pressure to get these items. Every day there was a shortages meeting where all items were reviewed. Haynes was getting agitated: "I don't think you are getting the point [thumping the table] – when am I going to get the finished parts from our parts supplier?" The parts buyer responded, "I've been told we will get them this week – I have been pushing them for two weeks." Haynes retorted, "Will you please send them a fax saying we need a minimum finished quantity here on site this week." Later in the meeting there was some confusion about how many parts were work in progress. Haynes started to look hot under the collar slammed down his pen saying, "it's too loose – get it right – get it right!"

Meanwhile, Bruce the sales manager could be seen physically pushing trolleys of stuff out of the factory for sale. His target had now risen from £2,000 a day to £3,000 a day. Later Haynes walked into Bruce's office where he was standing looking exhausted in rolled up shirtsleeves. Smiling Haynes said, "what do you think Bruce – £4,000 a day!" (Laughter from Bruce as he looks absolutely exhausted).

As the deadline for full production neared on August 5, it was clear that cash was dangerously low. With just £1,400 in the bank, Haynes had just signed £1,600 of cheques and had to sign a further £1,600 of cheques in two days' time. With the highest wages bill yet, cash was running out and Haynes' wife was in the office in tears in the evening as she thought she had written too many cheques and wouldn't be able to pay the wages. Thinking they didn't have the money in the bank to cover the amount, she couldn't sleep that night.

CRISIS AVERTED?

The following morning Haynes' wife phoned the bank first thing to find out how much funds Reliant had in its account. She learned a cheque had just come in which was enough to cover the wages. At the end of that day Reliant had just £400 in the bank. Relieved she said, "That is the closest I have ever, ever been [to bankruptcy] and I don't want to be that close again."

The corner had been turned and the factory was now working flat out. It was employing just 60 people, half the number of the previous owner – and Haynes wanted them to make twice as many cars as the largely handmade nature of the car and increased automotive safety regulations was putting pressure on car prices. In the mold shop car bodies were being made in the traditional way – largely by hand. There were 20 people and many had left jobs to come back, showing their commitment to Reliant. However, Haynes was not happy. In a meeting with the mold shop manager Haynes said, "I am horrified that we have to have 20 people in the body shop to produce bodies." The manager responded, "it used to be more than that!" Haynes retorted, "well I am even more horrified!" The manager told him, "but even outside they have to employ people and buy materials." Haynes was still not happy; "But it is still cheaper to do it outside. Last year we produced 3 cars per man and I want 15 cars per man."

Haynes focused on labor-saving technology by saying to the manager, "With a chopper gun you can have the bodies done with two people." But the manager disagreed: "Can I say that

2 people cannot do a body, like you say a body, with a chopper gun." Haynes said, "I've seen it being done, Bryan – I'm not having the labor. You have got to prove to me very quickly why you need the labor [rapping the table with his knuckles]. I am not having 20 people in that mold shop – it's an important thing. You can see from my body language – I am not having 20 people in that body shop. We have got to find a way around it. Go and get a chopper gun now and do your floors in chopper gun." Leaning forwards and nodding his head repeatedly Haynes said, "Please go out and buy a chopper gun and please go and do your floors now – go – that's an instruction. Go and buy one, no, go and borrow a chopper gun as I am sick to death of the argument. Please go and borrow a chopper gun from whoever it is and do a floor panel in chopper gun and then I'll start listening." At this point Bryan stood up and left the meeting room. To the remaining executives Haynes says, "I'm pushing you – I'm testing you. If I give in and say you can have 20 people in the body shop – it's an awful lot of money. It's a bill of £250,000 a year in the mold shop on labour. I can do a lot with a quarter of a million pounds."

Later walking along the production line Haynes asked an employee fixing wheels to a Reliant how things were going. "At the moment we are supposed to be doing 12 a week but we never made the target last week. There's lots of new chaps on and they ain't learned the job – so we're training them and trying to catch up at the same time." Having finished off the wheels the employee then pushed the car along the track to the next workstation.

At the end of August Reliant had fallen well short of the 50 cars they planned, producing 36 cars, but they were back in production and, with the cash from parts sales, Haynes's backers were convinced to put up more money and keep the company safe. Haynes, sitting in his office, with drawings for a new sports car in front of him, was not too disappointed. By November the factory was running more smoothly. There were still 20 people working in the mold shop working in the traditional way and chopper guns were not being used. The workforce now numbered around 70 employees and production now stood at 20 vehicles per week. As the works force manager remarked to Haynes, the workforce had been brilliant.

THE FUTURE

Haynes, still interested in sports cars, had recently commissioned a designer to come up with some contemporary designs that embodied British values. Clustered around some preliminary sketches with the designer and engineers, Haynes remarks, "I am a sports car man – I grew up with sports cars – wind in the hair motoring is what I like. It's not every day you can have a company where you can develop, with a very good team, what you want to do." "I am particularly buoyant at the moment as our investors have seen our drawings of our next generation of sports car for Reliant using the Scimitar brand." Smiling, he says, "I am particularly pleased they like what I have shown them and I have engaged a very good clay stylist and clay modelers in the West Midlands and the project has got the green light from the investors – and that excites me."

Meanwhile, outside the office is proof of Haynes's plans for new Robin models with the first 12 of 100 special edition Robins in British racing green with alloy wheels and redesigned dashboard being dispatched to buyers. Reliant Cars now had a full order book and with the economy as a whole growing, and with rising optimism from customers and dealers, the future looks bright.

The atmosphere in the factory by the end of the year was quite different from when Haynes first took over the company. As the manager of the works remarked, "Christmas this year – by gum we shall enjoy ourselves – is entirely different to last year where we didn't know where the next one from coming from. This year I can see a lot more years in front of us." Also reflecting upon the year, Haynes' wife said, "its been fun, its been long hours, its been jolly hard work, its been no family life and its been Reliant seven days a week." For Haynes the turnaround of Reliant has been a success:

> I feel proud that we have got this far and saved it. When it started it wasn't emotion driven – it was let's turn this business around, but it's become far more emotional. I totally believe in Reliant. I love the car. It's a funny old sight, but it works. At this point production is on target and there is £1m of orders.

Looking forwards, the company confidently expected to make profits in 1997 and to show their new four-wheeled sports car at the Birmingham motor show in the Fall.

QUESTIONS

1. Using the ESCO model suggest why Reliant may have declined.
2. In terms of Praxis, what immediate actions were taken to achieve a turnaround?
3. Identify the main practices in the case. Discuss their role in facilitating and inhibiting the changes that Haynes intended to achieve.
4. In terms of Praxis, what actions were taken to build a sustainable future for the firm?
5. Critically evaluate the turnaround of Reliant using the 3P framework.
6. Using Hart's (1998) integrative framework (reviewed in Chapter 1) argue for the type of integrative model present during Reliant's recovery

SOURCES

A brief history of the firm and its cars can be found on: www.3wheelers.com/reliant.html; http://en.wikipedia.org/wiki/Reliant;
http://en.wikipedia.org/wiki/Reliant_Robin.
BBC (1996) Trouble at the top. Reliant Motors. www.youtube.com/watch?v=Cm3RgR9-91M.
Daily Mail (2011) Three wheels are better than four! Reliant drivers are the safest on the road. London: Dailymail.co.uk. June 13, 2011.
Simpson, D. (2014) How we made the Reliant Robin. *The Guardian*, January 7.

MARCONI: WHEN STRATEGISTS HIT THE PERFECT STORM[1]

THE DEEP HISTORICAL BACKGROUND: GEC PLC

In 1996 Lord Weinstock finally stepped down as Managing Director of GEC (General Electric Company) plc. He had led the company for many years, after playing an instrumental role in the creation of the company. From humble beginnings, he had progressively built, through acquisition, merger, and organic means, the leading UK-based company in defence, electrical, and electronic markets. Weinstock was a hero to some and a villain to many. Although he had managed to build a profitable industrial empire with £11billion of revenues, and a strong balance sheet (the famous GEC cash mountain), he was seen by many to have underinvested, and was generally not liked by the investor community.

There was no doubt that the business was strategically challenged. It was a diverse conglomerate, ranging from warships to washing machines (or battleships to bacon slicers!), and although it was profitable, it was increasingly coming under pressure from a process of globalization in its markets. Most of its businesses enjoyed a competitive position in the domestic UK market, but few of them had a leading position internationally – indeed, in many of the businesses, export focus was predominantly centred on UK Commonwealth territories. The three largest businesses in the group were the defense business (then called GEC-Marconi), its power systems business (GEC Alstom), and its telecommunications business (GPT). All of these markets were undergoing an increasing process of globalization (even in defence where domestic presence was becoming less critical in the procurement processes of the UK government), and it was clear that the long-term winners in each market were going to be those that succeeded internationally.

---

[1]This case was prepared by Sotirios Paroutis and Neil Sutcliffe for the purposes of class discussion and is not meant to illustrate effective or ineffective handling of administrative situations.

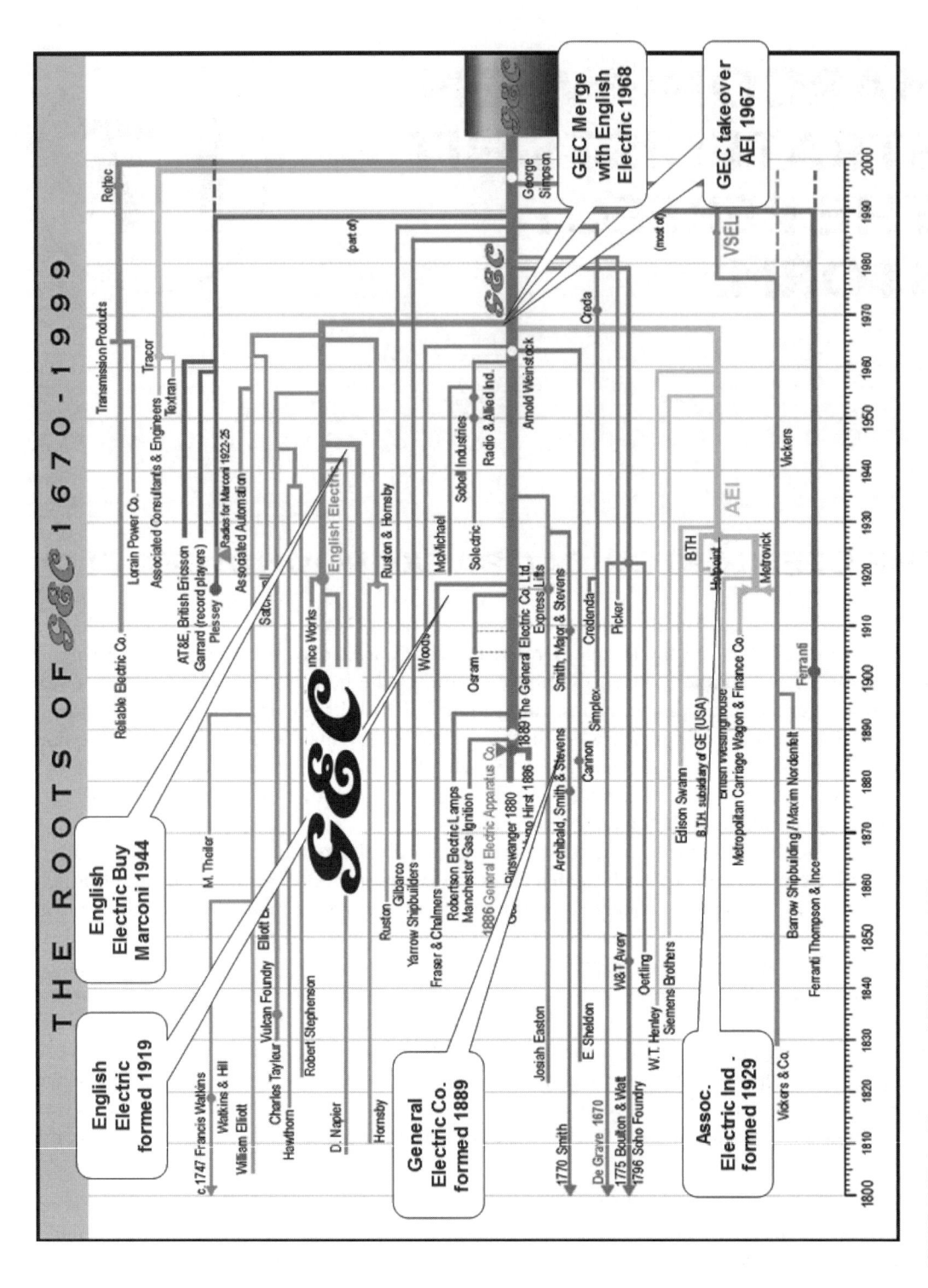

FIGURE 17.1 The roots of GEC 1670–1999

MARCONI: WHEN STRATEGISTS HIT THE PERFECT STORM

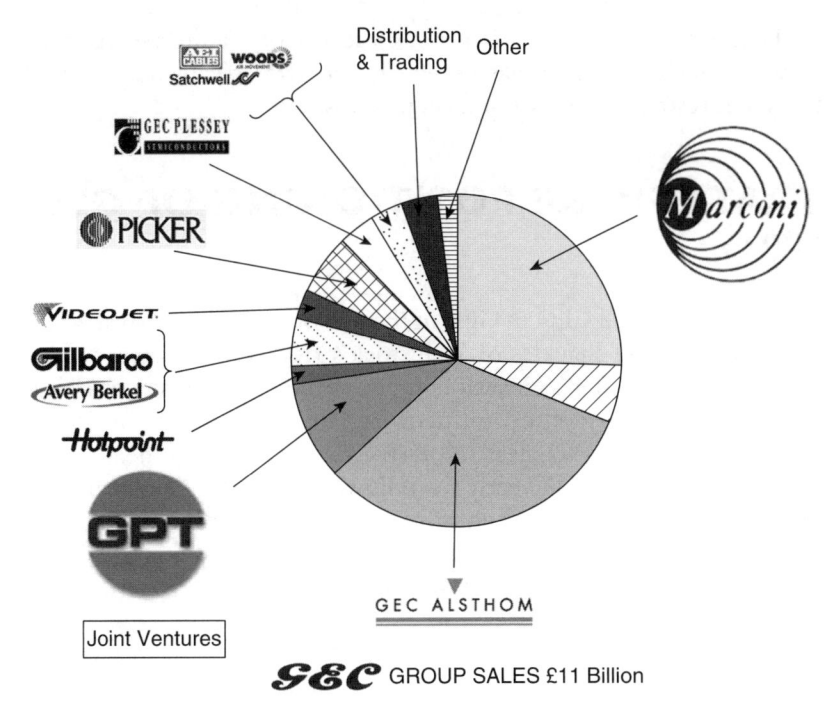

FIGURE 17.2 GEC in 1996

GEC had a history of failing to build international success on the back of its UK dominance. Indeed, it had also repeatedly managed to squander leading technology positions in a number of industries, through a failure to commit the investment in the infrastructure necessary to build export markets. It is worth noting some of the areas where GEC had failed to convert leading technology positions. It is recognized to have been the first to bring mobile telephony solutions to market, but had no significant presence at all in mobile in 1996. It had been an early player in computer technologies, with its GEC Computers business, which had now disappeared. In its semiconductor company (GEC Plessey Semiconductors) it had brought leading technologies through from the R&D lab, but was only a niche player in terms of global market share, and was confined to specializing in certain market segments.

So the challenge was clear – the group comprised of a portfolio of generally low-growth businesses, being sweated for profit and cash on the back of their domestic strength, but each increasingly failing to generate the funds to invest properly to compete internationally. Lord Weinstock had recognized this problem but his solution only made the strategic challenge even greater. His response was to seek international joint ventures in many of his bigger businesses. GEC Alstom, the power systems business was a 50/50 joint venture with Alcatel of France. GPT, the telecommunications business was a 60/40 joint venture with Siemens of Germany (who were also a competitor!), and the defense business, GEC Marconi had a number of joint ventures in it, such as that with Matra of France.

So this was the inheritance for Lord Weinstock's successor – a diverse portfolio of domestically strong, internationally weak companies, which were strategically hamstrung due to a series of joint ventures that restricted control of its biggest assets.

THE STRATEGIC RE-POSITIONING OF GEC (1996-2001)

George Simpson was appointed CEO of GEC in the Fall of 1996. His arrival was heralded as an opportunity to throw off the shackles of Weinstock's risk-averse legacy, and to strategically reposition the company, and offer its investors superior returns. Simpson was clearly up for the challenge, having built a reputation for restructuring business at Rover, British Aerospace, and Lucas Industries. His intentions to meet the restructuring challenge head on became all the clearer when he selected his new CFO early the following year. His appointment of John Mayo, a successful ex-UBS investment banker, most recently CFO of Zeneca, was clearly the result of a search that was looking for someone who could mastermind a strategic transformation. Mayo was acknowledged as the driver behind the successful separation of ICI into separate chemicals and pharmaceuticals businesses.

So the game was on – but what were Simpson and Mayo's options, and which one did they ultimately choose? Essentially he faced two choices – remain as a diverse conglomerate, or become much more focused on one, or a few, vertical markets.

In January 1999, Simpson sold off GEC's defense operations for £7.7bn and used the cash to embark on a spending spree in telecoms, mainly in the USA. In 1998 GEC purchased the 40% share of GPT owned by Siemens. At the time GPT was a UK-centric company with a major dependence on its System X switch sales to BT. Soon after, GEC merged GPT with its Italian company Marconi SpA, which already had overlapping product portfolios and a larger international business, to form Marconi Communications.

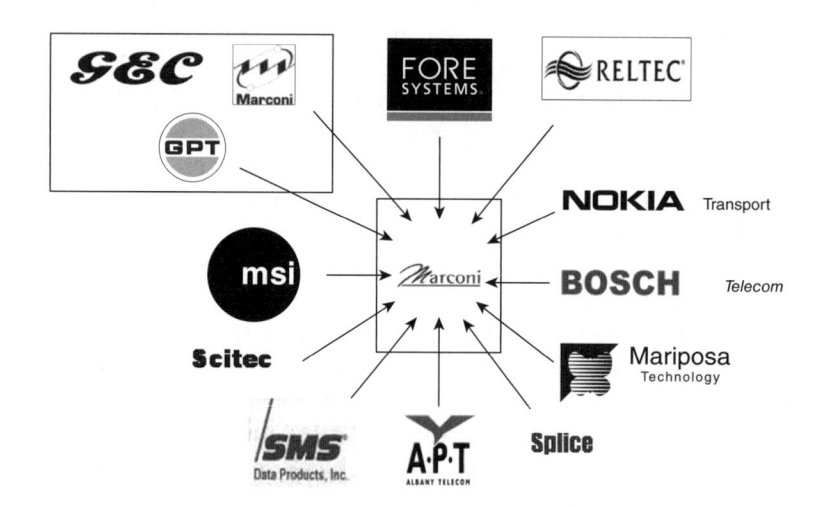

FIGURE 17.3 Marconi Acquisitions 1999–2001

MARCONI: WHEN STRATEGISTS HIT THE PERFECT STORM

Over the course of 1999/2000, the company completed the separation of the defense business and merged it with British Aerospace. With the acquisition of Reltec Corporation for $1.7bn, this ensured that Marconi gained entry into the US communications equipment market.

The GEC network equipment portfolio and reach was further strengthened with the acquisition of FORE Systems for $4.5bn in June 1999. For the first time Marconi had a world-leading position in broadband and access solutions but also gained an established footprint within the Northern America market, providing solutions for Carriers and Enterprise markets.

In November 1999 GEC was reborn as Marconi and listed on the London stock exchange, marking the completion of the company's transformation. Between the time of announcing and completing the watershed transaction, the company had built a strong global position in the fast-growing market for communications and network equipment.

The Marconi position was enhanced further by the acquisition of RDC, a wireless IP company, the transport business of Nokia, the Bosch Public Access division, and ACS, which combined has expanded Marconi's customer base, portfolio in local loop access and increased their in-territory support in Australia.

Marconi

2000
- GEC renamed Marconi and listed as Marconi plc
- Further disposals of non core businesses

1999
- Buys Fore Systems for $4.5 Billion Cash
- Buys RELTEC for $2.1 Billion Cash
- Demerges Marconi Electronic Systems (defence electronics) to British Aerospace for $10.8bn in shares returned to GEC shareholders

1998
- Forms Marconi Communications
- Buys Siemens' stake in GPT telecom for $1.05bn Cash
- $6 Bn flotation of GEC-Alsthom

1997
- Sells 8 non-core businesses for $1bn

GEC

FIGURE 17.4 GEC to Marconi

After year end, came the announcement of the acquisition of MSI, a global consultancy to the wireless communications industry and a provider of planning services and business software to deliver wireless infrastructure. In July APT was also acquired. It specialized in telecommunications services, including site acquisition and the design, construction, and maintenance of aerial masts. Further strategic acquisitions included SMS, a leading provider of outsourcing, Web hosting services, systems integration and application development, enabling Marconi to offer an integrated approach to infrastructure and application provision and management.

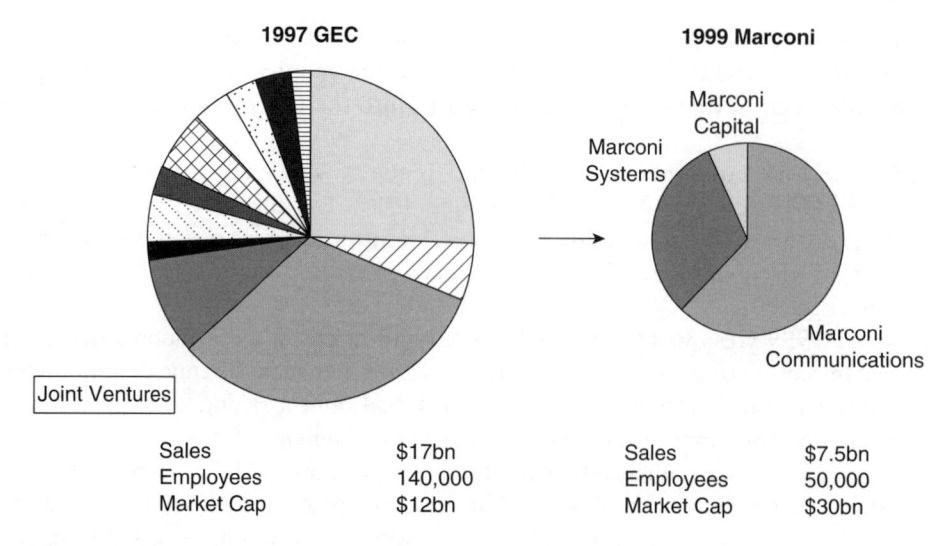

FIGURE 17.5 GEC in 1997 vs. Marconi in 1999

	1997 GEC		1999 Marconi
Sales	$17bn	Sales	$7.5bn
Employees	140,000	Employees	50,000
Market Cap	$12bn	Market Cap	$30bn

THE TELECOMMUNICATIONS BOOM AND BUST

By the turn of the millennium, the transition of GEC into a focused telecommunications business was largely complete. The company had divested its Power Systems business through an IPO, and the demerger of its defense business into British Aerospace was also complete. In addition, a number of significant acquisitions in the telecommunications sector had been undertaken, including Reltec and Fore Systems in the USA, Bosch Telecoms in Germany, and a number of smaller services companies. The company had been re-named, and re-listed as Marconi plc and was now organized in three main operating divisions. These were Marconi Communications, which contained all of the groups' telecommunications equipment businesses, Marconi Services, which comprised the groups' entire telecommunications services infrastructure, and Marconi Systems, which housed all of the non-telecommunications assets, including a number of businesses designated for sale.

The telecommunications industry was going through a period of unprecedented growth. This was driven by three major factors:

a Massive growth in volumes of data traffic, driven by the rapid uptake of internet services. Operators were responding by building huge capacity transport networks in anticipation of the expected growth.
b Rapid deregulation of national telecommunications markets, enabling domestic competition, and international expansion. New operators were springing up, both as local competitors to national incumbents, and also international carriers.
c The rapid build out of mobile networks on the back of the rapid take up of mobile services throughout the 1990s.

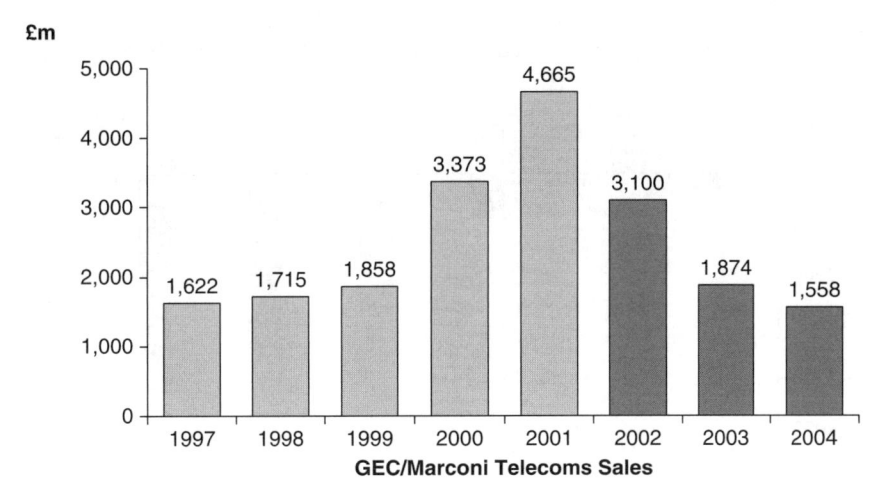

FIGURE 17.6 GEC / Marconi Telecoms Sales

Year	Sales (£m)
1997	1,622
1998	1,715
1999	1,858
2000	3,373
2001	4,665
2002	3,100
2003	1,874
2004	1,558

This created a "perfect storm" situation where the combination of these drivers led to a massive growth in build out of network infrastructure.

Marconi, like all equipment vendors, was enjoying rapid growth on the back of this surge in demand. The investment community responded well to Marconi's strategic transition. The share price had risen from £4 at the beginning of 1998 to £12 in the Fall of 2000. Indeed, despite the fact that Marconi revenues in 1999 were less than half those of GEC in 1997, the value of the company had more than doubled! Weinstock's cash mountain was no longer there – it had been invested in the acquisitions and, as such, was now working for the investors aiming at delivering superior returns. Indeed, the cash mountain had been replaced with debt – almost £3billion of it. But with the market capitalization of the group nudging £30billion, this was not, on the face of it, an unacceptable level of leverage.

In November 2000, the party ended. It became suddenly obvious that the situation was unsustainable. The CLEC's (new competitive operators in the USA) could no longer raise new capital, and so their spending was immediately suspended. They defaulted on supplier credit, and many started to fail. In response to the waning competition the ILEC's (incumbent operators) were under less pressure, and also curtailed network investment. This rapidly spread across the Atlantic, and within six months the revenues of equipment providers was in freefall.

In the first quarter of 2001, international telecoms groups such as Nortel, Alcatel, Nokia, and Ericsson warned that sales and profits would be down. However, Marconi's top management remained optimistic, delaying what seemed inevitable: a profits warning.

On May 16, Simpson told shareholders: "We anticipate the market will recover around the end of this calendar year, initially led by European established operators … we believe we can achieve growth for the full year, as a result of our relative strength supplying these operators."

Marconi hit the storm just like everybody else. Revenues in 2001/2 were 30% down on the prior year, and still falling (having risen by 30% in the prior year!). By the end of the financial

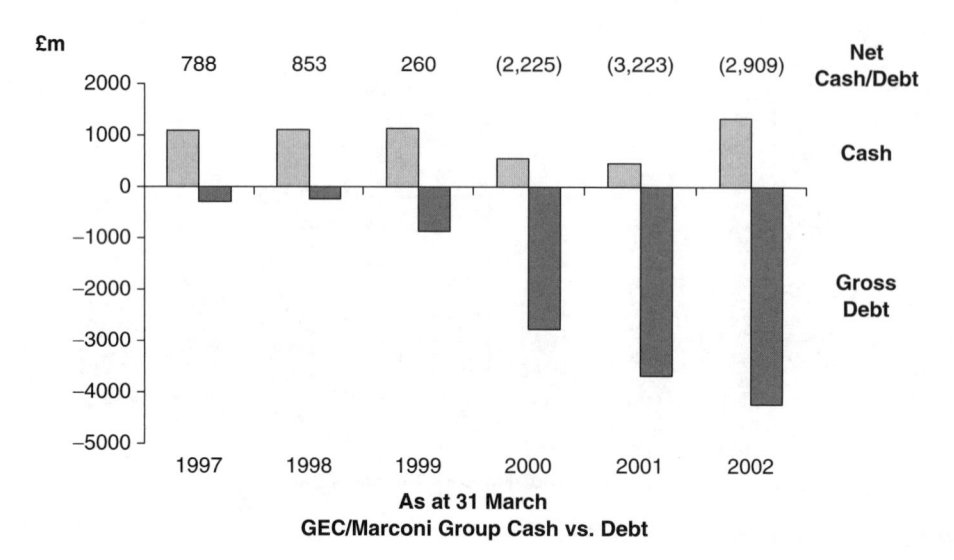

FIGURE 17.7 GEC / Marconi Group Cash vs. Debt

year 2002/3, revenues (at £1,874m) were 60% down on 2000/1 (£4,665m). There was no possibility of reacting quickly enough to protect the balance sheet from the inevitable impact of this reversal in sales. The combined impact of redundant inventories and mounting losses were adding to the debt mountain, and by 2002, the debt had ballooned to over £4.5billion.

The share price went into a downward spiral. As the business shrank in scale, and the debt ballooned, it was clear that the business was rapidly becoming over leveraged, to the extent that questions were starting to be asked as to whether the company would be able to meet its obligations to its creditors. Fortunately, the company's debts were free of covenants, and so despite the massive degradation in company performance it had not actually breached any of its obligations.

By the middle of 2001, the share price had collapsed to less than £1. However, there was little to justify even this value – with historical valuations in the industry of one times revenues, and with a debt burden of £4.5 billion, the company was to all intents and purposes worth nothing.

STRATEGISTS HITTING THE STORM

Simpson and his deputy John Mayo started facing serious questions from institutional investors, who had lost faith in Marconi's strategy. Media reports stressed that many loyal Marconi shareholders, who had been with the company since the "boring" GEC days, would inevitably be looking back to Weinstock's cash-pile and wishing it still existed. In its place were £2.5bn of debt and underperforming assets. These investors were demanding change, and in July 2001 John Mayo left the company. Lord Simpson, and the Chairman Sir Roger Hurn tried to steady the ship, and undertook a rapid strategic review, but the die was cast. On September 4, 2001, Simpson and Hurn were ousted.

Derek Bonham, the senior non-executive director took over as Chairman, and Mike Parton, the head of the Marconi Communications division was appointed CEO. They had inherited an unenviable situation. The company was losing money at a startling rate and, despite the recent sale of the Medical Systems division had less than 12 months' cash in hand. If the company ran out of cash, it would be impossible to raise any further debt, and the company's creditors would put the company into administration in order to recoup as much of the debt as possible. Whatever the recovery plan was to be, it had to be radical, and it had to be speedy.

Bonham and Parton were facing two key challenges: they had to realign the fundamentals of their business to cope with the global high-tech slowdown, and at the same time perform the delicate high-wire act of rebuilding Marconi's shattered reputation. Parton was a long-term Marconi insider, first joining GEC in 1980, and rising through the ranks to end up as head of its core networks division. In the eyes of the investors, as boss of high-tech division Marconi Communications during the 1990s, he was linked with the telecoms gamble. Marconi shares fell by another 12% on Wednesday during the week when this new team was announced and as a swathe of investment banks again cut their ratings on the company.

THE END GAME

By the end of 2004, following the huge hiatus after the bubble burst in 2001, the decline in the telecommunications equipment market had ended. Although the market had not returned to growth, it had experienced a period of stable activity and the equipment vendors were experiencing flat revenues. This enabled them to complete the operational restructuring, against a backdrop of reliable sales, and restore profitability.

Marconi had reduced its cost base by over 60%, reducing headcount from 25,000 to fewer than 10,000. The restructuring had been traumatic, but a core base of critical skills had been retained, and the core technology base in the critical product areas had been secured. The financial restructuring had left the company with a manageable level of debt, and as the business was now generating cash, the management team were starting to consider paying off the debt early. On the face of it, this financial stability would also give Marconi's customers the confidence that it was secure as a vendor for the foreseeable future.

However, normality had not been fully restored. Although the collapse in the market had ended, and virtually all vendors had successfully restructured themselves, and apparently survived, the market landscape was now very different. Three things had changed.

First, the market was less than half the size that it had been in millennium year and was at best stagnant in terms of growth. Like a lake that evaporates in a drought, there were now too many hungry fish competing for the next meal.

Second, after the insatiable desire to adopt exciting new technology in the 1990s, telecom's operators' attitudes to spending changed significantly. They were no longer under huge pressure from new operators to provide the latest whiz-bang service – on the contrary, they now turned their attention to providing traditional services at minimum cost. This meant that vendors could not compete through product functionality – it became a battle to do the simple things most cheaply.

Third, a new generation of competitors was appearing in China. In the early 1990s there were essentially no domestic telecommunications vendors in China. Towards the end of the century, a handful began to emerge, most notably Huawei, ZTE, and UTStarcom. These suppliers were using their increasing share of the domestic Chinese market to invest in generations of products that were fit for the international market. At the same time, the "dumbing down" of operators' requirements meant that the Chinese suppliers were better able to compete earlier than otherwise would have been the case. Operators were asking for simple, functional, and cheap equipment – exactly what the Chinese vendors could offer.

So the market was smaller, competition was on price rather than functionality, and a generation of new vendors was entering the game. The Marconi executive team were naturally concerned – indeed they were more anxious about the long-term future than they were during the freefall collapse of the market a few years before. It seemed inevitable that consolidation would happen. Rumors started to circulate about which global players would make a move against others. The question was – how would this play out, and how should the Marconi team play their hand to maximize the out turn for their new shareholders.

Their instinct was to move early rather than late – generally the first movers in a period of consolidation gained the most. The turning point was to come when BT announced their adjudication on the long-awaited 21st Century Network (21CN) contract. 21CN was a bold strategy by BT to massively upgrade the technology of their network to be able to provide new generation services to customers with a massively streamlined network design. It would involve the retirement of huge swathes of legacy technology in their network, to be replaced by the new generation equipment. BT was the first operator globally to embark on such a plan, and so the vendors that won, would be well positioned for other global operators who followed. Marconi was widely tipped to win business in one or more of three separate areas of the network. When the award was announced they won nothing. This was a strategically devastating blow. If Marconi could not win in their domestic market, with their biggest customer, then how could they compete elsewhere?

BT said that the decision was motivated on product and price, although few people think that this was the case. Certainly Marconi's technology was recognized by the BT team to be better in some areas, largely because of Marconi's intimate knowledge of BT's network. It is more likely that the real reason is that BT considered itself vulnerable to a relatively small vendor like Marconi, particularly considering the deep financial distress of a few years previously. Quite simply, BT wanted vendors who were likely to be around for the long term, and Marconi didn't look like it would.

The Marconi team rapidly initiated a further strategic review – time was now of the essence if the value of the company was to be maximized. BT's decision was only going to make life harder for the company everywhere else. An analysis of the competitive landscape was carried out, and strategic options considered.

QUESTIONS

What options does the Marconi management team have?
Compile a set of consolidation scenarios for the telecommunication market in 2005.
Critically analyze Marconi's pedigree as an independent vendor, and recommend potential transactions that the Marconi team should aim for in order to maximize value for shareholders.

SOURCES

BBC (2001) Analysis: Where did Marconi go wrong? Jeff Randall's view. July 5. Available at: http://news.bbc.co.uk/1/hi/business/1423642.stm (date accessed: April 10, 2011).

BBC (2001) Tough task ahead for Marconi duo. Available at: http://news.bbc.co.uk/1/hi/business/1526604.stm (date accessed: April 10, 2011).

Brummer, A. and Cowe, R. (1998) *Weinstock: The Life and Times of Britain's Premier Industrialist*. Harper Collins.

GEC 1990–2000. Annual Reports.

Marconi 2001–2005. Annual Reports.

LAFARGE VS. BLUE CIRCLE: PRACTICES IN A HOSTILE TAKEOVER[1]

18

INTRODUCTION

On January 31, 2000, the €12.1 billion French giant buildings materials group, Lafarge, launched an all-cash hostile bid for €4.7 billion UK company Blue Circle PLC ('Blue Circle'), the sixth largest cement producer in the world. At 430 pence per share, the offer valued the target at €5.6bn and represented a premium of just 1.4% over Blue Circle's closing middle market price. At the time the dot.com bubble was in full swing, and fund managers were desperate to release money tied up in unfashionable "old economy" stocks as these appeared overvalued. Lafarge was the only real bidder for Blue Circle and was confident after an earlier acquisition. The slim premium offered seemed a shrewd move. If the takeover bid succeeded, Lafarge would become the largest cement company in the world.

Newly appointed CEO of Blue Circle, Rick Haythornthwaite was spurred into action. Contacting his advisors, they immediately informed him that a formal offer document would arrive within 28 days and a rapid response was necessary in order to reduce investor uncertainty in the markets. His advisers suggested that the offer be denounced as derisory and for the team to work on a defense plan.

BACKDROP

The unsolicited bid for Blue Circle took place against a backdrop of massive global M&A activity. The stock market it seemed liked big M&A, particularly horizontal, within industry deals. In terms of the cement industry large-scale consolidation had been taking place over the last four years. By

---

[1] This case is prepared for the purposes of class discussion and is not meant to illustrate the effective or ineffective handling of administrative situations.

the end of 1999, the top six multi-national producers had 30% of global capacity compared with 11% in 1988. Further M&A opportunities existed in the industry but the largest companies were family controlled, which restricted their ability to expand but also provided a defense against acquisition. For large M&A anti-trust issues could also be problematic amongst UK companies. Nevertheless consolidation M&A remained on the agenda for larger cement companies as investors remained unhappy with the sector, seeing underperformance in relation to high-tech stocks. Also the nature of the cement business was that it benefitted from economies of scale and M&A would reduce retaliatory pricing between competitors in different regions.

Tactics

The bid for Blue Circle was not a spur of the moment decision. Bertrand Collomb, Chairman and CEO of Lafarge, had been planning the takeover for two years. He was confident of success after recently purchasing another smaller cement company in the UK and, although the premium being offered to investors for their shares was slim at just 1.4%, he was aware that all cash hostile offers, such as the one he was now offering (Haythornthwaite having rejected any possibility of a friendly takeover in a recent telephone conversation), had succeeded every time in the UK for the last 15 years. He knew his timing was good as investors were seeking to sell off "old economy stocks" in order to invest in dot.com companies and Blue Circle had just announced a profits warning which had shaken investor confidence. He was also aware that there were really no other bidders for Blue Circle and so a higher premium was not warranted. Furthermore his analysis of Blue Circle revealed mistakes in its strategy including over-diversification in the 1980s and early 1990s with acquisitions such as Birmid Qualcast and Myson. In his view this diversification was a strategic error as subsequent disposal of these acquisitions resulted in losses. Blue Circle had then not expanded internationally through cement acquisitions to the same extent as its competitors causing them to fall behind its international competitors. In Collomb's eyes this meant that Blue Circle was now heavily dependent on "too few countries" and its profitability was inherently volatile. He was also aware that Rick Haythornthwaite was the architect of Blue Circle's strategy of investing in Malaysia and so this hostile bid was not just an attack on Blue Circle's strategy but also upon his tenure as CEO.

Rick Haythornthwaite knew he needed to embark on a sustained campaign to counter Lafarge's attacks. Working closely with his financial advisors, Lazards, they would need to persuade markets and investors through formal communications that Blue Circle's previous strategy was the best one for the group. They would also need to promise a far more rosy future as an independent company than as a Lafarge subsidiary. He knew Blue Circle investors would be considering selling their shares to Lafarge, although he felt that they would probably want more than just a 1.4% premium. He would have to fight his case through 60 grueling days[2] of fighting for positive media coverage and facing key stakeholders, attempting to win their support for his management team and not succumb to the allure of cash.

Once Lafarge announced the formal bid, Blue Circle's defense team organized themselves at headquarters with power breakfasts for all key advisors to coordinate and control actions. The

---

[2]This is the maximum amount of time allowed by the Competition Commission in the UK for a takeover bid to take place (from Announcement to Completion).

first thing to do was to reject the bid as significantly undervaluing Blue Circle. City analysts' valuations at the time were generally around 500 pence per share. Lazard's valuation, based on Blue Circle's internal business plan, was in line with this and seemed reasonable provided profit forecasts were achievable. Haythornthwaite recognized however that the firm tended to achieve actual results lower than plan, and instructed them to reduce their profit forecasts. A revised discounted cash flow valued the business at a relatively conservative 486 pence. This figure supported Blue Circle's claim that Lafarge's bid of 430 pence significantly undervalued the group. As Rick Haythornthwaite was reported as saying "We are not rejecting the bid out of stubbornness. We genuinely believe the offer undervalues the company. If Lafarge want our assets, they have to be prepared to pay a good price for them" (*Telegraph*, February 22, 2000). The Lafarge bid is a "quest for our Asian assets," which "validates the investment strategy" of the group.

Blue Circle's first formal document released to the financial markets on February 21, 2000 was the group's 1999 results. These results were launched earlier than had been intended as it was thought that it was important to provide a solid base from which to launch the defense of their strategy. It stated that: "Lafarge's chairman has congratulated our management for 'doing all the right things'. He is right to;

- We have a business that is fundamentally changed, refocused on our strengths in cement, aggregates and concrete.
- We have invested carefully, building leading positions in our chosen markets.
- We have exciting growth prospects.
- We will deliver substantial performance improvement and cost savings in the near term."

The final dividend for the year was also announced in the document. It was raised to 10.95 pence per share, which was now in line with the industry. This was an increase compared with internal plans. Nonetheless the financial media clearly expected more, asking Blue Circle to explain why it was a better owner of its assets than Lafarge and how it might release cash from under-performing assets.

In response Blue Circle issued a string of communications that included the open market value and development value of the group's land holdings. On March 28, 2000 it issued forecasts for profits for Asia (2000–2) to convince shareholders that those investments would pay off in the short term. In defending management's strategy the document stated that: "Blue Circle has followed a deliberate strategy of increasing investment in Asia in anticipation of what is now a strong and sustainable recovery." Subsequently an operational improvements programme (OIP) was announced on April 6. This detailed projected benefits arising from cost savings estimated to be of the order of £116m (£193m) per annum by 2002. Finally Blue Circle announced it would return £800 million (£1333m) to shareholders in advance. This can be interpreted as a down payment to shareholders, demonstrating management confidence in delivering on their promises. Blue Circle's gearing increased significantly (17.2% (1999) to 107.7% (2000)) as a consequence, and free cash flow available for future projects was reduced dramatically. The document detailing the OIP was entitled "'Blue Circle is a business with renewed momentum". In it the main defense themes of property, performance improvement, Asia, and strong market positions were emphasized.

While making announcements to the financial markets, Blue Circle and its team of advisors were also considering a range of other strategic options. In Haythornthwaite's words, "We reviewed what made sense to shareholders. Many options were dismissed because they did not give cash to shareholders." One option was an MBO that would have been the eighth largest ever. However, financing couldn't be raised in time and it was divisive in the group. An alternative was to proceed with an acquisition of Southdown, a US cement manufacturer. Both parties were close to a deal before Lafarge's bid, and if a deal was agreed, then Blue Circle would have been too expensive for Lafarge. However, Southdown would not consider this option until Lafarge had gone away. Another possibility was a white squire defense where a third party investor is approached to acquire a large block of shares in the target company. Although there were discussions with Votorantim for this type of defense, it was not pursued. Blue Circle also had discussions with a number of other cement and building materials companies for potential merger. This White Knight defense would have been attractive to Blue Circle as the sought-after suitor would be more acceptable than Lafarge. The problem however was that none of the white knights would provide the cash that shareholders wanted and all were reluctant to be involved. It is also possible that Betrand Collomb had already spoken with potential white knights warning them not to become involved.

Coup de grace?

Forty-six days after the announced bid, Lafarge launched a dawn raid. This is when the acquirer and its brokers buy up as many shares as they can in early trading in the market, before other investors can react. Lafarge gained 19.9% of Blue Circle directly from the market and a further 9.6% through its bankers. With nearly 30% of Blue Circle, its senior executives thought the end was in sight. At this point Lafarge increased its offer to £4.50 (7.53) per share. Surely victory was assured?

Blue Circle had very few legal or regulatory defenses left. Clearance from competition authorities were a formality, and although Blue Circle did appeal to the Canadian regulatory authorities, where they argued that Lafarge had not made divestitures as required, no action was taken against them.

Apart from these specific strategic options, Haythornthwaite was also fully engaged in a media campaign during the takeover process. He had to get Blue Circle's message out to the investment community. This was a physically very demanding time for him as he was appearing in person on radio and television, commenting upon the bid in newspapers whilst also running Blue Circle. However, for most of the process his shareholders did not want to talk to him – underlining their dissatisfaction with the company. It was only in the last 10 days of the offer period that the institutional shareholders relented and meetings could be held. Rick Haythornthwaite and his finance director used the meetings in order to persuade investors to back management and their promises to refocus Blue Circle. The lobbying paid off. As the final day, day 60, of the bid approached, the *Wall Street Journal* reported, "The deciding factor seems to have been a blitz of shareholders visits by Blue Circle CEO Rick Haythornthwaite during the two weeks before the offer deadline" (*Wall Street Journal*, May 4, 2000). Total acceptances for the bid on May 3 totalled 44.5% of Blue Circle shares – Rick Haythornthaite and his team had won. It was the first all-cash bid for a FTSE 100 company to fail for 15 years.

POST DEAL ANALYSIS

Following the failure of the hostile bid, the media interpreted Blue Circle's success as due in part to the "spirited defense put up by Haythornthwaite himself" (BBC online, April 19, 2000) and the meanness of the Lafarge offer. It showed "institutional shareholders had confidence that Haythornthwaite could deliver on his promises of returning funds to investors and refocusing the company" (BBC online, May 4, 2000). The group's sizeable cost-savings program was seen as an important component of the takeover defense and there was general consensus that, although offers for battered Old Economy stocks were welcome, this was "not at any price" (*FT*, May 4, 2000).

Meanwhile in France Betrand Collomb was severely shaken. He had controlled nearly 30% of Blue Circle and his heavy personal involvement in the deal meant that the failure to win the bid was seen by many as a personal failure. This was particularly the case as it was rumored Lafarge's advisers recommended a revised offer in the range 460–70 pence in April 2000.

For Blue Circle, although the defense had been a success it was something of a pyrrhic victory with Lafarge holding so many shares. With 30% of Blue Circle shares in their control, the "defender is left looking over its shoulder" (*FT*, December 19, 2000). As a substantial minority shareholder Blue Circle was also obligated to share internal information with them. How could Blue Circle continue to remain independent with a major competitor inside the company? Some of the earlier options of making further acquisitions might have made a difference, but still potential partners were unwilling to be involved whilst Lafarge was present. The group also had to deliver on defense promises that analysts suspected might have been too ambitious. Haythornthwaite also realized that forecast operating profits were significantly below analysts' estimates and earnings quality appeared to be deteriorating.

As Collomb was now a major shareholder Haythornthwaite had to brief him on the results. Between them they agreed that, although Haythornthwaite was not willing to sell, a much-improved price might make all the difference. There was also the possibility that Lafarge might sell for a dignified exit. The discussions that followed between the two executives were conducted in great secrecy. Had there been any leaks, no deal would have happened.

To begin with Lafarge tabled £4.70 with no dividend. This was not acceptable to Haythornthwaite who needed a figure of at least £5.00 per share to recommend it to shareholders. Working right up to Christmas and beyond the advisers finally agreed £4.95 per share plus a final dividend, totalling £5.09p. One of the notable points in the negotiations was the movements of the currency markets, particularly in the exchange rate between Euros and Sterling, which meant that although the Blue Circle shareholders received an increased offer of 10%, Lafarge shareholders were only increasing their costs by 3%. Following a revised discounted cash flow analysis by advisors Lazards that gave a group value of £4.95, the Blue Circle Board had no hesitation in recommending the new offer to shareholders.

City analysts welcomed the new offer as being "a sensibly priced deal" and the vast majority of Blue Circle's shareholders, large institutions, readily agreed to the deal. However, many individual shareholders, who were mainly ex-employees with an emotional attachment, voted against the takeover, as they saw Blue Circle as a 'British Institution'. Nevertheless the takeover succeeded and Lafarge's shares jumped 20% on announcement, remaining relatively stable at this higher level.

QUESTIONS

1. Using the strategy-as-practice framework (presented in Chapter 3) explain why Blue Circle found itself being subjected to a hostile takeover bid.
2. In defending itself from Lafarge, many practice elements are presented in the case study. Show how Blue Circle was able to defeat Lafarge through effective alignment of these elements during the hostile bid.
3. Although Blue Circle was successful in its defense against Lafarge, it was subsequently taken over. Using the strategy-as-practice framework to analyze the post-bid period, suggest reasons why this came about.

ROOM FOR IMPROVEMENT? RELOCATING A BUSINESS SCHOOL[1]

INTRODUCTION

One of the older business schools in the UK, part of Oxford Brookes University, is located in a large leafy campus outside the city of Oxford, renowned for its universities and colleges. Oxford Brookes University Business School (OBBS) offers a full range of degree courses including taught undergraduate and postgraduate courses as well as research degrees. OBBS also engages with a wide range of for-profit and not-for-profit enterprises, offering taught courses, consultancy, and research. Courses are taught in a wide variety of buildings ranging from bespoke modern centers to inter-war and post-war structures of varying quality and size. They make up a substantial part of the campus, which is just one of several distributed across the city.

OBBS and its university have experienced sustained success over a long period of time but in the last few years there has been a significant increase in the levels of competition in the sector. Mindful of this the university announced in January 2015 that OBBS would be relocated as part of its 10-year estates development plan. OBBS's new location would be a completely refurbished building on the main campus of the university some five miles away in the city. The move is scheduled to take place in Summer 2016.

Following the announcement a series of staff briefings have been taking place at OBBS and at these meetings it is clear that opinions are divided about the move. Over and above the disruption of the impending move, of particular concern to the staff are the practicalities of the

---

[1]This case study was prepared by Duncan Angwin and Matt Thomas. It is intended as a basis for class discussion. We would like to thank those people at the organization who generously gave their time for the interviews upon which the case is based. The case is not intended to be an illustration of good or bad practice.

new location. Some seem to be happy that the city location will bring many benefits to staff, students, and the wider community, while others believe opportunities for OBBS at the current campus will be lost and the new location may seriously affect the style and character of the school. On one thing all are agreed: this strategic move will not be reversible and the consequences will be enduring.

BACKGROUND

Oxford Brookes University (OBU) is of medium size with around 16,000 students distributed across several campuses. The main campus and one other are located in the city with OBBS and two other campuses several miles away.

OXFORD BROOKES UNIVERSITY BUSINESS SCHOOL (OBBS)

OBBS has approximately 280 staff including administrative and academic positions. It is mostly contained on the rural out-of-city campus although approximately a quarter of the school is located at Headington in the city of Oxford. Historically OBBS has had a good reputation for its courses and is well regarded academically. It has often been viewed as highly innovative in its engagement with business and not-for-profit organizations and in the past this has resulted in significant grants being won for investment into infrastructure.

Transport

OBBS's campus is located among 80 acres of parkland. It is approximately five miles from the center of the city and its railway station. Some members of staff and students cycle from the city and this takes around 45 minutes. The university offers an attractive cycle scheme for the purchase of equipment. There are basic shower and cycle facilities on campus and a bike doctor. Although cycling is quite attractive during part of the year, traveling by car or bus is generally the preferred manner of transport, particularly for longer distances and when the weather is inclement. There is a bus service (see Image 19.1) that connects the campus to Oxford City railway station (approximately 40 minutes) and the main city campus (approximately 20–25 minutes depending on traffic). Feedback from students on their experience of studying at the campus has often cited the bus journey as diminishing the student experience. One member of staff likened it to being "Herded like cattle." The university has an eco-friendly policy and so encourages staff to use the bus or to cycle. Car parking is quite expensive although generally fairly available. Staff living close to a bus route are no longer permitted to have a parking permit. However, for those who live some distance away, the campus is in easy reach of a motorway giving rapid access to the site by car.

IMAGE 19.1 The "Brookes Bus"

Used with permission

The fabric

The buildings at the campus range in quality from a few modern lecture rooms, a café and a recently refurbished restaurant, to many poor-quality structures. The most recent investment in new buildings was in 2007 (see Images 19.2 and 19.3) when the university opened a state-of-the-art facility dedicated to engineering, and an Undergraduate Centre – a social space, providing an alternative to lecture halls, libraries, and study bedrooms.

Despite the out-of-town, parkland location, the site is dominated by a large 12 storey concrete tower block surrounded by lower buildings of the same design. The fabric of these elderly buildings, constructed from brick and prefabricated concrete slabs have deteriorated over time. The lack of recent investment in the buildings and low levels of maintenance is increasingly evident to staff and students. The staff describe the environment as "lacking visual appeal" (see Images 19.4 and 19.5) and even being "grotty." Students also downgraded their assessment of their experience of studying on the campus because of the condition of the infrastructure. This is a source of frustration to staff as it has damaged OBBS's student satisfaction rankings and yet is outside their direct control.

User experience

Staff are based in a number of buildings across the campus. The buildings range widely in style and type and, due to organic growth over a long period of time are linked in complex and

ROOM FOR IMPROVEMENT? RELOCATING A BUSINESS SCHOOL

IMAGES 19.2 AND 19.3 Buildings added to the out-of-city campus in 2007

Used with permission

IMAGES 19.4 AND 19.5 Out-of-city campus and an office interior

Used with permission

inefficient ways. Staff are situated in cellular offices (see Image 19.5) with one or two members allocated to each. These offices are based off dark and narrow corridors and generally poorly maintained. The offices are large enough to meet with students and many have whiteboards for instructional use. There is space for several filing cabinets and in one-person offices, a table. All offices have significant amounts of shelving for books and journals. There is seating in the corridors for students waiting for appointments. On some corridors are small kitchen areas where staff often speak with each other. The large size of departments means that colleagues are often spread across several floors or even across several buildings. Colleagues also meet at the Simon Williams Café – a light, open, airy space mid-way between the car park and the main campus buildings.

Students generally do not stay around after their lectures, due to the difficulties in travelling to and from the campus. Also, the buildings are not so comfortable and so they prefer to return to their accommodation on a different campus or meet in Oxford city. A new major building at the main city campus has also acted as a magnet to students as it offers a far more comfortable environment for studying and socializing. This exodus of students led a number of business school staff to describe Wheatley as a "dead" campus.

Despite the shortcomings of the out-of-city campus there is affection for the site among many of the staff. They suggest that, with investment, there is almost unlimited scope for expansion and the site is attractive to businesses due to its easy road access.

Nonetheless, the 10-year university estates plan, published in early 2015, made clear the future of the out-of-city campus by stating; "It is intended that all teaching, research and supporting activity will be moved from the out-of-city campus over the next ten years." (https://www.brookes.ac.uk/about-brookes/news/ten-year-investment-plan-for-oxford-brookes--estate/)

CITY CAMPUS

The year 2015 marked the 150th anniversary of Oxford Brookes University and was marked at the city campus by the opening of a new, prestigious, state-of-the-art building. At a cost of £160m, the new building seemed to fulfil the aspirations of the university. As the long-term estates planning programme titled "Space to Think" stated: "We're creating an estate to inspire students, strengthen our place as a leading university and further enhance the status of a degree from our University." The new building is a flagship development that demonstrates the seriousness of ambition. It won a RIBA (Royal Institute of British Architects) award for "building of the year" and in their citation stated, "the space made us wish we could go back to university again."

This development forms a new and impressive gateway to the university; staff, students, and visitors arriving onto the central campus do so via the "Piazza" (see Image 19.6), off Headington Road, a main thoroughfare into the city of Oxford. Newly planted mature trees provide a leafy "guard of honor" around the boundaries of the Piazza and one side is flanked by a Colonnade (see Image 19.7).

The Colonnade provides a new retail area for the campus and together with the Piazza forms a new cosmopolitan public space for Headington, with shops and amenities for the local community as well as the university.

The main building is designed as, and has quickly become, a new hub for students at the university. A dynamic social zone with multi-functional spaces where students are able to choose the area that best suits their needs. There are relaxing sofas to enjoy a coffee, areas for collaborative working and more traditional-style study spaces.

The library in the main building is an inspiring place for students to study, with lots of light, airy spaces and reading rooms with views across a central courtyard. The building stays open 24 hours a day during term time and with café's, restaurants, and bars also serves as an afterhours meeting place for many students and staff.

ROOM FOR IMPROVEMENT? RELOCATING A BUSINESS SCHOOL

IMAGE 19.6 The Piazza (www.architecture.com/StirlingPrize/Awards2014/South/JohnHenryBrookes Building.aspx)

Copyright © Photographer Nick Kane (www.nickkane.co.uk). Used with permission

IMAGE 19.7 The Colonnade (www.brookes.ac.uk/space-to-think/campuses/headington-campus/john-henry-brookes-building/jhbb-in-focus/colonnade/)

Copyright © Oxford Brookes University and Richard Sills. Used with permission

IMAGE 19.8 The Forum (www.brookes.ac.uk/space-to-think/campuses/headington-campus/john-henry-brookes-building/jhbb-in-focus/forum/)

Copyright © Oxford Brookes University and Paul Tait. Used with permission

IMAGE 19.9 The 320-seat lecture theatre (www.brookes.ac.uk/space-to-think/campuses/headington-campus/john-henry-brookes-building/jhbb-in-focus/teaching/)

Copyright © Oxford Brookes University and Paul Tait. Used with permisssion

The building contains a wide variety of places to study including silent areas for reflection and study, quiet spaces where you can work alone or maybe with a friend, busier zones for when you need more stimulation, bookable group presentation rehearsal rooms, informal group working spaces, and a graphics studio with computers and facilities dedicated to design. Furniture was designed and commissioned specially for working together around computer screens, informal seating with views across the Forum (see Image 19.8), and vending machines. These areas are popular with students and staff who are currently on-site.

Much of the teaching on the city campus takes place in the main building, in high-quality spaces dedicated to providing high-quality teaching. Facilities comprise: a 320-seat lecture theatre (see Image 19.9) with the facility to live-stream lectures and cinema-quality projection, three floors with a total of 24 teaching rooms, including three seminar rooms (seating up to 100), and three computer teaching rooms, alongside smaller, flexible teaching rooms.

The location of the city campus is just one mile from the "dreaming spires" of central Oxford and just under two miles from the central railway station, a 10-minute cycle ride. The city of Oxford offers students a vibrant lifestyle with countless coffee shops, bars, restaurants, night clubs, theatres, museums, and parks within modest walking distance.

COMPETING IN HIGHER EDUCATION

The competitive environment in higher education has been increasing in intensity for many years with increased pressure to win students and manage costs. Government-controlled caps on the number of students that can attend each university were removed at the end of the 2014/15 academic year and it is generally accepted that this will increase competition in the university sector for students.

To compete in this environment, OBBS is pursuing a strategy to develop a strong reputation for teaching and a distinctive research agenda. It is accepted that these objectives will sometimes conflict and tension between teaching and research is almost inevitable. For example, research involves sustained periods away from the university to collect field data or to attend international conferences. With teaching commitments this is often hard to achieve during term time.

In order to improve the university's competitiveness in teaching and research excellence, estates development had been put center stage for several years:

> Over the last few years, the Higher Education sector has become significantly more competitive and, in order to continue to attract and retain high calibre staff and students, Oxford Brookes University needs to ensure that its excellent reputation for teaching and research is matched by a high quality estate. The University knows that the physical environment is an important factor for students when choosing where to study, with 77% saying that facilities play a significant role in their university choice. Staff and students at Brookes also know, from recent experience, the transformative impact of new facilities and buildings, with the John Henry Brookes building having significantly enhanced the learning environment as well as the look and feel of Headington campus. (https://www.brookes.ac.uk/space-to-think/estate-investment-plan/frequently-asked-questions/)

OBBS has invested in research capabilities in recent years by creating a research office that provides dedicated support to researchers, and encourages cooperation and collaboration in research between members of OBBS by forming research clusters around related academic topics. The aim is to build some differentiation in these areas to enhance the international reputation of OBBS. Academic staff are drawn from a wide range of disciplinary areas and their employment contracts with the university vary according to the proportion of time given for active research versus teaching.

OBBS has enjoyed some recent success with student satisfaction ratings increasing, an improvement in position on academic league tables and a good result in the most recent assessment under the Research Excellence Framework (REF). Despite this there were some concerns at a falling quality of applications to OBBS and some believe that the fabric of the buildings might be a partial explanation.

FUTURE LOCATION FOR OBBS

The successful opening of the prestigious main building on the city campus has freed up space in a number of adjacent older buildings. OBBS will move into the Clerici building and former library once modernization of these buildings has taken place.

The refurbished Clerici building (see Images 19.10 and 19.11) will form a second "gateway" onto the Oxford Brookes University city campus and the ground floor will provide clear pathways to the main building and other facilities on the site. The refurbishment will also provide a major new 250-seat lecture theatre and several new teaching rooms. These facilities will be based on the ground floor of the Clerici building and pooled for use with the university as a whole.

OBBS will be based on the second and third floors of the Clerici building, which will include a mix of office space for staff, meeting rooms, social areas, and an area for the use of local businesses (see Image 19.12).

The footprint of the building has fixed the area allocated to OBBS. However, the precise layout of the space has not been fixed and could be influenced by the members of OBBS within the overall space constraints.

IMAGE 19.10 Aerial view of Clerici building

Copyright © BGS Architects. Used with permission

IMAGE 19.11 Main hall and Clerici external

Copyright © Blink Image and BGS Architects. Used with permission

IMAGE 19.12 Possible meeting room appearance
Used with permission of NxtWall Architects (www.nxtwall.com).

All the draft plans prepared by the architects show the office space to be "open plan," although the preferred phrase is "clustered seating." In early discussions on the move a staff member asked if the offices were definitely going to be open plan, to which the clear response was: "The space will be modern and contemporary designs not like a call centre or 'cubicle farm.' However, we do plan for staff to be in shared offices with appropriate support. How the accommodation will be configured will be something on which we plan to consult fully."

A QUESTION OF SPACE?

Long in the planning and sudden in the announcement and implementation, the relocation of the Business School from the out-of-city campus to the city campus has come as a shock to many OBBS staff. They have six months to come to terms with the move and contribute to the design of the new building within the overall constraints of the space available and the policies of the university estates department. With the clock ticking it is essential that as many stakeholders as possible are consulted in the design of the new space.

What is clear from the outset is that the layout into which OBBS will move will be very different to that used on the current site. Almost all aspects of the day-to-day work carried out by OBBS, and the working practices employed, will be affected by this change. Determined to ensure that these changes would be beneficial to the performance of OBBS, the Dean has set up a widespread communication and consultation program to involve as many staff and other stakeholders as possible. From the middle of February to the middle of April 2015, four faculty forum meetings have been held where OBBS senior management and a representative from the architects described the plans. Questions raised in these fora have been posted on a website dedicated to communicating progress on the move and, where possible, answers given to the questions raised. In addition, five consultation groups have been created with the aim that they should consult with relevant constituencies on matters relating to the layout of the new OBBS building on the city site. The five groups are: external engagement with the business community; full-time student experience; part-time and distance learning student experience; research; and staff experience. In addition, a sixth group has been created to visit other business schools with varied layouts, to learn from their experience.

The consultation groups, formed in April, are expected to meet six times and incorporate their recommendations into the architectural plans by late June.

Midway through this process a number of significant issues are becoming clear from differing stakeholder perspectives. The following commentary highlights some of the key debates in progress at this stage.

ROOM FOR IMPROVEMENT?

External engagement

From the consultations a number of issues emerged as important to staff. These are: 1) OBBS identity; 2) Journey to work experience; 3) Social spaces; 4) Collaborative working.

1) OBBS Identity

This is of concern particularly in dealing with external parties such as the business community.

> I'd like to add a few comments about space and identity. I don't doubt the benefits for wider collaboration across the university of being located at Headington. But all the design and space usage ideas seem to attach very little significance to the need for a clear Business School identity in the new location. If we are to collaborate meaningfully in increased partnerships both within and outside the university, we need to do that from a firm understanding of who and what we are. And our space is part of that understanding and identity.
>
> Senior Lecturer

This concern about the identity of OBBS in its new location was driven by the university's strict space-planning guidelines, which stated:

> Space is owned by Oxford Brookes University and is allocated to faculties & directorates based on their specialist need. Generic space such as standard teaching, social space, catering & balance (circulation, toilet & service facilities, etc) will be held centrally. It is accepted that all space will be flexible & multi-use allowing cross-team and faculty sharing of facilities to achieve high utilisation rates, where appropriate.

The Clerici building, in which the new OBBS will be situated, will form the second most important "gateway" into the university. The entrance will be branded Oxford Brookes University with no reference to the OBBS on the outside of the building and the ground floor will consist of pooled teaching facilities and pathways to other parts of the campus. The first space dedicated to OBBS will be on the first floor of the Clerici building.

However, unlike the existing entrance on the out-of-city site, the entrance to the business school will be impressive and modern in appearance (see Image 19.11). Visitors to the business school will first see a large double-height glazed wall, highlighted in a way that associates itself with the primary gateway to the university in the main building. The visitor will enter through revolving glass doors into a large bright atrium. This atrium will signal clear pathways to other parts of the university. Where and how visitors may be greeted to the OBBS is yet to be decided.

The Dean of the OBBS believes that the strong positive identity being developed by the university on the main campus will have a trickle-down effect on the Business School, improving the perception of teaching and research and ultimately the reputation of staff themselves.

2) Journey to work experience

Although the city campus is just five miles from the out-of-city campus, the logistics for many staff in travelling to the new campus are significant. The out-of-city campus is located less than a mile from junction 8 on the M40, there is also ample parking on this site for staff and many staff joined the organization with this commute in mind:

> From a staff perspective I think that many of us joined Brookes from other organizations having factored location into our decision-making. Parking (or lack of) always seems to be a "no discussion" topic but the realities for many of us is a big issue that will add significant time onto our daily commute.

Head of MBA programs

The new location for OBBS on the city campus has negligible parking and all staff will be expected to find other ways to arrive for work. Alternatives include arriving by train from which the two-mile journey to the city campus will take 15 minutes either by Brookes Bus or by cycling. Various bus routes from around Oxford also come within a short walk of the campus, however, this does not work for everyone:

> Can we start tip sharing for how to get to Headington from a variety of locations in the easiest way (having researched using ALL Park & Rides, public transport, even signing up to a gym and trying to negotiate free parking for the whole day) this may help everyone. Having reviewed these so far I know for example that I will be adding cost and at least an hour (or more) to my daily commute, but maybe I am missing a key bus route etc.

> Head of MBA programmes

Many staff live far from Oxford and travel to the out-of-city campus by car. The possibility of this campus becoming a park and ride had been raised, with the Brookes Buses continuing to run regularly between the two campuses. However, as these comments from a senior lecturer describe, this arrangement is still likely to add two hours to the daily commute to work for these staff:

> I currently travel 54 miles to get to Wheatley which takes me 1 hour because it is virtually all motorway driving. When teaching I like to arrive just after 8am so currently leave home at 7am. After relocating, to get to Headington by 8am, realistically I will need to arrive at Wheatley by 7am because the bus journey itself can be more than 30 minutes, especially in rush hour and I will have to allow 15 minutes to park my car and wait for the next bus. This means I will be leaving home at 6am.

> Senior Lecturer

3) Social spaces

The university's 10-year estate investment plan confidently asserts "the move will improve staff and student experience." Many staff agree, with one senior lecturer suggesting that the social spaces on the current campus are limited. She explains:

> Kitchens are great places for informal meetings that can lead to an unexpected exchange of ideas that prove valuable, however, the kitchens in the buildings where our offices are currently located are in poor positions and too small. I often choose to use a kitchen on a different floor to my office because it is larger and I am more likely to bump in to a colleague or two. Of course many of my colleagues are based in separate buildings. In addition, there is no after hours socialising amongst staff, people tend to get away after lecturing or at the end of office hours.

The opportunities to meet colleagues from other Faculties are also limited on the out-of-city campus. One of the main occasions for such interaction is at seminars or sessions organized with guest speakers, which are organized by all of the universities' faculties and departments. Invitations to these events are sent across the university to all staff and may be run either at lunchtime or in the evening. Given the teaching commitments of staff on the out-of-city campus and the logistics of reaching the city campus, they are rarely able to take advantage of these opportunities.

Opportunities to meet other academics in a less formal or social environment extend beyond Oxford Brookes University. The University of Oxford also organizes such events and regularly extends the invitation to Oxford Brookes staff.

4) Collaborative working

Senior managers see the relative isolation of the Wheatley campus as a serious impediment to the progress of OBBS. The previous Dean of OBBS suggested that collaborative work is made more difficult than it needs to be and contributes to a view of OBBS by other academics in the university as being conservative and myopic. The current Dean gave an example of where better cooperation would help advance the teaching agenda and reputation. OBBS had recently secured the necessary approvals to run a prestigious BSc programme that had been co-developed with a locally based industrial giant and the engineering faculty, who were also located on the out-of-city campus. He is confident that a closer physical presence with other faculties would lead to other degrees being developed with management as a common underpinning, such as Management in Life Sciences or Management in Design. The University's 10-year estate investment plan also asserts, "the move will allow for more cross-faculty and cross-university working."

A Professor echoed this view by saying; "OBBS should be at the core of Oxford Brookes University both physically and symbolically. We are marginalized in our current campus when Business should be the flagship of the University."

The improved opportunity for cooperation with other faculties is also seen to provide the possibility of enhancing research interests. An early career researcher in OBBS, who already collaborates with academics in other international universities, believes that the ability to attend seminars run by other departments will lead to productive new collaborations with other faculties within the university.

However, the view that the move to the city campus will benefit research interests was not universally held.

Research Experience

Among other things, a universities' reputation is formed from the quantity and quality of research that is published. This forms the basis of direct funding to the university from the government. In turn, academic staff are measured and rewarded by their writing output and scholarship. As publishing deadlines loom and journal committees demand the final re-write, all researchers agree that what is needed is complete focus and concentration. This requires a comfortable and familiar space with complete quiet and easy access to core reference material. The cellular offices on the out-of-city campus allow researchers to shut their office doors and work in silence with networked computers, surrounded by shelves and filing cabinets of personally collected books and journal articles. Many researchers also choose to work from home; "my best research is done between 7pm and 2am at home. It has become a ritual. By then, the children have eaten and are on their way to bed, I can retire to my study with no interruptions". (Professor)

Rumors suggested that the move to the city campus will result in the loss of individual offices and this is a great concern to active researchers. This became clear in a recent research meeting of one department where a senior lecturer was also on a committee involved in planning the move to Headington campus.

Departmental research meeting

The research meeting took place in a large lecture room. A couple of attendees seated themselves in second and third rows, but to make the meeting more congenial, tables and chairs were moved around in order to make more of a circle – better for informal discussion.

The meeting opened with a discussion about research clusters, an idea being actively pursued by OBBS to improve cooperation and collaboration between faculty on key research topics with the outcome of improving the quality and quantity of research published.

Senior Lecturer:	"We already have some well performing research centres such as diversity and coaching and mentoring, and we are beginning to see some fully functioning research clusters such as critical management studies. But in other areas such as international business and entrepreneurship the clusters do not appear to be active as yet."
Researcher A:	"The reason progress hasn't been made is because there has been no investment. The research centers were heavily invested in to get them off the ground – it wasn't just by talking."
Professor:	"It's a question of who one talks to. External networks are critical to pursuing high quality research with international recognition and impact. As time is limited, forcing focus on internal clusters might not be as advantageous as building external research networks."
Researcher B:	"Internal capability is important as well. Working with colleagues matters."
Senior Lecturer:	"The move of OBBS to the city campus is relevant to this discussion. The spatial set up will encourage collaboration between research colleagues because unlike our existing accommodation, where all staff have cellular

	offices with one or two occupants, the new accommodation will be open plan office for whole group."
Professor:	"What's behind this thinking?"
Senior Lecturer:	"It meets the principal of open access for students."
Researcher B:	"Well teaching faculty will like it."
Researcher C:	"What about my books?"
Senior Lecturer:	"Administrators say that most books are not needed anyway so it's an opportunity to get rid of them."
Professor:	"What about personalized books – I don't want to be rid of them – and if there are no offices, anyone could take them from open shelves."
Senior Lecturer:	"There will be an archive."
Professor:	"Where exactly?"
Senior Lecturer:	"This hasn't been organized yet."
Researcher B:	"Is there no personal space?"
Senior Lecturer:	"A group of research area heads argued for this and it seems the architects will create spaces for groups of seven people."
Researcher C:	"How big are these spaces?"
Senior Lecturer:	"About seven foot by 10 foot."
Researcher C:	"That's pretty small."
Researcher A:	"How will that work?"
Professor:	"Is there open access to students and administrators at any time? How popular would one be if colleagues in the office are trying to write and others in the office are conducting supervisions?"
Senior Lecturer:	"They are supposed to book an office for that."
Professor:	"How many offices are available?"
Senior Lecturer:	"One per twelve staff."
Researcher C:	"Well we would have to book these offices – another layer of bureaucracy."
Researcher A:	"Staff are supposed to put up their office hours so students are managed."
Researcher C:	"That's not my experience – they will just turn up."
Researcher A:	"But isn't this a good thing? One of the important criticisms of us in the student survey is that students say it's not always easy to access staff."
Professor:	"In order to write a research article, one needs sustained concentration. It's virtually impossible to concentrate if there is continuous noise and disruption."

Senior Lecturer:	"Well other universities have done it, for example Coventry, Nottingham, East Anglia. It's the way the sector is going."
Researcher B:	"And I bet the Academics sit there with headphones on?"
Researcher A:	"Rather like the way our students learn, listening to music and chat."
Professor:	"But where will we do our research?"
Senior Lecturer:	"In the library?"

On leaving the meeting, the Professor was deeply concerned for the practice of research in the department. He was not alone in his concerns. In an interview shortly after the meeting another Professor said, "this move could be devastating in terms of people's work. This is a violent imposition on professors; a professor will feel like a prostitute in an open plan office and the move will see a diminishing of their professional autonomy."

Although the current practice of working from home will continue, the view of many researchers is that the open-plan nature of the new offices will encourage people to work at home more than is currently the case. This has the potential problem of driving a wedge between research active staff and teaching staff because the absence of researchers will be more apparent. This will add to a culture of "presenteeism" – you have to be there – that is said to already exist in the faculty.

Teaching and the student experience

Although students of OBBS make it clear that their experience at Oxford Brookes University will be improved by better facilities and a location more central to Oxford, members of staff other than researchers have doubts about the layout in the new building on the city campus:

> Shared offices for academic staff is not going to work. Consider the need for Office Hours for academic staff where there is a need for "private space" where they can have confidential meetings with students or colleagues, this should be paramount.
>
> (Masters Programme Administrator)

Although not all discussions with students require privacy, staff are also concerned about the potential of disrupting colleagues trying to concentrate. This is also true of the distance-learning MBA program where tutors regularly conduct Skype conversations with students from around the world at their desks.

In response to these queries about privacy and disruption it has been made clear by the architects, through the staff communication programme, that meeting rooms and smaller interview rooms will be incorporated into the layout plans, there will be 26 such rooms and 1 larger faculty meeting room that will accommodate 30 people.

Given the excellent track record of Oxford Brookes University in obtaining high ratings for student experience there is some confidence among staff that these real issues will be tackled successfully in the consultation process.

Reflecting upon space

To researchers at OBBS, it seemed that a core issue in the move was the issue of space, or more accurately spaces. The move would change the nature of spaces within which OBBS and its staff existed. In line with the research that a number of colleagues were involved in, they realized that people affect and are affected by their spaces. Indeed space might affect how organizational strategies are worked out in practice. In considering the importance of space they realized these might include place and distance as well as day-to-day lived experience, where spatial concerns change the processes and routines people use in their work. They also realized space is the materialization of power, status, and identity. All of these related dimensions of space would have a role to play in the move to the new location. The question, however, is whether this would be room for improvement?

QUESTIONS

1. Discuss the practices and spatial arrangements of OBBS at its current location. Consider each stakeholder group.
2. Consider the spatial arrangements intended at the new building. What sorts of practices are likely to be enhanced and which are likely to be inhibited within the department?
3. Which stakeholder practices will benefit most from the relocation and which will be most adversely affected?
4. In your view how will OBBS strategy evolve in its new location over the next few years? What lessons can you suggest for the role that space plays in strategy practice?

STRATEGY-MAKING 2.0: STRATEGY DEVELOPMENT PROCESS AT THE WIKIMEDIA FOUNDATION[1]

THE WIKIMEDIA MOVEMENT

BACKGROUND – LAUNCHING WIKIPEDIA

On January 15, 2001, Wikipedia was launched as a complement to its predecessor Nupedia that was meant to become an expert-written, peer-reviewed online encyclopaedia. Due to the slow, labour-intensive peer review process involved, however, Nupedia had only produced 12 articles within its first year. On the other hand, Wikipedia's application of open-source software principles enabled anyone connected to the internet to create new wiki entries as well as edit existing ones. As a consequence, Wikipedia quickly outpaced Nupedia in content and popularity. It has become the largest and most popular general online reference work, which by 2011 had over 19 million articles in 281 languages written by volunteers around the world, which increased steadily to 33 million articles in 288 languages by 2014. In that year alone, 75,000 writers added over 4.5 million new articles. All content on Wikipedia is covered by the Creative Commons Attribution-ShareAlike license, a copyright license provided by the Creative Commons Corporation that entitles anybody to reuse and re-distribute it at no charge (Wikipedia, 2011a). Issues such as inaccuracies, level of reliability, plagiarism, and privacy concerns have been constant areas of criticism and challenge for Wikipedia. Much of its content, however, is of

---

[1]This case study was authored by Julia Gößwein and Loizos Heracleous. It is not meant to illustrate effective or ineffective handling of an administrative situation but to be used as a basis for class discussion.

astonishingly high quality as shown by a quality comparison of selected articles in Wikipedia and the *Encyclopaedia Britannica* (Giles, 2005).

As of December 2011, Wikipedia ranked sixth on Alexa's list of top 500 global sites (Alexa, 2011), after Google, Facebook, YouTube, Yahoo, and Baidu.com; a position it still retained by March 2015. Innovation has flourished at Wikipedia. Over the years, Wikibooks (textbooks and manuals), Wiktionary (dictionary and thesaurus), Wikiquote (collection of quotations), Wikiversity (free learning tools), and other wiki-based projects have emerged as part of Wikimedia's free knowledge initiative (Wikimedia Meta-Wiki, 2011a). Compared to Wikipedia, however, the size and impact of these projects remains modest.

THE WIKIMEDIA FOUNDATION AND CHAPTER ORGANIZATIONS

The Wikimedia Foundation was founded on June 20, 2003 as the parent, non-profit organization of Wikipedia and its sister projects and with the aim of encouraging their growth and development. Led by Sue Gardner as Executive Director and headquartered in San Francisco, California, USA, the foundation had around 100 permanent employees in 2011 (Wikimedia Foundation, 2011a); a number that rose to 252 in 2014. Its Board of Trustees consisted of 10 members, five of whom were elected by the Wikimedia community and five were appointed, and functioned as the corporate authority for Wikimedia. Its functions were to manage the foundation, articulate its mission and vision, oversee the disposition and solicitation of donations, and specify legal parameters for projects as necessary (Wikimedia Foundation, 2011b). The Advisory Board was an international network of experts who supported and advised the board and Wikimedia staff with respect to a variety of topics ranging from organizational development and technology to policy and outreach (Wikimedia Foundation, 2011c).

Over time Wikimedia has developed various partnerships with galleries, libraries, archives, museums and educational institutions, even telecommunication providers that sell mobile phones featuring Wikipedia, in an effort to support its vision: "Imagine a world in which every human being can freely share in the sum of all knowledge. That's our commitment" (Wikimedia Meta-Wiki, 2011j). The movement's unique governance structure has been undergoing constant change and attracted both public interest and academic debate. Characterized by community self-governance on the one hand, and the institutional influence of the Wikimedia Foundation on the other, much attention has been paid to the hybrid character of Wikimedia's ecosystem (Morell, 2011: 325–6).

Since Wikimedia refrains from utilizing advertising as a means of raising funds, the foundation's financing exclusively relies on volunteer donations. Between November 2011 and January 2012, a "crowdfunding" initiative of the Wikimedia Foundation and affiliated chapters has raised a total of US$20 million, which made it, with a 25% increase over the previous year's campaign, the most successful to date (Wikimedia Meta-Wiki, 2011c; Deals&More, 2012). Wikimedia's statement of activities and balance sheet are shown in Appendix 20.A.

Individual community members were the driving force behind the creation of Wikimedia Chapters, independent organizations aiming to support and promote Wikimedia projects within

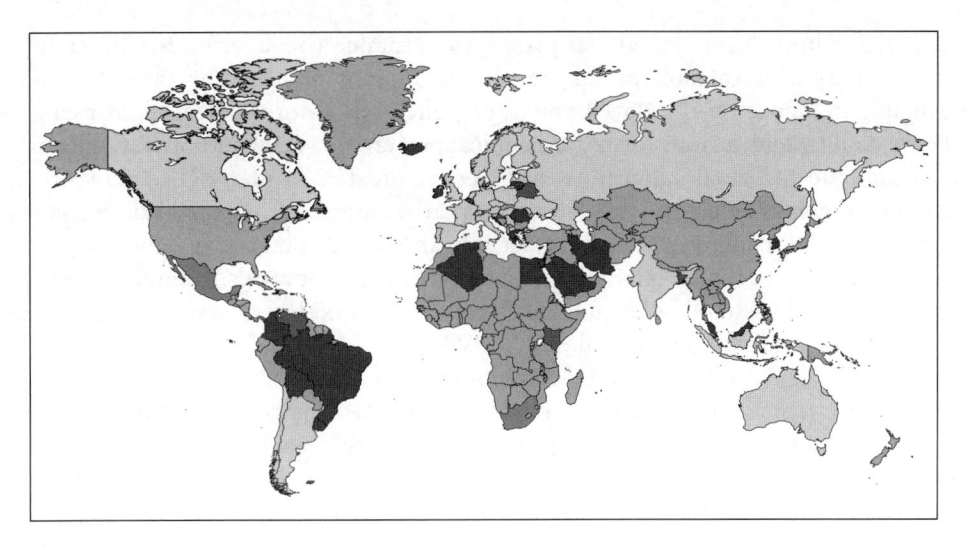

FIGURE 20.1 Existing chapters (dark blue), approved chapters (dark turquoise), planned chapters (green) and chapters in discussion (light blue) as of August 8, 2011

Source: Wikimedia Meta-Wiki 2011b.

specified geographical regions. Composed of community members, chapters formed a structural link between the foundation governing Wikimedia's infrastructure and the wider volunteer movement. Their local focus enabled them to more effectively engage in areas such as partnership development, fundraising, community-building activities, or media and stakeholder communications. Chapters were governed by their own Board of Directors or Trustees rather than the Wikimedia Board, and remained decentralized in that there was no central governing body overseeing them (Beaudette, 2012). By 2012, more than 30 Wikimedia chapters had been established and several others were planned or in discussion, as shown in Figure 20.1 and Appendix 20.B (Wikimedia Strategic Plan, 2011; Wikimedia Meta-Wiki, 2011b). By March 2015, the number of Wikimedia chapters had risen to 41 (Wikimedia Meta-Wiki, 2015).

The institutional governance provided by the Wikimedia Foundation and local chapter organizations helped to shape the effective functioning of the Wikimedia movement. Neither founder Jimmy Wales, nor the Board and other Wikimedia staff, commonly intervened in content and local governance decisions. They acknowledged the movement's decentralized character, emphasized that Wikimedia was not a place for hierarchy and rules, and offered support and advice instead (Beaudette, 2012). The Wikimedia board and staff bypassed the community only in situations that, for example, demanded swift action due to potential legal implications (Konieczny, 2010).

THE WIKIMEDIA COMMUNITY

Social roles and power relationships in the Wikimedia community were strongly affected by members' user states, which formed an important component of the movement's structure and were crucial for both local and global project governance (Beaudette, 2012). Anonymous, unregistered users were valuable participants in the creation and maintenance of content; but had negligible influence on the development of policies and norms. Registered users, on the other hand, could wield various forms of technical power and social authority. Frequently, they joined formal and informal subgroups that were dedicated to ideological, functional, and content-related themes based on their areas of expertise or interest. Trusted Wikimedians could apply for one of the many levels of volunteer stewardship, could receive administrator rights, and then move on to become "bureaucrats" and eventually "stewards." Stewards were elected individuals equipped with full access to all of Wikimedia's wiki interfaces, holding considerable authority in the community (Forte et al., 2009, Wikipedia, 2011b).

Jimmy Wales' role has changed as the community grew over time. In the early years "Jimmy was project governance and structure" (Beaudette, 2012), engaged in day-to-day operations such as content management and language projects. Over the years and given the development of community-based, decentralized governance, and robust norms, he has taken on the self-described role of "spiritual leader," engaged in overall leadership and policy debates (Forte et al., 2009: 57). He is widely respected by Wikimedians, referred to as "god-king" or "benevolent dictator" (O'Neil, 2011: 313)

Rewarding faithful volunteers with "barnstars" or "personal user" awards for their continuous work and diligence has emerged as a tradition within the Wikimedia community (Wikipedia, 2011c). Although many new users are joining the community, the one-year editor retention rate has been approximately 10%; and the number of active editors has hovered near 100,000. Large segments of the world's population did not engage with Wikimedia projects proportionately to their real-world representation (Wikimedia Strategic Planning, 2011b), and less than 15% of editors were women (Collaborative Creativity Group, 2010); 60% of contributors never edited again 24 hours after their registration (Wikipedia, 2011a).

COMMUNICATION AND COORDINATION – THE WIKI MODEL

While Wikimedia Meta-Wiki, a dedicated online platform, serves as a shared community site for all of the foundation's projects, focused wikis such as Wikimedia Outreach, Wikimedia Strategic Planning, and local wikis of Wikimedia chapters have been established for the coordination of specific projects (Wikimedia Meta-Wiki, 2011c). In addition to the Wikimedia Foundation Blog, Wikimedia Signpost serves as a weekly community newspaper covering a range of topics, events, and reports concerning Wikipedia and other projects of the Wikimedia family that followers can subscribe to at no charge (Wikipedia, 2011d). The Wikimedia Foundation also operates the weblog aggregator Planet Wikimedia in an effort to inform the community about the latest blog posts regarding Wikimedia projects, the wisdom-of-crowds and other topics of interest for the Wikimedia movement (Wikimedia Meta-Wiki, 2011d). Furthermore, various mailing lists are utilized by the foundation to communicate with and inform specific stakeholder groups and the wider community about relevant movement developments (Wikimedia Meta-Wiki, 2011e). On an annual basis, the Wikimedia Foundation organizes Wikimania, an international conference for Wikimedians that features presentations and discussions about projects the foundation operates, "other wikis, open source software, free knowledge and free content, and the different social and technical aspects which relate to these topics" (Wikipedia, 2011f).

Dedicated article talk pages serve as the primary means for reaching consensus regarding the scope and structure of an article, negotiating changes, deliberating on vandalism, and requesting peer review from other editors on Wikipedia (Viégas et al., 2007a: 83f). Moreover, numerous IRC (internet relay chat) channels based on the freenode network software enable real-time chats between Wikimedians about the foundation, chapters, cross-wiki issues, as well as specific wiki projects (Wikimedia Meta-Wiki, 2011f). Most edits on Wikimedia projects are done by only a small fraction of the users who have shared mental models how entries should look, and on appropriate action in different situations, thus enabling coordination through norms. Core contributors' leadership provides direction for peripheral editors on a variety of issues (Kittur and Kraut, 2008: 39).

POLICIES AND GUIDELINES

A large amount of different guidelines, policies, and formal processes arose from specific situational contexts and pressures exercised by stakeholders at different stages of Wikimedia's development (Forte et al., 2009: 58). They stand in sharp contrast to "naïve depictions of Wikipedia as an anarchic space" (Viégas et al., 2007b: 445). Written and edited by community members like any other Wikipedia page, they can be seen as dynamic and evolving collective-choice agreements (Wikipedia, 2011a) rather than unchanging rules.

All Wikimedia projects aim for decision-making based on "consensus over credentials," a fundamental principle that has been labelled anti-elitism (Wikipedia, 2011a). "Neutral Point of View" (NPOV), "verifiability," and "no original research" have emerged as the movement's non-negotiable, core content policies aimed at determining and implementing quality standards and control. The claims for verifiability and no original research require that content published on the site needs to be based on reliable scientific sources. According to the NPOV principle, articles must represent "all significant views fairly, proportionately, and without bias" (Wikipedia, 2011g). It therefore serves as an important collaborative tool to manage inter-editor conflict resulting from divergent positions on content, by encouraging people with competing views to work together on the same topic. Complementing the NPOV policy, a myriad of pages specify the community's communication standards. Contributing editors, for example, are advised to apply Wikipedia's etiquette (Wikipedia, 2011h), refrain from personal attacks (Wikipedia, 2011i), aim for consensus (Wikipedia, 2011j), avoid edit wars (Wikipedia, 2011k), as well as act on and assume good faith (Wikipedia, 2011l). Wikipedia's "five pillars" contained in Appendix 20.C, briefly summarize the most fundamental principles upon which the community operates (Wikipedia, 2011n), which aim to lower the increasingly high barriers of bureaucracy that new editors encounter. Since conflicts, however, remain an everyday issue between editors, a process of dispute resolution has emerged involving inter-editor negotiation, formal mediation and, if all other resolution mechanisms have failed, the enforcement of binding solutions based on arbitration (Wikipedia, 2011m).

WIKIMEDIA'S STRATEGIC PLANNING PROJECT

Project Motivation and Philosophy

Prior to the formation of the Wikimedia Foundation in 2003, strategic planning discussions generally took place within the respective wiki projects. Based on the application of traditional "wiki" processes, decisions concerning new languages, projects, or policies were made by either community members or movement leaders. Wikimedia's strategic planning efforts began to take more concrete shape after the first Board was formed in 2004. Public brainstorming pages were created and users encouraged to suggest strategic priorities to the Board. Participation, however, remained slim (Wikimedia Meta-Wiki, 2011g). By 2007, Wikimedia's Board undertook several strategic planning efforts: community wide, Board, staff, and project committees were formed (Wikimedia Meta-Wiki, 2011h), the foundation's mission (Wikimedia Meta-Wiki, 2011i) and vision (Wikimedia Meta-Wiki, 2011j) statements revisited, a SWOT analysis conducted (Wikimedia Meta-Wiki, 2011k) and several resolutions passed.

At its April 2009 Board meeting, however, the Wikimedia Foundation Board of Trustees decided to take a fresh approach to strategy-making, drawing on the principles of building a transparent, collective vision, open collaboration, and stakeholder involvement (Wikimedia Strategic Planning, 2011c). "The fastest way to develop a strategy," said Executive Director Sue Gardner, responding to a user who had commented on the contradiction between having groups focused on a specific topic and a process of open collaboration, "would be to have me and Michael [Michael Snow, Chair of the Board of Trustees at the time] create it alone in a room in a single day, or have Michael tell me what the strategy is, or have me recommend one to him. But it wouldn't necessarily be a very good strategy, and it certainly wouldn't be as good as what we can accomplish collectively:-)." (Wikimedia Foundation, 2011d).

The principles on which the strategic planning process was built are also apparent in the statement released by Michael Snow:

> The work of the Wikimedia Foundation is founded in the premise that open, mass collaboration is the most effective method for achieving high-quality decision-making. Therefore, we ask that the strategic planning process be designed to include input from a wide range of sources, including Wikimedia volunteers and supporters representing a diversity of geographies and projects. We ask that the process also aim to solicit input from parties who are currently not part of the Wikimedia community, in an effort to broaden our knowledge base and benefit from new ideas and information.
>
> The principles guiding this process should include:
>
> * Transparency. As much as possible, work should be done in public, and be visible to all.
>
> * Participation. The mechanisms used to solicit input should be designed to be as open as reasonably possible, and to encourage broad participation.
>
> * Collaboration. We recognize that we will not develop a consensus strategy that pleases everyone. We will need to make difficult decisions that may prove unpopular. But we believe that people who want to have a voice in the process, should be heard.

(Wikimedia Foundation, 2011e)

While pointing out that Wikimedia's official institutions – the Wikimedia Foundation and Wikimedia Chapters – needed to conduct planning processes of their own, Wikimedia's Board of Trustees and Foundation managers still understood well how institutional decision-making impacted the movement as a whole and that the success of Wikimedia's projects depended crucially on the support of their membership. For example, as mentioned by Philippe Beaudette, currently Director of Community Advocacy for Wikimedia, and in July 2009 employed by the foundation as facilitator of the strategic planning project (Wikimedia Strategic Planning, 2011c): "If we attempted to go off into a board room somewhere and design a strategy, it would most likely have been universally decried as not being 'the Wikimedia way' […] Experience has shown that when things are 'imposed' upon the Wikimedia community they usually are not adopted wholeheartedly" (Beaudette, 2011).

Even though the success of the project depended on the work of volunteers, Jimmy Wales made a point of distinguishing its philosophy from that of crowdsourcing, an increasingly popular method for tapping into the wisdom of the crowd:

> I don't like the term "crowdsourcing" because it is offensive to genuine communities and leads people to make poor business decisions. The etymology of the term comes from the term "outsourcing" – the idea of hiring people in a nation with cheaper labor. The idea of crowdsourcing is to get the cheapest labor of all by getting the public to do some piece of work for free. That's the wrong approach. Nobody works for free. Starting with some work that you want done, and working out how to "crowdsource" it is a generally delusional activity that takes matters the wrong way around. What does make sense: think about what people want to do in communities, and find a way to help them achieve that aim. This is the genuinely community-centric approach. (Wales, 2011)

DESIGNING THE PROCESS: OPENNESS AND FLEXIBILITY VS. CENTRALIZATION AND CONTROL

Although ultimately the design of the strategic planning process was characterized by four phases ("Level-setting," "Deep-dives," "Synthesis," and "Business Planning/Call to Action") with specific timeframes and goals, these were not clearly defined at the outset. Talking about his experiences in an online webinar, project manager Eugene Eric Kim from Blue Oxen Associates, describes some of the challenges the team encountered while designing the process phases:

> If you look at the bulk of the contributors to the Wikimedia project, what we know about the demographics is, that they are largely students; they are people under the age of 30 […]. Well, the problem with that is – if you don't have experience with strategic planning processes, then how do you participate in an open strategic planning process? How do you come to content on even what the processes should be? Even those people who have participated in strategic planning processes know that no process, or most processes are never identical and so coming to consensus on process and moving forward and all those things was going to be challenging. (Kim, 2011b)

The process design was caught in the tension between the opposing needs for process flexibility but also process clarity; and the interplay between openness but also a structure able to inform and drive decisions. On the one hand, the unpredictability of both the quantity and quality of volunteer contributions and the lack of contributors' prior experience in the design of collaborative strategic planning efforts demanded a flexible process structure that could easily be adapted. On the other hand, however, the project team realized that clear direction giving was needed to lead the volunteers through the process, to demonstrate appreciation for their time and effort and to make use of them as resources both efficiently and effectively:

> We also need to make sure that we deliver results. There can and should be an on-going conversation about the details of this process, but we can't wait until we all agree on everything before moving forward. We have to be both open and agile, meeting our individual needs, being thoughtful and deliberative, and at the same time, moving to action. This means that the process needs to be highly iterative, and that it needs to account for the specific needs of individual stakeholders. (Wikimedia Strategic Planning, 2011c)

Wikimedia's project team realized that its strategic planning initiative was different from any other project of the Wikimedia family. First and foremost, "a democratic process was never a goal for this project. Rather, it was a community facing/community influenced process" (Philippe Beaudette, Wikimedia Strategic Planning, 2011e). The same message comes across when project manager Eugene Eric Kim argues that,

> you can't have that principle [Neutral Point of View] in strategic planning [...] Strategic planning is about making choices. And so, again, what that sort of culture was going to be in terms of how people interacted with the strategic planning wiki in particular, we knew that was going to be different from an open source project. [...] We knew it was even going to be different from Wikipedia. Because we could not use all of the same principles at strategic planning and so on that Wikipedia uses. (Kim, 2011b)

In an effort to introduce a governance model for the process of engaging in the strategic planning project, a set of community principles were introduced at the outset rather than being allowed to gradually develop as collective-choice agreements, as would have been typical for other projects of the Wikimedia movement:

1. "This is a wiki. You are encouraged to edit pages.
2. Although this content is open and editable, this is also a 'safe space'. No ideas here are bad ones. If you disagree, make your case, but try not to flame or become agitated.
3. Although we strive for an open decision-making environment, there may be times when decisions must be made by the convenors.
4. There is no core set of project 'rules' here; that is, we didn't import over all the rules from one of the other projects. This wiki is managed with the assumption that everyone here has a 'clue' and will not forget and leave their 'clue' somewhere else. Administrative actions (such as block and ban) could happen here. And I'm sure that vandalism will occur.
5. In general, this wiki operates under a golden rule, and assumes good faith. Trust others to do what's right, and expect them to trust you to do what's right." (Wikimedia Strategic Planning, 2011f)

Thirty-seven dedicated Wikimedians offered to become hosts (convenors) to the strategic planning process with the primary goal of creating and maintaining a user-friendly wiki environment. In general, their work involved organizing and merging proposals, facilitating participation, welcoming new contributors, encouraging conversations, and resolving disputes constructively

(Wikimedia Strategic Planning, 2011g). Coordination between hosts took place through a regularly updated to-do list. Utilizing Wikimedia's IRC channel infrastructure, they conducted regular chats during office hours where real-time discussions took place and questions from volunteers were answered. Following Wikimedia's quest for openness and transparency, summaries and entire IRC logs can be accessed online on the strategy wiki (Wikimedia Strategic Planning, 2011h). As a complement to the work of hosts, appropriate governance of the four project phases was aimed for through experienced users equipped with "sysop" (system operator or administrator) rights, the appointment of six "bureaucrats" and engagement of the Wikimedia Foundation's steward team (Wikimedia Strategic Planning, 2011i).

Despite the open, collaborative nature of the process that was received positively by many Wikimedians, the top-down initiation of the project, which went contrary to the established culture of community-led projects, did not escape resistance from within the community as the following discussion illustrates:

Comment by User Mr. Quickling, September 21, 2009:

This whole project raises several "red flags" for me. First is the fact that it seems to come from top-down rather than bottom up. There is nothing in the Board of Trustees resolutions about starting a project like this, and it certainly did not come from the community. By process of elimination, it must have come from the small executive paid staff of the Foundation. Another issue is the addition of two names to the paid staff, Eugene Eric Kim and Philippe Beaudette, on the Wikimedia Foundation website. These people have vague titles, no information as to their duties, do not appear on the organization chart, and were not brought on using the usual open process for hiring new staff for the Foundation. There is also no information regarding the cost of this whole project, but I suspect it is high. While the aims of this project are noble, these areas of concern, taken together, make me very concerned about the whole thing. It looks and smells way too much like many money wasting projects done by for-profit corporations that end up with lots of harmful "programs" and benefit no one except the external consulting companies. In particular, I think the following things should be done:

- Clearly describe [name] and [name] duties on the Wikimedia Foundation website as well as who they are accountable to.
- State the cost of this whole project so the community can decide if it is worth it.
- In general, run this more like the Wikimedia Usability Initiative, which is doing great work and has none of the bad smell this has. (Wikimedia Strategic Planning, 2011e)

Response from Eugene Eric Kim, September 21, 2009:

Process/Background links to the April 2009 board resolution that started this whole process. Philippe is paid staff; I'm a contractor. I report directly to Sue Gardner, the executive director of the Foundation, and Philippe reports to me. Both of us came on board through an open hiring process that was widely advertised on the Foundation website in May 2009. I will publish a budget for the project in a few weeks; I'm ironing out a few details now.

In the meantime, I hate to think the project smells, and I'll do my part to clear the air. :-) I hope you'll do your best to Assume Good Faith about my role and intention as well. This is about the future of Wikimedia, and we hope that everyone who cares will come together to help shape it. And, FYI, these are the original job postings (and job descriptions) for which Philippe and Eugene applied, along with many other candidates. (Wikimedia Strategic Planning, 2011e)

Response from Erik Möller,
Deputy Director of the Wikimedia Foundation, September 22, 2009:

Please give the project a chance and specifically check out some of the great proposals that have been submitted already in a completely bottom-up fashion (a good way to find the best ones is to check out the Favorites pages that several users have built). (Wikimedia Strategic Planning, 2011e)

Response from user Jolieg, September 24, 2009:

Hello! I am new here but was drawn to join and post (which I assume is done with an edit) by "wikimedia's" corporate marketing efforts. You contacted me with this marketing effort! Seeing the "This smells bad" section made me feel like this was the place for it. Wikipedia was (and is) a beautiful creation. But why can't the creators have a success like Wikipedia and then humbly step back to serve its genius, as have so many volunteers? Why must you try to turn it into a corporate modeled opportunity to advance a career, a persona? From where I sit, the bad smell is that of ego and careerism. So as you go in circles, trying to figure out what is wrong or going wrong or may go wrong with Wikipedia, consider that the answer is, most likely, YOU! (Wikimedia Strategic Planning, 2011e)

Phase 1: "Level-setting"

The creation of a strategic planning platform, "strategy wiki," that was to facilitate the process of collecting, analysing, and synthesizing relevant information at a central location stood at the outset of this first project phase. By asking strategic questions such as "Where is Wikimedia now?" and "Where should Wikimedia go?" the project team aimed to encourage strategic thinking among contributors.

> The naïve way of thinking about how to do it might be – put the questions [Where are we now? Where do we want to go? How do we get there?] up on the wiki and if you wait long enough and if you have people to go there, then hopefully people come, they look at the questions, they have all sorts of these conversations and a few months later the strategic plan magically appeared. [...] However, reality of the situation is: this is not how wiki works. It is no magical thing where you put something up and if you build it, they will come. (Kim, 2011b)

Consequently, Wikimedia's project team approached the conduct of the level-setting phase in a more directive fashion, by shaping the context in which conversations took place. The team established a shared knowledge base, "Wikimedia-pedia," which aimed to illuminate the larger context of the planning process and support the identification of knowledge gaps. Structured according to the movement's goals (reach, quality, participation, and operations), Wikimedia-pedia contains a large collection of facts, existing research, and analysis relevant to the Wikimedia movement that may be accessed by everyone (Wikimedia Strategic Planning, 2011j). In addition, it contains interviews conducted by the Bridgespan Group, a non-profit consulting firm working with the Foundation, of Advisory Board members, Board of Trustees members, external experts, and Wikimedia Foundation employees, discussing what they believe to be an appropriate direction for Wikimedia (Wikimedia Strategic Planning, 2011k).

A process to develop formalized proposals stood at the center of the level-setting phase and was introduced by the project team to encourage wider community engagement, spur strategic thinking by members of the movement, and motivate individuals to participate actively in the implementation of the resulting strategic plan (Wikimedia Strategic Planning, 2011l). The team developed a basic template with a standardized proposal format as a way to improve the quality of submissions. Once published, a traditional wiki process was applied to polish, translate, debate, group, and merge the proposals. A box at the bottom of each proposal page enabled visitors at the site to rate it in terms of its priority, impact, feasibility, and desirability from very low to very high. A page listing all proposals was introduced and the suggestions were categorized according to their aims (see Appendix 20.D). The page further provided an overview of the most active proposals, the proposals that received the highest ranking, and those which most contributors volunteered to implement (Wikimedia Strategic Planning, 2011m). In contrast to activity on other wikis, however, Wikimedia discouraged the deletion of radical, merged, or irrelevant proposals, since it viewed the project as a larger brainstorming and sense-making process rather than an encyclopaedia.

Even though the sheer size of the movement provided a large talent pool for Wikimedia's strategic planning efforts characterized by cultural and geographical diversity, recruiting volunteers from the community proved to be a constant challenge (Beaudette, 2011). The project team therefore heavily engaged in relationship building with individual volunteers as well as Wikimedia Chapter Organizations, online and on a face-to-face basis. The design of an "outreach plan" was aimed at reaching as many of Wikimedia's stakeholders as possible early on in the process. Posters, mass mailings, stickers, and blogs were employed to spread the word about the process and a list of blogs featuring the strategic planning project was posted on strategy wiki (Wikimedia Strategic Planning, 2011n). Beyond that, the plan encouraged the utilization of Wikimedia's language ambassadors to tackle cross-language challenges and discussed opportunities to strengthen the commonly underrepresented voice of developing countries in the strategic planning project through, for instance, the participation in national electronic forums or the execution of regional workshops.

The launch of a broad Call for Participation on September 21, 2009 comprised the final milestone of Wikimedia's outreach plan. An appeal letter written by Wikipedia founder Jimmy Wales and Michael Snow (Chair of the Board of Trustees) was translated into 69 languages, highlighting six main ways in which volunteers were encouraged to support the yearlong planning process. These were contributing to proposals, joining a task force, offering expert advice, hosting independent conversations about Wikimedia's strategy, communicating feedback, and donating (Wikimedia Strategic Planning, 2011d, 2011o, 2011p). During the first year, 31 strategy face-to-face meetings took place in 19 different countries, from which minutes were shared online (Wikimedia Strategic Planning, 2011o).

To increase exposure, the Call for Participation was displayed across all Wikimedia projects as a top-of-page message. This being a standard approach for Wikimedia to communicate with readers and editors, existing infrastructure was applied to address logged-in users, anonymous users, and readers separately. For evaluation purposes, the project team developed an overview of the number of edits and page creations completed by the 20 most active editors throughout October 5, 2009, the last day of the "level-setting" phase. Given his function, most edits could be ascribed to project facilitator Philippe Beaudette. Apart from project manager Eugene Eric Kim from Blue Oxen Associates and John Fowler and Serita Cox from the Bridgespan Group, however, the remaining particularly active editors were not affiliated Wikimedia staff members but volunteers with diverse geographical and demographic backgrounds (Wikimedia Strategic Planning, 2011q). According to Philippe Beaudette, "the volunteers for our planning process came (predominantly, and with very few exceptions) from within our current volunteer community. In fact, it would be almost criminal to develop a new corps of volunteers for a planning process, because they wouldn't be able to speak for our existing volunteer community" (Beaudette, 2011).

Phase 2: "Deep-Dives"

In October 2009, the Wikimedia Foundation appointed a Task Force Selection Committee comprised of 15 members, thereby initiating phase 2, the so-called "deep-dives" phase of the strategic planning process. The committee's core responsibilities were to define the mandates and select suitable individuals among over 1,923 confirmed applications for a set of 14 task forces related to the three emerging strategic priorities of sustainability, development, and accessibility as depicted in Table 20.1 (Wikimedia Strategic Planning, 2011r).

The committee categorized the applications by individuals who offered to participate in a task force, most of which were received from India, followed by the USA, the Russian Federation, the United Kingdom, and the People's Republic of China. The criteria were availability, country, fluency, and specialty of applicants. Thirty percent of task force applicants were offering to invest 10 hours or more into the process on a weekly basis (Wikimedia Strategic Planning, 2011s).

Ultimately, each task force comprised of 5 to 10 members, one of whom was in charge of the group's coordinative and administrative tasks; the working language was English. Even though the work of task forces occurred transparently on strategy wiki and theoretically everyone was allowed to participate, task force members were considered "responsible and accountable […] for seeing that the work is done and the deliverables are in on time" (Wikimedia Strategic Planning, 2011t). The task forces were advised to aim for decision-making based on consensus among all participants. Nevertheless, individual group members with final decision-making powers had been identified at the beginning of the process in order to address situations in which reaching consensus was not feasible (Wikimedia Strategic Planning, 2011u). While receiving support from Wikimedia staff facilitators, the community members themselves were responsible for success or failure of the task forces (Grams et al., 2011).

Figure 20.2 illustrates the development of the number of content pages, editors, and proposals developed from August 2009 to March 2010. The two spikes visible on August 21 and September 21, 2009 correspond to the online Call for Proposals and Call for Participation. Initially, the number of page editors (green) and total proposals (red) paralleled each other.

TABLE 20.1 Strategic task forces (Wikimedia Strategic Planning, 2011r)

Sustainability	Development	Accessibility
Advocacy	Reader Conversion	Offline
Financial Sustainability	Expanding Content	Local language projects
Alliances and Partnerships	Wikipedia Quality	Arabic
Community Health	Technology	China
Movement Roles		India

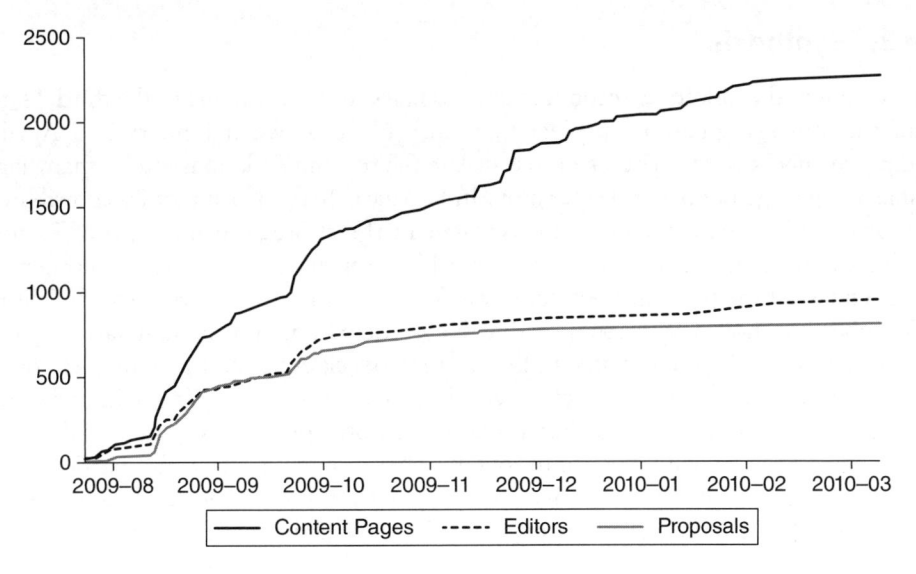

FIGURE 20.2 Content pages, page edits and proposals statistics from August 2009 to March 2010

Source: Wikimedia Strategic Planning, 2011v.

This indicates that at the time, the majority of contributions stemmed from volunteers adding a single, new proposal. After the official Call for Participation and the subsequent formation of task forces, however, the number of content pages continued to grow while the number of editors and proposals remained at around the same level, reflecting an increased engagement in the elaboration of existing proposals (Wikimedia Strategic Planning, 2011q).

Nevertheless, and despite tremendous relationship building efforts by the project team (Kim, 2011a), the deep-dives phase was less successful than had been hoped for, with only 9 of the 14 task forces delivering recommendations and only 4 of those being of the quality that had been anticipated (Newstead, 2010). The foundation's deliberation on the causes led to diverging explanations ranging from design failures of specific task forces (Newstead, 2010; Beaudette, 2011), asking too much from volunteers (Grams et al., 2011), resource limitations of the project team (Beaudette, 2011), or driving away engaged volunteers by misframing the question (Kim, 2011a).

According to Beaudette:

> The reasons for failure to deliver results varied. In one case, the theme of the task force was poorly designed ... "technology" is far too broad a topic. That particular task force was essentially paralyzed by the scope of their remit. Attempts to reboot it midway through were too little, too late. In another case, there was a failure by the person who was leading the task force to schedule, and a failure on our part, administratively, to reassign the task force to someone else. In an ideal world, the administrative team would have been quick to intervene, but because of resource limitations, we simply couldn't. That's the hazard of dealing with volunteers – sometimes things don't happen. But without volunteers none of it would have happened. I'd have been a little surprised if every task force had delivered the results on time, frankly. (Beaudette, 2011)

Phase 3: "Synthesis"

The publication of the task force recommendations marked the beginning of the third, "synthesis" phase of the strategic planning project that took place between January and April 2010. Community members were encouraged to translate the recommendations into as many languages as possible and engage in further deliberation. In February 2010, a group of 20 contributors who had demonstrated particularly deep involvement in the strategic planning process formed a Strategy Task Force that was to serve as the central hub for further discussions. In order to maintain the openness of the process, everybody was free to join the task force through February 28, 2010. Membership, however, presupposed active participation and the familiarity with a large amount of relevant background material. In four three-week cycles and with the help of a guidelines page defining the characteristics of good, movement-wide goals (Wikimedia Strategic Planning, 2011w), this Strategy Task Force synthesized previous discussions, amounting to over 900 proposals and recommendations, into roughly 1,500 content pages with a particular focus on the feasibility of their implementation. By April 30, 2010, this work had resulted in a first, rough draft for Wikimedia's five-year strategic plan, which was structured as follows:

1. Background and Context
2. Shared Beliefs and Principles of the Wikimedia Movement
3. Movement Priorities
4. Role of the Wikimedia Foundation in Supporting and Building the Movement
5. Movement Initiatives Helping to Grow the Movement and the Projects.

(Wikimedia Strategic Planning, 2011x)

Phase 4: "Business Planning/Call to Action"

During the fourth and final part of Wikimedia's strategic planning process the community was once more invited to review and refine the five strategic goals depicted in Figure 20.3, the rationales underlying them, key indicators, possible targets, and other measures. In June 2010 Wikimedia's "Theory of Change" was then circulated. Assuming the existence of a virtuous circle (Figure 20.4) between participation, quality, and reach that can be driven by both positive and negative feedback loops, it informed the development of the Wikimedia Foundation's business plan in collaboration with the Bridgespan Group (Wikimedia Strategic Planning, 2011y).

In the last month of the project, Michael Snow and Jimmy Wales launched an official "Call to Action" to enthuse volunteers to implement the directions identified throughout the process:

> As we bring this process to a close, our biggest challenge is to put these ideas into action. Here on Wikimedia's strategic planning wiki, you'll find a list of action opportunities organized around the priorities they support. We'd like to invite you to volunteer for and take ownership of these action opportunities. Here are just a few examples:
>
> - Developing a framework for expert review of Wikimedia content
> - Building a central repository of inter-language links and data
> - Awarding an annual prize for the best featured content
> - Launching a "be bold" campaign to invite people to contribute to Wikipedia.
>
> (Wikimedia Strategic Planning, 2011aa)

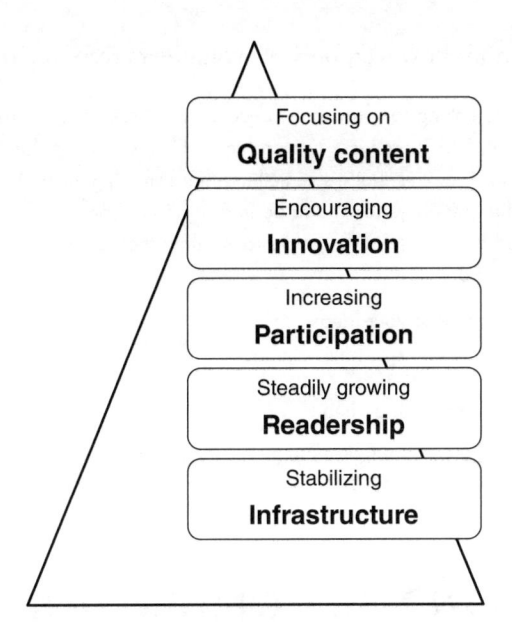

FIGURE 20.3 Wikimedia strategic priorities

Source: Wikimedia Strategic Planning, 2011z.

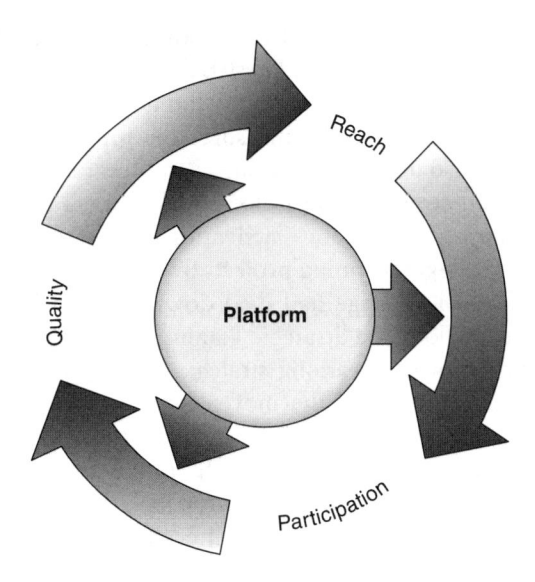

FIGURE 20.4 Virtuous cycle between participation, quality, and reach

Source: Wikimedia Strategic Planning, 2011z.

Following this Call to Action, however, only 35 volunteers responded. According to Eric Kim:

> People assumed that we were asking for proposals, because we were going to review them and then act on them, which was not the point. [...] There were two problems. First, we called this whole process a "proposal" process. The word, "proposal," implies that it's something that some higher body will review, a notion seemingly bolstered by the fact that people perceived to be in a position of power were the ones doing the asking. This was further exacerbated by our use of the active rather than the passive voice, a point that Samuel Klein underscored many times. Compare:
>
> Please post proposals so we can hear your ideas.
>
> versus:
>
> Please post proposals so your ideas can be heard.
>
> The former is stronger – it's how we're taught to write in school – but there's an implicit hierarchy in the language. Not so with the latter. (Kim, 2011a)

REFLECTING ON THE CONCLUSION OF THE PROCESS

As the strategic planning process came to an end, Wikimedia launched a dedicated celebration page and encouraged contributors to share their experiences and thoughts about the process, award barnstars to committed volunteers, and post a Virtual Champagne Toast. Volunteers who had been deeply engaged in the project and representatives of the Wikimedia Foundation commented on a variety of topics, as shown in Table 20.2 (Wikimedia Strategic Planning, 2011b).

In May 2011, Ting Chen, the new Chair of the Wikimedia Board of Trustees, turned again towards the community for support after the latest Editors Trends Study (Wikimedia Strategic Planning, 2011b) confirmed the decline in participation and retention of new editors. Chen's resolution titled "openness" highlighted the measures the foundation was taking to ensure a stable editing community but also urged the movement to promote openness and collaboration. The fact that Wikimedians on strategy wiki followed the appeal to discuss the issue at hand and contribute new ideas appeared to be a reactivation of the community that formed itself around Wikimedia's initial strategic planning project. By August 2011, however, the volunteer-led conversation on the discussions page had died down without having delivered any clear recommendations or results (Wikimedia Strategic Planning, 2011d).

The final, official document of the yearlong strategic planning process, entitled "Wikimedia Strategic Plan: A collaborative vision for the movement through 2015," was distributed and published on strategy wiki in February 2011. Publicly available, it elaborates on the five strategic priorities for Wikimedia, their corresponding critical targets and operational implications for the Wikimedia Foundation, as well as consequences for local Wikimedia Chapter organizations (Wikimedia Strategic Plan, 2011). In correspondence after the completion of the strategic planning process, Jimmy Wales emphasized how "all [...] investment at the Foundation is now driven by the strategic plan," and noted that the project left him with the same insight that he got from Wikipedia itself many years ago: "people can cooperate and can produce great value with harmony as long as some fundamental values of mutual respect are used to set the ground rules" (Wales, 2011).

TABLE 20.2 Volunteer comments (Wikimedia Strategic Planning, 2011b)

Topic	Comments
Formal recognition of volunteer contributions	**Bodnotbod:** "I think Phillip mentioned that there was some possibility that letters would be sent out thanking participants for their work on Strategy. I would be extremely grateful for such a letter as my family and friends often don't take my work on Wikimedia stuff very seriously, so it would be great to have something tangible."
	KrebMarkt: "About the letter, I want one too because it will be a first implementation of one volunteers recognition recommendation."
Strategy implementation	**Bodnotbod:** "Even though the latest documents to come out of the WMF don't appear to express an intention to carry out some of my favourite ideas I think they can still come to fruition via grassroots support for them."
	KrebMarkt: "[…] however we are not done yet. We have years of implementation & thick skulls cracking ahead of us."
	Randomran: "I hope some of those ideas will translate into action, or even just a *specific* call to action from someone with the leadership to influence the projects. A strategy without action is just wallpaper."
	Dafer45: "Now I hope we take these opportunities and make the best out of them."
Social / collaborative characteristics of project	**Randomran:** "I met a lot of great people through this process, and I realized how great a wiki can be when it functions like a co-operative neighborhood."
	Theo10011: "It is a great place to have discussions and talk with like-minded people […]."
	Dafer45: "I have been amazed by the amount of people that actually are willing to help with the mission, not only on this wiki, but on all the other Wikimedia projects, as well as on other projects. It has also been enlightening to see how much individuals are able to do if someone just empowers them by trusting in their ability to do it well."
	~Philippe (WMF): "[…] but there's no question that where we ended up is quite different from where we thought we'd be – and, I think, better. The sum of all of us took us to a really spectacular place. I'm proud to be a part of it."
Individual experiences and personal development	**Theo10011:** "I joined strategic planning during one of the early phases, took part on one of the task forces, wrote multiple proposals, became an admin and a host, helped other new users and felt like I was really involved in the process. […]. I got a chance to visit Wikimania and really felt like I was involved in some of the decision making process that goes on."
	Dafer45: "Throughout this process I have learnt a lot. […]. And it has been great to see how such an organic and decentralized movement can achieve such goals as has been achieved to this day, and how it can organize and aim for even greater goals in the future. […]. I do also appreciate that through this process I have learnt that solving problems is not as much about overcoming obstacles as it is about taking care of opportunities."
	~Philippe (WMF): "I've spent a year of my life with this process and it feels a little disconnected to be moving on to other things. It's been amazing, overwhelming, fear inducing, charming, enlightening, panic-stricken … just about any adjectives one can come up with, I've felt during this process."

In February 2015, Wikimedia announced a two-week strategy consultation with the community, on what they saw as major trends relating to the internet, in addition to the growth of mobile access and the next billion users going online (Wikimedia Meta-Wiki, 2015). A Wikimedia blog piece by the Philippe Beaudette, Director of Community Advocacy, gave some background to this consultation:

> Instead of launching a comprehensive (and expensive!) process and creating a formal document, like the last strategic planning initiative, we see this as the first step. We are interested in an iterative, discursive strategic process – one that continues to reflect changes in knowledge creation, user behavior, and the internet as a whole, while remaining agile and responsive to our mutual thoughts and needs. (Beaudette, 2015)

APPENDICES

APPENDIX 20.A Wikimedia Financials

1. Statement of Activities (in thousands of US dollars)

	2013–14	2010–11
Support and revenue		
Donations and contributions	49,612	23,686
In-kind service revenue	370	350
Other income, net	989	712
Investment income, net	244	37
Release of restrictions on net assets	1,589	----
Total revenue	**52,804**	**24,785**
Expenses		
Salaries and wages	19,980	7,312
Awards and grants	5,705	471
Internet hosting	2,529	1,800
In-kind service expenses	371	350
Operating expenses	12,485	5,761
Travel	1,966	1,159
Depreciation and amortization	2,722	1,001
Other expenses, including special events	143	36
Total expenses	**45,900**	**17,890**
Increase in net assets	**6,904**	**6,895**

2. Balance Sheet (in thousands of US dollars)

	2013–14	2010–11
Assets		
Cash and cash equivalents	27,880	12,026
Current portion of contributions receivable	1,800	1,000
Accounts receivable	----	695
Investments	23,261	5,849
Prepaid expenses & other current assets	1,600	1,215
Total current assets	**54,541**	**20,785**
Property, plant, and equipment	4,053	3,402
Noncurrent portion of contributions receivable	1,967	1,979
Total assets	**60,561**	**26,166**
Liabilities		
Accounts payable and accrued expenses	5,606	1,431
Deferred revenue	18	345
Other liabilities	1,462	168
Total liabilities	**7,086**	**1,974**
Net Assets		
Unrestricted net assets	49,825	20,772
Temporarily restricted net assets	3,650	3,420
Total net assets	**53,475**	**24,192**
Total liabilities and net assets	**60,561**	**26,166**

Source: Wikimedia Foundation Annual Reports, 2011 and 2014

APPENDIX 20.B Wikimedia Chapters

AR Wikimedia Argentina	IN Wikimedia India
AT Wikimedia Österreich	IT Wikimedia Italia
AU Wikimedia Australia	MK Викимедија Македонија
BD Wikimedia Bangladesh	MO Wikimedia Macau

(Continued)

APPENDIX 20.B *(Continued)*

CA Wikimedia Canada	MX Wikimedia México
CH Wikimedia CH	NL Wikimedia Nederlands
CL Wikimedia Chile	NO Wikimedia Norge
CZ Wikimedia Česká republika	PH Wikimedia Philippines
DE Wikimedia Deutschland	PL Wikimedia Polska
DK Wikimedia Danmark	PT Wikimedia Portugal
EE Wikimedia Eesti	RS Викимедија Србије
ES Wikimedia España	RU Викимедиа РУ
FI Wikimedia Suomi	SE Wikimedia Sverige
FR Wikimédia France	TW Wikimedia Taiwan
GB Wikimedia UK	UA Вікімедіа Україна
HK Wikimedia Hong Kong	US-NYC Wikimedia New York City
HU Wikimédia Magyarország	US-DC Wikimedia District of Columbia
ID Wikimedia Indonesia	VE Wikimedia Venezuela
IL Wikimedia Israel	ZA Wikimedia South Africa

APPENDIX 20.C The Five Pillars Of Wikipedia (*Source*: Wikipedia, 2011n)

"**Wikipedia is an online encyclopaedia.** It incorporates elements of general and specialized encyclopaedias, almanacs, and gazetteers. Wikipedia is not a soapbox, an advertising platform, a vanity press, an experiment in anarchy or democracy, an indiscriminate collection of information, or a web directory. It is not a dictionary, newspaper, or a collection of source documents; that kind of content should be contributed instead to the Wikimedia sister projects.

Wikipedia is written from a neutral point of view. We strive for articles that document and explain the major points of view in a balanced impartial manner. We try to avoid advocacy and we characterize issues rather than debate them. In some areas there may be just one well-recognized point of view; in other areas we describe multiple points of view, presenting each accurately and in context, and not presenting any point of view as "the truth" or "the best view." All articles must strive for verifiable accuracy: unreferenced material may be removed, so please provide references. Editors' personal experiences, interpretations, or opinions do not belong here. That means citing verifiable, authoritative sources, especially on controversial topics and when the subject is a living person.

Wikipedia is free content that anyone can edit, use, modify, and distribute. Respect copyright laws, and do not plagiarize your sources. Non-free content is allowed under fair use, but strive to find free alternatives to any media or content that you wish to add to Wikipedia. Since all your contributions are freely licensed to the public, no editor owns any article; all of your contributions can and will be mercilessly edited and redistributed.

Editors should interact with each other in a respectful and civil manner. Respect and be polite to your fellow Wikipedians, even when you disagree. Apply Wikipedia etiquette, and avoid personal

STRATEGY DEVELOPMENT PROCESS AT THE WIKIMEDIA FOUNDATION

attacks. Find consensus, avoid edit wars, and remember that there are 3,677,238 articles on the English Wikipedia to work on and discuss. Act in good faith, never disrupt Wikipedia to illustrate a point, and assume good faith on the part of others. Be open and welcoming. When conflict arises, discuss details on the talk page, and follow dispute resolution.

Wikipedia does not have firm rules. Rules in Wikipedia are not carved in stone, and their wording and interpretation are likely to change over time. The principles and spirit of Wikipedia's rules matter more than their literal wording, and sometimes improving Wikipedia requires making an exception to a rule. Be bold (but not reckless) in updating articles and do not worry about making mistakes. Your efforts do not need to be perfect; prior versions are saved, so no damage is irreparable."

Wikipedia (2011n)

APPENDIX 20.D Categorization Of Proposals (Adapted From Wikimedia Strategic Planning, 2011m)

1. WMF structure and function	5. Proposals by project	8. Enable features
Distributed infrastructure	Commons	
Funding	Wikinews	9. New features
Policy and governance	Wikipedia	API
Regional organization	Wikisource	Data
Strategic planning	Wikiversity	Graphics
		Instruction
2. Extending coverage	Wiktionary	Interwiki
Adding media	Wikispecies	Semantic MediaWiki
Content partnerships	Wikibooks	Social
	Wikiquote	Technical improvement
3. Volunteer support	6. Improving content	10. New projects
	Quality	New languages
4. Outreach	Peer-review	
Collaboration	Restricted editing	
Events	Ending anonymity	
Funding		
Multimedia	7. Improving usability	
Schools	Accessibility	
Supporting other communities	Avenues of access	
Text	Language issues	
	Media	

REFERENCES

Alexa (2011) Top sites. The top 500 sites on the web. Available at: www.alexa.com/topsites (date accessed: December 20, 2011).

Beaudette, P. (2011) Email interview by case authors, July 27.

Beaudette, P. (2012) From Wikipedia to Wikimedia: How not to structure a movement. Presentation, January 30.

Beaudette, P. (2015) Join the Wikimedia strategy consultation, February 23. Available at: http://blog.wikimedia.org/2015/02/23/strategy-consultation/ (date accessed: March 17, 2015).

Collaborative Creativity Group (2010) Wikipedia survey – overview of results. Available at: www.wikipediasurvey.org/docs/Wikipedia_Overview_15March2010-FINAL.pdf (date accessed: July 13, 2011).

Deals&More (January 2, 2012) Wikimedia fundraiser ends with $20M in the bank. Available at: http://venturebeat.com/2012/01/02/wikipedia-20-million/). (date accessed: February 2, 2012).

Forte, A., Larco, V., and Bruckman, A. (2009) Decentralization in Wikipedia governance. *Journal of Management Information Systems*, 26(1): 49–72.

Giles, G. (2005) Internet encyclopaedias go head to head. *Nature*, 438: 900–1.

Grams, C., Beaudette, P., and Kim, E. (2011) Strategic planning the Wikimedia way: Bottom-up and outside-in. Available at: http://www.managementexchange.com/story/strategic-planning-wikimedia-way Management Exchange (date accessed: July 13, 2011).

Kim, E. E. (March 22, 2011a) Followup to strategic planning for networks webinar by Eugene Eric Kim. Available at: http://leadershiplearning.org/blog/natalia-castaneda/2011-03-22/strategic-planning-networks-webinar (date accessed: July 20, 2011).

Kim, E. E. (May 27, 2011b) Wikimedia: Strategic planning the open source way. Talk at Open Your World forum. Available at: http://www-waa-akam.thomson-webcast.net/us/dispatching/?event_id=2e9cb68dd5d9d207654ed53688b1dca1&portal_id=af9b227bf07c733390c2738ee0330646 (date accessed: August 5, 2011).

Kittur, A. and Kraut, R. E. (2008) Harnessing the wisdom of crowds in Wikipedia: Quality through coordination. Proceedings of the 2008 ACM conference on computer supported cooperative work. New York.

Konieczny, P. (2010) Adhocratic governance in the internet age: A case of Wikipedia. *Journal of Information Technology & Politics*, 7: 263–83.

Morell, M. F. (2011) The Wikimedia Foundation and the governance of Wikipedia's infrastructure: Historical trajectories and its hybrid character. In G. Lovin and N. Tkacz (eds.), *Critical Point of View. A Wikipedia Reader*. Amsterdam: Institute of Network Cultures, pp. 325–41.

Newstead, B. (2010) *Wikimedia Strategy: Ground covered and road ahead*. Available at: http://blogs.hbr.org/cs/2010/01/wikimedia_strategy_ground_cove.html (date accessed: December 23, 2011).

O'Neil, M. (2011) Wikipedia and authority. In G. Lovin and N. Tkacz (eds.), *Critical Point of View: A Wikipedia Reader*. Amsterdam: Institute of Network Cultures, pp. 309–24.

Viégas, F. B., Wattenberg, M., Kriss, J., and van Ham, F. (2007a) *Talk before you type: Coordination in Wikipedia*. Proceedings of the 40th Hawaii International Conference on Systems Sciences, 2007: 78–87.

Viégas, F. B., Wattenberg, M., and McKeon, M. M. (2007b) The hidden order of Wikipedia. *Online Communities and Social Computing*, 4564: 445–54 (also available at series Lecture Notes in Computer Science).

Wales, J. (2011) Email interview by case authors. 27 July.

Wikimedia Foundation, Annual Report (2011) The way the world tells its story. Wikimedia Foundation Annual Report 2010–11. Available at: https://upload.wikimedia.org/wikipedia/commons/4/48/WMF_AR11_SHIP_spreads_15dec11_72dpi.pdf (date accessed: January 27, 2012).

Wikimedia Foundation (2011a) Answers archive, September. Available at: http://wikimediafoundation.org/wiki/Answers_archive/September_2011/en#Foundation:_How_many_employees_does_Wikimedia_have.2C_and_what_do_they_do.3F (date accessed: December 22, 2011).

Wikimedia Foundation (2011b) Board of Trustees. Available at: http://wikimediafoundation.org/wiki/Board_of_Trustees (date accessed: June 20, 2011).

Wikimedia Foundation (2011c) Advisory Board. Available at: http://wikimediafoundation.org/wiki/Advisory_Board (date accessed: July 13, 2011).

Wikimedia Foundation (2011d) *[Foundation-l] More on Wikimedia strategic planning*. Available at: http://lists.wikimedia.org/pipermail/foundation-l/2009-April/051594.html (date accessed: August 10, 2011).

Wikimedia Foundation (2011e) [Foundation-l] Strategic plan resolution. Available at: http://lists.wikimedia.org/pipermail/foundation-l/2009-April/051565.html (date accessed: July 5, 2011).

Wikimedia Meta-Wiki (2011a) Wikimedia movement. Available at: http://meta.wikimedia.org/wiki/Wikimedia_movement (date accessed: July 11, 2011).

Wikimedia Meta-Wiki (2011b) Wikimedia Chapters. Available at: http://meta.wikimedia.org/wiki/Wikimedia_chapters (date accessed: June 23, 2011).

Wikimedia Meta-Wiki (2011c) Fundraising 2010/Fundraiser report. Available at: http://meta.wikimedia.org/wiki/Fundraising_2010/Fundraiser_report (date accessed: July 13, 2011).

Wikimedia Meta-Wiki (2011d) Planet Wikimedia. Available at: http://meta.wikimedia.org/wiki/Planet_Wikimedia (date accessed: July 14, 2011).

Wikimedia Meta-Wiki (2011e) Mailing lists/Overview. Available at: http://meta.wikimedia.org/wiki/Mailing_lists/overview) (date accessed: July 11, 2011).

Wikimedia Meta-Wiki (2011f) *IRC/Channels*. Available at: http://meta.wikimedia.org/wiki/IRC_channels. (date accessed: July 11, 2011).

Wikimedia Meta-Wiki (2011g) Strategy. Available at: http://meta.wikimedia.org/wiki/Strategy. (date accessed: July 12, 2011).

Wikimedia Meta-Wiki (2011h) Wikimedia committees. Available at: http://meta.wikimedia.org/wiki/Committees) (date accessed: July 12, 2011).

Wikimedia Meta-Wiki (2011i) Mission. Available at: http://meta.wikimedia.org/wiki/Mission (date accessed: July 12, 2011).

Wikimedia Meta-Wiki (2011j) Vision. Available at: http://meta.wikimedia.org/wiki/Vision (date accessed: January 2, 2012).

Wikimedia Meta-Wiki (2011k) SWOT. Available at: http://meta.wikimedia.org/wiki/SWOT (date accessed: July 12, 2011).

Wikimedia Meta-Wiki (2015) 2015 Strategy/Community consultation. Available at: http://meta.wikimedia.org/wiki/2015_Strategy/Community_consultation#The_scenario (date accessed: March 18, 2015).

Wikimedia Strategic Plan (2011) Wikimedia Strategic Plan. A collaborative vision for the movement through 2015. Available at: http://upload.wikimedia.org/wikipedia/commons/c/c0/WMF_StrategicPlan2011_spreads.pdf (date accessed: December 23, 2011).

Wikimedia Strategic Planning (2011a) Stakeholders. Available at: http://strategy.wikimedia.org/wiki/Wikimedia_stakeholders (date accessed: June 27, 2011).

Wikimedia Strategic Planning (2011b) Editor trends study. Available at: http://strategy.wikimedia.org/wiki/Editor_Trends_Study (date accessed: July 13, 2011).

Wikimedia Strategic Planning (2011c) Process. Available at: http://strategy.wikimedia.org/wiki/Process (date accessed: June 22, 2011).

Wikimedia Strategic Planning (2011d) Purpose and principles. Available at: http://strategy.wikimedia.org/wiki/Purpose_and_principles (date accessed: June 22, 2011).

Wikimedia Strategic Planning (2011e) Village pump/Archive1. Available at: http://strategy.wikimedia.org/wiki/Village_pump/archive1 (date accessed: August 10, 2011).

Wikimedia Strategic Planning (2011f) Community guidelines. Available at: http://strategy.wikimedia.org/wiki/Community_guidelines (date accessed: June 22, 2011).

Wikimedia Strategic Planning (2011g) *Hosts*. Available at: http://strategy.wikimedia.org/wiki/Hosts (date accessed: June 20, 2011).

Wikimedia Strategic Planning (2011h) *IRC office hours*. Available at: http://strategy.wikimedia.org/wiki/IRC_office_hours (date accessed: June 24, 2011).

Wikimedia Strategic Planning (2011i) *Process/Administrators*. Available at: http://strategy.wikimedia.org/wiki/Process/Administrators (date accessed: June 27, 2011).

Wikimedia Strategic Planning (2011j) *Wikimedia-pedia*. Available at: http://strategy.wikimedia.org/wiki/Fact_base (date accessed: June 30, 2011).

Wikimedia Strategic Planning (2011k) Interviews. Available at: http://strategy.wikimedia.org/wiki/Interviews (date accessed: June 30, 2011).

Wikimedia Strategic Planning (2011l) Proposal: Call for proposals. Available at: http://strategy.wikimedia.org/wiki/Proposal:Call_for_Proposals (date accessed: June 22, 2011).

Wikimedia Strategic Planning (2011m) List of proposals. Available at: http://strategy.wikimedia.org/wiki/Proposals (date accessed: June 22, 2011).

Wikimedia Strategic Planning (2011n) Writings. Available at: http://strategy.wikimedia.org/wiki/Writings (date accessed: June 25, 2011).

Wikimedia Strategic Planning (2011o) Meetups. Available at: http://strategy.wikimedia.org/wiki/Meetups (date accessed: June 25, 2011).

Wikimedia Strategic Planning (2011p) Call for participation/appeal letter. Available at: http://strategy.wikimedia.org/wiki/Call_for_participation/Appeal_letter (date accessed: June 22, 2011).

Wikimedia Strategic Planning (2011q) Process/evaluation/phase1. Available at: http://strategy.wikimedia.org/wiki/Evaluation/Phase_1 (date accessed: July 1, 2011).

Wikimedia Strategic Planning (2011r) Task force/phase 2. Available at: http://strategy.wikimedia.org/wiki/Task_force/Phase_2 (date accessed: June 20, 2011).

Wikimedia Strategic Planning (2011s) Evaluation/call for participation. Available at: http://strategy.wikimedia.org/wiki/Evaluation/Call_for_participation (date accessed: July 1, 2011).

Wikimedia Strategic Planning (2011t) Village pump/archive3. Available at: http://strategy.wikimedia.org/wiki/Village_pump/Archive3 (date accessed: August 7, 2011).

Wikimedia Strategic Planning (2011u) Process/decision-making. Available at: http://strategy.wikimedia.org/wiki/Process/Decision-making (date accessed: June 25, 2011).

Wikimedia Strategic Planning (2011v) Process/evaluation/proposals. Available at: http://strategy.wikimedia.org/wiki/Evaluation/Proposals (date accessed: July 1, 2011).

Wikimedia Strategic Planning (2011w) Task force/strategy/goal guidelines. Available at: http://strategy.wikimedia.org/wiki/Task_force/Strategy/Goal_guidelines (date accessed: July 4, 2011).

Wikimedia Strategic Planning (2011x) Task force/strategy/plan overview. Available at: http://strategy.wikimedia.org/wiki/Task_force/Strategy/Plan_overview (date accessed: December 23, 2011).

Wikimedia Strategic Planning (2011y) Strategic plan/role of the WMF. Available at: http://strategy.wikimedia.org/wiki/Strategic_Plan/Role_of_the_WMF (date accessed: July 10, 2011).

Wikimedia Strategic Planning (2011z) Strategic plan/movement priorities. Available at: http://strategy.wikimedia.org/wiki/Strategic_Plan/Movement_Priorities (date accessed: July 8, 2011).

Wikimedia Strategic Planning (2011aa) Call for action. Available at: http://strategy.wikimedia.org/wiki/Call_for_action (date accessed: July 2, 2011).

Wikipedia (2011a) Wikipedia. Available at: http://en.wikipedia.org/wiki/Wikipedia (date accessed: July 13, 2011).

Wikipedia (2011b) Wikipedia: User access levels. Available at: http://simple.wikipedia.org/wiki/Wikipedia:User_access_levels (date accessed: June 24, 2011).

Wikipedia (2011c) Wikipedia: Awards. Available at: http://en.wikipedia.org/wiki/Wikipedia:Awards (date accessed: July 11, 2011).

Wikipedia (2011d) Wikipedia: Wikipedia Signpost/About. Available at: http://en.wikipedia.org/wiki/Wikipedia:Wikipedia_Signpost/About (date accessed: July 13, 2011).

Wikipedia (2011e) Wikipedia: Neutral point of view. Available at: http://en.wikipedia.org/wiki/Wikipedia:Neutral_point_of_view (date accessed: June 24, 2011).

Wikipedia (2011f) Wikimania. Available at: http://en.wikipedia.org/wiki/Wikimania (date accessed: July 12, 2011).

Wikipedia (2011g) Wikipedia: Neutral point of view. Available at: http://en.wikipedia.org/wiki/Wikipedia:Neutral_point_of_view (date accessed: June 24, 2011).

Wikipedia (2011h) Wikipedia: Etiquette. Available at: http://en.wikipedia.org/wiki/Wikipedia:Etiquette (date accessed: July 11, 2011).

Wikipedia (2011i) Wikipedia: No personal attacks. Available at: http://en.wikipedia.org/wiki/Wikipedia:No_personal_attacks (date accessed: July 11, 2011).

Wikipedia (2011j) Wikipedia: Consensus. Available at: http://en.wikipedia.org/wiki/Wikipedia:Consensus (date accessed: July 11, 2011).

Wikipedia (2011k) Wikipedia: Edit warring. Available at: http://en.wikipedia.org/wiki/Wikipedia:Edit_warring (date accessed: July 11, 2011).

Wikipedia (2011l) Wikipedia: Assume good faith. Available at: http://en.wikipedia.org/wiki/Wikipedia:Assume_good_faith (date accessed: December 20, 2011).

Wikipedia (2011m) Wikipedia: Dispute resolution. Available at: http://en.wikipedia.org/wiki/Wikipedia:Arbitration (date accessed: June 27, 2011).

Wikipedia (2011n) Wikipedia: Five pillars. Available at: http://en.wikipedia.org/wiki/Wikipedia:5P (date accessed: July 11, 2011).

INDEX

AA (Automobile Association), 200–202, *201*, *203*
Academy of Management (AOM), 87
Accounting Standards Committee (ASC), 133
activity theory, 7–8
Ahmed, A. M., 84–85
Alcatel, 247
Alvesson, M., 76
Amazon, 176
Amelio, G., 170
Andriopoulos, C., 151
Angwin, D., 32–33, 136, 141
App Store, 173
Apple
   CEOs at, **187**
   competitive landscape of, 174–176, 186
   Cook and, 152, 179, 184–187
   corporate culture of, 179–180
   decline of, 169–170
   deep collaboration and, 176–177
   Jobs' role and leadership at, 23–25, 152, 168–174, 175–176, 179–181, 182–185
   organization design at, 182
   product and service portfolio of, *169*, 171–174
   proprietary ecosystem and, 177–178
   strategic alliances and, 178–179
   strategic ambidexterity and, 152–154
Apple Watch, 173–174, 186–187
Argenti, P. A., 97–98
Argyris, C., 165
Aristotle, 23, 24
Austin, B., 204, 209

Bain & Company, 70, 73, 83–84
Balogun, J., 5, 97
Bank One, 134
Barrett, F. J., 98
Barrett, M., 100–101
Barry, D., 95
Beaudette, P., 285, 289–290, 291, 296
Beech, N., 151
Beiersdorf UK, 62–63
Berger, P., 96
BG plc, 193–194, *194–195*
Bhattacharyya, O., 217–218, 222, 226
Bilodeau, B., 83–84
Blue Circle, 256–260

Bond, C. H., 161–162
Bonham, D., 253
Booz Allen Hamilton (BAH), 69–70
Boston Consulting Group (BCG), 69
Boulding, K., 95
Bower–Burgelman (BB) process model of strategy making, 2–3
Bower, J. L., 2
Breene, T. R. S., 31, 32
Brew, A., 162, 163
British Aerospace, 249
British Borneo Oil & Gas, 199
British Gas, 192–196, *194–195*
British Gas Communications, 203
British Gas Financial Services, 197
British Gas Home Energy, 197
British Gas Services, 196–197
British Gas Trading, 197
Broadbent, R., 42
BT Group, 64–65, 254
Buckley, C., 206
Burgelman, R. A., 2–3, *4*
Burrows, P., 173, 182

Calori, R., 86
Cameron, K. S., 146, 148
Carter, C., 22
Central Electricity Generation Board (CEGB), 191
Centrica
   acquisitions and, 199–204, *201*, *203*
   Centrica model and, 197–200, **199**, 205–207, *207*
   choice of name and, 197
   demerger from British Gas and, 193–196, *194–195*
   deregulation and, 191–193, *192–193*
   employees and, 204–205, **205**
   organizational structure of, 197, 209
   strategy process at, 207–211, *208*, **210**, *210*
Chaffee, E. E., 95
Chandler, A. D., 2
charismatic leadership, 23–25
Chen, T., 294
Chief Executive Officers (CEOs)
   case studies, 20–21, 23–25
   upper echelons theory and, 19–22, *20*
   use of discourse and myths and, 22–26
Chief External Officers, 26–27

INDEX

Chief Strategy Officers (CSOs)
    activities, capabilities, and networks of, 34–37, 40
    case study, 41–42
    definition of, 30–31
    role, location, and types of, 31–34, *33*, **39**, 40–41
    strategy teams and, 45
    tools and formal outputs of, 38
Christensen, C. M., 77
Christiansen, L. C., 112
Cisco, 48–49
Clark, T., 75
Clarke, P., 42
Cognizant Technologies, 222–223
Collomb, B., 257, 260
communication skills, 37
Compaq, 175
consulting interventions, 72–75, *73*, **74**
Controlling Science, 101–102
Cook, P., 205, 206–207
Cook, T., 152, 179, 184–187
core competencies, 110–111
corporate failure
    ESCO model and, *122*
    Nortel Networks and, 116–120, **118–119**
    perspectives on, 113–115, **115**
    stages of, 120–121, **120**
    strategic misalignment and, 113
    WorldCom and, 116–120, **116–117**
Cox, S., 289
Creative Commons Corporation, 279
critical discourse studies, 101
culture, 37, 112–113
Cunningham, J., 61
Cuno, J., 97

Dana Petroleum, 199
Dell, 53–54, 175–176
Denning, S., 77
Devonshire, E., 162, 163
Dimon, J., 134
Direct Energy Marketing Ltd, 203
discourse
    approaches to strategy and, 97–101
    case studies, 99–100, 101–102
    definition of, 95
    leadership and, 22–26
    role of, 95–97
    strategy tools and, 90
distributed activity, 58
Doh, J., 26–27
Duncan, R. B., 145
Dye, R., 32

Ebbers, B., 117
Eisenberg, E. M., 96
Eisenhardt, K. M., 148

electricity market, 191–192, *192*, 198. *See also* Centrica
Elkind, P., 184
Ellison, L., 171
Elmes, M., 95
Elop, S., 148–150
Elton, L., 162
emergent school, 2
Energy America, 203
environmental velocity, 86, *87*
ESCO (environment, strategy, core competencies and organization) model
    domains of, 110–112
    elements of, 6–7, *6*, 10, *11*, *121*
    misalignments and, 6–7, *122*
    performance and, 110–113
    3P framework and, 109–110
eSolar, 20–21

Fadell, T., 178
Fincham, R., 75
Finkelstein, S., 19
Fiol, M., 96
flexibility, 38
Floyd, S. W., 59
Ford, J. D., 97, 98
Ford, L. W., 97
Foster, J., 200, 207
Foucault, M., 101
Fowler, J., 289
Fredrickson, J. W., 3–4
Freeman, J., 111, 114
Friesen, P. H., 3
Frost, A., 62
functional approaches, 97–98
Furusten, S., 75

Ganguly, D., 227
Gardner, R. *See* Centrica
Gardner, S., 280, 284
Gasse, J.-L., 183
GEC (General Electric Company) plc, 245–254, *246–252*
Ghosh, D., 212
Giddens, A., 102
Glaxo Welcome, 133
Gokhale, K., 216
Goldfish, 197, 202–203
Good, J., 195, 201, 206, 209
Google, 176, 181–182, 186
Grand Metropolitan, 133
Grant, D., 98
Gratton, L., 60
Greenwood, R., 98
Greiner, L. E., 165
Gross, B., 21
Grossman, L., 183
Grover, R., 173, 182

Hambrick, D. C., 19–20
Hannan, M. T., 111, 114
Hardy, C., 101
Harrison, B., 134
Hart, S. L., 2, 3
Hartigan, P., 216
Haynes, J., 237–244
Haythornthwaite, R., 256–260
healthcare industry, 213–216. *See also* Narayana Health (NH)
Hendry, J., 95
Heracleous, L., 23, 98–99, 100–102, 116, 153.
Hewlett-Packard (HP), 22–23, 50–52, 175
Higginson, A., 41–42
Higgs, M., 112
Hirsch, P. M., 96
Hodgkinson, G. P., 88
Hogg, M. K., 77
Holbrook, N. J., 162, 163
Human Computer Interaction (HCI), 88
human resource management, 111–112
Hurn, R., 252

IBM, 170, 174, 178
iBook, 171
iCare, 222–223
iCloud, 173
Idealab, 20–21
iMac, 171
Indian Space Research Organisation (ISRO), 225
Indira Gandhi National Open University (IGNOU), 221
industrial organization, 113–114, **115**
inertia, 115
information technology (IT), 139, 140
Intel, 170, 178
interaction abilities, 62
interpretive approaches, 95, 98–99
iPad, 173
iPhone, 172–173, 178
iPod, 172, 178
Isaacson, W., 177
iTunes, 172, 178
iWork, 173

Jacob Suchard, 132–133
Jacobs, C., 98, 101–102
Jarratt, D., 86
Jarzabkowski, P.
  interpretive approach and, 98
  on strategy-as-practice, 7, 8, 9, 162–163, 164
  on strategy tools, 86–87, *87*, 88
  structurational approach and, 100
Jenkins, A., 161, 162
Jobs, S.
  deep collaboration and, 175–176
  discourse and, 98

Jobs, S. *cont*.
  proprietary ecosystem and, 177–178
  role and leadership at Apple and, 23–25, 152, 154, 168–174, 179–181, 182–185
  secrecy and, 179–181
Johansson, A., 76
Johnson, G., 7, 10, 22
JP Morgan Chase (JPM), 134

Kachaner, N., 31, 45
Kahney, L., 178
Kaplan, S., 86, 166
Karantinou, K. M., 77
Kawasaki, G., 183
Kazmin, A., 216, 217
Kelby, S., 184
Kim, E. E., 285–288, 289, 294
Klaering, A., 23, 98
Klasson, K., 32
Knott, P., 86
knowledge intensity, 86–87, *87*
Kropp, T., 26

La Ville, V., 134
Lafarge, 256–260
Lane, M., 26–27
Lane, P. J., 59
language, 94–95. *See also* discourse
Lashinsky, A., 179, 180, 185
Lassen, A. H., 147
Lawrence, T. B., 8
leadership
  case studies, 20–21, 23–25, 26–27
  corporate failure and, 119–121
  Jobs and, 23–25, 152, 154, 168–174, 179–181, 182–185
  upper echelons theory and, 19–22, *20*
  use of discourse and myths and, 22–26
  Wales and, 282
Leahy, T., 41
learning and teaching, 161–166, *163*, **164**, *165*
Lenovo, 175–176
Leschley, J., 133
Lewis, M. W., 148, 150–151
Liedtka, J. M., 97
Lindsay, R., 161
Linnarsson, H., 77
Linzmayer, O. W., 184
Livingston, I., 64
Luckmann, T., 96
Lufthansa, 26
Lumsden, C., 76

macro level, 1, 4–8, *5*, 10
Madhavan, N., 216
Maitlis, S., 8

INDEX

March, J. G., 145–146
Marconi, 248–251, *250–251*
Marshak, R., 98–99
Mason, P. A., 19–20
Matra, 247
Mayo, J., 248, 252
McGrath, J. E., 49
McKinsey, 70, 72, 74
McLarty, R., 76
Melin, L., 4–5
mergers and acquisitions (M&A)
    case studies, 133–141, *138*
    complexity of, 127–129
    strategy-as-practice approach to, 128–135, *130*, *132*, 141–142
meta-level abilities, 62
micro level, 1, 4–8, *5*, 10, 12. *See also* 3P framework
Microsoft, 168, 170, 174–175, 178
middle-level managers
    engaged strategy participation and, 61–63
    roles of, **58**, 59–60, *60*, 65
    strategy communities and, 63–65
Milberg Weiss, 134
Miles, R. E., 111, 112
Miller, D., 3
Mintzberg, H., 2
Mitroff, I. I., 95
Mom, T. J. M., 148
Monitor Group, 77
Mounoud, E., 134
multi-business firms, 58–59
myths, 22–26

Narayana Health (NH)
    as business model, 227
    characteristics of, 212–214, **213**, **228–229**, *228*, *231*
    cross-subsidized pricing model and, 218–219
    culture of, 226
    daily accounting system and, 219–220, *230*
    efficiency and, 217–218
    fixed salary model and, 218
    healthcare industry and, 213–216
    ideas from other industries and healthcare systems and, 223–224
    lean management of, 226–227
    low-cost model of, 223
    micro-insurance schemes and, 224–225
    mobile outreach clinics and, 225
    process improvement and standardization at, 220–221
    qualified personnel and, 221–222
    technology and, 222–223, *230*
    telemedicine and, 225
    vision of, 212–213, 216–217
National Grid Company (NGC), 192
National Power, 192

natural gas market, 192–193, *193*, 198. *See also* Centrica
Neil, J., 239
Nestlé, 132–133
networks and networking, 35
NeXT, 170
Nichols, C., 61, 87–88
Nokia, 148–150
Norman, D. A., 88
normative fit, 110
Noser, T. C., 162
Novell, 170
Nuclear Electric, 192
Nupedia, 279

Oakes, L. S., 8
Ofgas, 193
Oil and Gas (Enterprise) Act (1982), 192
One.Tel, 203
organization studies, 114–115, **115**
organizational ambidexterity, 145–147
organizational development (OD) approach, 76
organizational ecology, 114, **115**
organizational psychology, 114, **115**
Oxford Brookes University Business School (OBBS)
    city campus and, 266–268, *267–268*
    competitive environment of, 268–269
    current location of, 263–266, *264–265*
    relocation of, 262–263, 269–278, *270–271*

Palmer, G., 165
Panopticism, 102
paradox theory, 148–154, **152**
Paroutis, S., 22–23, 45–47, 61, 87–88, 89, 165
Parton, M., 253
Patterson, A., 62–63
Payne, A., 76
Penglai Electric, 21
PESTLE (Political, Economic, Social, Technological, Legal, Environmental) framework, 84
Pettigrew, A. M., 45–47
planning school (rational school), 2
Podolny, J., 185
Pondy, L. R., 95
Porter, M. E., 47, 111, 114, 153
PowerGen, 192, 199
practice-informed teaching, 163
practice-inquiry teaching, 164
practice-skills teaching, 163–164
practices, 9, 10, 11–12, *11. See also* discourse; strategy tools; 3P framework
practitioners, 9, 9, 11–12, *11*, 57–59, **58**. *See also* 3P framework; *specific types of practitioners*
praxis, 9, 10, 11–12, *11. See also* mergers and acquisitions (M&A); strategic alignment; strategic ambidexterity; 3P framework

Price, I., 97
PwC Consulting, 174

Quinn, R. E., 146, 148

Raghuvanshi, Dr., 219, 220, 226
Rake, M., 64
Ramamurti, R., 219, 220
Rank Hovis McDougall, 133
rational school (planning school), 2
Ravasi, D., 89
Reddy, S., 217
reflection, 47
Regnér, P., 8, 58
Reid, D., 42
Reliant Car Company, 235–244, *236–237*, *240*
resource allocation process (RAP) model, 2
resource-based view, 10, 110
Reynolds, M., 164
Rigby, D. K., 83–84
Robertson, J., 161–162
Robinson, T., 76
Rosenblum, J. W., 97
Rowntree, 132–133

Samsung, 176, 186
Saxton, T., 77
Schön, D. A., 47
Schumpeter, J. A., 114
Scientific Management, 102
Scottish Gas, 197
Scottish Hydro, 192
ScottishPower, 192
Sculley, J., 170, 182
Seidl, D., 89
7-S Framework, 110
Sharma, A., 98
Shells LPG, 200
Shetty, D. *See* Narayana Health (NH)
Shetty, V., 223
Shirley, D., 42
Shrader, R. W., 69–70
Siemens, 247, 248
Sillince, J. A. A., 98
Simpson, G., 248, 251–252
Singapore Airlines, 152–154
Smith, R. C., 96
Smith, W. K., 148, 151
SmithKline Beecham, 133
Snow, C. C., 112
Snow, M., 284, 289, 292
social networks, 35
social psychology theories, 50
Spender, M., 208
Spindler, M., 170

Stanford University, 221
Stewart, S., 31, 45
Stichcombe, A. L., 114
Stigliani, I., 89
Stiles, D., 86
strategic alignment, 110, **112**. *See also* corporate failure; ESCO (environment, strategy, core competencies and organization) model
strategic ambidexterity
  case studies, 146–147, 149–150, 153–154
  individual-level ambidexterity, 147–148
  organizational ambidexterity, 145–147
  paradox-based approach to, 148–154, **152**
strategic management research, 2–5, **3**, *4–5*
Strategic Management Society (SMS), 31
strategizing
  definitions of, 4–5, *5*
  level and mode of, 49–51, *51*
strategizing capabilities, 61–62
strategy analysts, 45
strategy-as-practice
  analysis of practice in case studies and, 165–166, *165*
  micro- and macro-level aspects and, 1, 4–5, 8, 10, 12
  questions in, 12
  scholars of, 7–9
  teaching strategy for, 161–166, *163*, **164**, *165*
  See also 3P framework
strategy communities, 63–65
strategy consultants
  case studies, 69–71, 73
  characteristics and roles of, 68–71, **72**, **75**, 78
  consulting interventions and, 72–75, *73*, **74**
  perspectives on, 76–77
strategy consulting teams, 72–73, *73*
Strategy Directors (SDs). *See* Chief Executive Officers (CEOs)
strategy managers, 45, 47. *See also* strategy teams
strategy teams
  activities of, 45–49, **46**, 55
  capabilities of, 50–51
  case studies, 49, 51–54
  composition of, 45
  level and mode of strategizing in, 49–51, *51*
  3P framework and, 54, *54*
strategy tools
  as cognitive artifacts, 88–89
  discourse and, 90
  as material artifacts, 89
  types of, 83–85
  use of, *85*, 86–87, *87*
structurational approach, 100–101
Sturdy, A., 71
subjugation, 136–137
Suddaby, R., 98
Sutton, R., 183

INDEX

SWOT (Strengths, Weaknesses, Opportunities, and Threats) analysis, 84–85
Sykes, R., 133
Systech, 99–100

Tata Consultancy Services, 26–27
Taylor, G., 62
Taylorism, 102
teaching and learning, 161–166, *163*, **164**, *165*
team reflexivity, 47
technical abilities, 62
Tesco, 41–42
Texas Instruments, 21
Thomas, R., 101
3P framework
  Chief Strategy Officers and, **39**
  elements of, 9–10, *9*
  ESCO model and, 109–110
  mergers and acquisitions and, 128–135, *130*, *132*, 141–142
  middle-level managers and, 58
  pathways of influence in, 85–86, *86*, 90
  strategy consultants and, 75
  strategy teams and, 54, *54*
  See also practices; practitioners; praxis
Trigo, S. P., 72
Tsoukas, H., 22
Twitter, 146–147

upper echelons theory, 19–22, *20*

Vaara, E., 8, 9
Van Leeuwen, T., 22
Van Scoter, J., 21
Veba Oil and Gas UK, 200
Venkatraman, N., 110

Wadhwani Foundation, 221
Wales, J., 282, 285, 289, 292
Wei, H., 161
Weinstock, Lord, 245–248
Werle, F., 89
Werr, A., 77
Werres, K., 116
West, M. A., 47
Whittington, R.
  on practices, 10
  on strategy-as-practice, 7, 8, 9, 12, 97, 162–163, 164
  on strategy teams, 47
  on strategy tools, 85
Wikimedia Foundation
  communication and coordination at, 282–283
  as community, 281–282
  organizational structure of, 280–281, *281*, **296–298**

Wikimedia Foundation *cont.*
  policies and guidelines at, 283, **298–299**
  strategic planning project of, 284–296, **290**, *291*, *293*, **295**, *299*
  Wikipedia and, 279–280
Wikipedia, 279–280
Williams, T. L., 235
Wilson, D. C., 86–87, *87*
Wooldridge, B., 59, 60
workshops, 36
Worren, N., 86
Wright, R., 88

CASE STUDIES

Apple
  CEOs at, **187**
  competitive landscape of, 174–176, 186
  Cook and, 152, 179, 184–187
  corporate culture of, 179–180
  decline of, 169–170
  deep collaboration and, 176–177
  Jobs' role and leadership at, 23–25, 152, 168–174, 175–176, 179–181, 182–185
  organization design at, 182
  product and service portfolio of, *169*, 171–174
  proprietary ecosystem and, 177–178
  strategic alliances and, 178–179
  strategic ambidexterity and, 152–154

Bain & Company, 70–71, 73
Beiersdorf UK, 62–63
Blue Circle, 256–260
Booz Allen Hamilton (BAH), 69–70
BT Group, 64–65

Centrica
  acquisitions and, 199–204, *201*, *203*
  Centrica model and, 197–200, **199**, 205–207, *207*
  choice of name and, 197
  demerger from British Gas and, 193–196, *194–195*
  deregulation and, 191–193, *192–193*
  employees and, 204–205, **205**
  organizational structure of, 197, 209
  strategy process at, 207–211, *208*, *210*, *210*
Chief External Officers, 26–27
Cisco, 49
Controlling Science, 101–102

Dell, 53–54

eSolar, 20–21

GEC (General Electric Company) plc, 245–254, *246–252*

Hewlett-Packard, 51–52

Narayana Health (NH)
　as business model, 227
　characteristics of, 212–214, **213**, **228–229**, *228*, *231*
　cross-subsidized pricing model and, 218–219
　culture of, 226
　daily accounting system and, 219–220, *230*
　efficiency and, 217–218
　fixed salary model and, 218
　healthcare industry and, 213–216
　ideas from other industries and healthcare systems and, 223–224
　lean management of, 226–227
　low-cost model of, 223
　micro-insurance schemes and, 224–225
　mobile outreach clinics and, 225
　process improvement and standardization at, 220–221
　qualified personnel and, 221–222
　technology and, 222–223, *230*
　telemedicine and, 225
　vision of, 212–213, 216–217

Oxford Brookes University Business School (OBBS)
　city campus and, 266–268, *267–268*
　competitive environment of, 268–269
　current location of, 263–266, *264–265*
　relocation of, 262–263, 269–278, *270–271*

Reliant Car Company, 235–244, *236–237*, *240*

Systech, 99–100

Tesco, 41–42
Twitter, 146–147

Wikimedia Foundation
　communication and coordination at, 282–283
　as community, 281–282
　organizational structure of, 280–281, *281*, **296–298**
　policies and guidelines at, 283, **298–299**
　strategic planning project of, 284–296, **290**, *291*, *293*, **295**, *299*
　Wikipedia and, 279–280